Teaching and
Studying the Holocaust

Related Title

Teaching Holocaust Literature
Samuel Totten, Editor
0-205-27402-1

Teaching and Studying the Holocaust

Edited by

Samuel Totten
Stephen Feinberg

Foreword by

John K. Roth

Russell K. Pitzer Professor of Philosophy
Claremont McKenna College

Allyn and Bacon

Boston ■ London ■ Toronto ■ Sydney ■ Tokyo ■ Singapore

Series editor: *Traci Mueller*
Series editorial assistant: *Bridget Keane*
Marketing manager: *Stephen Smith*

 Copyright © 2001 by Allyn & Bacon
A Pearson Education Company
Needham Heights, MA 02494

Internet: www.abacon.com

Library of Congress Cataloging-in-Publication Data

Teaching and studying the Holocaust / editors, Samuel Totten, Stephen Feinberg.
    p. cm.
    Includes bibliographical references (p.).
    ISBN 0-205-18495-2
    1. Holocaust, Jewish (1933–1945)—Study and teaching.   I. Totten, Samuel.
II. Feinberg, Stephen.

    D804.33 .T46 2000
    940.53'18'07—dc21

                                00-056918

Cover: Arnold Kramer. Photograph of Majdanek shoes. USHMM Photo Archives, worksheet no. N00031. Copyright © United States Holocaust Memorial Museum.

Acknowledgments: The editors gratefully acknowledge the United States Holocaust Memorial Museum for permission to reprint the following:

    Der Giftpilz (The Poison Mushroom). Book cover. 1988.25.1 USHMM Collection.

    Kurant. Lodz Ghetto Policeman. Drawing. 1991.124.1 USHMM Collection.

    Halina Olamuscki. *Le dernier chemin Korczak et les enfants* (The Last March of Janusz Korczak and the Children [on Their Way to Deportation]). Drawing. 1989.33.1 USHMM Collection.

    Petr Kien. *Uniformschneiderei* (Uniform Tailor Shop). Print. 1989.2.124 USHMM Collection.

    Arnold Kramer. "Railway Cars," "Shoes," and "Stars, Triangles and Markings." Photographs. USHMM Collection.

Printed in the United States of America

10 9 8 7 6 5 4 3 2 1   04 03 02 01 00

*Samuel Totten dedicates this book to
Henry Friedlander, Sybil Milton, William S. Parsons,
and Elie Wiesel, all of whom have inspired and
informed his work in the field of Holocaust education.*

*Stephen Feinberg dedicates this book to his
wife, Patt Moser, and to his children,
Joshua and Sara Feinberg.*

CONTENTS

FOREWORD

The Courage to Try

DR. JOHN K. ROTH

Russell K. Pitzer Professor of Philosophy
Claremont McKenna College

I do not know / if you can still / make something of me /
If you have the courage to try . . .

—Charlotte Delbo, *Auschwitz and After*

Active in the Resistance against Nazi Germany's occupation of her native France, Charlotte Delbo (1913–1985) was not Jewish, but after her arrest she was deported to Auschwitz in January 1943. Caught in the Holocaust, she witnessed Nazi Germany's destruction of European Jewry while she saw what happened to the 230 French women in her Auschwitz convoy—she was one of the 49 who survived. In 1946, she began to write the trilogy that came to be called *Auschwitz and After* (*Auschwitz et après*), whose anguished visual descriptions, profound reflections on memory, and diverse writing styles make it an unrivaled Holocaust testimony.

As *Auschwitz and After* draws to a close, Delbo says, "I do not know / if you can still / make something of me / If you have the courage to try . . ."[1] She contextualizes those words in two ways that have special significance as one thinks about *Teaching and Studying the Holocaust*—both the book you are presently reading and the issues that its title suggests. First, Delbo stresses that her experience in Auschwitz and then in Ravensbrück—it was a Nazi camp outside Berlin, maintained especially for women, to which she was eventually sent—gave her what she called "useless knowledge," a concept to which I will return.[2] Second, just before the lines I have quoted from *Auschwitz and After*, Delbo remembers Françoise, one of the French women who survived Auschwitz with her. Memory makes Françoise mourn. When she thinks of what has happened, Françoise insists that the "advice" one often hears—start over, begin again, put the past behind you—rings hollow as it mocks what cannot be forgotten. "Make one's life over, what an expression," Françoise protests.[3]

Françoise was not the only survivor on Charlotte Delbo's mind in *Auschwitz and After*. Delbo had not forgotten Poupette, Marie-Louis, Ida, and many others who were with her in the camps. Nor could Delbo forget how Auschwitz forever divided, besieged, and diminished her own life. Thus, as if she were speaking for her survivor friends, as well as for herself, Delbo wondered "if you can still / make something of me."

Teaching and Studying the Holocaust is not about Charlotte Delbo, and yet it is, for this book definitely confronts the challenge that Delbo poses about the Holocaust: What can and cannot be done with the Shoah (as the Holocaust is often called)? What must and must not be made of that catastrophe? If we have the courage to try to teach about the Holocaust, to learn from that disaster, and to learn from our teaching as well, what awareness should that courage embody, what questions must it raise, what pitfalls does it have to avoid if the outcomes are to be worthwhile?

Samuel Totten and Stephen Feinberg, the editors of *Teaching and Studying the Holocaust,* have brought together a superb group of Holocaust educators to reflect on issues of that kind. Significantly, they do so from a variety of perspectives. It is often observed that the Holocaust's scope was vast, its destruction immense. The perpetrators came from virtually every sector of German society. Scarcely any part of the targeted populations—Jews first and foremost, but non-Jewish groups as well—went unharmed. Hence, research, teaching, and learning about the Holocaust require sound rationales that take advantage of multiple approaches. Sound historical work is foundational and indispensable. However, as *Teaching and Studying the Holocaust* also makes clear—and this is one of its most distinctive contributions—knowledge about the Holocaust depends on study that concentrates on art, film, music, drama, poetry, fiction, and even Internet developments, along with the documents and eyewitness testimonies that are of such basic importance in historical studies.

While emphasizing these multiple approaches, *Teaching and Studying the Holocaust* also makes valuable contributions because it courageously raises questions, including some that have long been on my mind during more than twenty-five years of Holocaust-related teaching at Claremont McKenna College and other educational centers in the United States and abroad where I have been privileged to learn and teach about the Shoah. On the first day of courses that I teach on the Holocaust, I normally distribute a questionnaire to my students. Following a suggestion echoed in this book—namely, that student input can helpfully focus rationales for Holocaust teaching—I want to find out what students think initially about questions such as: Why should the Holocaust be studied? What goals should be emphasized in teaching and learning about the Holocaust? How should the Holocaust be investigated or taught? What criteria should be used to judge whether study and teaching about the Holocaust are successful? A word about my findings to such questions can help to highlight the courage to try that *Teaching and Studying the Holocaust* so admirably inspires.

When I polled my college class at the time of this writing—the autumn of the 1999–2000 academic year—my students' responses to the question "Why should the Holocaust be studied?" included the following: We should study to remember and honor those who were victimized. We should study to try to understand. We should study for the sake of the future. Other respondents said that we should study the Holocaust because it is the twentieth century's defining moment, because of the extreme evil it involved, and because "it happened." As for the goals that should be emphasized, the students repeatedly stressed two: One goal in teaching and learning about the Holocaust, they said, should be *understanding* how and why it happened. The other goal should be *prevention*. By prevention the students meant "no more genocide." With respect to the question about how the Holocaust should be studied, the following themes were most pronounced: There should be historical objectivity, but facts alone are "not enough." "All sides," some said, "should be explored." Multiple approaches, more claimed, are required. Virtually everyone thought that first-hand reports (especially from survivors) are crucial.

The students' responses to the first three questions were direct and even confident. At times these young women and men, most of them studying the Holocaust seriously for the first time, were not yet aware, could not yet have realized, how much their responses assumed. It is a good question, for example, whether anyone can *understand* the Holocaust—at least it is a good question when we think about all that understanding entails, especially where the Holocaust is concerned. When they came to the question about criteria for successful Holocaust teaching, however, the students were more tentative. Several of them wondered whether there could be such criteria. Others stressed greater understanding—that word again—of the Holocaust's history. Still others said that measures of success might include: never forgetting the Holocaust, less Holocaust denial, greater tolerance, and prevention of related disasters in the future.

The most succinct and focused student comment said that success in Holocaust education would depend on answers to three questions: Has one learned about what happened? Has one been affected (emotionally and spiritually) by the teaching? Has one wrestled deeply with and been disturbed by the content of the study? After we discussed these responses, I played a short video vignette in which the Holocaust survivor Elie Wiesel can be heard to say that, from his point of view, there is one fundamental reason to study the Holocaust: namely, *to make us more sensitive*.

To a large degree, my students' responses pleased me. Their content, including its unspoken assumptions, helped to set the agenda for my teaching. I played the Wiesel video clip, moreover, because my own study and teaching about the Holocaust are governed largely by ethical concerns, and I think that his emphasis on sensitivity is rightly placed. Among other things, my Holocaust-related ethical concerns involve dispelling what Inga Clendinnen, author of *Reading the Holocaust* (1999), identifies as "the 'Gorgon effect'—the sickening of imagination and curiosity and the draining of the will which afflicts so many of us when we try to look squarely at the persons and processes implicated in the Holocaust."[4] Clendinnen calls such perplexity dangerous, "an indulgence we cannot afford."[5] As I understand her point, it bolsters my belief—it is also, I sense, a governing conviction in *Teaching and Studying the Holocaust*—that a primary reason, if not *the* primary reason, for Holocaust education is not only to learn *about* the Holocaust but to learn *from* it in ways that encourage sound ethical reflection, more respect for human life, and greater determination to mend the world.

Neither learning about nor learning from the Holocaust is easily done. First, there are critical voices who question how or whether the latter happens *even if* we have learned *about* the Holocaust. Second, there are also critics who question how or whether learning *from* the Holocaust takes place *because of* what we learn about the Holocaust. Critics of the first kind can point out that, as far as the history of genocide in the twentieth century and beyond is concerned, "Never again" has become a cliché that is mocked by "Again and again." I want to concentrate, however, on the second case. Raising a more subtle but no less crucial issue for Holocaust pedagogy, it sharply focuses why learning about the Holocaust cannot glibly or easily let us make much of the Shoah when it comes to lessons, moral insights, and determination to check genocidal tendencies.

To mark those challenges in this preface, before they are judiciously addressed, implicitly and explicitly, as they are in *Teaching and Studying the Holocaust*, three persons need to be mentioned. One of them is Charlotte Delbo, whom we have encountered already. Recall that Delbo spoke about the "useless knowledge" that Auschwitz and Ravensbrück impressed upon her. Such knowledge is useless not simply because it is so dark as to be unforgettable, but also because such knowledge is so overpowering that, the more we encounter its stark realities, the more we are likely to be overpowered by them. If we are to learn from the Holocaust, that prospect looms large. Delbo makes us wonder how we should try to cope with the likelihood that what we try to learn from the Holocaust will be overwhelmed by the "useless knowledge" we obtain as we learn about it.

One of the first American interpreters of Charlotte Delbo—and she taught him a great deal—is the literary critic Lawrence Langer. Echoing Delbo, Langer suggests that "there is nothing to be learned from a baby torn in two or a woman buried alive."[6] The Holocaust, he thinks, is "the central event of our time."[7] Nevertheless, knowledge about the Holocaust leaves us largely estranged from a moral universe that we might nostalgically yearn to inhabit but that has been ruined by Auschwitz and Treblinka. If I read Langer correctly, the perplexity that Inga Clendinnen wants to mitigate is less his problem than what he identifies as an understandable but problematic inclination to "pre-empt" the Holocaust. Pre-empting the Holocaust, says Langer, means "using—and perhaps abusing—its grim details to fortify a prior commitment to ideals of moral reality, community responsibility, or religious belief that leave us with space to retain faith in their pristine value in a post-Holocaust world."[8] Langer makes us wonder how we can learn from the Holocaust without pre-empting it. This pitfall is one of the most important that the courage to try to teach about and learn from the Holocaust must guard against. *Teaching and Studying the Holocaust* shows us how to take many of the right steps in that direction.

In a *New York Times* essay published on June 27, 1999, Langer credited the author of the book he was reviewing for drawing the "sensible if unpopular conclusion that we should study a historical event like the Holocaust not to extract lessons but to appreciate its complexities and contradictions." Adding that such a conclusion "will please a few readers but probably upset many more," Langer made those comments about Peter Novick and his controversial book, *The Holocaust in American Life,* which also puts complicating questions before all of us who try to be Holocaust educators.

In addition to asking "Why now? and "Why here?" when it comes to discerning the American concern about the Holocaust that, among other things, leads to the publication of *Teaching and Studying the Holocaust*, Novick expressed skepticism about the value of such concern. In particular, he is dubious about "the idea of 'lessons of the Holocaust.'"[9] Early on in his book, he emphasizes two reasons for his skepticism. Both deserve serious consideration. The first is *pedagogic*. The Holocaust's very extremity, argues Novick, makes it an unlikely source of "lessons for dealing with the sorts of issues that confront us in ordinary life."[10] He doubts that there is anything that is necessarily "morally therapeutic" in "the mere act of walking through a Holocaust museum, or viewing a Holocaust movie," or, we might add, teaching or taking a course on the Holocaust or genocide.[11] Here I think Novick's challenge is a version of "show me the money." As one's reading of this book will reveal, *Teaching and Studying the Holocaust* helps to show how we can best identify and teach the Holocaust-related lessons that are needed most.

The second reason for Novick's skepticism is *pragmatic*, which is to say that he is dubious that there will be much "money" to show when one asks "what is the payoff" of learning from the Holocaust that is supposed to be ethical. Novick does not deny that Holocaust study might sometimes sensitize people against "oppression and atrocity," but he contends that emphasis on the Holocaust (especially emphasis that insists on the Holocaust's "uniqueness") "works in precisely the opposite direction, trivializing crimes of lesser magnitude."[12] For most Americans, Novick contends, "contemplating the Holocaust is virtually cost-free: a few cheap tears," but in another sense he reckons that such contemplation is not cost-free at all, because "it promotes *evasion* of moral and historical responsibility" as far as our own American history is concerned.[13] Here Novick's challenge seems to go like this: How do we study and teach about the Holocaust and genocide without evading moral and historical responsibilities that belong to us as we confront our American past, present, and future? If we do not evade those responsibilities, will efforts to learn about and from the Holocaust deserve the attention that are now being devoted to them?

One thing leads to another, and in Holocaust studies there are more questions than answers, which is one of the most important reasons to study Holocaust history. Be that as it may, where teaching about and learning from the Holocaust are concerned, the courage to try confronts us with challenges about what can and cannot, what must and must not, be made of the Holocaust. How should we cope with the likelihood that what we try to learn from the Holocaust will be overwhelmed by the "useless knowledge" we obtain as we learn about it? How can we learn from the Holocaust without pre-empting it? Can we learn from the Holocaust without evading important moral responsibilities? What is, after all, the "payoff," pedagogic and pragmatic, of Holocaust and genocide studies? This foreword can end by raising those questions, because what follows in *Teaching and Studying the Holocaust* provides a sound basis for answering them, not only in the words on its pages but also in the responsible teaching that this book will help to promote as it inspires the proper courage to try.

NOTES

1. Charlotte Delbo, *Auschwitz and After,* trans. Rosette C. Lamont (New Haven, CT: Yale University Press, 1995), 352.

2. The second part of the *Auschwitz and After* trilogy is called *Useless Knowledge* (*Une connaissance inutile*).

3. Delbo, *Auschwitz and After,* 351.

4. Inga Clendinnen, *Reading the Holocaust* (Cambridge: Cambridge University Press, 1999), 4.

5. Ibid., 5.

6. Lawrence L. Langer, "Pre-empting the Holocaust," *The Atlantic Monthly,* November 1998, 108. The ideas in this article are elaborated by Langer in *Preempting the Holocaust* (New Haven, CT: Yale University Press, 1998).

7. Lawrence L. Langer, ed., *Art from the Ashes: A Holocaust Anthology* (New York: Oxford University Press, 1995), 7.

8. Langer, "Pre-empting the Holocaust," 105.

9. Peter Novick, *The Holocaust in American Life* (Boston: Houghton Mifflin, 1999), 13.

10. Ibid.

11. Ibid.

12. Ibid., 14.

13. Ibid., 15.

PREFACE

STEPHEN FEINBERG

SAMUEL TOTTEN

The Holocaust is one of the most significant historical events of the twentieth century. Where once it was viewed as a mere footnote to World War II, it is now seen as an event that is extraordinarily significant in its own right. The systematic destruction of Jews and Gypsies, along with the persecution of other victims, is one of the most incomprehensible and perplexing events facing humanity *and* educators. Indeed, it is the very singularity of the event that increasingly demands the attention of teachers and students.

Within the past decade, the study of the Holocaust has become more and more commonplace within the world of education, in the United States and beyond. As of 2000, seventeen states have required, recommended, or encouraged the inclusion of a study of the Holocaust in their school systems. Various state and private agencies and organizations have helped craft either entire curricula devoted to the Holocaust or have developed guidelines to assist classroom educators with the teaching of this extraordinary and complex history. Furthermore, entire courses have been developed by teachers in both public and private schools connected to this history, while individual lessons on the Holocaust also have been added to existing courses of study.

This increasing concern with the Holocaust highlights the need for conscientious teachers to confront not only the underlying educational issues associated with the Holocaust but also the pragmatic concerns of addressing this history in an accurate and thorough fashion within the context of secondary school classrooms.

It is our hope that this book, *Teaching and Studying the Holocaust*, will serve as a resource guide for those who want to teach the Holocaust. In that regard, the authors in this book address a host of fundamental issues and questions that we believe teachers need to consider as they design and implement lessons and units on the Holocaust:

- Why need a teacher address this catastrophe?
- What does the teacher want to accomplish by teaching about the Holocaust to secondary school students?
- What historical knowledge must a teacher possess?
- In what specific sources can a teacher find historical and literary information on the Holocaust?
- What is the connection between the rationale(s) for teaching the Holocaust and the pedagogical strategies selected?
- What are among the most pedagogically sound ways to teach this history?

This book also includes information for those teachers who are looking for specific suggestions in regard to the selection and use of content information and resources:

- What are some ways to use primary documents?
- How should first-person accounts be incorporated into the study?
- Which literature is appropriate for middle school students and which is appropriate for high school students?
- How can use of the Internet help students learn about the Holocaust?
- What are some key films that can be used in the teaching of the Holocaust, and what are the most effective methods for using them?
- What are the most efficacious methods to incorporate drama, art, or music into a study of the Holocaust?

Ultimately, it is our hope that the use of this book will assist educators and students to wrestle with the fundamental issues and themes raised by this extraordinary history.

ACKNOWLEDGMENTS

Samuel Totten and Stephen Feinberg wish to acknowledge their appreciation of the United States Holocaust Memorial Museum for granting the use of various photographs and documents used in this book. They also wish to thank Mr. Steven Vitto, Research Librarian, for his critical assistance.

Their appreciation also goes to the following reviewers for their helpful comments on the manuscript: Dr. Geoffrey Short, University of Hertfordshire; Dr. Carol Rittner, The Richard Stockton College of New Jersey; Dr. Sanford Gutman, State University of New York, Cortland; and Dr. Michael Berenbaum, former Director of Research, United States Holocaust Memorial Museum.

Samuel Totten also wishes to sincerely thank William Fernekes for his contributions to the conception and early development of this book.

ABOUT THE CONTRIBUTORS

About the Editors

Stephen Feinberg is the director of National Outreach in the Education Division of the United States Holocaust Memorial Museum. He also served as the original coordinator of the Mandel Teacher Fellowship Program in the Education Division of the United States Holocaust Memorial Museum. The goal of this program is to develop a national corps of skilled secondary schoolteachers who will serve as leaders in Holocaust education in their schools, communities, and professional organizations. A graduate of UCLA, where he studied history, and the Harvard Graduate School of Education, he was a social studies teacher and supervisor in the Wayland Public Schools, Wayland, Massachusetts, for eighteen years. He served as a Peace Corps volunteer in Morocco from 1967 to 1970 and in Thailand from 1974 to 1975. He served as co-editor, with Samuel Totten, of the 1995 special issue, "Teaching about the Holocaust," of *Social Education,* the official journal of the National Council for the Social Studies. Feinberg has developed curricula in the areas of Holocaust education and American constitutional history. He has made presentations on Holocaust education at professional conferences and workshops in the United States and Europe.

Samuel Totten is currently a professor in the Department of Curriculum and Instruction at the University of Arkansas at Fayetteville. Before entering academia, he taught English and social studies at the secondary level in Australia, Israel, California, and Washington, D.C. He also served as a K–8 principal in northern California. He has an earned doctoral degree in curriculum and instruction from Teachers College, Columbia University, in New York City.

Prior to, and several years into, its operation, Totten served as an educational consultant to the United States Holocaust Memorial Museum. In this later capacity he co-authored, with William S. Parsons, *Guidelines for Teaching about the Holocaust* (Washington, D.C.: United States Holocaust Memorial Museum, 1993).

His essays on Holocaust education have appeared in such journals as *The British Journal of Holocaust Education; Canadian Social Studies; The Journal of Holocaust Education;* the *Journal of Curriculum and Supervision; Social Education;* and *The Social Studies.*

Currently he is editing two books on the Holocaust—*Teaching Holocaust Literature* (Boston: Allyn and Bacon, 2001) and *Remembering the Past, Educating for the Future: Educators Encounter the Holocaust* (Westport, Conn.: Greenwood)—and is editing another entitled *Genocide Education: Issues and Approaches.*

About the Authors

Roselle K. Chartock is a professor of education at the Massachusetts College of Liberal Arts in North Adams, Massachusetts. She has taught and written about the Holocaust for over twenty-five years. In 1972, while teaching history at Monument Mountain Regional High School in Great Barrington, Massachusetts, she and her colleagues created what they believe to be the first interdisciplinary unit of instruction on the Holocaust at the secondary level of schooling. She described this unit in depth in an article, "A Holocaust Unit for Classroom Teachers," published in *Social Education* in 1978, and subsequently wrote several related articles that appeared in *Today's Education; Massachusetts Teacher; Commonwealth Review,* and *The Reference Librarian.* The curriculum also resulted in the development of an anthology of readings, *The Holocaust Years: Society on Trial,* edited by Chartock and Jack Spencer (New York: Bantam Books, 1978). The anthology was republished in 1995, with new readings, as *Can It Happen Again? Chronicles of the Holocaust,* by Black Dog and Leventhal.

Chartock teaches a course in her college's Honors Program entitled "The Holocaust and the Nature of Prejudice." Besides writing and teaching about the Holocaust, Dr. Chartock has lectured and presented workshops for teachers throughout the nation. The focus of many of these workshops was on the music of the oppressed and the oppressor.

Steven Cohen is currently a lecturer in education at Tufts University in Medford, Massachusetts. He was a high school history teacher at Cambridge School of Weston from 1976 to 1988, Fenway Middle College High School (Boston) from 1992 to 1997, and Boston Arts Academy in 1999. At the college level, he has taught at the Experimental College at Tufts (1989–1990), Cambridge College (1993–1994), and now at Tufts University (1996–present).

He started teaching about the Holocaust in 1979 and has worked with the Facing History and Ourselves Foundation since that time as a member of its teacher team and as a program associate. His pedagogical efforts are highlighted in Melinda Fine's study of the Facing History and Ourselves program, *Habits of Mind: Struggling over Values in America's Classrooms* (San Francisco, Calif.: Jossey-Bass Publishers, 1995).

Cohen served as the chief researcher on the revised edition of Facing History and Ourselves' *Holocaust and Human Behavior* book. He also co-authored, with Mary Johnson, a study guide entitled "Kristallnacht" that appeared in *Dimensions: A Holocaust Journal* (Fall 1988), and co-authored, with John Michalczyk, *The Cross and the Star: A Study Guide* (St. Louis, Mo: Albion Press, 1992).

Bibliographies and timelines developed by Cohen appear in John Michalczyk's (ed.) *Medicine, Ethics, and the Third Reich* (Kansas City, Mo.: Sheed and Ward, 1994), and John Michalczyk's (ed.) *The Resister, the Rescuer, and the Refugee* (Kansas City, Mo.: Sheed and Ward, 1997).

David M. Crowe is a professor of history at Elon College, where he teaches the Holocaust and Russian history. He is also a visiting scholar at the Harriman Institute at Columbia University, a member of the Education Committee of the United States Holocaust Memorial Museum in Washington, D.C., President of the Association for the Study of Nationalities at Columbia University, and former chairman of the North Carolina Council on the Holocaust.

His books include *The Holocaust: Roots, History, and Aftermath* (Boulder, Colo.: Westview Press, 2000), and *A History of the Gypsies of Eastern Europe and Russia* (New York: St. Martin's Press, 1995), which was a History Bookclub selection. He is currently writing a biography of Oskar Schindler.

Judith E. Doneson received her B.S. in film from Boston University and her M.A. and Ph.D in contemporary Jewish history from The Hebrew University of Jerusalem. She has lectured at the Yad Vashem Institute, a program of Yad Vashem—The Holocaust Martyrs' and Heroes' Remembrance Authority, in Jerusalem, and was a Fellow at the Center for Jewish Studies at the University of Pennsylvania. Doneson has taught at Tel Aviv University and Saint Louis University, and was visiting professor of history at Washington University in St. Louis where she currently teaches Holocaust and Film.

Doneson is the author of *The Holocaust in American Film* (Philadelphia, Penn.: The Jewish Publication Society, 1987), soon to be reissued by Syracuse University Press, and a contributor to *Spielberg's Holocaust: Critical Perspectives on Schindler's List* (Bloomington, Ill.: Indiana University Press, 1997), and *Lessons and Legacies, Volume II and Volume III* (Evanston, Ill.: Northwestern University Press, 1998 and 1999). Her essays have also appeared in *Holocaust and Genocide Studies, Studies in Contemporary Jewry,* and other journals.

William R. Fernekes is supervisor of social studies at Hunterdon Central Regional H.S. in Flemington, New Jersey. A twenty-five-year veteran classroom teacher and department supervisor, he has published extensively in the fields of social studies curriculum; issues-based curriculum design and pedagogy; human rights education; and Holocaust/genocide studies.

Among the articles and essays he has published on the Holocaust are: *Teacher's Guide: Illustrative Lesson Plans,* for the textbook series entitled *Holocaust* (Woodbridge, Conn.: Blackbirch Press, 1998); "The Holocaust: A Central Issue for Citizenship Education," in *Social Science Record,* Fall/Winter 1997; "Studying the Holocaust Using Internet Resources" (with Hilarie Bryce Davis and Christine Hladky), in *The Social Studies,* January/February 1999; and "The Holocaust, Human Rights and Citizenship Education" (with David A. Shiman), in *The Social Studies,* March/April 1999. Among the book chapters he has published on the Holocaust are: "The Babi Yar Massacre: Seeking Understanding Using a Multimedia Approach" in Samuel Totten's (ed.) *Teaching Holocaust Literature* (Boston, Mass.: Allyn and Bacon, 2001); "Education about the Holocaust, Human Rights and Social Responsibility," in Bernard Schwartz' and Frederick C. DeCoste's (eds.) *The Holocaust: Art, Politics, Law, and Education* (Edmonton, Alberta, Canada: University of Alberta Press, 1999); and, with Samuel Totten, "Education about the Holocaust in the United States" in Israel W. Charny's (ed.) *Encyclopedia of Genocide* (Santa Barbara, Calif.: ABC Clio Press, 1999).

Fernekes also serves as a consultant to the Education Department of the United States Holocaust Memorial Museum, where he has advised on development and implementation of educational programs since 1991.

Robert P. Hines teaches history at Richard Montgomery High School in Rockville, Maryland, where he is also chair of the History Department.

He is a graduate of the Yad Vashem Institute for Teachers, which is a program of Yad Vashem—The Holocaust Martyrs' and Heroes' Remembrance Authority, in Jerusalem, Israel. He has fifteen years of experience training teachers in Holocaust Education, and thirty years of experience in the classroom teaching Advanced Placement and International Baccalaureate European History.

John J. Michalczyk is chair of the Fine Arts Department and co-director of Film Studies at Boston College. For two decades he has lectured on Holocaust film, and has produced two films dealing with the Holocaust: *The Cross and the Star: Jews, Christians and the Holocaust* (1992) and *In the Shadow of the Reich: Nazi Medicine* (1997), both distributed by First Run Features in New York. He has also published two books based on international conferences convened at Boston College: *Medicine, Ethics, and the Third Reich: Historical and Contemporary Issues* (Kansas City, Mo.: Sheed & Ward, 1994) and *Resisters, Rescuers, and Refugees: Historical and Ethical Issues* (Kansas City, Mo: Sheed & Ward, 1997).

Karen Shawn, Ph.D., formerly a teacher of English in Lawrence, Long Island, is an assistant principal at Moriah School of Englewood, a Hebrew Day School in New Jersey. She is the regional director of Educational Outreach for the American Society of Yad Vashem, and teaches the pedagogical component of the Yad Vashem Summer Institute for Educators from Abroad in Jerusalem, Israel. She is also a consultant to the Ghetto Fighters House (GFH) in D.N. Western Galilee, Israel, and co-author of the teacher's guide for the GFH International Reading Project. She is the author of *The End of Innocence: Anne Frank and the Holocaust* (New York: Anti-Defamation League, 1994), and editor of *In the Aftermath of the Holocaust: Three Generations Speak* (Englewood, N.J.: Moriah School, 1995).

Derek Symer is the editor and publisher for history products at Chadwyck-Healey Publishing in Alexandria, Virginia. From 1990 to 1996, Symer worked in the Office of the Historian and Exhibitions Department at the United States Holocaust Memorial Museum in Washington, D.C. He is a 1990 graduate of Dartmouth College where he studied history and German language. In 1995, he earned his M.A. in European history at the American University.

Shari Rosenstein Werb is a Museum Educator at the United States Holocaust Memorial Museum (USHMM). She has created educational programs and materials to help students learn more about Holocaust history through examination of artifacts, artwork, music, documents, and historical photographs. She is also the founding coordinator of the National Art Contest at the United States Holocaust Memorial Museum. She has lectured on the topic of art and the Holocaust to hundreds of educators and students throughout the United States.

Paul Wieser is currently the director of Social Studies at the Pendergast School District, Phoenix, Arizona. He has been involved with Holocaust education since the early 1970s when he completed graduate work in the field at the University of San Francisco. He has continued his study at the Yad Vashem—The Holocaust Martyrs' and Heroes Remembrance Authority in Jerusalem; Haifa University; and the Ghetto Fighters' House in Israel.

Wieser has been the recipient of several National Humanities Council Fellowships, which have allowed him to further his research into the history of the Holocaust. Additionally, he is a Mandel Fellow of the United States Holocaust Memorial Museum and frequently gives workshops across the United States on the subject of the methodology and pedagogy associated with Holocaust education. During the summer of 1999 he served as a museum educator at the United States Holocaust Memorial Museum.

Wieser is the author of several articles, the most notable of which appeared in a special edition of *Social Education* (October 1995), devoted to teaching about the Holocaust. His efforts in the field have been recognized by the Arizona School Board Association which awarded him its Golden Bell Award. He is also the recipient of the Shofar Zachor Award, presented by the Phoenix Holocaust Survivors' Association for furthering the cause of Holocaust education. His close association with the National History Day Program has resulted in his students (all of whom research a Holocaust topic for one year) winning nine consecutive state titles and the national title in 1993.

Belarie Zatzman, Ph.D., teaches in the Department of Theatre in Atkinson College at York University, Toronto, Canada. She regularly presents workshops in schools about Holocaust and the fine arts, and has worked with the Atlantic Jewish Council; Dalhousie University; the Holocaust Memorial Museum of the Jewish Federation of Greater Toronto; the Toronto Board of Education; the Faculties of Education at the University of Toronto and York University; and the Toronto Jewish Board of Education.

Over the past 15 years Zatzman has also directed Yom Hashoa events and Holocaust plays. Recent publications include: "Traces of the Past: Practice and Research as Shifting Structures in Drama and Holocaust Education" in *Second International Drama Education Research Institute* (Victoria: University of Victoria, British Columbia, 1999) and "Creating Narrative Memorials: Drama and the Holocaust" in *Drama Now! and the Challenge of Tomorrow?* (Conference Proceedings—Christchurch College, Canterbury) (London: National Drama Publications, London Drama at Central School of Speech and Drama, 1999).

Teaching and Studying the Holocaust

The Significance of Rationale Statements in Developing a Sound Holocaust Education Program

SAMUEL TOTTEN

STEPHEN FEINBERG

WILLIAM FERNEKES

When preparing to teach about the Holocaust, it is essential to establish a solid set of rationales. Holocaust lessons and units bereft of controlling principles often lack a sound historical focus, including the critical need to address the "whys" of the historical events versus focusing solely on the "whats" of the history. Ultimately, a sound set of rationales helps teachers to design and implement clearly delineated goals, objectives, content, and assessment strategies.

In this chapter, we discuss numerous concerns regarding rationale statements including but not limited to the following: their purpose, their use in developing goals and objectives, their value in guiding content selection, their influence in selecting pedagogical strategies and resources, their use in avoiding pitfalls common to many studies of the Holocaust, and the critical need to revisit them throughout the study.

The Purpose of Rationales

In his essay, "Toward a Methodology of Teaching About the Holocaust," Henry Friedlander (1979), a scholar and survivor of the Holocaust, expressed great concern about the sudden proliferation of courses of study and curricula about the Holocaust:

> The problem with too much being taught by too many *without focus* [italics added] is that this poses the danger of destroying the subject matter through dilettantism. It is not enough for well-meaning teachers to feel a commitment to teach about genocide; they also must know the subject. . . . The problems of popularization and proliferation should make us careful about how we introduce the Holocaust into the curriculum; it does not mean we should stop teaching it. But we must try to define the subject of the Holocaust. Even if we do not agree about the content of the subject, we must agree on its goals and on its limitations. (Friedlander, 1979, pp. 520–521, 522)

The issues raised by Friedlander in 1979 remain central concerns today, perhaps even more so. Within the last decade, there has been an even greater surge in the development of curricula, teacher guides, resources, and organizational programs addressing the subject of the Holocaust. Although many of the resources and programs are engaging and pedagogically sound, many are not (Totten and Parsons, 1992, pp. 27–47). In particular, rationales for some curricula are extremely weak, often providing superficial justifications for the study of the Holocaust. That poses a serious problem to teachers and students alike, making the need for sound rationales, goals, and objectives for teaching about the Holocaust that much more significant.

As the authors of the U.S. Holocaust Memorial Museum's *Guidelines for Teaching about the Holocaust* note:

> Because the objective of teaching any subject is to engage the intellectual curiosity of the student in order to inspire critical thought and personal growth, it is helpful to structure lesson plans on the Holocaust by considering throughout questions of rationale. Before addressing what and how to teach, one should contemplate the following: Why should students learn this history? What are the most significant lessons students can learn about the Holocaust? Why is a particular reading, image, document, or film an appropriate medium for conveying the lessons about the Holocaust which you wish to teach? (Parsons and Totten, 1993, p. 1)

Issues of rationale are also not emphasized enough in the classroom. For example, some teachers plunge into their courses without asking students questions such as, "Why study the Holocaust?" or "Why study this particular aspect of the Holocaust?"

Regardless of whether the teacher is experienced or inexperienced in teaching about the Holocaust, questions of rationale should always be considered. Teachers should *constantly* ask themselves, "Why am I teaching this subject in the first place?" "What are the most essential topics/questions that need to be addressed within this subject matter, and why is that so?"

It is impossible, of course, to teach all history, so each community, school, and individual educator must select and organize those historical events and deeds that best assist students to understand both the past as well as the world in which they live today. This means that rationale statements must clearly identify why a particular period of history should be incorporated into the school curriculum. If this is not done, there is the danger that this history may become marginal and irrelevant to the students. As Friedlander (1979) suggests, equally significant is the need for the teacher (hopefully in conjunction with the students) to decide what aspects of the history should be taught and why. Developing clearly stated rationales will assist teachers in emphasizing particular aspects of the history, thus helping to assure that the study is neither so broad nor so limited that it becomes meaningless.

All that said, to ignore the history of the Holocaust is to distort the history of humanity and, particularly, that of the twentieth century. Indeed, we are in complete agreement with Eisner's (1979) perceptive thesis that

> . . . what schools do not teach may be as important as what they do teach. I argue this position because ignorance is not simply a void; it has important effects on the kinds of options one is able to consider, the alternatives one can examine, and the perspectives with which one can view a situation or problem. (p. 83)

Finally, those teachers who have understood the importance of rationales for teaching the Holocaust have sound responses and answers to those individuals—students, parents, administrators, school board members, or other citizens in the community—who question the importance of this history. When teachers are asked why they are teaching something that may be perceived as "outside the curriculum" or controversial, they often lack sound explanations for curricular decisions. The development of sound rationales can help to alleviate this painful situation.

Developing Rationale Statements

When developing rationale statements, teachers find it helpful to ask themselves a series of questions:

- Why is the Holocaust important to study?
- What do I perceive as the most important lesson(s) to be learned from a study of the Holocaust, and why?
- If I only have time to teach, for example, five different topics/aspects of the Holocaust, what would they be and why?
- What do I want my students to walk away with after a study of the Holocaust, and why?
- If I can only plant one seed in my students' minds for them to ponder over the long haul of their lives about the Holocaust, what would it be and why?

When developing rationale statements, one should concentrate on both cognitive and affective levels—the mind, knowledge, and thinking, as well as the heart, dispositions, and feelings. To address one of those components and not the other is likely to result in an incomplete curriculum, one that is bereft of the essential components that make us human.

If, after designing a series of rationale statements, one discovers that the focus is on the "whats, wheres, and whens" of the history but bereft of the "whys," then it is imperative that the teacher reconsider the goals, objectives, and content for the lesson or unit. Likewise, if one discovers that the focus is solely on a series of facts versus the importance this history has for both the individual and post-Holocaust society, then it would be wise to consider adding components that are likely to engage students in pondering long and hard what meaning this history has for their own lives and the world in which they live. Indeed, this process is imperative. As historian Yehuda Bauer (1978) has stated, ". . . [T]he crucial problem is how to anchor the Holocaust in the historical consciousness of the generation(s) that follow it" (p. 45). And, we would add, moral consciousness.

By examining the causes and consequences of the policy decisions made by the Third Reich, as well as those by other societies during the Holocaust period, we help students gain a deeper understanding of how governmental policies can lead to persecution, discrimination, and the destruction of human life. The moral and ethical dimensions of Holocaust study, often embedded in the context of memoirs, diaries, and other first-person accounts, help students reexamine their own values and actions, and provide opportunities for reflection on genuinely caring responses to patterns of prejudice and discrimination.

If a key goal in teaching the Holocaust is to "make a student both knowledgeable and different" (Lipstadt, 1995, p. 29), then teachers need to consider how to accomplish this. A key place to begin this process is in the development of their rationale statements. As Rosenberg and Bardosh (1982–1983) correctly assert:

> There is a fundamental distinction between the process of learning and the process of integrating the meaning and implications of an important event into consciousness and conscience. One can learn about an event by consuming and assimilating the factual details that have gone into its making. But learning does not necessarily indicate understanding. The latter is the result of integration. By integration we mean that the actions of individuals who have successfully absorbed an event into their moral and intellectual world will display an awareness of that event in their everyday activities. (p. 3)

Examples of Rationale Statements for Teaching the Holocaust

> *If the study of genocide is not also the study of humanity and inhumanity, if it does not add to our understanding of human behavior, then what is its purpose in the curriculum?*
>
> —Margaret Drew

Over the past twenty years, a number of thought-provoking rationales have been generated by educators in regard to the question: "Why teach about the Holocaust?" Those that we find the most thought-provoking and/or interesting are as follows:

- to study human behavior;
- to teach students why, how, what, when, and where the Holocaust took place, including the key historical trends/antecedents that led up to and culminated in the "final solution";
- to explore concepts such as prejudice, discrimination, stereotyping, racism, antisemitism, obedience to authority, the bystander syndrome, loyalty, conflict, conflict resolution, decision making, and justice;
- "to illustrate the effects of peer pressure, individual responsibility, and the process of decision making under the most extreme conditions" (Schwartz, 1990, p. 101);
- to become "cognizant that 'little' prejudices can easily be transformed into far more serious ones" (Lipstadt, 1995, p. 29);
- to "make students more sensitive to ethnic and religious hatred" (Lipstadt, 1995, p. 29);
- to develop in students an awareness of the value of pluralism and diversity in a pluralistic society;
- to reflect on the roles and responsibilities of individuals, groups, and nations when confronting life in an industrial/technological/information age, including the abuse of power, civil and human rights violations, and genocidal acts;
- "to develop a deeper appreciation of the relationship of rights and duties, and to realize that human rights and the corresponding duties they entail are not the birthright of the few but the birthright of all—every man, woman, and child in the world today" (Branson and Torney-Purta, 1982, p. 5);
- to examine the nature, structure, and purpose of governments;
- to "become sensitized to inhumanity and suffering whenever they occur" (Fleischner in Strom and Parsons, 1982, p. 6);
- to provide a context for exploring the dangers of remaining silent, apathetic, and indifferent in the face of others' oppression;
- to teach civic virtue . . . [which is related to] the importance of responsible citizenship and mature iconoclasm" (Friedlander, 1979, pp. 532–533);
- to understand that the Holocaust was *not* an accident in history; it was not inevitable (Parsons and Totten, 1993, p. 1);
- to develop an understanding that the Holocaust was a watershed event not only in the twentieth century, but in the entire history of humanity (Parsons and Totten, 1993, p. 1);
- to demonstrate how a modern nation can utilize its technological expertise and bureaucratic infrastructure to implement destructive policies ranging from social engineering to genocide;
- to illustrate that the Holocaust resulted from a cumulative progression of numerous historical events and deeds, *and* that it was not an event in history that was inevitable (Parsons and Totten, 1993, p. 3).

Teachers—in conjunction, if they wish, with their students—need to decide what the focus of the study will be, and then develop appropriate rationale statements. Just as each class of students is unique, each study of the Holocaust by necessity will be unique. To a certain extent, this is likely to be dictated by the teacher's knowledge base, what the teacher perceives as being of the utmost significance vis-à-vis the history, the levels and the abilities of the students, the time alloted for the study, the type and amount of resources available, and/or a combination of these concerns.

Although some teachers explain why the subject of the Holocaust is important to their students, they do not always encourage student responses. This approach is apt to set a "preachy" tone that may cause students some consternation and/or even to question the motive(s) of the teacher. This style of teaching also signals to students that their views and thoughts are not as important as those of the teacher.

Finally, some educators (particularly curriculum developers) have a tendency to borrow noble-sounding rationales from others and posit them as goals for their own curricula. To use other educators' rationale statements in this fashion is the same as never designing a rationale statement in the first place.

The Need for Careful Use of Language in Rationales

The language used in creating the rationale(s) is critical. Of the utmost importance is that rationales not constitute "comparisons of pain." That is, one should not assert that "the Holocaust is the most horrific example of genocide in the history of humanity." To make such an assertion minimizes the horror and suffering experienced by humans in other genocides.

Terms such as *"unimaginable"* or *"unbelievable"* are often used when speaking about the Holocaust, but these terms may send a message to students that the Holocaust was so "unreal" that it is pointless to try and learn about what happened. Indeed, students may begin to believe that the Holocaust was a one-time aberration, and that it has no message for humanity today. The simple but profound fact is that the Holocaust did happen. It was systematically planned and implemented by human beings, and thus it is not "unimaginable" or "unbelievable." As Lawrence Langer (1978) states:

> What does it mean to say that an event is beyond the imagination? It was not beyond the imagination of the men who authorized it; or those who executed it; or those who suffered it. Once an event occurs, can it any longer be said to be "beyond the imagination"? Inaccessible, yes; . . . contrary to "all those human values on which art is traditionally based," of course. What we confront is not the unimaginable, but the intolerable, a condition of existence that so diminishes our own humanity that we prefer to assign it to an alien realm. (p. 5)

One should also avoid the use of clichés in rationale statements. Too often teachers and curriculum developers have mindlessly latched on to such phrases as "Never Again," "Always Remember," "Never Forget," and "Those Who Do Not

Remember History are Condemned to Repeat It," without giving ample thought and consideration as to their meaning.

Spoken by survivors, these admonitions *are* powerful *and* meaningful. They are *not* powerful and meaningful, though, when they are spoken by politicians, after-dinner speakers, conference participants, and teachers who neglect to acknowledge the fact that genocide has been perpetrated, time and again, since 1945.

If and when curriculum developers use such phrases as "Never Again," they should ask themselves what they mean by them. That is, do they mean that the Holocaust, involving the same people (in which Jewish men, women, and children are the victims and the Nazis are the tormentors and executioners) must never take place again? Or, do they mean that no genocide should ever take place again? Both, of course, are legitimate goals and something that everyone should strive for and be vigilant about.

To use such phrases simply because they sound good is problematic at best. (For a more detailed discussion of this issue, see Totten [1999], "Teaching the Holocaust: The Imperative to Move Beyond Clichés.")

Factors Influencing the Focus of Rationale Statements

Among the most important factors influencing the focus of rationale statements are: (1) one's aims in teaching the history; (2) one's knowledge of the history of the Holocaust; (3) the particular course one is teaching; (4) the levels and abilities of one's students; (5) the available time for study of the Holocaust; and (6) the instructional resources available.

Quite obviously, the major factor influencing the focus of one's rationale statements is one's aim in teaching this history. Is it to provide a deep understanding of how Germany became a fascist, totalitarian, and genocidal state? Is it to focus on both the incremental nature of the assault against the Jews and others as well as the extermination process? Is it to focus on the complexity and danger of the bystander syndrome both within and outside the Nazi sphere of influence and power? Is it to focus on the literature (fiction, poetry, drama) of the Holocaust? Is it to teach lessons about living in a world where genocide is still perpetrated on a regular basis?

Even those who have a working knowledge of this history need to seriously consider what their goals are for such a study. In doing so, it is wise to consult key historical works, pedagogical essays, comprehensive chronologies of the Holocaust, and the most accurate and pedagogically sound lessons and curricula available on the Holocaust in order to develop strong rationale statements. If, by contrast, one has an extremely limited knowledge of the history, then *it is imperative the teacher educate him/herself about this history prior to teaching it.*

The particular course one teaches will also dictate the focus of the rationale statements. For example, the rationale statement in a history course will differ from one in a literature course because the focus of each is bound to be fundamentally different. That said, there is bound to be overlap in the content of the rationale statements. The study of human behavior could very well be the focus of both a historical and literary rationale statement. By contrast, a social studies teacher emphasizing the study of change over time may develop rationale statements that stress the impact of the past on present societal conditions and decision making, or on how contemporary democratic institutions reflect the relative success or failure of citizens to embody democratic values and processes in their daily lives.

In developing a course on the Holocaust, it is vital to take into consideration the levels, abilities, and backgrounds of one's students. The factors inherent in these concerns will dicate the sophistication and depth of the study, the resources used, and the pedagogical strategies and learning activities employed. To neglect these issues is pedagogically unsound. Furthermore, it is an invitation to a study that will likely be either too sophisticated or too simplistic. For students with limited reading ability, one can create a study of the Holocaust through a blend of graphic, visual, and audio resources, as well as appropriate reading materials that are accurate but not beyond their ability to comprehend. Many resources, including those available on selected Internet sites, can be utilized effectively with those who have reading difficulties, particularly when in-depth discussion of the resources is regularly employed to facilitate student comprehension and understanding of how specific cases (i.e., personal audio testimonies) are illustrative of larger historical trends.

Time is always a critical factor in the classroom. Many teachers are extremely limited in how much time they can allot to this history. That results in the need to make some difficult decisions in regard to what one can and cannot include in such a study. An in-depth study of topics is generally preferable to superficial coverage of a plethora of topics. As Fred Newmann (1988) states, ". . . less in this context does not mean less knowledge or information, for depth can be achieved only through the mastery of considerable information. Rather, less refers to less mastery of information that provides only a superficial acquaintance with a topic" (p. 347). Newmann (1988) correctly observes that:

> . . . we usually try to teach too much. . . . We are addicted to coverage. This addiction seems endemic in high school, especially in history. . . . Beyond simply wasting time or failing to impart knowledge of lasting value, superficial coverage has a more insidious consequence: it reinforces habits of mindlessness. Classrooms become places in which material must be learned—even though students find it nonsensical because their teachers have no time to explain. Students are denied opportunities to explore related areas that arouse their curiosity for fear of straying too far from the official list of topics to be covered.
>   . . . The alternative to coverage, though difficult to achieve, is depth: the sustained study of a given topic that leads students beyond superficial exposure to rich, complex understanding. (p. 346)

Teachers who do not consider the issue of time when developing rationale statements may be in for a rude awakening when it comes to teaching the course predicated on such rationale statements.

The instructional resources a teacher has available for a study of the Holocaust will likely influence the focus of the study; and that, in turn, will likely impact the type of rationale statements one devises. Simply stated, one can develop all the rationale statements one wants, but if one does not have the resources to teach the information, concepts, and issues, then it is likely that the focus and intent of the rationale statements will not be realized. Given that the range of available instructional resources will influence classroom practices, the development of rationales should coincide with a determined effort to expand available resources to encompass the broad goals of the course. While this is time consuming and costly, over time a comprehensive set of instructional resources, including books, first-person accounts, primary documents, online resources, computer software, audiovisual materials, fiction and poetry, and lists of community members, can be developed to support curricular rationales and programs.

The Use of Rationale Statements to Develop Goals and Objectives for the Study

Limited value exists in developing rationale statements if they do not influence the actual goals and objectives of the course. Together, the rationale statements, goals, and objectives will assist one in developing the content, the pedagogy, the resources, and the learning activities to be employed.

Learning objectives should take into consideration the developmental level of prospective students in the course, address all levels of Bloom's taxonomy or a comparable taxonomy of thinking or cognitive operations, include both content and process concerns, and provide opportunities for extension of learning beyond the classroom so that other "communities" experience the benefits of what students have learned in the course.

Rationales Should Direct the Content Used in the Study

Over the course of the past five years, both educators (Shawn, 1995) and noted scholars (Dawidowicz, 1992; Lipstadt, 1995) have criticized the content of courses being offered on the Holocaust in many of our nation's public schools. In doing so, they have addressed everything from the weakness of curricular goals and objectives to the weaknesses inherent in the depiction of the history in various curricula.

In an article entitled "Current Issues in Holocaust Education," educator Karen Shawn (1995) argued that "The ill-considered rush to educate may lead to the trivialization and distortion of the memory of the Holocaust. This is evident in the recent alarming proliferation of poorly conceived and executed textbooks, teaching aids, and lesson plans flooding our schools" (p. 18). She concluded her article by stating, ". . . today Holocaust education is threatened by ignorance, arrogance, superficiality, and commercialism" (p. 18).

Teachers need to carefully select from the mass of topics and information available that specifically and accurately address the emphases in their rationale statements. The key here is to narrow the information without watering it down, and to strive for depth over superficial coverage. (See the annotated bibliography at the end of this text for a list of many of the best resources available for conducting a study of the Holocaust.)

In addition to the question, "Why teach about the Holocaust?" there are several other key questions that teachers must ask themselves prior to engaging their students in a study of the Holocaust: "What are the most important lessons we want our students to learn from the Holocaust?" (Parsons and Totten, 1993), and, as the Coalition of Essential Schools personnel (1989) continually ask in the course of their pedagogical efforts, "So what? What does it [the information and newfound knowledge] matter? What does it all mean?" (p. 2). This process should guide teachers to develop and implement a study that is relevant and meaningful for their students as well as assist them in shaping an unwieldy and massive amount of information into something more manageable.

Historian Lucy Dawidowicz (1992) correctly asserts that most Holocaust curricula are "better at describing what happened during the Holocaust than explaining why it happened" (p. 69). In a survey of twenty-five curricula Dawidowicz (1992), found that "most curricula plunge right into the story of Hitler's Germany; a few provide some background on the Weimar Republic, presumably to explain Hitler's rise to power. Though all curricula discuss Nazi anti-Semitism, preferring generic terms like 'racism' and 'prejudice' instead of the specific 'anti-Semitism,' fifteen of the twenty-five never even suggest that anti-Semitism had a history *before* Hitler. Of those that do, barely a handful present coherent historical accounts, however brief. . . . A small number of curricula include lessons which survey the pre-Nazi history of Jews in Europe, presumably to humanize the image of the Jews depicted in Nazi propaganda" (p. 69).

In regard to antisemitism—which often is the issue that most curricula developed for use by secondary level teachers neglect to address—Dawidowicz (1992) persuasively argues that avoidance of that topic, "and especially its roots in Christian doctrine" (p. 71), skews history and provides a distorted picture of the cause of the Holocaust. "To be sure, Christianity cannot be held responsible for Hitler, but the Nazis would not have succeeded in disseminating their brand of racist anti-Semitism had they not been confident of the pervasiveness, firmness, and durability of Christian hatred of Jews" (Dawidowicz, 1992, p. 71). "Omitting all references to Christian anti-Semitism is one way some curricula avoid the sensitivities of the subject. The more acceptable and common pedagogic strategy is to generalize the highly particular nature and history of anti-Semitism by subsuming (and camouflaging) it under general rubrics like scapegoating, prejudice, and bigotry. . . . These abstract words suggest that hatred of the Jews is not a thing in itself, but a symptom of 'larger' troubles, though no explanation is given as to why the Jews, rather than dervishes, for instance, are consistently chosen as the scapegoat" (Dawidowicz, 1992, p. 73).[1] (For additional insights into similar as well as other problems in various Holocaust curricula, see Totten and Riley [under review] "The

Problem of Inaccurate History in State Developed/Sponsored Holocaust and Genocide Curricula and Teacher Guides: A Challenge to Scholars of the Holocaust and Genocide.")

The complexity of the subject matter of the Holocaust is daunting. The era itself—leaving aside consideration of major antecedents or postwar issues—spanned a period of twelve years (1933–1945), the geographic area covered all of continental Europe and beyond, and the people involved numbered in the millions. Numerous "parties" were involved, including the perpetrators, collaborators, the bystanders, and the victims—none of whom were monolithic. Inherent in this are issues and concerns such as the Nazis' rise to power, the life of the Jews in Germany and Europe prior to the Holocaust period, and so on. Over and above that, there are the host of critical historical trends (antisemitism, racism, social Darwinism, extreme nationalism, totalitarianism, industrialism, and the nature of modern war) that one needs to be conversant with in order to even begin to understand the Holocaust (Niewyk, 1995, p. 175). It is imperative that teachers provide students with a solid knowledge base regarding the antecedents of the Holocaust as well as the whys, hows, whens, and wheres.

It also is essential to place the study of the Holocaust within a historical context that will allow students to see the relationship of political, social, and economic factors that impacted the times and events that resulted in that history (Totten and Feinberg, 1995, p. 325). The content that teachers and other curriculum planners select for a study of the Holocaust should facilitate the understanding of the historical context of the period. For example, depending on the emphasis in one's course, familiarizing students with the history of antisemitism or the impact of the German defeat in World War I or the consequences for Germany of the Great Depression will greatly influence the construction of a unit on the Holocaust. If emphasis is placed almost exclusively on the political factors leading to the rise of the Nazis, while scant attention is paid to a social phenomenon such as antisemitism, the ultimate organization of the unit and its historical context will be directly affected. Similarly, creating a context that primarily emphasizes the economic misery brought on by the depression as the *main* "cause" of the Nazis' assumption of power to the exclusion of the social and political factors that motivated large and significant segments of the German public will, likewise, impact the final organization of the teaching unit. The development of historically accurate lessons and units on the Holocaust demands that teachers and curriculum planners attempt to integrate thoroughly and accurately the political, economic, and social factors associated with this history. The role of rationale statements in guiding content selection is crucial.

It also is incumbent on teachers to show that behind the statistics are real people, comprised of families of grandparents, parents, and children. First-person accounts provide students with a way of "making meaning" of collective numbers. Although students should be careful about overgeneralizing from first-person accounts—such as those from survivors, journalists, relief workers, bystanders, and liberators—personal accounts can supplement a study of the Holocaust by moving it "from a welter of statistics, remote places and events, to one that is immersed in the 'personal' and 'particular'" (Totten, 1987, p. 63). And as Friedlander (1979) has noted, one of the best ways to study human behavior in such extreme situations as genocide is "to consult the memoir literature as an original source" (p. 526). Yet again, if rationale statements focus on individuals as well as groups, then it will be more likely that teachers and students will come to understand and appreciate that real people are behind the mind-numbing statistics.

In some cases, teachers focus on one or two aspects (pieces of the history, issues, perspectives) of the Holocaust to the exclusion of other key issues. For example, some focus on the crimes of the perpetrators but not the antecedents of the history; the actions of the perpetrators but not the lives of the victims; the fact of the death camps versus the ever-increasing discrimination that marginalized and isolated the Jews and other victims in the first place; the role of the rescuers to the exclusion of the policies and/or actions of the perpetrators, victims, and bystanders; the passivity of Jews but not the varied forms of resistance they put up; the notion that Jews allowed themselves to be herded into ghettos, camps, and gas chambers but nothing about the deceit and overwhelming power of the Nazis, the abject fear experienced by the potential and actual victims, or the "choiceless choices" people were forced to make; and the obedience to authority but nothing about the terror induced by the Nazis.

By developing strong rationale statements that focus on the whys and hows of the Holocaust, as well as those pertaining to the whats, wheres, and whens, teachers are more likely not only to include absolutely critical information about the Holocaust but also a more well-rounded perspective of the events. Concomitantly, they also are more likely to include a balanced and accurate view of the perpetrators, collaborators, bystanders, rescuers, and victims. To skip over this initial work (e.g., developing rationale statements that will lead an accurate and comprehensive view of the history) is to enter a study blind.

Developing a rationale statement, however, is simply the first step. Once teachers and students develop rationale statements, they must carefully scrutinize them in regard to the type of study they are about to undertake. If, after developing a set of rationale statements, the teacher and the class discover that their primary focus is going to be on just the victims or just the perpetrators or just the rescuers or simply the what and whens of the Holocaust but not the whys and hows, then they need to ask themselves the following: Is this sensible? If not, why not, and what can we do to rectify the situation? Is such a study valuable? If so, how and why? And if not, why not? Will such a study provide the students with a solid sense of the history of the Holocaust? What is the point of solely focusing on one aspect of the Holocaust to the exclusion of another that is equally important? Is there a way to balance the study in order to make it more inclusive, more comprehensive, more valuable?

At the risk of being redundant, thoroughly examining and weighing rationale statements assists the teacher in determining whether a course of study is comprehensive, thorough, and historically accurate versus one that is going to be unduly limited in some form or manner.

Using Rationales to Guide the Type of Pedagogy and Resources Used during the Study

Strong rationales should guide the selection of effective pedagogical strategies and appropriate instructional resources. To develop rationales and then ignore them when developing or selecting teaching strategies, learning activities, and resources is likely to weaken the value of the overall study.

The complexity and emotionally charged nature of this history dictates that not just any instructional strategy, learning activity, or resource will do. Each must be of the highest quality, thought-provoking, and not be comprised of those that, even inadvertently, minimize, romanticize, or simplify the history. As Totten (1991a) noted, "A major flaw endemic to much of the current curricula on [the Holocaust], at least at the secondary level, is that the suggested teaching methods are routine and predictable, and the learning activities are comprised of memorizing facts and pencil-and-paper exercises that call for answers to lower level cognitive questions" (p. 198). Numerous Holocaust curricula also include activities as "word scrambles" or crossword puzzles, many of which may lead to the creation of a "fun and games" atmosphere rather than one of serious study. In turn, this tends to trivialize the importance of studying this history (Parsons and Totten, 1993, p. 7).

Some teachers have a propensity to engage their students in simulations where they, the students, supposedly act out actual situations experienced by the perpetrators, victims, and others. As the authors of the U.S. Holocaust Memorial Museum's *Guidelines for Teaching About the Holocaust* state, this is a dubious practice: "Even when teachers take great care to prepare a class for such an activity, simulating experiences from the Holocaust remains pedagogically unsound. The activity may engage students, but they often forget the purpose of the lesson, and even worse, they are left with the impression at the conclusion of the activity that they now know what it was like during the Holocaust. . . . The problem with trying to simulate situations from the Holocaust is that complex events and actions are over-simplified, and students are left with a skewed view of history" (Parsons and Totten, 1993, pp. 7, 8).

There is absolutely no way that students will *ever* be able to experience what it was like for the victims to be forced from their homes, herded into ghettos, crammed into suffocatingly hot or freezing cattle cars for days on end, or to have been subjected to torture and murder at the hands of the Nazis. Simulations that purport to provide students with such experiences trivialize and mock the experiences of those who were killed and those who survived.

Those teachers who are prone to use simulations as part of a unit on the Holocaust should ask the question, "Why should simulations be used when there already exists a wealth of actual case studies?" It is one thing for a teacher to broaden student perspectives by asking "What *might* you have done" (which is more appropriate than asking, "What *would* you have done?"), and quite another to launch a class into a simulation that attempts to recreate choices and human behavior that defy the imagination. Statements of rationale will hopefully prod teachers to reflect on the content and purposes of classroom practices. (For a more detailed discussion of simulations, See Totten [2000].)

Strong rationales also can assist with the opening and closing of lessons and units on the Holocaust. Opening and closing lessons in a study of the Holocaust are important because they set the tone and context for the entire course. For example, if one of the rationales for the study is "to help students think about the use and abuse of power, and the roles and responsibilities of individuals, organizations, and nations when confronted with civil rights violations and/or policies of genocide," an opening can easily be tailored to begin to explore such issues. Additionally, strong openings are able to dispel misinformation students may hold prior to the study of the Holocaust; set a reflective tone, whereby students come to appreciate the need to make careful distinctions when weighing various ideas, motives, and behaviors; indicate to the students that their ideas and opinions about this history are important; tie the history to the students' lives; and/or establish that the history has multiple interpretations and ramifications. By contrast, a strong closing can encourage students to synthesize the various aspects of their study, connect this history to the world they live in today, and encourage them to continue to examine this history. (For a detailed discussion of various ways to begin a lesson or unit on the Holocaust, see Samuel Totten's [1998] "The Start Is as Important as the Finish in a Holocaust Study"; and for a detailed discussion of various ways to close a lesson or unit on the Holocaust, see Samuel Totten's [in press] "Nothing About a Study of the Holocaust Should Be Perfunctory, Including Its Close: Suggestions for Closing a Lesson, Unit or Study on the Holocaust.")

The pedagogy used in such a study should be one that is student-centered; that is, one in which the students are not passive but rather actively engaged in the study. It should be a study that, in the best sense of the word, complicates the students' thinking, engages students in critical and creative thought, and involves in-depth versus superficial coverage of information. It also should involve students in reading and examining primary sources (e.g., contemporaneous documents issued during the Holocaust period, diaries and letters written by the victims and others, and so on). Using first-person accounts and other primary sources about the Holocaust (e.g., documents, photographs, trial records, spoken word recordings, and documentary film footage) helps students establish direct connections with the ideas of those who were involved in this historical period, thus helping them examine the broader historical themes in a more personal dimension. The vast scope and complexity of the Holocaust can be difficult to comprehend; therefore, it is critical that teachers choose resources that not only facilitate the achievement of course goals but that help students grapple with the choices and decisions made by perpetrators, bystanders, victims, and rescuers. This also is true of the many choiceless choices—as Lawrence Langer (1982) deems them—that the victims were often forced to make.

Because the history itself as well as many of the primary sources available on the Holocaust have the power to generate powerful emotional responses in students, the use of personal journals is highly recommended to provide a means for young people to express their feelings privately to the teacher about the information and issues they are encountering. At appropriate junctures, the teacher can determine if journal entries should be shared with other students, but this is clearly a pedagogical decision that requires careful consideration. (For ideas along this line, see Chris M. Anson and Richard Beach [1995], *Journals in the Classroom: Writing to Learn*. Norwood, MA: Christopher Gordon.)

Clearly stated and well-thought-out rationale statements not only are capable of assisting a teacher in selecting appropriate resources but can also help to avoid materials that detract from the study, diminish its importance, and/or move the study far afield. Unfortunately, in an ostensible effort to engage students' interest, some curriculum developers have incorporated such questionable pieces as Mick Jagger's "Sympathy for the Devil," Lenny Bruce's "My Name Is Adolf Eichmann," and The Boomtown Rats' "I Never Loved Eva Braun" into their curricula on the Holocaust. As a wealth of powerful resources on the Holocaust exists that students find extremely thought-provoking and engaging, marginal materials are to be avoided. The latter materials, although possibly interesting at first glance, tend to trivialize and oversimplify the study of the Holocaust, reducing its significance to the level of a popular culture artifact taken out of context. In contrast, poetry, fiction, and artwork that reflects deeply on the Holocaust and its legacy is highly appropriate for use, because it illustrates and deepens understanding of core themes about the era without resorting to artistic techniques or conventions that transform the Holocaust into just another topic of mass popular culture, devoid of deep meaning or long-term significance. (For a discussion of appropriate and powerful literary, artistic, and musical responses to the Holocaust, see the chapters in this book by Karen Shawn, Samuel Totten, Shari Werb, Belarie Zatzman, and Roselle Chartock.)

Involving Students in the Development of Rationale Statements

A good place to begin with the development of rationale statements for a study of the Holocaust is with the students themselves. This immediately encourages students to begin thinking about why one would want or need to study this history; and, in doing so, it begins to personalize the study for them. It may also motivate them to become more engaged in the study and to begin to see the relevance it has for their own lives as well as the society, country, and world in which they live.

Initially, the teacher can ask the students to think of reasons why young people *should* study the Holocaust. After the students record their responses in journals or on a sheet of paper, the teacher can write a variety of the responses on the board or overhead projector. Later, the responses can be transferred to a bulletin board, where they could remain during the course of the study in order to highlight and draw attention to them. As the unit progresses and students learn more about the actual history of the Holocaust, the class can return to the initial responses during which they could reexamine and, if need be, revise their initial statements.

An even more engaging way to get the students involved in the examination of rationales is to have them write down those questions they have about the Holocaust and/or that they wish to have answered during the course of the study. For example, during a special week-long, four-hour-a-day, summer course on the Holocaust, a group of high school students came up with the following questions (all quoted exactly as they were written):

- Why exactly did the Holocaust happen?
- What was the main factor that caused this genocide?
- What percent of Germany's population was Jewish during the time of the Holocaust's beginning?
- Why were Jews blamed in the first place?
- How many people actually survived the Holocaust?
- How did Hitler get into office?
- Why did Hitler have so much power?
- What was Hitler's main motive for killing all the Jews?
- How did the Jews become so hated?
- Did this affect America?
- Why are we usually only taught that Jews were persecuted?
- Why didn't all the people in the camps rebel at once, so that their [sic] may have been a hope for freedom?
- Who else was eventually included with the Jews, and why?
- Was there any dissention [sic] among the German ranks regarding following orders which lead to the mass extermination of Jews?
- Why didn't the U.S. try and step in sooner?
- What are the warning signs of something like the Holocaust, and how can we stop if from happening again?
- Why???

Many of the student questions penetrate to the core of the tragedy of the Holocaust, while others are more concerned with key facts (chronology, the number of people who were murdered by the Nazis, number of survivors). With teacher guidance, students could take such questions as the above and fashion them into rationale statements. These statements, in conjunction with the teacher's, could set the stage for the study.

Using Rationale Statements to
Avoid Pitfalls during the Course of Study

Another use of rationale statements is to safeguard against some of the many pitfalls (e.g., assaulting students with one horrific image after another, minimizing the horrific nature of the Holocaust, romanticizing the Holocaust, skewing the history by minimizing or overstating various situations or aspects of the history, providing simple answers to complex questions/situations) that have plagued Holocaust lessons and units. As one can readily ascertain, teaching this history involves, at least to a certain extent, a "balancing act" of sorts.

Teachers need to be judicious in their approach to the Holocaust and be sure that in teaching about the history they do not constantly bombard their students with one horrific image after another, to the point where the students are overwhelmed with the horror. Students are essentially a "captive audience." Assaulting them with horrific images outside of any constructive context is antithetical to good teaching. The assumption that students will seek to "understand" human behavior after being exposed to horrible images is a fallacy. Instead of becoming engaged with the history, students may have a tendency to ignore it or "shut down" their attention in order to protect themselves from the ghastly images.

Teachers also need to avoid denying the reality of the Holocaust by minimizing the fact that the perpetrators committed ghastly crimes against the Jews and others. What is required is a fine balancing act. To attempt to teach the Holocaust without presenting the hard facts is impossible. To attempt to teach the Holocaust without presenting the "full story" is miseducative. As Jan Darsa (1991) states, the facts of the Holocaust may be uncomfortable for the students to learn, but "in discomfort there is struggle and growth" (p. 181). When the horror is explored, it should be done only to the extent necessary to achieve the objective(s) of the lesson.

Some teachers have a tendency—often inadvertent—to "romanticize" the Holocaust. For example, some teachers try to leave the students with a rosy view; that is, they place an inordinate emphasis on the themes of hiding and rescue. Many place a heavy emphasis on the Allies' liberation of the camps, while ostensibly ignoring the fact that for years and years the fate of the Jews fell on deaf ears. Still others tend to conclude the study in a way that leaves students with a sense that "all is well with the world." This is often done by focusing on the postwar trials of the Nazis and insinuating that, in the end, "justice was done."

The fact that some people reached out to support or rescue Jews is vitally significant, but to place it at the center of such a study skews the history. Teachers and students need to keep the facts in mind, and the fact is "at best, less than one-half of one percent of the total population [of non-Jews] under Nazi occupation helped to rescue Jews" (Oliner and Oliner, 1991, p. 363). And, while the "liberation" of the camps was a monumental event, it is also true that the liberation of the camps was never really an objective of the Allies so much as a duty they more or less encountered as they drove toward the unconditional surrender of Germany and her allies. It is also a deplorable fact that the vast majority of the perpetrators and collaborators never were brought to trial. And, of course, all did not end well. Six million Jews perished at the hands of the Nazis, and millions of others (including Gypsies, the physically and mentally handicapped, Soviet prisoners of war, Poles, and other Slavs) also had their lives taken by the Nazis. Many Jews lost entire families and had neither homes nor communities to which they could return. Others tried to return to their towns but were met with everything from contempt to outright antagonism to murder. And, over fifty years later, many survivors remain traumatized by the events they experienced and the losses they suffered. Students need to learn the hard facts of the Holocaust, and rationale statements should reflect that.

Many teachers tend to teach the Holocaust as a totally unique event in the history of humanity or as a vehicle for making universal statements about humanity. There are aspects of the Holocaust that are unique and there are key aspects that are of universal significance. There is a critical need to examine both the uniqueness of the Holocaust as well as its universal nature. This must be done by avoiding the pitfall of establishing a false dichotomy between the two. The latter simply degenerates into a situation that removes the students from the history and the myriad ramifications it has for them and the world in which they live.

Why is it important to consider the issue of the uniqueness of the Holocaust? As this history is taught or studied, some are apt to equate it to the long and tortured history of man's inhumanity to man. Yet, one must recognize that while other groups throughout history have been persecuted and murdered, the complete and total physical annihilation of an entire people as official state policy brings a solitary character to the study of the Holocaust. As Steven T. Katz (1994) writes, "It is this unconstrained, ideologically driven imperative that *every* Jew be murdered that distinguishes the Sho'ah (Holocaust) from prior and to date subsequent, however inhumane, acts of collective violence, ethnocide, and mass murder" (p. 26). And, as Elie Wiesel (1979) has noted, "While not all victims [of the Nazis] were Jews, all Jews were victims, destined for annihilation solely because they were born Jewish. They were doomed not because of something they had done or proclaimed or acquired but because of who they were: sons and daughters of the Jewish people" (p. iii). Few statements graphically illustrate the systematic, sustained, and unprecedented nature of this genocidal act as well as the following one by Wiesel (1984):

> The Nazis' aim was to make the Jewish world shrink—from town to neighborhood, from neighborhood to street, from street to house, from house to room, from room to garret, from garret to cattle car, from cattle car to gas chamber.
>   And they did the same to the individual—separated from his or her community, then from his or her family, then from his or her identity, eventually becoming a work permit, then a number, until the number itself was turned into ashes. (p. 1)

It also is important to focus on the universal dimensions and significance of the era. Although it was undeniably unique within the context of human civilization, those who fell victims to the Nazi reign of terror experienced prejudice, discrimination, scapegoating, denial of fundamental human rights, barbarous treatment, and other lawless actions against them, just as did victims of other genocides.

When selecting content, every effort should be made to avoid depicting groups (Jews, Gypsies, Germans, Poles, rescuers, bystanders, etc.) as one-dimensional. The multifaceted aspects of all groups must be acknowledged. Simplistic views and stereotyping take place when groups are viewed as monolithic in attitudes and actions. Thus, while Jews have long been the target of antisemitism and were the central victims of the Nazi regime, students should not view Jews as solely being victims. Jewish resistance also should be examined. Likewise, Germans should not be perceived only as Nazis or perpetrators, nor should Poles and Ukrainians solely be characterized as collaborators. Further, to focus exclusively or almost totally on the role of the rescuers to the exclusion of role of the bystanders is to distort the history. While the role of the rescuers is vital to address, it also is critical to acknowledge and ponder the fact that many more stood by and allowed the events that ultimately culminated in the Holocaust to unfold.

It also is important to keep in mind that generalizations without modifying and qualifying words (e.g., sometimes, usually, etc.) tend to stereotype group behavior and historical reality (Parsons and Totten, 1993, p. 4).

When teaching any history, it is imperative to avoid allowing simple or simplistic answers or notions to explain complex behavior or situations. This is even more significant when myths or misnomers abound about a subject—as is the case with the Holocaust. *Common knowledge of an historical event does not constitute accurate knowledge.* Rather, accurate knowledge of an historical event is based on the collection of accurate data. Its effective interpretation is predicated on using organizing principles and concepts drawn from legitimate scholarship. It is this type of information and data that should be used in the classroom. A good method to assess the accuracy of information is to do ample reading of the major historians of the Holocaust and to check and cross-check their sources against the best sources available.

In an attempt to make history relevant to students, some curricula have a tendency to distort it. As Lipstadt (1995) has noted, certain Holocaust curricula "elide the differences between the Holocaust and all manner of inhumanities and injustices." [Such curricula often] "address a broad array of injustices" (p. 27), and many other types of mass murder. Some tend to suggest that all genocidal acts are the same in their genesis and/or implementation. Some also draw direct or near direct parallels between Nazi Germany and the issue of racism, prejudice, and economic and social disenfranchisement in the United States.

Although it is pedagogically sound to make connections between the historical and moral issues of the Holocaust and contemporary life, it is pedagogically unsound to equate the Holocaust with any and all civil and human rights violations. Rationale statements that clearly delineate the distinctions are more likely to result in a study that is both historically accurate and pedagogically sound.

Too often, the Holocaust is simply taught because teachers think it might prove to be a "hook" to engage students' interest or because they are interested in the subject matter. A case in point is the fact that many teachers in the late 1990s were swayed by popular culture that *Schindler's List* was "the thing to do/see," and thus took their students to see the film without providing them with any background information in which to contextualize or understand it. With such sensitive subject matter, this is both egregious and unconscionable. Once again, this highlights the need for educators to establish well-thought-out rationales before proceeding with the teaching of the Holocaust.

Revisiting Rationales throughout the Study of the Holocaust

It is vital to revisit issues of rationale throughout the study. This is especially important during an in-depth study of the Holocaust, because learners can lose sight of why they are studying and concentrating on the experiences of a particular group.

As teaching about complex human behavior often results in examining multiple aspects of events and deeds, students need to continuously think about why they are studying this history. By repeatedly highlighting questions of rationale throughout a course, a signal is sent to students that *this is not simply another piece of history to wade through,* but that it has important lessons for both contemporary and future generations. What those lessons are will have to be extrapolated, discussed, and wrestled with by the teacher and the students. Finally, by continually revisiting and wrestling with issues of rationale, students will more likely gain a greater understanding as to how and why the Holocaust is important to their own lives as well as to society.

The Issue of Teaching and Learning about Other Genocides

There is nothing, of course, that precludes teachers from addressing other genocides that have been perpetrated prior to or following the Holocaust (e.g., the Armenian genocide and the Cambodian genocide, respectively). In fact, it is an important and extremely worthwhile pedagogical activity. Be that as it may, the focus of *this book* is, as its title states, teaching about the Holocaust. For that reason, the editors and authors have not addressed how to teach about other genocides. Each genocide is a complex topic unto itself. Indeed, each is comprised of a series of historical trends that combined to make each possible, and these need to be studied in a good amount of detail in order to begin to understand the causes and facts of each. That, in our minds, is another book altogether.

The Issue of Holocaust Denial

Up to this point, we have purposely avoided addressing the issue of Holocaust denial. The only reason we are even addressing the issue of denial herein is due to the fact that some students are apt to broach the issue in class, either because they have received misinformation at home or from friends or have come across denier's sites on the Internet. That said, *it is our firm belief that the discussion of denial has no place in the classroom during a study of the Holocaust.* There are numerous reasons for this, but among those we consider the most significant are as follows: First, we strongly believe that it is ludicrous to "give time" to such foolish and totally fallacious assertions. The deniers are not, despite their incorrect and euphemistic use of the term "revisionism," historians; instead, what they spew out are outright lies that deserve no attention by clear-thinking individuals. The fact of the matter is, deniers are antisemitic individuals who are out to poison the minds of others. Second, to devote time to the deniers' words in class constitutes, quite literally, a waste of time. This is true, for the simple but profound reason that most teachers simply do not have enough time as it is to address any subject matter in depth, let alone one as complex and detailed as the Holocaust. Thus, to take time to address the issues the deniers raise sucks precious time away from the study of critical issues germane to the Holocaust. Even if even one-half or one-quarter of a period is allocated to address deniers' falsifications, it is likely that another topic is not going to be addressed at all, or that a topic that is addressed will be done so in less depth than it could or should have been. Third, students who either believe in or are enamored of the arguments of deniers often sound "authoritative" in what they have to say, when, in fact, most are talking off the top of their heads, largely ignorant of the historical record. For a teacher to attempt to engage such individuals in a "discussion" is futile, not to mention counterproductive.

Realizing that some teachers may feel compelled to "offset" or argue against the deniers assertions, we are in total agreement with Ronnie S. Landau, author of *Studying the Holocaust: Issues, Readings and Documents* (New York: Routledge, 1998) when he asserts that ". . . the most effective ways of countering the potentially harmful influence of Holocaust deniers are to keep in mind the following: that care should be taken not to dignify their opinions, accusations and assertions. . . . In other words, it is quite unnecessary and probably counter-productive to write a book, teach a class or deliver a lecture with the *express* purpose of refuting their work; a corollary of this is that every serious word that *is* written or uttered on this subject is *implicitly* working counter to the revisionists' aims and desires. In short, we should guard against . . . providing the very publicity they seek . . . (p. 11).

For those students insistent on learning more about issues of denial, teachers would be wise to refer them to the Anti-Defamation League (823 United Nations Plaza, New York, NY 10017) for information on denial and the deniers. They should also be encouraged to read such works as Deborah Lipstadt's thought-provoking and instructive *Denying the Holocaust: The Growing Assault on Truth and Memory* (New York: The Free Press, 1986). Despite making such recommendations, teachers should make it clear that the students are to do this on their own time and that such issues will not be addressed in class.

Conclusion

Well-constructed rationales for Holocaust study represent the foundation for successful curriculum design, instructional planning, selection of curricular resources, and evaluation of student progress. The ongoing refinement of rationales is a critical dimension of reflective practice, because it fosters a critical approach to the improvement of Holocaust education and can engage both students and teachers in dialogues about the significance and meaning of the Holocaust in contemporary society.

NOTE

1. Speaking of the need to address the issue of antisemitism but taking a different slant than that of Dawidowicz, Friedlander (1979) has suggested that "Studies of modern anti-Semitism are more useful. They analyze the social roots and political uses of modern anti-Semitism; they trace

the birth of the anti-Semitic parties and of their transformation into totalitarian movements. They show how the new anti-Semitism based on race differed qualitatively from the preceding type based on religion. They thus delineate the radical nature of modern anti-Semitism. But because they usually do not include the demonic, they fail to provide a fully satisfying explanation of how this ideology could lead to genocide" (p. 528).

REFERENCES

Anson, Chris M., & Beach, Richard. (1995). *Journals in the Classroom: Writing to Learn.* Norwood, MA: Christopher Gordon.

Bauer, Yehuda. (1978). *The Holocaust in Historical Perspective.* Seattle: University of Washington.

Branson, Margaret S. & Turney-Purta, Judith. (Eds.) (1982). International Human Rights, Society, and the Schools. Washington, DC: National Council for the Social Studies.

The Coalition of Essential Schools. (1989, June). "Asking the Essential Questions: Curriculum Development." *Horace, 5*(5):1–6.

Darsa, Jan. (1991). "Educating about the Holocaust." In Israel W. Charny (Ed.), *Genocide: A Critical Bibliographic Review* (pp. 175–193). Volume Two. London: Mansell Publishing Limited.

Dawidowicz, Lucy S. (1992). "How They Teach the Holocaust." In Lucy S. Dawidowicz, *What is the Use of Jewish History?* New York: Schocken Books.

Eisner, Elliot. (1979). *The Educational Imagination: On the Design and Evaluation of School Programs.* New York: Macmillan.

Friedlander, Henry. (1979). "Toward a Methodology of Teaching about the Holocaust." *Teachers College Record, 80*(5):519–542.

Katz, Stephen T. (1994). *The Holocaust in Historical Context: Volume 1: The Holocaust and Mass Death Before the Modern Age.* New York: Oxford University Press.

Landau, Ronnie S. (1998). *Studying the Holocaust: Issues, Readings and Documents.* New York: Routledge.

Langer, Lawrence L. (1978). *The Age of Atrocity: Death in Modern Literature.* Boston: Beacon Press.

Langer, Lawrence L. (1982). *Versions of Survival: The Holocaust and the Human Spirit.* Albany, NY: State University of New York.

Langer, Lawrence L. (1995). *Admitting the Holocaust: Collected Essays.* New York: Oxford University Press.

Lipstadt, Deborah (1986). *Denying the Holocaust: The Growing Assault on Truth and Memory.* New York: The Free Press.

Lipstadt, Deborah. (March 6, 1995). "Not Facing History." *The New Republic,* pp. 26–27, 29.

National Council for the Social Studies. (1991, February). Special Issue ("Teaching About Genocide") of *Social Education, 55*(2). [Edited by Samuel Totten and William S. Parsons.]

Newmann, Fred. (1988, January). "Can Depth Replace Coverage in the High School Curriculum?" *Phi Delta Kappan,* pp. 345–348.

Niewyk, Donald L. (1995). "Holocaust: The Genocide of the Jews." In Samuel Totten, William S. Parsons, and Israel W. Charny (Eds.), *Genocide in the Twentieth Century: Critical Essays and Eyewitness Accounts* (pp. 167–184). New York: Garland Publishing.

Oliner, Pearl M. & Oliner, Samuel P. (1991). "Righteous People in the Holocaust." In Israel Charny (Ed.), *Genocide: A Critical Bibliographic Review* (pp. 363–385). London and New York: Mansell Publishing and Facts on File.

Parsons, William S., & Totten, Samuel. (1993). *Guidelines for Teaching about the Holocaust.* Washington, DC: United States Holocaust Memorial Museum.

President's Commission on the Holocaust. (1979). *Report to the President.* Washington, DC: Author. [One-page handout.]

Rosenberg, Alan, & Bardosh, Alexander. (Fall/Winter 1982–1983). "The Problematic Character of Teaching the Holocaust." *Shoah,* pp. 3–7, 20.

Schwartz, Donald. (1990, February). " 'Who Will Tell Them After We're Gone?': Reflections on Teaching the Holocaust." *The History Teacher, 23*(2):95–110.

Shawn, Karen. (1995). "Current Issues in Holocaust Education." *Dimensions: A Journal of Holocaust Studies, 9*(2):15–18.

Sizer, Theodore R. (1984). *Horace's Compromise: The Dilemma of the American High School.* Boston: Houghton Mifflin.

Strom, Margot Stern, & Parsons, William S. (1982). *Facing History and Ourselves: Holocaust and Human Behavior.* Watertown, MA: Intentional Educations.

Totten, Samuel. (1987). "The Personal Fate of Genocide: Words of Witnesses in the Classroom." Special issue of the *Social Science Record* ("Genocide, Issues, Approaches, Resources") 24(2):63–67.

Totten, Samuel. (1991a). "Educating about Genocide: Curricula and Inservice Training." In Israel W. Charny (1991) *Genocide: A Critical Bibliographic Review* (pp. 194–225). Volume 2. London: Mansell Publishing.

Totten, Samuel. (1991b). *First-Person Accounts of Genocidal Acts Committed in the Twentieth Century: An Annotated Bibliography.* Westport, CT: Greenwood Press.

Totten, Samuel. (1994, November). "Educating about Genocide: Progress Is Being Made, But Much Still Needs to Be Done." *Internet on the Holocaust and Genocide,* Special Triple Issue, 51/52/53.

Totten, Samuel. (Summer 1994). "The Use of First-Person Accounts in Teaching about the Holocaust." *The British Journal of Holocaust Education, 3*(1):53–76.

Totten, Samuel. (1998, February). "The Start Is as Important as the Finish in a Holocaust Study." *Social Education, 62*(2):70–76.

Totten, Samuel. (Spring 1999). "Teaching the Holocaust: The Imperative to Move Beyond Clichés." *Canadian Social Studies, 33*(3):84–87.

Totten, Samuel. (in press). "Nothing about a Study of the Holocaust Should Be Perfunctory, Including Its Close: Suggestions for Closing a Lesson, Unit or Study on the Holocaust." In Samuel Totten's *Holocaust Education: Issues and Approaches.* Boston: Allyn and Bacon.

Totten, Samuel. (2000, April). "Diminishing the Complexity and Horror of the Holocaust: Using Simulations in an Attempt to Convey Historical Experiences." *Social Education, 64*(3):165–171.

Totten, Samuel, & Feinberg, Stephen. (1995, October). "Teaching about the Holocaust: Rationale, Content, Methodology, & Resources." *Social Education, 59*(6):323–327, 329, 331–333.

Totten, Samuel, & Parsons, William S. (Spring 1992). "State Developed Teacher Guides and Curricula on Genocide and/or the Holocaust: A Succinct Review and Critique." *Inquiry in Social Studies: Curriculum, Research, and Instruction. The Journal of the North Carolina Council for the Social Studies, 28*(1):27–47.

Totten, Samuel, & Riley, Karen. (under review). "The Problem of Inaccurate History in State Developed/Sponsored Holocaust and Genocide Curricula and Teacher Guides: A Challenge to Scholars of the Holocaust and Genocide."

U.S. Holocaust Memorial Museum. (1995). "Frequently Asked Questions about the Holocaust." Washington, DC: Author. [Handout.]

Wiesel, Elie. (1978). "Then and Now: The Experiences of a Teacher." *Social Education, 42*(4):266–271.

Wiesel, Elie. (1979). "Preface." *Report to the President.* Washington, DC: President's Commission on the Holocaust.

Wiesel, Elie. (1984). "All Was Lost, Yet Something Was Preserved." Review of *The Chronicle of the Lodz Ghetto, 1941–1944.* " *New York Times Book Review,* pp. 1, 23.

CHAPTER 2

The Holocaust, Historiography, and History

DAVID M. CROWE

The roots of the Holocaust lie in the deep traditions of historic and religious anti-semitism that became an integral part of the fabric of Western civilization in the past two thousand years. In the nineteenth century, political and racial antisemitic writings appeared that added to the religious body of traditional Christian anti-semitism, which had haunted Jews for centuries. This new form of antisemitism was an indirect product of the dramatic changes that had taken place throughout the Western world during and after the Enlightenment, the French Revolution, and the Industrial Revolution. Jewish emancipation slowly followed on the heels of the political and social transformations that swept Europe during this period. As new nations emerged throughout Europe, questions began to be raised as to what was a German, an Italian, a Serb, or a Hungarian. The most vocal respondents to such nationalistic questions were extreme nationalists who were more often than not affected by distorted interpretations of social Darwinism.

This social theory was loosely drawn from Charles Darwin's 1859 work on animal evolution, *On the Origin of Species*. Throughout the rest of the nineteenth and early twentieth centuries, writers and social commentators began to apply and distort Darwin's theory to all sorts of social, political, and economic issues. One of Europe's most prominent social Darwinists, Herbert Spencer, coined the phrase "survival of the fittest," which racial extremists used in their discussion of racial superiority and inferiority. They were stimulated not only by the new spirit of nationalism that swept through during this period, but also by the aggressive push of European nations in Asia and Africa.

One extreme German nationalist, Wilhelm Marr, created the phase "anti-semitism" in his 1879 *Der Sieg des Judenthums das Germanthum (The Victory of Jewry over Germandom)*. Marr blamed the Jews for the serious economic difficulties of the new German state (Germany was created in 1871), and said the "Jewish problem" was not a religious issue but a social one. Future German, Austrian, and other anti-Jewish writers now began to inaccurately view Jews as a race, not as a religious group. Another German writer, Alfred Ploetz, created the term *Rassenhygiene* (racial hygiene), and talked of negative and positive forces, such as war, revolution, and health care that helped or hindered the strengthening of "superior races" over "inferior ones."

Ploetz drew his ideas from a large body of writings that surfaced in the second half of the nineteenth century, which blamed the Industrial and French revolutions for much of the political and social upheaval that had shaken Europe during that period. The Industrial Revolution had changed the face of Europe dramatically and triggered a significant shift in population from rural to urban areas. Over time, rural "family values" became a lost ideal to those who saw urbanization, industrialization, and political liberalization as the core reasons for Europe's decay. These conservative writers and commentators blamed the Jews, who over the centuries had been legally forced to live only in Europe's urban areas, for most of these changes. Jews now became identified with the urban intellectual, political, and social ideas so deeply hated by Europe's growing body of conservative racist writers.

Yet, the Holocaust also should be seen as a byproduct of another aspect of the political and socioeconomic upheavals that swept Europe—industrialization and war. The factory system that was so central to the Industrial Revolution gave European manufacturers and their government sponsors the ability to kill on an impersonal scale never before imagined. It was not until World War I that the full force of industrial mass killing truly showed itself in all of its horror. A war that most combatants thought would last only a few months lasted over four years. Though estimates vary, eight to ten million people died in this conflict. This was the war that introduced to the world new, inhumane, impersonal weapons of death such as gas. World War I so traumatized the Western world that its leaders did everything possible in the 1930s to cater to Germany, Italy, and Japan's growing aggression. By the time that world leaders finally awoke to the true nature of this aggression, it was too late. Adolf Hitler was also deeply affected by his role as a combat soldier in World War I. He returned from the battlefield a determined German nationalist, one who blamed the Jews for Germany's failure in this conflict. This belief was based on the rabid antisemitism that pervaded nationalist thought at this time. When one combines these ideas with the humiliation associated with the Treaty of Versailles and the economic devastation of the Great Depression, one can see that the die for the Holocaust was now cast.

Historiographical Overview

The Holocaust is one of the most horrible, complex crimes in modern history. In an effort to try to explain how Germany could foment such criminal acts against the Jewish people and other minorities, historians and other specialists have produced a vast literature dealing with all aspects of this tragedy. To specialist and nonspecialist alike, the current body of material available for the study of this subject is massive and daunting. Moreover, the subject is complicated by a number of controversies that have surfaced since the end of World War II. This chapter will discuss the evolution of various interpretations of Holocaust causation, examine the numerous controversies that have complicated the historical study of this subject, and survey the major works in the field of Holocaust history since 1945.

A good starting point for this discussion would be a look at the plight of the survivors of the Holocaust. Of the almost six million Jews who died in the Holocaust, more than half lost their lives in the horrible complex of death, concentration, and forced or slave labor camps. According to Yehuda Bauer and Robert Rozett (1990), 5,596,000 to 5,860,000 European Jews out of a prewar population of 9,797,000 died in the Holocaust (pp. 1797–1799). Estimates are that 250,000 to 500,000 Gypsies (Roma and Sinti) and 200,000 to 250,000 handicapped also died as a result of German genocidal policies from 1933 to 1945 (United States Holocaust Memorial Museum, n.d.-a., np).

One of the earliest studies to deal with the Holocaust was Léon Poliakov's *Bréviare de la haine* (1951), which was published three years later in the United States as *Harvest of Hate: The Nazi Program for the Destruction of the Jews of Europe.* Poliakov's study sets out the basic outline of the Holocaust, beginning with the origins of German Nazi antisemitism. He concentrates mainly on the evolution of the more deadly phases of the Holocaust from the German conquest of Poland in 1939 through the implementation of the Final Solution in 1941, the German plan to mass murder all of the Jews of Europe. Poliakov spends a good amount of time on Jewish resistance, and discusses the plight of non-Jewish victims, such as the Roma (Gypsies), the Russians, Poles, and Czechs.

Soon after the publication of the French edition of Poliakov's study, Gerald Reitlinger published *The Final Solution: The Attempt to Exterminate the Jews of Europe, 1933–1945* (1953). In this and later editions of his work, Reitlinger discusses the evolution and history of the Holocaust in each country in Europe. His impassioned work is balanced with some scholarly detachment, and he sees the Holocaust as principally aimed at the Jews of Europe. Reitlinger does not cover the issues of Jewish resistance and the plight of other minorities with the same depth as Poliakov. However, according to Abraham J. Edelheit (1990), Reitlinger's work also suffers from an overdependence on German documents, "to the extent of repeating German evaluations of Jewish behavior in extremis" (Edelheit, 1990, p. 667).

In 1961, a new Holocaust work appeared in the United States that would become a genuine classic, and dominate the field of Holocaust studies for some time. Raul Hilberg's *The Destruction of the European Jews* (1961) was intended to be a study of the Holocaust through the eyes of the perpetrators—the Germans. The major topics of discussion in Hilberg's work centered around the expropriation of Jewish property, the forced concentration of Jews in the Greater Reich and Poland, the development of the mobile killing program of the Einsatzgruppe in 1941 and later, the deportation of Jews from the Greater Reich and Europe to the General Government's ghettos and killing centers, the creation and operation of the "factories" of death, and a detailed look at the actual killing process during the Final Solution. Hilberg's clinical study of the Holocaust from the German perspective meant that he relied heavily on German documentation. Critics fault him for his failure to use the new body of Jewish survivor testimony that was available to scholars, and particularly for his criticism of the Judenräte (Jewish Councils used by the Germans throughout Europe to help oversee administration of the complex of ghettos) and ineffective Jewish resistance.

The entire dynamics of Holocaust study changed dramatically in the early

1960s as the world learned of the story of Adolf Eichmann. One of the key figures in the mass deportation of Jews from throughout Europe to the death camps and ghettos in Poland and the occupied parts of the Soviet Union, Eichmann had been living in Argentina since 1950. He was kidnapped by Israeli agents in 1960, and was tried in Jerusalem the following year. Eichmann's eight-month trial ended on December 15, 1961, and resulted in his execution the following spring. Although questions quickly arose regarding the legality of Eichmann's kidnapping and trial, nothing stirred up the incipient Holocaust field more than Hannah Arendt's (1963) series of articles in *The New Yorker*, and subsequent book, *Eichmann in Jerusalem: A Report on the Banality of Evil* (1963b). Arendt tried to put the Holocaust into the greater context of the German Nazi dictatorship. She raised questions about the right and impartiality of the Israelis to try Eichmann. Perhaps most troubling was Arendt's critical evaluation of the role of Jewish leaders and the Judenräte in Europe, which Arendt felt lacked moral courage and worked to protect a select few in their individual communities. Though Arendt had drawn some of her facts from *The Destruction of the European Jews*, her critics felt that her conclusions reflected a superficial knowledge of the Holocaust. Jacob Robinson (1965), for example, argued in *And the Crooked Shall Be Made Straight* that many of Arendt's major points were wrong. In particular, her criticism of the Judenräte was incorrect (Weiss, 1988, p. 685). In *The Informed Heart*, Bruno Bettelheim (1960) was sympathetic to some of Arendt's ideas, and criticized the Jewish failure to rise up against the Germans. Richard Rubenstein (1975) obliquely criticized both the Judenräte and Jews throughout Europe for their seeming passivity against the Germans and their collaborators. This approach tended to help strengthen the myth of "like sheep to slaughter" that would haunt Jewish survivors of the Holocaust for several decades. (Elon, 1993, p. 3; Segev, 1993, pp. 159–60, 179–181)

By the mid-1960s, several important works appeared that traced the antisemitic roots of the Holocaust back to its Christian origins. The first significant book on this subject was written by a Jesuit priest, Edward H. Flannery (1965). In *The Anguish of the Jews: Twenty-Three Centuries of Anti-Semitism,* Flannery took a blunt and direct approach to this sensitive subject. He traced the origins of historic antisemitism to its Greek and Roman roots, but laid the principle blame for the institutional development of this horrible and deadly prejudice on the shoulders of Christian Europe. Father Flannery's shocking work was soon followed by a study of historic antisemitism, Werner Keller's *Diaspora: The Post-Biblical History of the Jews* (1969). A prominent German biblical scholar, his excellent study of the history of the Jewish people from the end of the Roman republican era, until the creation of the state of Israel in 1948, provided a detailed, scholarly investigation of not only the history of the Jewish people during this period but also the evolution of Western antisemitism. Other works that later broached this subject include William Nicholls' *Christian Antisemitism: A History of Hate* (1993), and two excellent documentary studies, Alexis P. Rubin's *Scattered Among the Nations: Documents Affecting Jewish History, 49 to 1975* (1995), and Paul Mendes-Flohr's and Jehuda Reinharz's, *The Jew in the Modern World: A Documentary History* (1995).

The most important work to come out during this period was Lucy S. Dawidowicz's *The War Against the Jews, 1933–1945* (1976). Still in print, this often read and cited study looks at the Holocaust from the perspective of the major Jewish communities in Central and Eastern Europe and the Soviet Union. It also explores questions regarding German motivation for the mass killings of Jews, the lack of response to this tragedy in the West, and questions about Jewish resistance. Its appendices examine the plight of the Jews in each country in Europe. Dawidowicz would later publish *The Holocaust and the Historians* (1981), which questions the failure of Western scholars to include the Holocaust in their principle works on that period in history. In 1976, she also published *A Holocaust Reader*, which includes primary and secondary sources on the Holocaust.

Other important general studies to come out during this period include Yehuda Bauer's *A History of the Holocaust* (1982), a textbook on the Holocaust by one of Israel's most prominent Holocaust scholars, and Martin Gilbert's *The Holocaust: A History of the Jews of Europe during the Second World War* (1985). Gilbert has written less of a traditional history of the Holocaust, as it relies heavily on the personal testimony of survivors and observers.

As Holocaust studies began to enter the mainstream of Western scholarship, particularly in the United States in the 1980s, new interest developed in Holocaust historiography. This was an indication that enough had been written on the Holocaust to begin to explore the various interpretations and perspectives taken by scholars in the four decades since the Holocaust ended. Other than Lucy Dawidowicz's classic *The Holocaust and the Historians,* there also appeared during this period Yisrael Gutman and Gideon Grief's *The Historiography of the Holocaust Period* (1988). This large collection of essays was taken from the papers of the Fifth Yad Vashem International Historical Conference in the spring of 1983. Gutman and Grief's (1988) excellent collection looks at the state of Holocaust studies and interpretation in most European countries, including the Soviet Bloc, the United States, and Israel. It was followed five years later by Michael R. Marrus's *The Holocaust in History* (1987). This classic and readable study looks at the vast body of historical literature that had been published on the Holocaust since 1945. Marrus breaks his study down topically, looking at the various works and interpretations on the Holocaust in the broader scope of Western history. He also discusses questions surrounding the Germans' decision to implement the Final Solution, the role of the various nations of Europe in this mass killing and persecution program, the attitudes of Europeans toward such policies, questions about the Jewish role in their own fate, Jewish resistance, and questions of rescue.

Current and Ongoing Debates in the Field of Holocaust Studies

"Intentionalists" versus "Functionalists"

As historians began carefully to examine the history of the Holocaust, schools of historical interpretation—the "intentionalists" and the "structuralists" or "functionalists"—emerged. In Germany, "intentionalists" underscored the importance of Hitler's antisemitism and drew a direct line from this to the implementation of the Final Solution, the plan for the mass murder of the Jews of Europe. "Functionalist" historians saw the origins and implementation of the Final Solution more in the partnership of various Nazi party and German government agencies and bureaucracies. Their analysis of the role or "function" played by these various agencies became the basis of their name, "functionalist" (Bracher, 1970; Browning, 1992; Jäckel, 1972; Low, 1994; Marrus, 1987).

The principle "intentionalist" West German historians were Karl Dietrich Bracher and Eberhard Jäckel. Bracher (1970) included a discussion of the role of anti-semitism and the mass murder of the Jews in *The German Dictatorship*. Bracher traced the roots of Hitler and the Nazis' antisemitism back to nineteenth-century Germany and Austria. He argued that the idea of gassing Jews went back to World War I, and underscored Hitler's reaction to being gassed late in the war. Bracher felt that, for Hitler, the Final Solution had priority over all other war issues (Low, 1994, p. 102). In *Hitler's Weltanschuung (Hitler's Philosophy of Life)*, Jäckel (1972), argued that the removal of Jews from German society was a goal Hitler dreamed of as early as 1919. Later, Jäckel (1984) would argue in his *Hitler in History* that it was Hitler who insisted on the Holocaust, although he doubted that the Führer ever gave a direct order for the implementation of the Final Solution. Other German "intentionalist" scholars included Erich Nolte, Andreas Hillgruber, and Karl Hildebrand (Low, 1994, p. 97).

One of the principle German "functionalists" was Martin Broszat (1969) who had published *Der Staat Hitlers (The Hitler State)*. This work later appeared in English as *The Hitler State: The Foundation and Development of the Internal Structure of the Third Reich* (Broszat, 1981). Drawing on this work, Brozat wrote a critique of "revisionist" historian David Irving's conclusion in Irving's *Hitler's War* (1977), that Hitler had nothing to do with the Final Solution. Broszat criticized Irving for his attempt to "normalize" Hitler. Elsewhere, Broszat (1977) argued that Hitler was too erratic, and German antisemitic policy too inconsistent, to draw a direct line from pre-1933 Hitlerian and Nazi antisemitic teachings to the Final Solution. Broszat (1977) saw the origins of the Final Solution more as an outcome of actions in the field once the invasion of the Soviet Union began. Another German historian, Hans Mommsen, (1983) argued even more forcefully that Hitler played little if any direct role in the Final Solution. Mommsen (1983) concluded that Hitler's anti-semitism, while real, was expressed more for propagandistic needs than anything else. Hitler, Mommsen argued, had no game plan for the destruction of Europe's Jews. Instead, Mommsen saw the Final Solution as the product of the competitive chaos of the Nazi regime, which was a direct result of Hitler's erratic administrative style. Uwe Dietrich Adam (1972), however, thought that it was a "belated Hitler decision" that led to the Final Solution (Browning, 1995, p. 87; Marrus, 1987, pp. 40–42).

Michael Marrus (1987) has pointed out that "intentionalists" see Adolf Hitler as the driving force behind the antisemitic policies that led to the Holocaust. Marrus further argues that Lucy Dawidowicz (1976) was the principle advocate for this perspective in *The War Against the Jews*. Browning (1995) argues in *The Pathway to Genocide* that the "intentionalists" centered much of their research on the diplomatic and political history of the Third Reich in an effort to prove their case, while the "functionalists" or "structuralists" concentrated on the complex, and often chaotic nature of the bureaucracy of the Nazi Party and government and the accompanying creative void used by Hitler's underlings as the reason for the Final Solution. Some of the early "functionalist" historians, such as Karl Schleunes (1990), now feel that both schools of argumentation have some merit (Browning, 1995, pp. 3–4).

In their search for justification for their point of view, the "intentionalists" point to early war speeches by Hitler, whom Gerald Fleming (1984) termed the "fighting prophet" (Marrus, 1987, p. 37). Perhaps the best example of non-German "intentionalist" historical writing on the Holocaust is Fleming's *Hitler and the Final Solution* (1984), which came out at the height of the "intentionalist"-"functionalist" debate. In his introduction to this work, Saul Friedländer dubbed Fleming an "ultra-intentionalist" (p. x). According to the "intentionalists," war gave Nazi leaders a cover to implement more deadly Jewish policies. The attack on the Soviet Union in the summer of 1941 provided the ultimate opportunity for implementation of the most deadly phase of the "war against the Jews," the Final Solution. For the "intentionalists," Hitler's antisemitic policies and war were deeply intertwined. "Intentionalists," however, have never been able to agree on when Hitler decided to implement his mass killing program for the Jews (Marrus, 1987, pp. 37–40).

Hitler also remains a central point in the arguments of the "functionalists," though in a very different way. According to Christopher Browning (1995), the "functionalists" were primarily social and institutional historians (p. 3). For "functionalists," Hitler's erratic and distant leadership style helped create a party and bureaucratic system, in which conflict and periodic chaos helped Hitler emerge as more of an arbiter than a true, visionary leader with firm goals and direction. The "functionalists" do accept the importance of antisemitism in German Nazi policy, but see more of an evolutionary, uneven development of policy leading to the Final Solution. Of particular importance to the final decision to mass murder Jews was the failed campaign in the Soviet Union, which some "functionalists" see as the final dumping ground for Europe's Jewish population (Browning, 1995, pp. 3–5; Marrus, 1987, pp. 40, 42–43).

As with most debates like this one, time has smoothed off the edges of the differing schools of thought. In reality, the truth lies somewhere in between. Perhaps the strongest case for this middle ground is put forward by Christopher Browning (1995), who argued in his *Pathway to Genocide* for what Michael Marrus (1987) calls a "moderate functionalist" position (p. 43). Browning (1995) believes it would be a mistake to dismiss Hitler's antisemitic statements in the two decades before the outbreak of World War II, yet he also feels that they should be put into the context of their times and not seen as part of the broader game plan that led to the Final Solution. What is evolutionary in German Nazi policy from 1939 to 1941 is the desire to rid German-occupied Europe of its Jewish populations through expulsion. The radicalization of German expulsion policies was very much a product of German military successes during this period (Browning, 1995, pp. 26–27).

The Final Solution

The Final Solution (in German, *Endlösung*), the German plan to systematically murder every Jewish person in Europe, was the culminating horror of the Holocaust. Christopher Browning (1995) argues that the Final Solution evolved into policy from the spring through the fall of 1941 and that it was driven by Hitler's elation over what appeared to be his military victory over the Soviets. Browning also feels that Hitler played the deciding role in the decision to implement the Final Solution (1995, pp. 8–38).

If Adolf Hitler was the spiritual force behind the Final Solution, then Heinrich Himmler was its architect. In the introduction to *The Architect of Genocide: Himmler and the Final Solution* (1991), Richard Breitman surveys the various disputes about the Final Solution that became part of the "intentionalist-functionalist" debate. Although his study centered around Himmler's role in implementing the Holocaust, Breitman emphasized the need for historians to be very precise in their chronology as they looked at the planning and implementation of the Final Solution. He thinks that those who see Hitler as the prime ideological mover and force behind the Final Solution fail adequately to weigh the impact of German policies toward Jews in the 1930s. Breitman also asserts that those who advocate the improvisational nature of planning for the Final Solution do not properly look at earlier events that might have undercut the "functionalist" perspective, which holds that mid-level Nazi leaders and bureaucrats were operating without any knowledge of a German masterplan for killing Jews. Breitman is particularly critical of Arno J. Mayer's (1988) *Why Did the Heavens Not Darken? The Final Solution in History,* for advocating the lack of a certain German plan of mass death. On the other hand, he is complimentary of Gerald Fleming's *Hitler and the Final Solution* (1984), which was written in response to Holocaust revisionist David Irving's contention (in *Hitler's War*) that Hitler knew nothing of the Final Solution. Breitman (1991) faults Fleming, though, for not showing "when Hitler committed his crimes, only that he did" (p. 27). Perhaps the best study on the complex issues surrounding the Final Solution is David Cesarani's collection of essays, *The Final Solution: Origins and Implementation* (1996). It brings together writings by some of the foremost specialists on the subject. Its major themes include an exploration of the timing of the Final Solution and the early stages of the invasion of the Soviet Union with the actual implementation of the German mass death program. In one of the most innovative essays in this collection, Henry Friedlander includes the Roma or Gypsies in the Final Solution, something he did in greater depth in his *The Origins of Nazi Genocide: From Euthanasia to the Final Solution* (1995).

The Judenräte (Jewish Councils) and Jewish Leadership in Europe during the Holocaust

One of the most sensitive controversies to emerge among historians, survivors, and others after the Holocaust centers around the role of the Jewish Councils, or Judenräte. Created after the German conquest of Poland in the fall of 1939, these councils acted as administrative intermediaries between the Germans and local Jewish communities. Because the Jewish Councils were responsible for the day-to-day running of ghettos, they wielded vast power. Sadly, what were for the most part well-meaning Jewish leaders working to do whatever possible to make life as tolerable for their communities, the Jewish Councils were soon required by the Germans to implement debilitating policies of forced or slave labor, property confiscation, and, once the Final Solution was underway, forced selection. Weiss (1990a) breaks down the reaction of Jewish leadership in Eastern Europe from 1939 to 1942 into four categories: (1) refusal fully to take part in any administrative alliance with the Germans; (2) limited willingness to play a role in the administrative work of the Jewish Councils, up to the point of handing over Jewish victims to the Germans; (3) an acceptance of the deadly nature of German policies; and (4) an active acceptance of Germany's deadly policies in an effort to save one's own life (p. 766).

To begin to understand the complexity of the problems faced by Jewish Council Members, it is important to look at individual cases and ghettos to ascertain the diversity of approaches. In the Lodz ghetto, Jewish Council chairman Mordechai Rumkowski believed that by making the Lodz ghetto economically valuable to the Germans, he could keep his community intact and alive. His efforts failed, and the Lodz ghetto was finally liquidated in the summer of 1944. Rumkowski and his family were murdered in Auschwitz in the fall of 1944 (Adelson and Lapides, 1989, p. 493). At the opposite end of this administrative spectrum was Adam Czerniakow, the head of the Warsaw ghetto's Jewish Council. Up until his suicide on July 23, 1942, Czerniakow worked to develop a diversified lifestyle for the population of the ghetto. He took his own life in reaction to the German demand to begin roundups of Jews for deportation (Hilberg, Staron, and Kermisz, 1979, p. 23).

Isaiah Trunk (1972) provides a more detailed examination at this complex issue in his classic, *Judenrat*. Of the 720 Jewish Council members discussed in his study, almost 80 percent were killed or died as a result of deportation. Only 12 percent of these Council members survived the Holocaust, compared to a general European Jewish population survival rate of 33 percent. Weiss's (1990a) analysis of the conduct and plight of 146 early Jewish Council members shows that almost 72 percent of these leaders were killed, resigned, dismissed (or committed suicide) for their refusal to carry out German orders. Only 14.4 percent of the early Jewish Council leaders openly complied with all German orders. Because of these reactions, the Germans appointed a new wave of Jewish leaders who proved more pliable to German demands. The level of compliance among this new group was much higher (Weiss, 1990a, pp. 766–768).

One of the most troubling issues surrounding the Jewish Council controversy was the role of the Jewish ghetto police, or the Jüdischer Ordnungsdienst. The Jewish ghetto police were responsible for carrying out all German decrees, regardless of their nature. They seized property and taxes, kept public order, rounded up Jewish forced or slave laborers, and helped guard victims for transport to the concentration and death camps. Once the mass deportations began in 1942, some members of the Jewish police began to question their roles, and chose to go to their death rather than send neighbors and family members for transportation to certain death (Trunk, 1972, pp. 516–517). As they had done with recalcitrant Jewish Council members, the Germans quickly replaced resistant Jewish police force members with more willing Jewish volunteers. In some cases, the Jewish police saw their powers increase as that of the Jewish Councils faded in the later years of the Holocaust. A number of Jewish policemen were tried for war crimes after the war by the American International Military Tribunal (IMT) Nuremberg war crimes trials, and in Israel. Most of those tried received little or no punishment but were ostracized by their Jewish communities (Weiss, 1990b, pp. 771–774).

The Plight of Other Minorities

Another controversy to emerge in Holocaust historiography is the plight of other minorities. Some Jewish historians, such as Steven T. Katz (1994) and Yehuda Bauer worry that inclusion of non-Jewish victims in the Holocaust diminishes the uniqueness of the Jewish tragedy (Berenbaum, 1990, pp. 23–25). Representatives of non-Jewish groups who suffered mistreatment at the hands of the Germans from 1933 to 1945 argue that the pain, suffering, and losses of these groups need to be acknowledged. With the growing popularization of the Holocaust, particularly in the United States, this controversy is likely to intensify as more groups try to be included as Holocaust victims.

What is most important here is to differentiate between those groups that were genocidal victims of the Germans and their collaborators, and those that were subjected to varying degrees of mistreatment based on their lifestyle, ethnicity, religious beliefs, political affiliation or opposition to German policies.

Two groups, the handicapped and the Roma (or Gypsies) were designated for mass murder because the Germans considered them a threat to German "Aryan" racial purity. German "racial pseudo-scientists" considered Jews and the handicapped to be Lebensunsvertes Lebens—"Life unworthy of life"—and the Gypsies as dangerous "asocials." As such, each of these groups were singled out during the Holocaust for varying degrees of mistreatment, punishment, and, ultimately, mass murder. In the first six years of Nazi power in Germany, the Jews were robbed of all of their political, social, and economic rights in an effort to force them to leave Germany, while three hundred thousand handicapped people were sterilized. The Gypsies were rounded up, placed in camps, and watched closely by the police. Once World War II broke out, the Germans set up the T-4 "euthanasia" program in the Third Reich for the handicapped, which resulted in the murder of seventy thousand to eighty thousand of these helpless victims. In 1941, the T-4 specialists were transferred eastward to provide the technological and expert nucleus for the Final Solution. Estimates are that in addition to almost six million Jewish victims, the Germans and their collaborators also killed 250,000 to 500,000 Roma (Gypsies) and 200,000 to 250,000 handicapped. (Friedlander, 1995, p. 110; Kenrick and Puxon, 1972, p. 184; Kenrick and Puxon, 1995, p. 150; Lifton, 1986, p. 142; Müller-Hill, 1988, pp. 64–65; United States Holocaust Memorial Museum, n.d.-e, p. 19.) Ian Hancock (1996) argues that it is possible that more than one million Roma died during the Holocaust (p. 50).

Other groups and individuals were also persecuted during the Holocaust, although they were not genocidal victims. It should be remembered that Nazi Germany was a racial state with a very well-defined body of German pseudoscience that defined all Europeans along "racial" lines. According to Henry Friedlander (1995), Jews and Gypsies were "racially alien" people who were dangerous to the purity of Aryan blood. The Nazis singled out Jews as a special threat to Aryan racial purity, and they became special "racial" targets of the German leadership. The Germans viewed the mentally and physically handicapped and the Roma as potential "pollutants" of Aryan blood. They also saw the Roma as an asocial criminal element. The Germans thought that some Slavic people were *untermenschen* (subhumans) who occupied the coveted Lebensraum that was to be the nucleus of the Thousand-Year Reich. As such, once the Germans murdered the Slavs' cultural and intellectual elite, particularly the Russians and the Poles, they were to become quasi-slaves in the Third Reich (Friedlander, 1995, pp. 14–18; Lukas, 1990, p. 4). Even though twenty-six to twenty-eight million Soviets, some of whom were not Slavic, and three million non-Jewish Poles died during World War II, not all of these victims were killed as a result of deliberate acts of genocide. This does not diminish the tragedy of these deaths but merely underscores the fact that few groups suffered from the determined, fanatical genocidal policies in the same way as the Jews. A number of works have appeared in the last twenty-five years that try to make a stronger case for the uniqueness and importance of the non-Jewish deaths in the Holocaust. Some scholars choose simply to detail the fate of a specific group, such as Donald Kenrick and Gratton Puxon (1972, 1995) in their *The Destiny of Europe's Gypsies* and their update, *Gypsies under the Swastika*. Crowe (1994, 1996) follows the same course in his *A History of the Gypsies of Eastern Europe and Russia*. A prominent Roma scholar, Ian Hancock (1991, 1996), takes a more aggressive position, and argues that Roma suffering, in terms of percentage of losses, was higher than that of Jews and other groups (p. 7 and p. 49, respectively). Katz (1994) has attempted to counter efforts by non-Jews to put their suffering from 1933 to 1945 on the same plane as Jews by writing the first volume of a planned three-volume work, *The Holocaust in Historical Context*. Katz tries to underscore the uniqueness of the Jewish tragedy during the Holocaust by pointing out the long Western traditions of antisemitism and comparing Jewish suffering during the Christian era in Western civilization to that of other groups.

Efforts have also been made by Polish historians to draw attention to the plight of Polish victims during the Holocaust, which Lukas (1990) detailed in his *Forgotten Holocaust: The Poles under German Occupation, 1939–1944*. In the introduction, Lukas (1990) claims that the reason for the omission of Polish victimization during the Holocaust is tied to efforts by Holocaust scholars to look at this tragedy in "exclusivistic" Jewish terms (p. ix). Statistically, Lukas (1990) argues, over six million Poles perished during World War II, half of them Jewish and half of them Christians. Some of the first Poles killed by the Germans were intellectuals, politicians, and priests whom the Germans viewed as an integral part of the Polish national leadership. Bauer differs and notes in his introduction to Yisrael Gutman's and Shmuel Krakowski's *Unequal Victims: Poles and Jews During World War II* (1986), that, although a minority of Poles tried to help Jews during the Holocaust, most were either indifferent or actively antagonistic toward the Germans' Jewish victims (p. ix). The question here, then, is whether the Poles' traditional anti-semitism and less than admirable reaction to Jewish victimization during the Holocaust somehow diminishes the significance of Polish losses during World War II and the Holocaust. Perhaps the most succinct view of the plight of the Poles during the Holocaust is provided in the United States Holocaust Memorial Museum's (n.d.-d) booklet, *Poles*. It correctly underscores the German view that, with few exceptions, the Poles were *untermensch* (subhumans) and deserved considerable mistreatment (United States Holocaust Memorial Museum, n.d.-d , p. 3).

Other groups that are commonly cited as Holocaust victims are Soviets, particularly prisoners of war (POWs), the Jehovah's Witnesses, homosexuals, Afro-Germans, Ukrainians, Belorussians, and political dissidents. Although all of these groups suffered varying degrees of mistreatment at the hands of the Germans and their collaborators during World War II, questions have emerged about whether such mistreatment, usually imprisonment, should be placed in the same category as the Germans' efforts to mass murder Jews, the handicapped, and Gypsies.

The Germans persecuted Jehovah's Witnesses throughout the Nazi era, because they were pacifists who refused to use the "Sieg Heil" salute to Hitler, and because they would not join any Nazi organization, register for the draft, or serve in the Wehrmacht. Witnesses openly but passively challenged Nazi laws and were jailed in large numbers. Witnesses who were willing to drop their objections to these practices could be released from prison, where they were strongly mistreated, and a small number did. Most of the ten thousand Witnesses arrested by the Germans during the Holocaust, however, remained in prison throughout this period, where they were viewed as model prisoners by the Germans (Höss, 1996, pp. 102–104; United States Holocaust Memorial, n.d.-c, pp. 1–19; Watch Tower Bible and Tract Society of Pennsylvania, 1993, pp. 693–694).

Homosexual males were persecuted because of their lifestyle. Nazi policy toward this group mirrored age-old Western prejudices against male homosexuals and centered around what ideologists called "socially aberrant" behavior (Plant, 1986, pp. 22–52; United States Holocaust Memorial Museum, n.d.-b, p. 1). In an Aryan nation that sought to expand the size of its pure "racial" base throughout Europe, the existence of a group that could not produce offspring through its sexual activity was considered harmful to German society. According to the United States Holocaust Memorial Museum, the Germans arrested one hundred thousand men for suspected gay activities from 1933 to 1945, and imprisoned about half, most of them in regular prisons. About five thousand to fifteen thousand of the imprisoned homosexual males were sent to concentration camps. In the camps, officials forced gay prisoners to wear a pink triangle, a badge of particular shame, and suffered severe persecution from their guards and other prisoners (Plant, 1986, pp. 148–150; United States Holocaust Memorial Museum, n.d.-b, pp. 4–7). Grau (1995) refers to this persecution as the "hidden Holocaust." Yet, in using this term, he is also careful to distinguish between the German program to murder all of the Jews of Europe and efforts to force those with homosexual inclinations to stop these practices (Fischer, 1995, p. 285; Grau, 1995, pp. 6–7).

One of the most problematic issues for Nazi leaders who waged a campaign of severe persecution against male gays in the Third Reich was the presence of homosexuals in the upper Party leadership. Ernst Röhm, the head of the powerful Nazi paramilitary organization, the SA (Sturmabteilung, or storm detachment), was an open homosexual, as were many of the SA's other leaders. In fact, Röhm's homosexuality was used as one of the justifications for the deadly "Night of the Long Knives" purge of the SA on June 28, 1934. In reality, Hitler approved of this action to rid himself of a leadership group that was a threat to his own leadership and a growing concern to German military leaders (Plant, 1986, pp. 61–67).

"Ordinary Men":
Christopher Browning and Daniel Goldhagen

One of the most divisive controversies to erupt in Holocaust scholarship over the past decade has centered around a book written by Daniel Goldhagen, *Hitler's Willing Executioners: Ordinary Germans and the Holocaust* (1996). The seed for this work was drawn from Christopher Browning's *Ordinary Men: Reserve Police Battalion 101 and the Final Solution in Poland* (1992). According to Hilberg (1997), the dean of American Holocaust scholars, Goldhagen used the phrase "Ordinary Germans" in his title as a "calculated attack on a senior scholar, Christopher Browning" (p. 721). Like Browning (1992), Goldhagen (1996) centered his work around the postwar trial transcripts of the members of this reserve police unit, in an effort to try to determine the personal feelings and motivations of those involved in mass killing operations in Poland and the occupied Soviet Union during the Final Solution.

Browning's (1992) work looks at the activities of the reserve policemen from the Hamburg area of Germany from the summer of 1942 until late 1943. Browning says that these "ordinary Germans," most of whom had no close ties to the Nazi Party, and were not deeply imbued with a special Nazis fanaticism, played a part in the murder of 83,000 Jews—38,000 from mass executions, 45,000 through deportation to Treblinka and death (pp. 177–189, 191–192). Browning points to a number of factors, such as group conformity and ideological indoctrination, that drove these five hundred men to commit mass murder. Browning was not able to determine conclusively what caused ordinary Germans to kill innocent Jewish men, women, and children (pp. 184–186).

If Browning was hesitant to point to any single or collective explanation for the actions of Reserve Police Battalion 101, Goldhagen (1996) was quick with a ready answer. According to Goldhagen, the answer centered around German "eliminationist" and later "exterminationist" antisemitism. (Goldhagen defines "eliminationist" antisemitism as "the belief that Jewish influence, by nature destructive, must be eliminated irrevocably from society" (Goldhagen, 1996, p. 48). He argues that "exterminationist" antisemitism, which called for the "physical extermination of the Jews," grew out of the "eliminationist" mindset (1996, p. 71). He argues early on in his lengthy study that such antisemitism "moved many thousands of 'ordinary Germans'—and would have moved millions more, had they been appropriately positioned—to slaughter Jews" (1996, pp. 69–72). As he does throughout his study, Goldhagen dismisses any other explanation for such atrocities, and insists that this deep-seated "eliminationist" German antisemitism, which he says existed in German society well before the Nazis came to power, was the principle reason for the Holocaust (pp. 9, 23, 71).

Goldhagen's thesis, which is based on a rather weak overview of antisemitic traditions in German history and new research in the postwar court records previously investigated by Browning (1992), has been severely criticized by some of the Western world's most prominent Holocaust scholars. Hilberg (1997) concludes that Goldhagen has overstated "the extent and depth of German anti-Semitism" (p. 723). He is particularly critical of the fact that the "Goldhagen thesis" leaves little room for the ethnic Germans and other Europeans involved in the mass killings of Jews. Overall, Hilberg feels Goldhagen's book is "lacking in factual content and logical rigor" (p. 724). More pointedly, Browning (1997) argues that Goldhagen's "'keyhole' approach to German history, its stereotypical generalizations about the perpetrators" (p. 104) and "the employment of the metaphor of disease to illuminate our understanding of a singular and uniform German anti-Semitism," very much "becomes an eery mirror image of how anti-Semites write about Jews" (p. 104).

Goldhagen's book sold hundreds of thousands of copies in Germany. Older Germans reacted strongly against the idea that there was something innate in the killing passions that drove the Germans to mass murder Jews, while younger Germans, who found Goldhagen's work attractive and informative, were more supportive of the "Goldhagen thesis," feeling that too much of the truth about the Holocaust had been clouded over by the older generation. Perhaps Volker Ullrich, an editor of *Der Zeit*, best explained the German reaction to Goldhagen's work in a German televised debate on the Goldhagen phenomena:

> Here finally is someone who expresses what has long been a taboo; that the distinction between "criminal Nazis" and "normal Germans" is false; that the readiness to murder millions came from the middle of German society. When someone utters this simple truth it acts on no few Germans as a kind of liberation. (Quoted in Elon, 1997, p. 44)

The Catholic Church and the Holocaust

The 1998 Vatican document, *We Remember: A Reflection on the Shoah*, was an effort by Pope John II and the leadership of the Roman Catholic church to put to rest one of the most delicate issues of Holocaust scholarship and memory—the reaction of Pope Pius XII (r. 1939–1958) and the Catholic church to news of the Holocaust. The Catholic church is the largest Christian denomination in the world, with one billion adherents, and the pope its most important spiritual and moral force. One would presume that with its large number of priests, nuns, and lay leaders in villages, town, and cities throughout the Roman Catholic parts of Europe, that the Vatican would have been very well informed about the mounting German killing program against the Jews (Lewy, 1964, pp. 295–308; Zuccotti, 1996, pp. 132–135). Charges of Vatican inaction, insensitivity, and outright antisemitism have periodically surfaced in the decades since the end of the Holocaust. What really set the stage for a more critical view of Pius XII's policies toward the Jews was Rolf Hochhuth's book and play, *The Deputy* (1963). Coming in the aftermath of Adolf Eichmann's trial and execution, it severely criticized Pius XII's failure to do more for Jews in the Holocaust (Hochhuth, 1963, pp. 289–295).

Since then, a number of historians, such as Guenter Lewy (1964) and Susan Zuccotti (1996), have strongly criticized Pius XII for his abject moral failure to speak out more forcefully against the growing campaign of atrocities and mass death against Europe's Jews (Lewy, 1964, pp. 300–304; Zuccotti, 1996, pp. 134–135). Defenders of the pope argue that he did quietly support efforts by Italian priests and nuns to help save individual Jews throughout Italy (Bokenkotter, 1990, pp. 351–352). They also point to story after story of individual Catholics who risked their lives throughout Europe to save Jews (Zuccotti, 1996, pp. 132–135). Moreover, they note that Pius XII's first responsibility was to his Catholic flock throughout Europe. His defenders argue that his failure to speak out forcefully against Hitler's "war" against the Jews was driven by the fear that if he did so, the Germans would take out their displeasure on priests, nuns, church institutions, and individual Catholics in Europe. They also point to the fact that some of the first victims of Nazi oppression in Germany, Poland, and elsewhere were Catholic clerics (Gallagher, 1998, p. F4; Zuccotti, 1996, pp. 133–134).

These explanations have proven to be most unsatisfactory to many Holocaust scholars and survivors. At issue, of course, is not just papal reaction to the Holocaust, but the deeper question of millenia-old Catholic antisemitism. Pius XII did little after the Holocaust to address his failures.

By contrast, his successor, Pope John XXIII (r. 1958–1963), who had served as Papal Nuncio in Turkey during the Holocaust and actively worked to save Jews, did a great deal during his brief reign to begin to build bridges to the world's Jewish community. In fact, John XXIII was one of the principle forces behind the 1965 Vatican document, *Nostre Aetate*, which acknowledged the special historical and spiritual ties between Christianity and Judaism. *Nostre Aetate* also condemned traditional antisemitism and its abuses (Rubin, 1995, pp. 298–302).

More recently, Pope John Paul II (r. 1978–present) has done a great deal to heal the deep historical rift between Catholics and Jews. John Paul II has publicly spoken out against the crimes against the Jews during the Holocaust. In 1986, he visited the Rome synagogue, and seven years later established diplomatic ties with Israel. In 1994, John Paul II had a menorah lit and a Kaddish (Jewish prayer for the dead) said in the Vatican to remember the Jews who were murdered during the Holocaust. Yet, the Vatican has never offered an apology for the church's inaction during the Holocaust, although Catholic bishops in Germany, France, Hungary, and elsewhere have issued statements to this effect. Jewish leaders had hoped that the long-anticipated 1998 Vatican document, *We Remember,* prepared by a special papal commission over an eleven-year period, would directly address the role of the church during the Holocaust. Sadly, although the fourteen-page document did admonish Catholics for their failure to speak out more forcefully against anti-Jewish atrocities and even criticized the Catholic church for its traditional anti-semitism, *We Remember* argues that the Holocaust was caused not by these excesses but by the nationalistic antisemitism of the Germans (John Paul II, 1998, p. A10). In the cover letter to *We Remember,* John Paul II said he hoped that the document would "help heal the wounds of past misunderstandings and injustices. May it enable memory to play its necessary part in the process of shaping a future in which the unspeakable iniquity of the Shoah will never again be possible" (John Paul II, 1998, A10). *We Remember* has been criticized for its historical inaccuracies, its failure to completely address Pope Pius XII's moral failings during the Holocaust, and the continued refusal of the Vatican to apologize for the church's failure to more force-fully take a moral stand against German outrages against Jews and other minori-ties during this tragedy (Bohlen, 1998, pp. A1–A11; Niebuhr, 1998, p. A11). In early 2000, during an official visit to Israel, Pope John Paul II, while at the Yad Vashem Holocaust Memorial, made reference to the barbarity of the Holocaust.

Swiss Neutrality and Nazi Gold

One Holocaust issue that received a great deal of attention in the late 1990s is that of gold and other financial deposits stored in secret Swiss bank accounts before and during the Holocaust. Some of these deposits were made by Holocaust vic-tims and survivors, while other secret reserves came from German gold stolen from Holocaust victims or occupied countries. Some of the German gold was taken from the bodies of murdered Jews, melted down, and then deposited as gold bars in German accounts in Swiss banks. In addition to questions about the nature and sources of some of this stolen gold, there also is controversy over Swiss claims of neutrality during World War II, and Switzerland's response to the flood of Jew-ish and other Holocaust victims seeking to enter the country during this tragedy.

According to Gustav Niebuhr (1997), the postwar Swiss created a mythology that kept alive Winston Churchill's comment that the Swiss were the world's only "decent neutrals" during the war. Niebuhr said part of this Swiss image centered around the idea that they were "an island of integrity amidst World War II's bar-barism" (1997, p. 14), ready to fight for their independence. The reality was quite different. In order to avoid the fate of many of their neighbors, Switzerland became an important contributor to the German economy during World War II. The Swiss allowed the Germans free access to their rail lines, while Swiss industry became an important contributor to the German war effort (Cowell, 1997a, p. A1; Cowell, 1997b, p. A6; Cowell, 1997c, p. A6).

As part of this special relationship with the Third Reich, Switzerland agreed to work with the Germans to restrict the flow of refugees into Switzerland—particularly

Jewish refugees. In fact, Swiss historian Jacques Picard told Israeli journalist Amos Elon (1997) that his country did not have a refugee policy during the Holocaust, just a Jewish policy (p. 42). Part of this policy centered around efforts by Heinrich Rothmund, an important Swiss police official, to convince the Germans to stamp the passports of all German Jews with a red "J." Berlin agreed, but insisted that the Swiss put the same marking on the passports of Swiss Jews. Rothmund told the Swiss cabinet that this would be a mere formality, and red "Js" were soon stamped on all passports held by Swiss Jews. Though about three hundred thousand refugees passed through Switzerland during the Holocaust, only a little over a third were allowed to remain in the country. In an interview conducted by Amos Elon (1993), Swiss historian Guido Koller said that there were seventy thousand to one hundred thousand Jewish refugees among the three hundred thousand refugees who passed through Switzerland during World War II. About twenty-five thousand to thirty thousand of the one hundred thousand refugees allowed to settle in Switzerland were Jews.

Equally troubling are the vast German gold reserves stored in secret Swiss bank accounts during the war. This gold, estimated to be worth as much as $5 billion at today's exchange rates, was taken from the various countries conquered by the Germans during the war. It has been estimated that these reserves helped prolong World War II in Europe from one to two years. About a sixth of the gold deposited in Swiss accounts by the Germans was stolen from Holocaust victims, some of it gold teeth and jewelry from the death camps. Between 60 percent and 85 percent of funds stolen by the Germans throughout Europe were deposited in Swiss accounts (Elon, 1997, pp. 41–42). According to Philip Miller, this gold was used to finance the German war effort (Miller, 1997, p. 9).

After the war, efforts by the Allies to force the Swiss to pay the claims of survivors and their relatives for legal or stolen deposits and other assets in Switzerland were largely unsuccessful. In 1946, the Swiss agreed to make a token payment of $58.4 million, though estimates are that the Swiss still held $200–300 million in stolen German assets in their banks. The Swiss payment was to be used to cover claims and also would be distributed to Jewish agencies for humanitarian relief efforts. The Polish and Hungarian governments were later able to get the Swiss to make small payments to compensate them for assets lost during the war. Over the next four decades, the secretive Swiss banks did everything possible to dismiss the numerous claims of Holocaust survivors (Cesarani, 1997, pp. 3–5; Miller, 1997, pp. 13–14; Sanger, 1997, p. A10).

All of this began to change in 1995, when the World Jewish Congress in New York pressed the Swiss government and the powerful Swiss Bankers Association to do more to try to uncover the mystery of stolen and hidden German and Holocaust deposits in Swiss banks. Spurred by a U.S. Congressional hearing in 1996 led by Senator Alfonse D'Amato, and a special American commission headed by Paul Volcker, a former U.S. Federal Reserve chairman, the Swiss parliament created an international committee of experts to look into these complex issues (Kramer, 1997, p. 77). Several statements by prominent Swiss leaders, critical of the World Jewish Congress' efforts, triggered something of an international crisis, followed by threats of a boycott of Swiss banks. Given that the Swiss banking industry derives much of its profits from abroad, the threat of a boycott seemed to do the trick (Elon, 1997, p. 43).

The Swiss Bankers Association (SBA) and the government agreed in early 1997 to set up a special Holocaust victims' fund, initially valued at $70 million but later increased to $192 million. Several months later, the Swiss government said it would establish a Swiss Foundation for Solidarity worth $4.7 billion to aid victims of the Holocaust and other genocides. This fund had to be approved by parliament and a public referendum in 1998, which was ultimately delayed because of strong Swiss public sentiment against it. As Swiss authorities scrambled to make up for their past, a scandal broke out when a Swiss bank guard, Christoph Meili, discovered in early 1997 two cartloads of Holocaust bank records about to be destroyed by the Union Bank of Switzerland where he worked. Meili, who turned the documents over to Jewish community leaders in Zürich, was fired, and later sought political refuge in the United States (Andrews, 1997, pp. A7, A11). As this controversy developed, an American presidential commission, headed by Stuart E. Eizenstat, U.S. Undersecretary of State for International Trade, put the finishing touches on an extensive report that claimed that the Swiss knew that much of the money deposited by the Germans in Swiss accounts was stolen. The Eizenstat report concluded, though, that there was nothing to indicate that the Swiss knew that some of the gold had come from Holocaust victims (Slany, 1997, pp. ix–x). This study finally spurred the SBA to dig more deeply into their secretive accounting system to locate the accounts of Holocaust survivors. On July 23, 1997, the SBA published a list of 1,756 dormant World War II accounts in the *New York Times* and other major newspapers. Although there were names of Holocaust victims on the list, it also included the names of prominent Nazis. Other accounts have since been "discovered," and, in early 1998, the Swiss government agreed to conclude a major settlement package with Holocaust survivors and various Jewish groups. On August 12, 1998, Switzerland's major banks agreed to a $1.25 billion settlement with the World Jewish Congress and other Jewish organizations. Twelve percent of this money is to go to non-Jewish victims and organizations (Goshko, 1998, pp. A1, A11).

Several months earlier, Estelle Sapir, a Holocaust survivor, announced in New York that Switzerland's Crédit Suisse had agreed to pay her a settlement, estimated to be about $500,000. As early as 1946, Miss Sapir had tried to recover her father's assets in the bank, only to be told that Crédit Suisse could do nothing until she produced a death certificate for her father. Since her father was murdered in the German death camp in Majdanek, Poland, this was impossible. Though Crédit Suisse went to great lengths to paint this payment as an exception, a nonprecedent-setting case, those involved in trying to get Swiss banks to be more generous in their settlement of individual claims hope the Sapir case will set the tone for future claims dispositions (Sanger, 1998, p. A27).

The Holocaust gold debate triggered a national soul-searching in Switzerland, particularly among the older generation. It has caused some Swiss to demand the reevaluation of the country's role in World War II. A panel of Swiss scholars is working on a more truthful accounting of Switzerland's history during this tragic period. Many older Swiss, though, resentfully feel the question of looted German and Holocaust gold is an attack on the Swiss national character and traditional neutrality (Cowell, 1997a, p. A1). At the core of this debate in Switzerland is truth and fiction. In varying degrees, most of the countries of Europe that were allied, conquered, or were even neutral during the Holocaust and World War II played some supportive role in the German war effort, and even in the Holocaust. Some countries, like Switzerland and Austria, have tried to hide behind claims of neutrality or victimization to mask their roles in the war, while the French, the Slovaks, the Romanians, and others have only recently begun to face the realities and guilt of collaboration.

National Views on the Holocaust

Holocaust studies throughout Europe and North America were (and still are) deeply affected by national perspectives on this tragedy. European scholarship was influenced by each nation's experience with the Nazis as well as the degree of collaboration and traditional antisemitism found in these countries.

In France, concerns over Holocaust culpability played a smaller role than the concern over collaboration. Over time, however, questions of war criminality and Holocaust involvement and responsibility entered the scholarly mainstream, so that today the Holocaust is a topic of great interest and concern to the French.

In Germany and Austria, a very different approach was taken on the Holocaust. In West Germany, questions of Holocaust guilt were taken quite seriously as the nation struggled with its Nazi past and faced the complex process of denazification and rebuilding. There was a strong tendency to hide behind the belief that it was the Nazi Party, not the German people, who were the villains in this history. Former soldiers followed the same tack, and asserted that the Wehrmacht—the German Nazi armed forces—had merely done its soldierly duty, and not taken part in the atrocities of the Holocaust. Contemporary scholarship, however, has shown that the Wehrmacht did collaborate in the mass killings (Bartov, 1986, pp. 106–141; Bartov, 1996, pp. 119–121; Streit, 1996, pp. 108–114).

In Austria, the Holocaust was a subject not to be discussed. When brought up, the Austrians, who had enthusiastically welcomed the Germans when their country was united with the Third Reich in the Anschluss of 1938, argued that they had also been victims of the Germans.

In the Soviet Bloc, most countries followed the Soviet line of refusing to acknowledge a specific tragedy for a single group of people. The official Soviet position, which was repeated in other parts of Eastern Europe, was that all peoples of the nation or region suffered horribly from German Nazi crimes. In many ways, war memory became a religion, and was used constantly to remind the Soviets, Hungarians, Poles, and others of the great sacrifices and leadership provided by their national communist parties against the hated "fascists." Thus, in the parts of Europe where the worst atrocities of the Holocaust took place, the Holocaust was a nontopic. Each of these national traditions, as well as those in Israel and the United States, would greatly affect the course of Holocaust studies in the Western world.

Germany

Germany bears the greatest responsibility for the Holocaust. What has complicated the ability of the German nation and people to come to grips with the historical responsibility for the Holocaust is the division of Germany from 1945 to 1991. The Soviet-style shroud that hindered a more mature reckoning with Holocaust responsibility in East Germany has complicated the ability of the Germans to deal more maturely with this issue throughout the reunited nation.

East Germany (German Democratic Republic, GDR)   The German Democratic Republic (GDR), which officially came into existence in 1949, was carved out of that part of Germany occupied by the Soviet Union at the end of World War II. The GDR became the most reliable of the Soviet Union's East European satellite states, and as such, mirrored much of Moscow's attitudes on Jews and the Holocaust.

Holocaust historiography began to emerge in the postwar period, influenced partly by public interest in the subject, and by events such as the 1961 Eichmann trial. Until this point, what GDR historians did discuss about the Holocaust tended to be filtered through the broader questions of antifascism and Nazism.

One of the best studies on GDR historiography on the Holocaust was published in 1976, Konrad Kweit's "Historians of the German Democratic Republic on Antisemitism and Persecution." Two years later, the fortieth anniversary of Kristallnacht ("Night of the Broken Glass;" the November 9–10, 1938 antisemitic pogrom in the territory controlled by the Third Reich) stirred new interest in the Holocaust among GDR historians. A series of publications followed, while government leaders took part in religious and commemorative services throughout the GDR. In 1976, the GDR offered a token reparations payment to Jewish victims of the Holocaust who had once lived in territory occupied by the GDR. This was rejected, because some of the survivors felt the payments should be offered to all Jewish Holocaust survivors; however, this first-time offer marked an important turning point in official GDR attitudes toward the Holocaust and Jews (Peck, 1996, pp. 459–460).

Over the next decade, interest in the Holocaust, and particularly Jewish victimization, continued to grow in the GDR's churches and other institutions. This spurred a considerable amount of activity among historians, especially in 1988, when the GDR faced the fiftieth anniversary of Kristallnacht. A number of major conferences, symposia, and lecture series were sponsored by Humboldt University, the Central Institute for History of the Academy of Sciences, and other institutions on the Jews in German history, antisemitism, and the Holocaust.

West Germany (Federal Republic of Germany, FRG)   Given the closed nature of the GDR, West Germany was to bear the brunt of Holocaust guilt and responsibility in the decades after World War II. Very little German historical work during this period dealt with the Holocaust, and what studies emerged were often done by German emigre scholars such as Fritz Stern, in his *Politics of Cultural Despair* (1961). Austrian historian Eugen Kogon touched on the fate of the Jews in his *Der SS-Staat: Das System der deutschen Konzentrationslager (The SS State: The System of German Concentration Camps)* (1946), which appeared four years later as *The Theory and Practice of Hell* (1950). Kogon, a Catholic writer and publisher, was sent to Buchenwald at the beginning of World War II for his anti-Nazi sentiments. *Der SS-Staat* was published a year after his release (Cargas, 1985, pp. 60–61).

The first significant work to appear in West Germany on the Holocaust did not appear until 1960, when Wolfgang Scheffler published *Judenverfolgung im Dritten Reich (The Persecution of Jews in the Third Reich)*. Scheffler detailed the Jewish response to Hitler in the 1930s. In 1962 Karl Dietrich Bracher, Wolfgang Sauer, and Gerhard Schultz, explored the significance of antisemitism to Nazi ideology in their *Die Nationalsozialistische Machtergreifung: Studien zur Erichtung des totalitären Herrschaftssystems in Deutschland, 1933–34 (The National Socialist Ascendance to Power: Studies on the Establishment of Totalitarian Rule in Germany, 1933–34)*. Bracher, Sauer, and Schultz (1962) argued that antisemitism was an integral part of Nazi teachings, and underscored Jewish efforts to maintain their own sense of cultural and religious identity in the face of the German Nazi onslaught. Bracher, Sauer, and Schultz (1962) along with Martin Broszat (1960), who published *Der Nationalsozialismus: Weltanschaung, Programm und Wirklchkeit (The National Socialist World View: Program and Reality)* the same year, saw antisemitism as one of the few constants in Nazism (Kulka, Birkenhauer, and Hildesheimer, 1997, pp. 16–17).

The appearance of these works and the trial of Adolf Eichmann had a profound impact on West German Holocaust historiography. According to Kulka, Birkenhauer, and Hildesheimer (1997), an article by British historian Hugh Trevor-Roper (1960) triggered a wave of new scholarship on the ideological underpinnings of National Socialism, particularly as it related to Hitler's war aims and racism. What emerged in this growing field of German Holocaust studies were the earlier discussed schools of interpretation—the "intentionalists" and the "structuralists" or "functionalists."

What is important about the West German debate regarding "intentionalism" versus "functionalism" in the 1960s and 1970s is its impact on an even more intense struggle among German historians in the 1980s, known as the Historikerstreit or "historians' debate." Some of the West German historians who were engaged in the "intentionalist"-"functionalist" debate now took part in an intellectual struggle that went public in Germany in the mid-1980s and raged over the "normalization" of the Holocaust in West German scholarship and society. As Michael L. Morgan (1997) has pointed out in his "To Seize Memory: History and Identity in Post-Holocaust Jewish Thought" (pp. 153–154), the Historikerstreit evolved out of the efforts among some conservative German intellectuals and politicians to place the Holocaust in the broader context of twentieth-century European history. This debate was triggered by the showing of the American television series "Holocaust" in West Germany in early 1979, efforts to build German national museums in Bonn and Berlin, and the controversy surrounding President

Ronald Reagan's plans to visit a cemetery in Bitburg, West Germany, where Waffen SS troops were buried. All of the major articles and lectures of the Historikerstreit debate are collected in *Forever in the Shadow of Hitler?*, translated by James Knowlton and Truett Cates (1993).

The debate began in 1986 with a speech delivered by Erich Nolte, which was later published in the conservative *Frankfurter Allgemeine Zeitung* as "Die Vergangenheit, Die Nicht Vergehen Will" *(The Past That Will Not Pass)*. In his speech and article, Nolte linked the Final Solution to fears among the Nazi leadership that if the Soviet Union occupied Germany, the Soviets would begin to mass murder Germans. According to Nolte, with the exception of gassing, all of the mass murder techniques used by the Germans had already been used in the 1920s and 1930s by the Soviets. Nolte claimed the German mass murder of Jews was an "Asiatic deed" in response to the potential Soviet mass murder of Germans after Stalingrad. He even posed the question "Was the Gulag Archipelago [Soviet prison camp network] not primary to Auschwitz?" (Nolte, 1993, p. 22). Another German historian, Andreas Hillgruber (1986), expressed similar feelings in his *Zweierlei Untergang (Two kinds of Destruction)*, which pointed to the mass murder of German civilians by Soviet forces in East Prussia during the war (Habermas, 1993, p. 35). Jürgen Habermas led the opposition to these views and was soon joined by other prominent West German historians, such as Hans Mommsen and Eberhard Jäckel. Jäckel strongly disagreed with the idea that fear of Soviet atrocities was the stimulus for the Holocaust. In his essay, "A Kind of Settlement of Damages: The Apologetic Tendencies in German History Writing," Habermas (1993) criticized Hillgruber, Nolte, and others for trying to drive the shame of Auschwitz from the German collective consciousness. He argued that they were "destroying the only reliable foundation for our [constitutional and democratic] ties to the West" (Habermas, 1993, pp. 43–44). Perhaps Jürgen Kocka (1993) best captured the essence of antinormalization thinking in West Germany at this time:

> Neither by relativizing and leveling the National-Socialist period and other dark points of our past, nor by affectionately painting miniatures of the history of everyday life, nor through short-circuited geographism should historians react to the challenge to endow identity. Their task is to describe, explain, and present past reality with scholarly means within the context of the changing and never unitary future-oriented problems of the present. In doing that they help set the present in as enlightened a relationship as possible to the past—and that means an appropriate, comprehensive, common, and critical relationship; they fulfill important societal needs and contribute in a fundamental and indirect sense to finding identity, provided one employs a concept of identity that includes self-distancing and reflection, as well as constant change and always renewed criticism. (pp. 91–92)

Poland

Poland, which had a prewar Jewish population of 3.5 million, was a country with its own deep-seated traditions of antisemitism. To many Jews, the Poles emerged as villains second only to the Germans. Memories of historic Polish antisemitism blended with accusations that the Poles did little to help Jews during the Holocaust, and in some cases even aided the Germans. The Poles have countered by arguing that they also suffered heavily from German mistreatment, and point out that many Polish priests, nuns, and civilians helped a number of Jews survive this horror.

Significant postwar writing on the Holocaust centered around reports on the extensive war crimes trials conducted by the Poles in the years immediately after World War II. The trial record of Amon Goeth, the commandant of the Plaszow forced labor camp outside of Krakow—made famous in *Schindler's List*—was one of many accounts of German atrocities committed against Poles. This 1947 document, *Proces Ludobojcy Amona Leopolda Goetha (People's Trial against Amon Leopold Goeth)*, was published by the short-lived Central Jewish Historical Commission, and contained the testimony of a number of Jewish survivors. Over the next few decades, the government adopted an on-again, off-again official policy of anti-semitism, stimulated partially by Moscow and Warsaw's growing support of the Arabs in the Middle East. According to Michael C. Steinlauf (1996), the late 1960s saw a particularly venomous assault on all Jewish subjects, particularly from the West. "Zionist" became the common term throughout the Soviet bloc for all things Jewish, and from the Soviet bloc's perspective, evil. Works such as Leon Uris' *Exodus* (1957) and *Mila 18* (1960) as well as Jerzy Kosinki's *The Painted Bird* (1965), were accused of defaming the Polish nation (Steinlauf, 1996, pp. 122–124). The election of Karol Wojtyla, the archbishop of Krakow, as Pope John Paul II in 1979, and the emergence of the Solidarity dissident political movement in the following year, brought the question of the Holocaust to the surface, particularly after the new pope visited Auschwitz. As the shroud of communism began to be lifted in Poland, a newfound interest in the Polish past, and more particularly its Jewish past, began to surface. Very often, interest in Polish Jewry was linked to a more romantic longing for the Poland of old. Antoni Slonimski's postwar poem, "Elegy for the Little Jewish Towns" (1958) reappeared, while in 1985 *Polin: A Journal of Polish-Jewish Studies* was initiated. State publishing houses released a number of works on Jewish themes, and books by Isaac Bashevis Singer and other Jewish writers appeared throughout the 1980s. Yet, the Polish nation was not prepared to face its own responsibilties for its antisemitic past. When Claude Lanzman's *Shoah* appeared in 1985, it was venomously attacked in the press. Lanzman's film was felt to have sullied the Polish nation, and critics reminded their readers that the Germans also had plans to mass murder Poles (Steinlauf, 1996, pp. 133, 136–138).

The Holocaust remained in the mainstream of Polish academia and culture with the controversy over the construction of a Catholic convent at the edge of Auschwitz. A number of works appeared concerning this controversy, which went to the heart of Polish-Jewish relations. Some of the best works on this topic are Carol Rittner and John K. Roth's (Eds.) *Memory Offended: The Auschwitz Convent Controversy* (1991) and Wladyslaw Bartoszewski's *The Convent at Auschwitz* (1991). Despite these issues, interest in Polish Jewish history has grown over the past decade. Jewish studies programs have been established at Warsaw University and at Jagiellonian University in Krakow. Efforts to restore Jewish quarters in some of

Poland's more important cities have gained momentum, and even Poland's small Jewish population of five thousand has grown during this period.

The Soviet Union

Soviet scholars were not permitted by state censors to mention any special mistreatment of Jews during the long Soviet war with the Germans from 1941 to 1945. Memory of the Holocaust was almost completely erased from the Soviet collective memory. But the Soviet Union, with its large Jewish population, could not totally erase Holocaust memory. Early Soviet reports on war crimes trials included information on Jewish victims, as did press reports in the 1950s and 1960s. In many ways, as Lukasz Hirszowicz (1993) has pointed out in his "The Holocaust in the Soviet Mirror," these war crimes trial reports were the first glimpse into the Holocaust for many Soviet readers (pp. 39–46). Yet ample evidence of German genocide against the Jews in Soviet-occupied territory had been available to the Soviets since the latter part of the war. The Soviets had conducted the first major war crimes trial of the war in 1943 in the northern Caucasus city of Krasnodar. A local Soviet court tried thirteen Soviets for collaborating with Einsatzgruppe D in the killing of hospital patients throughout Krasnodar. The court sentenced eight Soviets to death and three got twenty-year prison terms (Spector, 1990, p. 1489). As the Red Army moved west in 1944, it began to discover the remains of much of the machinery of death set up by the Germans in Lithuania, Latvia, Estonia, Poland, and Ukraine. Moreover, throughout World War II, Ilya Ehrenburg (1944) had collected a vast body of Holocaust survivor testimony that was first published in 1944 in the Soviet journal *Znamya (The Banner)*, with the approval of Soviet authorities.

In 1945, Ehrenburg's collection appeared as *The Black Book in the Soviet Union*. A year later, it was published in Romania and the United States (Ehrenburg and Grossman, 1981). Initially, *The Black Book* was a portion of a three-part study on the Holocaust throughout Europe. The first volume, which was soon suppressed by Joseph Stalin, was the only part of the study ever to reach the West. *The Black Book* became the best source of primary material on the Holocaust in the Soviet Union. The various first-hand accounts are broken down according to republic—Ukraine, Byelorussia, the Russian Soviet Federative Socialist Republic (RSFSR), Lithuania, and Latvia.

With the collapse of the Soviet Union in 1991, a new body of historical writing on the Holocaust by former Soviet historians began to appear. Two important historiographical studies on Soviet perspectives on the Holocaust that surfaced during this period were Zvi Gitelman's "Soviet Reactions to the Holocaust, 1945–1991" (1993), and his "Politics and the Historiography of the Holocaust in the Soviet Union" (1997). These pioneering works opened the door for future study of the historiography of the Holocaust during the Soviet era. Gitelman (1997) argues that the uneven application of the policy of Holocaust suppression left a distorted view of this tragedy that has proven very difficult to overcome in the post-Soviet era (pp. 14–42).

Hungary

With the exception of the Soviet Union, Hungary had the largest Jewish population in Eastern Europe after World War II. Over two-thirds of prewar Hungary's 725,000 Jews died during the Holocaust, most of them in the final years of the war. Though Hungarian Jews suffered from some of the same antisemitism that swept through Eastern Europe and the Soviet Union, they were able to reconstruct some measure of traditional Jewish life. As in Poland, the first publications to surface in Hungary after the Holocaust dealt with the war crimes trials. Pro-Nazi accusations were often mixed with postwar political issues, particularly after the communists took power in 1948. According to Randolph L. Braham (1996), a number of survivor accounts also surfaced during this period. Of particular interest is a lengthy article by István Bibó, "Zsidókèrdès Magyarországon 1944 után (Hungarian Jews in 1944)" (1948). Bibó correctly underscored Hungarian responsibility for the death of so many Jews in the latter part of the war (Braham, 1996, p. 209).

After the Hungarian revolution of 1956, the new government of János Kádár allowed something of a modest rejuvenation of religious and cultural life for the country's eighty thousand to one hundred thousand Jews. A number of Holocaust-related works were published during this period. After the 1967 Six Day War in the Middle East, however, official Hungarian policy toward its Jews became more virulent, often mimicking that of the Soviet Union (Hoensch, 1988, pp. 200–202, 271; Kovacs and Crowe, 1985, p. 168). The winds of change shifted again in the 1970s, and a new generation of Jewish writers began to assert their own rediscovery of their Jewish identity through a growing body of forthright works on the Holocaust. They were influenced by Randolph L. Braham's 1977 study, *The Hungarian Labor Service System, 1939–1945,* and his two-volume classic, *The Politics of Genocide: The Holocaust in Hungary* (1981), which was published in Magyar in Hungary in 1988.

By the late 1980s and early 1990s prominent government and church leaders, such as Gyula Horn and the Hungarian Catholic Bishops Conference, also spoke out against and apologized for Hungarian responsibility in the death of Jews during the Holocaust.

France

Until the 1990s, successive French governments adopted the position that France was a conquered nation during World War II. The real, legal government in France was in exile, first in London and later in Algiers. The collaborationist regime of Marshal Henri Pétain that ruled Vichy France (as opposed to the German Occupied Zone in the northwest) was run by an illegal group of traitors who signed an unconstitutional armistice with the Third Reich. Since the Vichy regime was a puppet of the Germans and unconstitutional, its antisemitic legislation was illegal. This view was challenged by Michael R. Marrus and Robert O. Paxton in their *Vichy France and the Jews* (New York: Basic Books, 1981). They argued that the Vichy regime freely instituted the 109 antisemitic laws and decrees that formed the body of antisemitic legislation not only in Vichy France but also in the Unoccupied Zone.

Over the next decade, the mythical shroud that had prevented the French from honestly assessing national responsibility for the Holocaust in France was lifted, aided by the indictment or trials of Klaus Barbie and three prominent French Holocaust perpetrators—Paul Touvier, René Bousquet, and Maurice Papon. As several essays in Richard J. Goslan's *Memory, the Holocaust, and French Justice: The Bousquet and Touvier Affairs* suggest (Hanover, NH: University Press of New England, 1996), what was particularly troubling about the Touvier affair were efforts by the French Catholic church to have him pardoned. Bousquet's case was somewhat different, as he was a prominent French banker with close ties to the French President Francois Mitterand. His murder in 1993 prevented a full legal discussion of Vichy responsibility for French Jewish deaths during the Holocaust. Yet, the revelations brought up in the Touvier and Bousquet affairs and the trial of Maurice Papon did force a national soul searching. In 1995, President Jacques Chirac admitted that the Vichy regime had played a role in the Holocaust, while several years later Prime Minister Lionel Jospin made a similar admission.

The trial, conviction, and brief escape attempt of Maurice Papon in the late 1990s created new embarrassments for the French, as Papon was a highly placed government official who once held a cabinet position. Papon, a police supervisor in Bordeaux during the war, was accused of signing orders that led to the arrest and deportation of almost 1,700 Jews. His trial raised anew questions about the interrelationship between Vichy collaboration and postwar political ties and successes. The fact that Papon took advantage of his free status during his appeal and escaped to Switzerland to avoid incarceration embarrassed a nation already weighted down by the cloud of collaboration with the Germans during the Holocaust. Between seventy-five thousand and seventy-eight thousand of the Jews living in France during World War II died in the Holocaust.

Italy

It is important to keep in mind when discussing the Holocaust in Italy to look separately at developments in Italy proper and in the Vatican, the latter of which was technically a separate political entity ruled by the pope. This discussion deals solely with the historiography of the Italian state of Benito Mussolini during the Holocaust. Prewar Italy had one of the smallest Jewish populations in Europe—forty-seven thousand. There were also ten thousand foreign Jews in Italy during this period. About sixty-eight hundred Italian Jews would perish in the Holocaust.

In the first thirty years after the war, the Holocaust was not discussed in any depth in Italy. Jewish losses were equated with Gentile losses, since many Italians had died in POW camps or at the hands of the Germans, particularly after 1943. Mussolini's race laws were blamed on the Germans. Renzo De Felice's *Storia degli ebrei italiani sotto il fascismo (History of the Italian Jews under Fascism)* (Turin: Einaudi Publishers, 1960), which was commissioned by the Union of Italian Jewish Communities, was the first major study of the Jews in Italy before and during the Holocaust.

The most important study on the fate of Italy's Jews during the Holocaust was Liliana Picciotto Fargion's *Il libro della memoria. Gli Ebrei deportati dall'Italia (The Memory Book: The Deportation of Italian Jews)* (Milan: Mursia Publishers, 1991). It provided exacting details of the activities of Italian police in rounding up Jews, and stood in contrast to Nicola Caracciolo's three-part television series in 1986, "Hli ebrei e l'Italia durante la guerra, 1940–1945," which applauded the activities of Italian officials and individuals who aided Jews during the Holocaust. Susan Zuccotti balances all of these issues in her *The Italians and the Holocaust: Persecution, Rescue and Survival* (Lincoln: University of Nebraska Press, 1996). She links the high survival rate of Italian Jews to the lack of strong antisemitic traditions among the Italians, which she ties to the small size of the Jewish population and traditions of assimilation. Yet, she is also highly critical of those Italians who chose to collaborate and abuse or murder Jews.

The Netherlands

The Netherlands had a Jewish population of 140,000 Jews on the eve of World War II. About three-quarters of this population would die during the Holocaust, one of the highest death rates in Europe. The reasons for this level of mass murder centered around the strong presence of the SS in the Netherlands. The Reich Commissioner in the Netherlands, Arthur Seyss-Inquart, stubbornly pursued a course that deprived Dutch Jews of their property and forced most of them to live in Amsterdam. Gentile Dutch protests against Jewish roundups in preparation for shipment to the east in mid-1942 only strengthened Seyss-Inquart's determination to make the Netherlands *judenfrei*. About twenty-five thousand Dutch Jews went into hiding at this time, including Anne Frank and her family. While many Dutch citizens helped hide Jews during this period, it should be remembered that members of the Dutch Nazi Party and the Dutch Green Police played an important role in the Jewish roundups. Between 105,000 to 107,000 Dutch Jews were rounded up and sent to Auschwitz (sixty thousand) or Sobibór (thirty-four thousand). In the immediate postwar years, the Dutch viewed the war mainly as a battle between the Germans and the Dutch resistance movement. Between 1960 and 1965, however, Louis de Jong's twenty-one-part television series, "Occupation," included the persecution of the Jews. In 1965, Jacob Presser and Arnold Pomerans published the two-volume *Ondergang: Der Vervolging en Verdelging van het Nederlandse Jodendom, 1940–1945* (The Hague: 1965), which appeared in English in 1988 as *Ashes in the Wind: The Destruction of Dutch Jewry* (Detroit, MI: Wayne State University Press). The significance of Ondergang (Destruction), which was sponsored by the Dutch government's State War Documentation Institute, was that it made the Dutch question their role and culpability in the Holocaust. Ondergang also played an important role in forcing the Dutch to deal honestly with the guilt and shame of the Holocaust.

Israel

The Holocaust, for obvious reasons, has always had a special place in Israeli historiography. In the three years after Israel became a state in 1948, almost seven hundred thousand Jews returned to their ancient homeland. About half of these immigrants were Holocaust survivors. But even before 1948, questions of Holocaust memory and study were being explored in the Yishuv, or Jewish community in Palestine. Offices for Yad Vashem (later The Holocaust Martyrs' and Heroes' Remembrance Authority), were set up in Jerusalem in 1946. Yad Vashem legally became the official Israeli body to oversee the vast collection of Holocaust testimony and archives being collected not only in Israel but throughout the Western world. If there are any "deans" in Israeli Holocaust scholarship, they are Yehuda Bauer and Yisrael Gutman. Both were professors at the Institute for Contemporary Jewry at Hebrew University in Jerusalem and are now with the Yad Vashem, the major Holocaust research center in Jerusalem.

Bauer, who was born in Czechoslovakia in 1926, is very sensitive to the plight and actions of the Holocaust's Jewish victims. He is particularly interested in the reaction of non-European Jews to the Holocaust and the role they played in helping the Jews of Europe. Unfortunately, he pays little significant attention to the fate of the other genocidal victims of the Holocaust such as the Roma (Gypsies) and the handicapped. Bauer's works include *American Jewry and the Holocaust: A History of the American Jewish Joint Distribution Committee, 1939–1945* (Detroit, MI: Wayne State University Press, 1981), *Out of the Ashes: The Impact of American Jews on Post-Holocaust European Jewry* (Oxford, UK: Pergamon Press, 1989), and *Jews for Sale: Nazi-Jewish Negotiations, 1933–1945* (New Haven, CT: Yale University Press, 1994). Bauer has also written one of the earliest textbooks: *A History of the Holocaust* (1982). In *American Jewry and the Holocaust,* Bauer argued that the weak position of the American Jewish community in American society during the Holocaust helps explain its weak reaction to events in Europe (pp. 455–456). *Jews For Sale* deals with efforts by a variety of organizations and individuals, particularly from 1942 to 1945, to negotiate with various Nazi officials to save Jewish lives.

Yisrael Gutman, who was born in Warsaw, Poland, in 1923, was a member of the Jewish Fighting Organization (Zydowska Organizacja Bojowa, ZOB). The ZOB played a major role in Jewish resistance against the Nazis in Warsaw, culminating in the Warsaw Ghetto Uprising of April 19–May 16, 1943. Like Bauer, Gutman pays a great deal of attention to the Holocaust's Jewish victims. He celebrates the courage of the Jewish guerillas in the Warsaw uprising, and is critical of the failure of the leaders of the Polish underground to help the Jewish resistance against the Nazis. Yet he does note that there were individual Poles who did help Jews. Some of Gutman's major works include *Resistance: The Warsaw Ghetto Uprising* (Boston, MA: Houghton-Mifflin, 1994), and, with Shmuel Krakowski, *Unequal Victims: Poles and Jews During World War II* (New York: Holocaust Library, 1986). He has also coedited the four-volume *Encyclopedia of the Holocaust* (New York: Macmillan, 1990), *The Catastrophe of European Jewry* (Jerusalem: Yad Vashem, 1976), *Documents on the Holocaust* (Jerusalem: Yad Vashem, 1981), and, with Michael Berenbaum, *Anatomy of the Auschwitz Death Camp* (Bloomington: Indiana University Press, 1994).

As Elon (1993) has pointed out in his incisive article, "The Politics of Memory," immediate postwar Israelis reacted to news of Holocaust atrocities with "a mixture of awe and shame" (p. 3). Newly arrived survivors were overwhelmed with feelings of guilt and shame at having survived, while younger, Palestinian

Jews often questioned why those who had survived had passively "gone like sheep to slaughter" (Elon, 1993, p. 3).

Holocaust memory and studies would be transformed in Israel by the "Kasztner affair" and the trial of Adolf Eichmann. The former development centered around a libel suit brought by Rudolf Kasztner, a Zionist leader from Hungary who was accused of collaboration with the Germans by another survivor, Malkiel Gruenwald. Although Kasztner was initially the plaintiff, the four-year trial that he initiated brought into the mainstream of Israeli Holocaust memory several issues that would deeply affect Israeli scholarship and debate on the Holocaust for years. These included questions about the Jewish response to the Holocaust, the role of the *Judenrat*, the reaction of Jews living in Palestine at the time of the Holocaust, and conflicts between those Zionist Jews in Palestine and European Jews over their differing reactions to the Holocaust. Although Kasztner ultimately won his case after an appeal to the Israeli High (Supreme) Court, the trial brought to the surface the longstanding Yishuv Zionist criticism of the passive European Jewish response to the Holocaust, and suspicions about the collaborative role of the *Judenrat*. After Kasztner's assassination by Jewish extremists in 1957, Holocaust survivors in Israel concluded that it was best to maintain their traditional low profile (Segev, 1993, pp. 258, 283–284, 305–309).

This tendency among Israeli survivors to hide their experiences began to change after the Eichmann trial in 1961, which forced a more open discussion of the Holocaust throughout Israeli society. Most important, the testimony of survivors at the trial, which was broadly covered in the Israeli press, created a new sense of respect for the survivors. Now, instead of just the traditional definition of physical resistance so strongly promoted by older Israelis, a new form of "spiritual" resistance was discussed, which meant that any act of a survivor that maintained one's human dignity, faith, or traditions was celebrated throughout Israel (Ofer, 1996, pp. 877–878).

The Eichmann kidnapping and trial had helped pave the way for the creation of the chair of Holocaust studies at Bar Ilan University in 1961 and the opening of the Institute of Contemporary Jewry at Hebrew University of Jerusalem in 1962. Yad Vashem, though, remained the central institution for Israeli research and study of the Holocaust—particularly its journal and book series, *Yad Vashem Studies*. In 1968, Yad Vashem began to sponsor a number of international conferences on the Holocaust, and today conducts an array of workshops, symposia, and other gatherings on this subject.

Yet, even with this new interest in the Holocaust, the subject and its historiography remained deeply affected by Israeli politics and history to the extent, at least according to Tom Segev (1993), that it has distorted Holocaust history (p. 11). Segev (1993) feels that Israeli leaders have historically used the Holocaust to justify the existence of Israel as well as the creation of a Jewish homeland for the world's Jews (p. 514). Moreover, both in Israel and elsewhere, the Holocaust has often become a way for nonreligious Jews to reconnect with their Jewish heritage. In fact, according to Segev (1993), some Israelis feel it might be best to forget the Holocaust altogether, since Israelis were not properly learning its lessons. The

Holocaust, Segev writes, "often encourages insular chauvinism and a sense that the Nazi extermination of the Jews justifies any act that seems to contribute to Israeli security, including the oppression of the population in the territories occupied by Israel in the Six-Day War" (p. 517).

Part of the role of the historian in Israel over the past few decades has been to untangle the history of the Holocaust from this complex web of Israeli history and politics and transform it into a more honest, detached field of studies. A seemingly impossible task, the younger generation of Holocaust scholars in Israel have done a remarkable job of doing just that. Yehuda Elkana (1988) castigated Israelis for distorting the image of the Holocaust by using it to paint a picture of Jews as eternal victims. A special issue of the leftist journal *Politika* (1993) was quite critical of Yad Vashem for what it claimed was the narrowness of scholarship and perspective on the Holocaust (Ofer, 1996, pp. 888–889; Segev, 1993, pp. 502–504). What can best be said about Israeli historical scholarship and writing at this point is that it has matured considerably as evidenced by Leni Yahil's fine *The Holocaust: The Fate of European Jewry* (1990). Published originally in Hebrew in 1987, this comprehensive work takes a detailed look at the history of the Holocaust and its roots. The author obliquely tries to address some of the most important historiographical controversies in her work, such as the role of the *Judenrat,* the move to the Final Solution, Jewish resistance, and the rescue of Jews. She also has looked at the role of historic antisemitism, though in far less depth than other issues. She is equally sensitive to issues surrounding the response of Jews in the Yishuv and elsewhere to the plight of European Jews. She explores questions of rescue and the reaction of the Christian world to the fate of the Jews. Yahil's study is drawn from a rich body of documents, and reflects the maturation of Israeli scholarship on this subject.

Conclusion

At a distance, the complexity and diversity of the various historiographical debates that lie at the center of Holocaust studies seems overwhelming. For the most part, this is true. The Holocaust is an extremely complex topic of study, which presents anyone teaching the subject or certain aspects of it with considerable challenges. And, while there is no way to diminish the difficulty of the subject matter, there are some things than an educator can do to address the topic with honesty and accuracy. Because of the growing popularity of the Holocaust, its study has become prey to a growing body of mythology and half truths that distorts its history. A classic case in point is the story about Denmark's King Christian X's decision to wear the yellow Star of David to protest a German decision to force his country's eight thousand Jews to wear one. This never happened. Moreover, the perpetuation of this myth cloaks a much deeper lesson about the Danes and their Jewish countrymen. From the time that the Germans occupied Denmark in the spring of 1940, the Danish government let the Germans know that there was no "Jewish problem," since the Danes saw everyone in their country as Danish. Moreover, as news of a spreading Holocaust reached the Danish people, a Danish national debate took place about what the nation should do if the Germans tried to force restrictions on the Jews. The Danes concluded that if they allowed the Germans to harm or restrict one Danish Jew, this would compromise the essence of Danish democracy. Thus, it should come as no surprise that when a lower-level German diplomat informed the Danish government in the fall of 1943 of a German plan forcibly to deport the Jews, the Danish people rose up and spirited their Jewish community across the Baltic Sea to Sweden and safety. The point of this story is to underscore the need for accuracy in Holocaust education. This holds true whether a teacher spends two hours or two weeks teaching the Holocaust.

In addition, it is also important to try to put the Holocaust into the proper historical context of the war swirling around it. This failure is one of the traps that Holocaust historians and others often fall into when examining this subject. Innumerable Holocaust historiographical problems and conflicts have emerged because of this problem. One of the issues is the fate of other victims. If the Holocaust is seen as part of the greater moral, political, and social decadence that swept not only Germany but much of Europe at the time, then it should come as no surprise that the Germans should strike out not only against the Jews but also against others deemed as inferior. The failure to see a partial link between the early stages of the Final Solution and the unimaginable horror of war on the Eastern Front is also problematic, particularly in light of the fact that twenty-six to twenty-eight million Soviets died brutally at German hands. Finally, understanding the complexity of the environment of desperate, total war being fought throughout the world might help one be slightly more sympathetic to the difficulties faced by those who did seek to help save Jews and others.

Because of the complexity of the subject matter, it is very easy to get tunnel vision when teaching the Holocaust or parts of it. One must always try to keep it in its proper historical perspective. To do this requires a great deal of background reading. One of the purposes of this chapter is to provide educators not only with an overview of the major historiogaphical issues that have developed in the Holocaust field since the end of World War II, but also to provide them with a solid bibliography of sources, mainly in English, that they can consult when preparing lessons. It is most important to develop a simple reading list that blends together a solid, general work on the Holocaust with more specialized articles and books on that phase of the Holocaust to be taught by the educator. Again, accuracy and honesty are the keys to effective Holocaust education.

Finally, educators need to avoid making the Holocaust into something it is not. The popularization of the Holocaust has made it increasingly everyone's topic. The term Holocaust is becoming watered down by overuse and misuse, mainly because of the desire of individuals and groups either to jump on the Holocaust bandwagon or to compare their own personal or collective tragedies to the Holocaust. This is not wise.

What an educational discussion of the Holocaust does is pave the way for a more sympathetic exploration of not only other genocidal tragedies in world history but also an investigation into the how and whys of such events. The main thing to avoid in using the Holocaust as a pathway to looking at other genocidal tragedies is making it a contest of comparative pain. The death of that Roma (Gypsy) child in Auschwitz or that young Bosnian Muslim at Srebrenica is as tragic as the Jewish mother shot by the Einsatzgruppen at Babi Yar.

REFERENCES

Adam, Uwe Dietrich. (1972). *Judenpolitik im Dritten Reich (Jewish Policy in the Third Reich)*. Düsseldorf: Droste Verlag.

Adelson, Alan, & Lapides, Robert. (1989.) *Lódz ghetto: Inside a Community under Siege*. New York: Viking.

Amesberger, Hilga. (1995). *"Schindler's Liste" Macht Schule: Spielfilme als Instrument Politischer Bildung an Osterreichen Schulen*. Wein: W. Braumüller.

Andrews, Edward. (1997, January 17). "A Guard's Fateful Moment: Saving Swiss Bank Files." *The New York Times*, pp. A7, A11.

Arendt, Hannah. (1963, February 16). "Eichmann in Jerusalem, I." *The New Yorker*, 39(9):40–112.

Arendt, Hannah. (1963, February 23). "Eichmann in Jerusalem, II." *The New Yorker*, 39(10):40–111.

Arendt, Hannah. (1963, March 2). "Eichmann in Jerusalem, III." *The New Yorker*, 39(11):40–91.

Arendt, Hannah. (1963, March 9). "Eichmann in Jerusalem, IV." *The New Yorker*, 39(12):48–113.

Arendt, Hannah. (1963a, March 16). "Eichmann in Jerusalem, V." *The New Yorker*, 39(13): 58–134.

Arendt, Hannah. (1963b). *Eichmann in Jerusalem: A Report on the Banality of Evil*. New York: Viking.

Bartoszewski, Wladyslaw. (1991). *The Convent at Auschwitz*. New York: G. Braziller.

Bartov, Omer. (1986). *The Eastern Front, 1941–45: German Troops and the Barbarization of Warfare*. New York: St. Martin's Press.

Bartov, Omer. (1996). "Operation Barbarossa and the Origins of the Final Solution." In David Cesarani (Ed.), *The Final Solution: Origins and Implementation* (pp. 119–136). London: Routledge.

Bauer, Yehuda. (1982). *A History of the Holocaust*. New York: Franklin Watts.

Bauer, Yehuda, & Rozett, Robert. (1990). "Estimated Jewish Losses in the Holocaust." In Israel Gutman (Ed.), *Encyclopedia of the Holocaust* (Vol. 4, pp. 1797–1802). New York: Macmillan.

Berenbaum, Michael. (1990). "The Uniqueness and Universality of the Holocaust." In Michael Berenbaum (Ed.), *A Mosaic of Victims: Non-Jews Persecuted and Murdered by the Nazis* (pp. 20–36). New York: New York University Press.

Bettleheim, Bruno. (1960). *The Informed Heart: The Human Condition in Mass Society*. New York: Macmillan.

Bibó, István. (October–November 1948). "Zsidókérdés Magyarországon 1944 után." *Válasz* (8):778–877.

Blumenthal, Ralph. (1998, January 10). "Cries to Halt Publication of Holocaust Book." *The New York Times*, p. A13.

Bohlen, Charles. (1998, March 17). "Vatican Failure to Save Jews from Nazis." *The New York Times*, p. A1–A11.

Bokenkotter, Thomas. (1990). *A Concise History of the Catholic Church*. New York: Doubleday.

Bracher, Karl Dietrich. (1970). *The German Dictatorship: The Origins, Structure, and Effects of National Socialism*. New York: Praeger Publishers.

Bracher, Karl Dietrich, Sauer, Wolfgang, & Schultz, Gerhard. (1962). *Die Nationasozialistiche Machtergreifung: Studien zur Erichtung des Totalitären Herrschaftssystems in Deutschland, 1933–1934*. Koln: Westdeutscher Verlag.

Braham, Randolph L. (1977). *The Hungarian Labor Service System, 1939–1945*. Boulder, CO: East European Monographs.

Braham, Randolph L. (1996). "Hungary." In David Wyman & Charles Rosenzveig (Eds.), *The World Reacts to the Holocaust* (pp. 200–224). Baltimore, MD: Johns Hopkins University Press.

Braham, Randolph L. (1988). *A Magyar Holocaust* (The Hungarian Holocaust), 2 vols. Budapest: Gondolat.

Braham, Randolph L. (1981). *The Politics of Genocide: The Holocaust in Hungary*, 2 vols. New York: Columbia University Press.

Breitman, Richard (1991). *The Architect of Genocide: Himmler and the Final Solution*. New York: Knopf.

Broszat, Martin. (1977). "Hitler und die Genesis der 'Endlösung': Aus Anlass der Thesem von David Irving (Hitler and the Origins of the Final Solution: On the Occasion of David Irving's Thesis). *Vierteljahrshefte* 25(4):739–775.

Broszat, Martin. (1960). *Der Nationalsozialismus: Weltanschaung, Programm und Wirklichkeit*. Stuttgart: n.p.

Broszat, Martin. (1969). *Der Staat Hitlers*. Munich: Deutscher Taschenbuch Verlag.

Broszat, Martin. (1981). *The Hitler State: The Foundation and Development of the Internal Structure of the Third Reich*. London: Longman.

Browning, Christopher. (1985). *Fateful Months: Essays on the Emergence of the Final Solution*. New York: Houghton Mifflin.

Browning, Christopher. (1992). *Ordinary Men: Reserve Police Battalion 101 and the Final Solution in Poland*. New York: HarperCollins.

Browning, Christopher. (1995). *The Pathway to Genocide: Essays on Launching the Final Solution*. Cambridge, UK: Cambridge University Press.

Browning, Christopher. (1997). "Daniel Goldhagen's Willing Executioners." *History and Memory* 1:88–108.

Cargas, Harry James. (1985). *The Holocaust: An Annotated Bibliography*. Chicago, IL: American Library Association.

Central Zydowskiej Komisiji Historycznej w Polscie. (1947). *Proces Ludobojcy Amona Leopolda Goetha (The People's Lawsuit Against Amon Leopold Goeth)*. Warsaw: Central Zydowskiej Komisji Historycznej w Polsce.

Cesarani, David. (1996). *The Final Solution: Origins and Implementation*. New York: Routledge.

Cesarani, David. (1997). "Jewish Victims of the Holocaust and Swiss banks." *Dimensions* 11(1):3–6.

Chalk, Frank, & Kurt Jonassohn, (1990). *The History and Sociology of Genocide: Analysis and Case Studies*. New Haven, CT: Yale University Press.

Cowell, Alan. (1997a, February 8). "Swiss Beginning to Question Image of Heroism in the War." *The New York Times*, pp. A1–A5.

Cowell, Alan. (1997b, March 7). "Swiss and Their Burden of Nazi Germany's Gold." *The New York Times*, p. A6.

Cowell, Alan. (1997c, June 6). "Swiss, Irked by Critics, Ask 'Why Single Us Out?' " *The New York Times*, p. A6.

Crowe, David. (1994, 1996). *A History of the Gypsies of Eastern Europe and Russia*. New York: St. Martin's Press.

Crowe, David. (1995). "The Holocaust Survivor and the U.S. Holocaust Memorial Museum." In Menachem Mor (Ed.), *Crisis & Reaction: The Hero in Jewish History* (pp. 299–306). Omaha, NE: Creighton University Press.

Dawidowicz, Lucy S. (1981). *The Holocaust and the Historians*. Cambridge, MA: Harvard University Press.

Dawidowicz, Lucy S. (Ed.). (1976). *A Holocaust Reader*. West Orange, NJ: Behrman House, Inc.

Dawidowicz, Lucy S. (1976). *The War Against the Jews, 1933–1945*. New York: Bantam.

De Felice, Renzo. (1960). *Sturia degli ebrei it aliani sotto il fascismo (History of the Italian Jews Under Fascists)*. Turin: Einardi Publishers.

Drobisch, Klaus, Rudi Goguel, Werner Müller, & Dohle Horst, (Eds.). *Juden untern Hakenkruez: Verfolgung und Ausrottung der Deutschen Juden, 1933–1945 (Jews Under the Hakenkruez [swastika]: The Persecution and Destruction of the German Jews)*. Frankfurt (Main): Roderberg-Verlag.

Edelheit, Abraham J. (1990). "Historiography of the Holocaust." In Israel Gutman (Ed.), *Encyclopedia of the Holocaust* (Vol. 2, pp. 666–672). New York: Macmillan.

Ehrenburg, Ilya. (1944). "Murderers of the People." *Znamya*, nos 1–2, not paginated.

Ehrenburg, Ilya, & Vasily Grossman. (Eds.). (1981). *The Black Book: The Ruthless Murder of Jews by German-Fascist Invaders Throughout the Temporarily Occupied Regions of the Soviet Union and in the Death Camps of Poland During the War of 1941–1945.* New York: Holocaust Library.

Elkana, Yehuda. (1988, March 2). "The Need to Forget." *Haaretz,* p. 4.

Elon, Amos. (1997, January 26). "The Antagonist as Liberator." *The New York Times Magazine,* pp. 40–44.

Elon, Amos. (1993). "The Politics of Memory." *The New York Review of Books,* 40 (16):3–5.

Eschwege, Helmut. (1966). *Kennzeichen j. bilder, dokumente, berichte zur Geschichte der Verbrechen des Hitlerfaschismus an der Deutschen Juden, 1933.* Berlin: Deutscher Verlag der Wisenschaften.

Fargion, Liliana Picciotto. (1991). *Il libro della mémoria Gliebrei deportati dalt'Italia (The Memory Book: The Deportation of Italian Jews).* Milan: Mursia Publishers.

Fikejz, Radoslav. (1998). *Oskar Schindler (1908–1974).* Svitavy: Mestské Muzeum a Gallerie Svitavy.

Fischer, Klaus P. (1995). *Nazi Germany: A New History.* New York: Continuum.

Flannery, Edward. (1965). *The Anguish of the Jews: Twenty-Three Centuries of Anti-Semitism.* New York: Macmillan.

Fleming, Gerald. (1984). *Hitler and the Final Solution.* Berkeley: University of California Press.

Frank, Anne. (1989). *The Diary of Anne Frank: The Critical Edition.* David Barnouw & Arnold Pomerans (Eds). New York: Doubleday.

Friedlander, Henry. (1995). *The Origins of Nazi Genocide: From Euthanasia to the Final Solution.* Chapel Hill: University of North Carolina Press.

Gallagher, James. (1998, March 29). "Defending the Pope: Pius XII Did Not Turn His Back on the Jews." *Greensboro News & Record,* p. F4.

Gelber, Yoav. (1988). "The Problematics of the Historiography of the Reaction of the Yishuv and the Jews in the Free World to the Holocaust." In Yisrael Gutman and Gideon Grief (Eds.), *The Historiography of the Holocaust Period* (pp. 571–584). Jerusalem: Yad Vashem.

Gerend, László. (1982). *Kiüzettünk városunkból.* Budapest: n.p.

Gilbert, Martin. (1985). *The Holocaust: A History of the Jews of Europe During the Second World War.* New York: Holt, Rinehart and Winston.

Gitelman, Zvi. (1997). "Politics and the Historiography of the Holocaust in the Soviet Union." In Zvi Gitelman (Ed.), *Bitter Legacy: Confronting the Holocaust in the USSR* (pp. 14–42). Bloomington: Indiana University Press.

Gitelman, Zvi. (1993). "Soviet Reactions to the Holocaust, 1945–1991." In Lucjan Dobroszycki and Jeffrey Gurock (Eds.), *The Holocaust in the Soviet Union* (pp. 3–27). Armonk, NY: M.E. Sharpe.

Goldhagen, Daniel. (1996). *Hitler's Willing Executioners: Ordinary Germans and the Holocaust.* New York: Alfred A. Knopf.

Goshko, John M. (1998, August 13). "Swiss Banks Agree to Holocaust Pact." *The New York Times,* pp. A1, A11.

Goslan, Richard. (1996). *Memory, the Holocaust, and French Justice: The Bousquet and Touvier Affairs.* Hanover, NH: University Press of New England.

Grau, Gunter. (1995). "Persecution, 'Re-education' or 'Eradication' of Male Homosexuals Between 1933 and 1945: Consequences of the Eugenic Concept of Assured Reproduction." In Gunter Grau (Ed.), *Hidden Holocaust? Gay and Lesbian Persecution in Germany, 1933–45* (pp. 1–7). London: Cassell.

Gruntova, Jitka. (1997). *Oskar Schindler: Legenda a Fakta.* Brno: Barrister & Principal.

Gutman, Yisrael. (1990). "Denial of the Holocaust." In Israel Gutman (Ed.), *Encyclopedia of the Holocaust* (Vol. 2, pp. 681–687). New York: Macmillan.

Gutman, Yisrael. (1988). "Jewish Resistance—Questions and Assessments." In Yisrael Gutman and G. Grief (Eds.), *The Historiography of the Holocaust Period* (pp. 641–678). Jerusalem: Yad Vashem.

Gutman, Yisrael, & Gideon Grief, (Eds.). (1988). *The Historiography of the Holocaust Period.* Proceedings of the Fifth Yad Vashem Historical Conference. Jerusalem: Yad Vashem.

Gutman, Yisrael & Shmuel Krakowski, (1986). *Unequal Victims: Poles and Jews During World War II.* New York: Holocaust Library.

Habermas, Jürgen. (1993). "A Kind of Settlement of Damages: The Apologetic Tendencies in German History Writing." In James Knowlton and Truett Cates (Trans.), *Forever in the Shadow of Hitler? The Dispute About the Germans' Understanding of History* (pp. 34–44). Atlantic Highlands, NJ: Humanities Press.

Hancock, Ian. (1991). "Gypsy History in Germany and Neighboring Lands." In David Crowe and John Kolsti (Eds.), *The Gypsies of Eastern Europe* (pp. 3–9). Armonk, NY: M.E. Sharpe.

Hancock, Ian. (1996). "Responses to the Porrajmos: The Romani Holocaust." In Alvin Rosenfeld (Ed.), *Is the Holocaust Unique? Perspectives on Comparative Genocide* (pp. 39–64). Boulder, CO: Westview Press.

Hilberg, Raul. (1997). "The Goldhagen Phenomenon." *Critical Inquiry,* 23(4):721–728.

Hilberg, Raul. (1961). *The Destruction of the European Jews.* 3 Volumes. New York: Quadrangle Books.

Hilberg, Raul, Stanislaw Staron, & Josef Kermisz, (Eds.). (1979). *The Warsaw Diary of Adam Czerniakow.* New York: Stein and Day.

Hillgruber, Andreas. (1986). *Zweierlei Untergang (Two Kinds of Destruction).* Cologne: Siedler Verlag.

Hirsch, Rudolf, & Rosemarie Schuder. (1987). *Der Gelbe Fleck. Wurzehn und Wirkungen des Judenhasses in der Deutschen Geschichte.* Berlin: Rütten & Loening.

Hirszowicz, Lukasz. (1993). "The Holocaust in the Soviet Mirror." In Lucjan Dobroszycki and Jeffrey Gurock (Eds.), *The Holocaust in the Soviet Union* (pp. 29–59). Armonk, NY: M.E. Sharpe.

Hochhuth, Rolf. (1963). *Der Stellvertreter (The Deputy).* Hamburg: Rowohlt Verlag.

Hochhuth, Rolf. (1964). *The Deputy.* New York: Grove Press.

Hoensch, Jörg K. (1988). *A History of Modern Hungary, 1867–1986.* London: Longman.

Höss, Rudolf. (1996). *Death Dealer: The Memoirs of the SS Kommandant at Auschwitz.* Steven Paskuly (Ed.). New York: DaCapo Press.

Initiative Sozialistisches Forum. (1994). *Schindler Deutsche: Ein Kinotraum von Dritten Reich.* Freiberg: Initiative Sozialistisches Forum.

Irving, David. (1977). *Hitler's War.* New York: Viking.

Jäckel, Eberhard. (1984). *Hitler in History.* Hanover, NH: University Press of New England.

Jäckel, Eberhard. (1972). *Hitler's Weltanschauung.* Middleton, CT, n.p.

John Paul II. (1998, March 17). "John Paul's Plea: 'Never Again.' " *The New York Times,* p. A10.

Karsai, Elek. (1988). "The Holocaust in Hungarian Literature and Arts, 1975–1985." In Yisrael Gutman and Gunter Grief (Eds.), *The Historiography of the Holocaust Period* (pp. 386–403). Jerusalem: Yad Vashen.

Katz, Steven T. (1994). *The Holocaust in Historical Context: The Holocaust and Mass Death Before the Modern Age,* Volume 1. New York: Oxford University Press.

Keller, Werner. (1969). *Diaspora: The Post-Biblical History of the Jews.* New York: Harcourt, Brace.

Kenrick, Donald, & Gratten Puxon, (1972). *The Destiny of Europe's Gypsies.* New York: Basic Books.

Kenrick, Donald, & Grattan Puxon, (1995). *Gypsies Under the Swastika.* Hatfield: University of Hertfordshire Press.

King, Christine. (1991). "Jehovah's Witnesses Under Nazism." In Michael Berenbaum (Ed.), *A Mosaic of Victims: Non-Jews Persecuted and Murdered by the Nazis* (pp. 188–193). New York: New York University Press.

Knowlton, James, & Cates Truett (Trans.). (1993). *Forever in the Shadow of Hitler? Original Documents of the Historikerstreit, the Controversy Concerning the Singularity of the Holocaust.* Atlantic Highlands, NJ: Humanities Press.

Kocka, Jürgen. (1993). "Hitler Should Not Be Repressed by Stalin and Pol Pot: On the Attempts of German Historians to Relativize the Enormity of the Nazi Crimes." In James Knowlton and Truett Cates (Eds.), *Forever in the Shadow of Hitler?* (pp. 85–92). Atlantic Highland, NJ: Humanities Press.

Kogon, Eugen. (1946). *Der SS-Staat: Das System der Deutschen Konzentrationslager.* Frankfurt am Main: Verlag der Frankfurter Hefte.

Kogon, Eugen. (1950). *The Theory and Practice of Hell.* New York: Farrar.

Kosinski, Jerzy. (1965). *The Painted Bird.* New York: Houghton Mifflin.

Kovacs, Martin L., & David M. Crowe, (1985). "National Minorities in Hungary, 1919–1980." In Stephen M. Horak (Ed.), *Eastern European National Minorities, 1919–1980* (pp. 160–189). Littleton, CO: Libraries Unlimited.

Kramer, Jane. (1997, April 28 and May 5). "Manna from Hell: Nazi Gold, Holocaust Accounts, and What the Swiss Must Finally Confront." *The New Yorker,* 73(10):74–88.

Kulka, Otto Dov, & Anne Birkenhauer, & Esriel Hildesheimer, (1997). *Deutsches Judentum unter dem Nationalsozialismus.* Tübingen: Mohr Siebeck.

Kweit, Konrad. (1976). "Historians of the German Democratic Republic on Antisemitism and Persecution." *Leo Baeck Institute Yearbook* XXI:73–198.

Lerman, Antony. (1989). *The Jewish Communities of the World.* New York: Facts on File.

Lewy, Gunther. (1964). *The Catholic Church and Nazi Germany.* New York: McGraw Hill.

Lifton, Robert Jay. (1986). *The Nazi Doctors: Medical Killing and the Psychology of Genocide.* New York: Basic Books.

Lipstadt, Deborah. (1993). *Denying the Holocaust: The Growing Assault on Truth and Memory.* New York: The Free Press.

Low, Alfred. (1994). *The Third Reich and the Holocaust in German Historiography: Toward the Historikerstreit of the Mid-1980s.* Boulder/New York: East European Monographs/Columbia University Press.

Loshitzky, Yosefa (Ed.). (1997). *Spielberg's Holocaust: Critical Perspectives on "Schindler's List."* Bloomington: Indiana University Press.

Lukas, Richard. (1990). *Forgotten Holocaust: The Poles Under German Occupation, 1939–1944.* New York: Hippocrene Books.

Markovits, Andrei, & Beth Simone Noveck, (1996). "West Germany." In David Wyman and Charles Rosenzveig (Eds.), *The World Reacts to the Holocaust* (pp. 391–446). Baltimore, MD: John Hopkins University Press.

Marrus, Michael R. (1987). *The Holocaust in History.* New York: Penguin Books.

Marrus, Michael R., & Robert O. Paxton, (1981). *Vichy France and the Jews.* New York: Basic Books.

Mayer, Arno J. (1988). *Why Did the Heavens Not Darken? The Final Solution in History.* Palo Alto, CA: Stanford University Press.

Mendes–Flohr, Paul, & Jehuda Reinharz, (Eds.). (1995). *The Jew in the Modern World: A Documentary History.* New York: Oxford University Press.

Miller, Philip. (1997). "Europe's Gold: Nazis, Neutrals and the Holocaust."*Dimensions,* 11(1):7–14.

Moldova, György. (1975). *A Azeme Imre—Induló.* Budapest: St. Emeric March.

Mommsen, Hans. (1983). *"Die Realisierung des Utopischen: die 'Endlösung der Judenfrage' im 'Dritten Reich.'"* (The Realization of Utopia: The 'Final Solution of the Jewish Question' in the 'Third Reich'). *Geschichte und Gesellschaft,* 9(3):381–420.

Morgan, Michael L. (1997). "To Seize Memory: History and Identity in Post-Holocaust Jewish Thought." In Alvin Rosenfeld (Ed.), *Thinking About the Holocaust: After a Half Century* (pp. 151–181). Bloomington: Indiana University Press.

Mueller, Werner, & Horst Dohle, (1973). *Juden Unterm Hakekreuz. Verfolgung und Ausrottung der Deutschen Juden, 1932–1945.* Berlin, n.p.

Müller-Hill, Benno. (1988). *Murderous Science: Elimination by Scientific Selection of Jews, Gypsies, and Others, Germany, 1933–1945.* Oxford: Oxford University Press.

Nicholls, William. (1993). *Christian Antisemitism: A History of Hate.* Northcale, NJ: Jason Aronson.

Niebuhr, Gustav. (1997, May 24). "Clergy Help the Swiss Face Their Past." *The New York Times,* p. 14.

Niebuhr, Gustav. (1998, March 17). "Several Voices: A Stand Bold and Cautious at Once." *The New York Times,* p. A11.

Nolte, Ernst. (1993). "Between Historical Legend and Revisionism? The Third Reich in the Perspective of 1980." In James Knowlton and Truett Cates (Eds.), *Forever in the Shadow of Hitler?* (pp. 1–15). Atlantic Highlands, NJ: Humanities Press.

Nolte, Erich. (June 6, 1986). "Die Vergangenheit, Die Nicht Vergehen Will." *Frankfurter Allgemeine Zeitung.*

Ofer, Dalia. (1996). "Israel." In David Wyman and Charles Rosensveig (Eds.), *The World Reacts to the Holocaust* (pp. 836–923). Baltimore, MD: Johns Hopkins University Press.

Ofir, Adi. (June–July 1986). "On the Renewal of the Name." *Politika 8*, pp. 2–7.

Pawolski, Franciszek. (1993). *Spielberg: w poszukiwaoiou ark.* Krakow, n. p.

Peck, Jeffrey. (1996). "East Germany." In David Wyman and Charles Rosenzveig (Eds.). *The World Reacts to the Holocaust* (pp. 447–472). Baltimore, MD: Johns Hopkins University Press.

Plant, Richard. (1986). *The Pink Triangle: The Nazi War Against Homosexuals.* New York: Henry Holt and Company.

Poliakov, Léon. (1954). *Harvest of Hate: The Nazi Program for the Destruction of the Jews of Europe.* Syracuse, NY: Syracuse University Press.

Politika, No. 8, June–July 1986. [In particular, see Adi Ofir's "On the Renewal of the Name," pp. 2–7.]

Presser, Jacob, & Arnold Pomerans, (1988). *Ashes in the Wind: The Destruction of Dutch Jewry.* Detroit, MI: Wayne State University Press.

Rittner, Carol, & John K. Roth, (Eds.) (1991). *Memory Offended: The Auschwitz Controversy.* New York: Praeger.

Robinson, Jacob. (1965). *And the Crooked Shall Be Made Straight: The Eichmann Trial, the Jewish Catastrophe, and Hannah Arendt's Narrative.* New York: Macmillan.

Rósza, Agnes. (1978). *Nürnbergi lágernapló, 1944–1945.* Budapest: n.p.

Rubenstein, Richard. (1975). *The Cunning of History.* New York: Harper & Row.

Rubenstein, Richard. (1996). "Religion and the Uniqueness of the Holocaust." In Alan Rosenbaum (Ed.), *Is the Holocaust Unique? Perspectives on Comparative Genocide* (pp. 1–9). Boulder, CO: Westview Press.

Rubin, Alexis P. (1995). *Scattered Among the Nations: Documents Affecting Jewish History, 49 to 1975.* Northvale, NJ: Jason Aronson.

Rummel, R. J. (1992). *Democide: Nazi Genocide and Mass Murder.* New Brunswick, NJ: Transaction Publishers.

Sanger, David. (1997, May 9). "Clinton's Choice on the Nazis' Gold: Press the Swiss, or Close the Door." *The New York Times,* p. A10.

Sanger, David. (1998, May 5). "Crack in the Vault: Swiss Bank Yields to a Nazi Victim's Daughter." *The New York Times,* p. A27.

Scheffler, Wolfgang. (1960). *Judenverfolgung im Dritten Reich.* Frankfurt am Main: Büchergilde Gutenberg.

Schleunes, Karl. (1990). *The Twisted Road to Auschwitz Nazi Policy Toward German Jews, 1933–1939.* Urbana: University of Illinois Press.

Segev, Tom. (1993). *The Seventh Million.* New York: Hill and Wang.

Slany, William. (1997). *U.S. and Allied Efforts to Recover and Restore Gold and Other Assets Stolen or Hidden by Germany During World War II.* Washington, DC: United States Government Printing Office.

Slonimski, Antoni. (1958). "Elegia miasteczek zydowski" ["Elegy for the Little Jewish Towns."] In Jan Winczakiewicz (Ed.), *Izrael w poezji polshiej: Anthogia,* p. 239.

Spector, Shmuel. (1990). "Krasnodar Trial." In Israel Gutman (Ed.), *The Encyclopedia of the Holocaust* (Vol. 4, p. 1489). New York: Macmillan.

Steinlauf, Michael C. (1996). "Poland." In David Wyman and Charles Rosenzveig (Eds.), *The World Reacts to the Holocaust* (pp. 81–155). Baltimore, MD: Johns Hopkins University Press.

Stern, Fritz. (1961). *The Politics of Cultural Despair: A Study in the Rise of the Germanic Ideology.* Berkeley: University of California Press.

Streit, Christian. (1996). "Wehrmacht, Einsatzgruppen, Soviet POWs and Anti-Bolshevism in the Emergence of the Final Solution." In David Cesarani (Ed.), *The Final Solution: Origins and Implementation* (pp. 103–118). London: Routledge.

(1997, July 29). "Swiss Bank Confirms Papers May Be Tied to Jewish Property." *The Washington Post,* p. A11.

Szulc, Tad. (1995). *Pope John Paul II: The Biography.* New York: Scribner.

Trevor-Roper, Hugh. (1960). "Hitler's Kriegziele" (Hitler's War Objectives). *Vierteljahrshelfte für Zeitsgeschichte,* 8: 121–133.

Trunk, Isaiah. (1972). *Judenrat: The Jewish Councils in Eastern Europe Under Nazi Occupation.* New York: Macmillan.

United States Holocaust Memorial Museum. (n.d.-a). *Handicapped.* Washington, DC: Author.

United States Holocaust Memorial Museum. (n.d.-b). *Homosexuals.* Washington, DC: Author.

United States Holocaust Memorial Museum. (n.d.-c). *Jehovah's Witnesses.* Washington, DC: Author.

United States Holocaust Memorial Museum. (n.d.-d). *Poles.* Washington, DC: Author.

United States Holocaust Memorial Museum. (n.d.-e). *Sinti & Roma.* Washington, DC: Author.

Uris, Leon. (1957). *Exodus.* New York: Doubleday.

Uris, Leon. (1960). *Mila 18.* New York: Doubleday.

Watch Tower Bible and Tract Society of Pennsylvania. (1993). *Jehovah's Witnesses: Proclaimers of God's Kingdom.* Brooklyn, NY: Watch Tower Bible and Tract Society of New York/International Bible Students Association.

"We Remember." (1998, March 17). *The New York Times,* p. A10.

Weiss, Aharon. (1988). "The Historiographical Controversy Concerning the Character and Functions of the Judenrats." In Yisrael Gutman and Gideon Grief (Eds.), *The Historiography of the Holocaust Period* (pp. 679–696). Jerusalem: Yad Vashem.

Weiss, Aharon. (1990a). "Judenrat." In Israel Gutman (Ed.), *Encyclopedia of the Holocaust* (Vol. 2, pp. 762–771). New York: Macmillan.

Weiss, Aharon. (1990b). "Jüdischer Ordnungsdienst." In Israel Gutman (Ed.), *Encyclopedia of the Holocaust* (pp. 771–774). New York: Macmillan.

Weiss, Christoph. (1995). *Der Gute Deutsche: Dokumente zur Diskussion am Stephen Spielberg's "Schindlers Liste" in Deutschland.* St. Ingbert: Rohrig Universitätverlag.

Yahil, Leni. (1990). *The Holocaust: The Fate of European Jewry.* New York: Oxford University Press.

Zuccotti, Susan. (1996). *The Italians and the Holocaust: Persecution, Rescue, and Survival.* Lincoln: University of Nebraska Press.

CHAPTER 3

Instructional Issues/Strategies in Teaching the Holocaust

PAUL WIESER

The Holocaust is not simply another event in the history of the world; it has immense ramifications. It colors who we are as human beings and what it means to live in a world in which genocide has become rather commonplace. For these reasons, it is vitally significant to devise powerful and pedagogically sound lessons that enable students to glean unique insights into the history of the Holocaust and leave them with something of importance to ponder far past the conclusion of the lesson itself.

—Totten, 1998, p. 30

For those of us who have invested a significant portion of our lives in teaching the Holocaust, Professor Totten's advice rings true. Far from being considered a mere footnote or aberration in history, the Holocaust is viewed as a watershed event, a defining moment, an event that represents an age. And although it has yet to earn a full place in the school curriculum, it is gradually being given some place in the classrooms of many schools across the nation.

A study of the Holocaust impacts on many issues—historical, ethical, social, religious, political, legal—all symbolic of problems found in today's world. For some, it is a thorny subject. Teaching it can be like trying to find one's way through a minefield. Some parents raise concerns over appropriateness. Not-so-well meaning groups with their own agendas question why this "Jewish" history must be a part of the curriculum. Then there is the often-raised question of how all of this is "relevant." Unfortunately, the sometimes controversial nature of the subject, and the desire not to offend, causes teachers to shy away from teaching it. When one factors in the "plate is already full" argument, it is no wonder that the teaching of the Holocaust has been characterized by a rather inconsistent pattern of implementation.

Several questions confront those educators who choose to take up this challenge. Why introduce this history to students? What lessons can be learned from this history? What methodologies will be used to create "powerful" and "sound" lessons that not only satisfy the stated objectives but stimulate students' further inquiry and reflection? Failure to clearly answer these questions *prior to* the implementation of the unit of study can only lead to lessons that lack focus, are uninspired, and, at best, result in a superficial treatment of the subject. As in all good teaching, unless the rationales and methods are clearly and firmly established, students have little chance in learning of and appreciating the significance of the Holocaust. (For an in-depth discussion regarding issues of rationale see Chapter 1 in this book.) Trivialization of this subject is the last thing to which students should be exposed.

The purpose of this chapter is to explore some of the many instructional concerns that teachers of the Holocaust deal with as they prepare their lessons and units of study. In an examination of the selection of content issue, questions abound. What topics need to be examined? What is appropriate? How detailed should the lessons be? How important is historical accuracy, and how can teachers insure that integrity in this area is maintained?

This chapter will also focus on a brief discussion of instructional materials. Among the issues to be addressed are: What is available for teachers' use? Can textbooks be relied on? What supplementary materials should be considered?

In addition to the issue of time constraints, other pedagogical issues that need to be considered when teaching this history are: Are there unintentional consequences if this history is taught poorly? Could antisemitism and denial actually be a product of poor teaching? Given the multidisciplinary nature of the content, should teachers other than history/social studies teachers be expected to develop lessons for teaching the Holocaust? If so, are they, in fact, teaching the "history" of the Holocaust? How can literature be used to illuminate this subject? Is the use of role playing/simulations a sound pedagogical practice? These are just a few of the methodological/pedagogical considerations that surround this field of study and warrant more than a cursory treatment.

Finally, there are considerations that involve parents and the community as a whole. Given the nature of what is to be taught to their children, parents need to made aware of what will take place in the classroom. And, depending on the type of community, there may be the real need to "sell" the course of study.

If the study of the Holocaust is to be effective and if it is to be engaging and thought-provoking for our students, then educators must utilize strategies, activities and resources that are uniquely suited for the task. It is not this author's intent to criticize the methods or materials that have proved productive for many teachers. Those of us who have been in the field long enough are well aware that there are any number of ways to teach an effective lesson and a myriad of materials available to help us do just that. Yet, there is now a large enough body of knowledge concerning Holocaust education that we can speak of methods and materials that are recognized as "sound" and "powerful." Educators in the field should be aware of these.

The study of the Holocaust is a compelling one. Indeed, teachers testify to the high level of interest among their students. Why? Largely because such a study raises questions about issues such as prejudice, bias, peer pressure, conformity, and fairness that they themselves have to deal with on a daily basis. As Ronnie Landau (1994) notes: "If taught properly, the Holocaust . . . has the power to sensitise them to the dangers of indifference, intolerance, racism and the dehumanization of others—the ideal educational formula for creating good, responsible citizens in a multicultural society" (p. 60).

Selection of Content

Once a teacher has determined the rationales for teaching this particular history, it is essential for teachers to follow clear and obtainable objectives. When objectives are well defined with specific references made to events associated with this history, teachers are much more likely to stay focused, and the content will be properly addressed.

Effective lessons are more likely to be taught if careful attention is paid to the selection of content—*and*, if this process is based on sound criteria. Good teachers know how crucial it is to the success of any teaching to first determine the developmental appropriateness of the content. The concern with teaching the Holocaust is not only whether the material is too difficult for students to master but the graphic nature of so much of this history.

In this author's estimation, historical accuracy is one criteria that perhaps has not had enough attention paid to it. Errors in fact and misconceptions will not only result in the miseducation of students but interfere with satisfying the very objectives the content was designed to address. The Holocaust is an extremely complex subject and not the easiest to teach. Lessons littered with inaccuracies call into question one's professional integrity. Errors in fact distort the historical record and misinform rather than educate our students.

All teachers confront the amount of content they wish to address versus the amount of time they have to do so. This is a particular headache to those in the field of social studies. That conflict colors the very nature of the presentation, whether it is detailed or superficial. Given the complex nature of the Holocaust, teachers need to "find" ample time for their students to deal with the issues and questions they are being introduced to. This latter course may not be feasible for all; however, not to aim for depth over coverage may lead to a cursory treatment of the history of the Holocaust itself. Since young people see a direct correlation between the importance of a subject and the amount of time devoted to it, any superficial type of study raises some rather serious ethical considerations.

With the above criteria in mind, what ought to be taught when dealing with the Holocaust? What are the essential topics that need to be addressed?

In a well-thought-out curriculum, where standards and teaching objectives are clearly defined, any serious study of the Holocaust should begin with a coherent historical account of the history of antisemitism—with particular attention paid to its roots in Christian doctrine. Students need to realize that although the fundamental responsibility for the Holocaust lies with the Nazi perpetrators and not with the teachings of the Christian faith, the Nazis would not have been as successful in "selling" their version of racial antisemitism had it not been for a long-standing tradition of Christian hostility toward Jews. Jumping right into the story of Nazi Germany without providing background on this complex issue leaves students with the impression that antisemitism had no history before Hitler and the Nazis. Omitting this history is a serious flaw found in many Holocaust curricula, one which leaves students with an incomplete and distorted understanding of the historical reality.

Trying to teach about the roots of antisemitism in Christianity is a sensitive issue for teachers as well as for students and parents. (How this impacts parents/communities will be discussed later in the chapter.) It is "... like leading a tourist party across crocodile territory" (Dawidowicz, 1992, p. 71). More than one teacher—not to mention school district—has chosen to give this issue a wide berth. But by detouring around the subject or attempting to "hide" it within general studies of prejudice or bigotry, educators will only fail to impart to their students the highly distinctive character and history of one of the more essential contributing factors to the Holocaust.

Within the context of a study of the history of antisemitism, a final consideration for teachers might be a brief examination of modern Jewish history. To understand why Jews became the target of the Nazis as well as to understand Jewish response to Nazi persecution, it is necessary to delve into the Jewish historical experience and the structure of Jewish communal life (Friedlander, 1979, p. 536). (See Box 3.1). For those who possess the "luxury" of time to devote to such lessons, their students will no doubt come away with an understanding of how vulnerable the Jewish position in Europe was and an appreciation of the fact the Nazis were a dominant and formidable force, not only to Jews but to other nations.

The second topic that should be included as part of core content in any study of the Holocaust is a thorough examination of the post-World War I years (1918–1933)—the period that produced Hitler and National Socialism. Unfortunately, due to the time constraints, this topic is frequently left unaddressed. An understanding of the historical setting in Germany during these years *is absolutely critical*, however, if students are to grasp how fascism triumphed. The loss of the war, the humiliation of Versailles, extreme nationalism, economic dislocation, the political instability of Weimar—all contributed to an atmosphere in which Nazism could grow, prosper, and ultimately seize control of the state (Bracher, 1970).

What could be labeled "Toward the Final Solution" should provide the focus for a third core of content. Dealing with the years 1933–1939, the course of study could follow Hilberg's "definition," "exploitation," and "concentration" phases of the process of destruction (Hilberg, 1985). Here, material dealing with anti-Jewish legislation, the opening of the concentration camps, Kristallnacht, and the development of ghettos, is a way to convey to students that the destruction of Europe's Jews evolved through stages and that it involved much more than an attempt to simply eliminate Jews from the German economy and society.

The one content area that seems to get most of the attention in teachers' lessons is that which deals with the Final Solution. The establishment of the concentration camps and death camps—the "arena" for the Holocaust—clearly provides the focus for much of today's classroom instruction. In this regard, students need to be made aware of the differences between the various types of camps and their functions. The role of the perpetrators (not all of whom were goose-stepping, black-uniformed fanatics, but "law-abiding" citizens such as bureaucrats, businessmen, doctors, and nurses), needs to be emphasized as a way of clearly indicating the scope of this horrific event. Additionally, attention should be paid to the systematic and bureaucratic actions that eventually led to what is known as the Holocaust. These include the activities of the Einsatzgruppen, plans for the Final Solution (e.g., the Wannsee Conference), and the evolution of the killing process. The part played by collaborators, both Jewish (ghetto police) and non-Jewish (camp guards, kapos), also needs to be examined. Lessons should be structured so as to impart to students the reality of the victims' trauma, that is, the transport by train and the arrival at the camps as they passed through what was to be the last stages of the Final Solution.

Finally any study of the Holocaust should include an examination of the role played by the bystanders. What were some of the moral dilemmas and dangers that non-Jews dealt with as they wrestled with the whole issue of assisting or rescuing Jews? How did the outside world behave relative to the fate of the Jews? And what about the response of the Allies? What did they know about the Holocaust? Why didn't the United States bomb Auschwitz in 1944? These questions broaden the scope of study and raise serious questions as to the culpability of certain individuals and groups, whose roles students must come to realize were much more than ancillary.

Teachers will read through the above suggestions and no doubt immediately start wondering why certain topics do not appear. "Why isn't resistance listed?" "Shouldn't there be a discussion on the liberation of the camps and the subsequent trials of the perpetrators?" "What about the churches' roles, in particular that of the Vatican?" Few would argue against including these areas if everyone had months to devote to the subject. But in the world of the classroom, where material must be covered and objectives have to be taught, some difficult choices must be made. This author's choices appear above. At best, they represent a listing of the most basic content areas that simply cannot be left unaddressed if the history of the Holocaust is not to be distorted and if our students are to come away with any meaningful understanding of this human tragedy.

Instructional Materials

Those who began teaching about the Holocaust years ago can testify to the dearth of instructional materials that were available. Textbooks were of no help, as there was little to nothing in them about the Holocaust. Finding multiple copies of anything to use in the classroom was a chore, and besides Anne Frank there was not much to choose from. Yet, the study of this history "limped" forward through the early 1970s as resourceful educators responded by creating their own materials.

In the mid-to-late 1970s, various organizations began developing curricula and certain boards of education seriously considered mandating teaching the Holocaust. By the mid-to-late 1980s, this "discovery" of the Holocaust led to a

B O X   3.1 The Importance of Addressing the History of the Jewish People

Oftentimes the history of the Jewish people is presented as a litany of one disaster after another. The Jew as victim is an image that is popularly portrayed in a variety of genre, one that, when associated with the Holocaust, is difficult to avoid. This cloud of "victimhood," though, obscures for the most part a rich historical record characterized by a dynamic, vibrant participation in the cultural, social, political, and economic life of Europe and beyond. The image of the hard, grinding subsistence existence of the shtetl, where bearded men were allowed to exist only at the fringes of a Gentile world, clashes dramatically with that of the assimilated, acculturated people, at home in metropolitan centers, whose legal existence in society was recognized and whose position, particularly in the business community, was well developed and of longstanding importance.

Students need to be made aware that between the segregation, economic restrictions, crippling taxes, pogroms and pillage, forced baptism, blood-libel charges, expulsions, and death, the Jews passed their gifts onto the surrounding society. In Poland-Lithuania from the fifteenth to eighteenth centuries, the Jews had built a vital and buoyant society. In spite of negative pressures in the cities from Christian businessmen, their economic base was relatively broad and secure. Through their links with their brethren in the Ottoman Empire, Jewish merchants played an important part in the overland transit trade between the Eastern Mediterranean and Western Europe. They obtained concessions for working salt mines and forests. They were involved in agricultural life as the stewards and lessees of large estates. In this capacity, they helped open up and settle tracts of undeveloped land in Eastern Poland. They also were engaged in a wide variety of crafts and service occupations, as doctors and chemists, goldsmiths, tailors, shoemakers, ferriers, weavers, butchers, and soapmakers. In

addition, intellectual life, which focused on religious learning and study, flourished, as numerous yeshivot sprang up. Many of these gained fame for their scholarship, in particular those in Vilna and Lublin. It was this East European Ashkenazic Jewry that would fashion a unique Jewish culture—the wellspring of Jewish creativity for Jewish communities throughout the world.

Likewise, Jews who found themselves living under Arab control adapted and built prosperous societies. Even though numerous restrictions were imposed on them, because Islam was not impregnated with a strong religious bias against Judaism and Jews, Jews were able to establish themselves in society and the economy more readily than had been the experience in Christian-dominated lands. Overwhelmingly, Jews became townspeople, traders, and artisans, inhabiting crowded Jewish quarters, such as those in Baghdad and Cordoba and Toledo in Moslem Spain.

On the social and cultural level, there was a steady adaptation to Arab life. Jews spoke Arabic as their daily tongue, wore Arab dress, and Arabized their names. Jewish scholars began absorbing and then contributing to Arab literature, philosophy, and medicine. This intellectual cooperation reached its zenith in the Golden Age in Moorish Spain, when Spain became the most cultured and enlightened country in Europe. In this environment the Jewish population flourished. By the tenth century, Spain was a major center of Jewish scholarship. During the next two centuries, the Spanish Jews were to demonstrate a remarkable capacity to develop their own religious and spiritual heritage while at the same time taking part in Arab life and culture of the country.

To the east, the rise of the Ottoman Empire saw a corresponding rise in Jewish fortunes. The Jews of this region enjoyed economic prosperity, a high level of culture,

(continued)

BOX 3.1   Continued

and developed important Talmudic academies. The Ottoman rulers actually encouraged the immigration of Jews from Christian lands where they were oppressed or had been expelled. As had been the case in Spain, sultans employed Jews as their personal physicians and advisers on various issues.

For students who might view all of this as "ancient history" and see little or no relevance to their lives or to the modern age, teachers might draw attention to the creative achievement of three German-speaking Jews—Karl Marx, Sigmund Freud, and Albert Einstein—each of whom had a profound influence on the modern world. They also could point to the fact that about a fifth of the Nobel Prize recipients since the first prize was awarded in 1901 have been Jewish.

But why is it important to see the Jews as more than victims and to appreciate the rich cultures developed by the Jews of Europe? As already suggested, if students are to grasp the reasons Jews became targets of the Nazis, if they are to understand why the Jews responded in the manner they did, and if they are to leave the classroom without the distorted view that the Jews must be guilty of something, then they must know more about this people other than their being the objects of genocide.

It is worth noting that for some educators teaching the Holocaust and emphasizing the victimization of the Jews has become the

means toward discouraging aggression against others. The thinking here is that through such an approach, the world will somehow become a safer place. Although these individuals may be well intentioned, this author thinks that in taking such an approach "they might as well believe that dying is good for your health." If tolerance is a lesson students are to learn from a study of the Holocaust, as it would seem they are suggesting, then kids need to know of what they are supposed to be tolerant. If they think of Jews as only victims of the Nazis, as the "perfect martyrs," how does this prepare them to appreciate and be tolerant of this highly particularistic people when they encounter them?

Within the perspective of Jewish history, the Holocaust is the most massive and disastrous catastrophe since the earliest days of that history. *It is not, however, the defining moment of Judaism nor the sound basis of a moral education. Yes, the Jews were victims but that fact should not overshadow the way of life it tried to destroy.*

And, finally, one last consideration for looking beyond the "cloud of victimhood": *When we teach the Holocaust separately from teaching about the Jews as a whole, we run the risk of abstracting and diminishing them.* As Ruth Wisse (1998/1999) points out, "Teaching the Holocaust as a secular crucifixion cuts off Jewish tragedy from the historical continuum, and distorts the rich reality of Jewish experience" (p. 5).

veritable explosion of instructional material. Once the question used to be, "How can I teach this subject with so few resources out there?"; now, it could easily be rephrased, "With so much material available, what do I select to augment my classroom lessons?" Indeed it becomes an extremely time-consuming, yet necessary task of sorting through the litany of offerings—books, videos, CD-ROMs, lesson plans, charts, filmstrips, atlases, activities, and even entire curricula—to determine what is credible and of the most use to teachers. Although it is not this author's primary intent to examine and evaluate all that is available or to provide an endless discussion of the merits of one title over another, some observations in this area are warranted.

Even today, in far too many cases, history and social studies teachers limit themselves to the use of textbooks, the best of which might recite the facts about the Holocaust but more often than not omit any discussion of the history of anti-semitism and fail to stress the centrality of premeditated mass murder as an instrument of policy. A few paragraphs and perhaps a photo is the typical treatment one can expect to find in texts. For example, John A. Garraty's highly acclaimed *Exploring America's Past* (1998) devotes three paragraphs to the Holocaust and includes a picture of children survivors. Such "passing references" are certainly not suitable for any true study of the "history" of the subject. As most texts are designed to be used in survey classes, they cannot be expected to address in detail every topic presented. This being the case, it makes the search for alternative materials even more necessary, if not critical, especially if students are to grasp the most rudimentary knowledge of the realities of this history. (There is at least one text that does include, relatively speaking, fairly "extensive" coverage of the Holocaust; that is *A History of U.S.* (1995) by Joy Hakim. An eight-page chapter—pages 110–117—with numerous photographs is dedicated to the subject.)

This author can recall thinking of all the great things he could accomplish if a classroom set of *Smoke and Ashes* by Barbara Rogasky (1988) were available, or marveling at what could be accomplished if English teachers could support what the social studies teacher was doing by having his/her students read *Friedrich, The Devil's Arithmetic, Number the Stars, The Devil in Vienna,* or *The Endless Steppe.*

Fortunately, supplementary materials abound. Museums (the United States Holocaust Memorial Museum being the foremost), Holocaust resource centers, archival facilities, memorials, research institutes, and certain publishers all provide educators with a wide array of materials intended to assist teachers in meeting their objectives.

Not only are particular books or videos available for purchase, but there are entire curriculums, replete with the objectives and activities, primary source readings, maps, charts, and enough historical background to make those who are new to the field feel a bit more comfortable. *That said, it is imperative to be cautious, for many of the extant curricula are not of a particularly high quality.* Errors in historical fact abound and many of the suggested activities are not pedagogically sound. In many cases, these curricula were the products of local efforts by educators who were trying to get "something" in place or perhaps to meet a particular mandate. Good intentions are fine, but it does take considerable expertise to develop an entire curriculum; one that is well defined in scope, historically sound, where goals and objectives are clearly stated, and where students come away with lessons that ideally will never leave them.

One of the more widely known of the above mentioned curricula is *Facing History and Ourselves,* a privately produced curriculum. This program focuses on a study of the Holocaust as a means ". . . to teaching about the dangers of indifference and the values of civility by helping schools confront the complexities of history in ways that promote critical and creative thinking about the challenges we face and the opportunities we have for positive change" (Facing History and Ourselves National Foundation, 1994, pp. xx). Far from being a "packaged" course of study with prescribed sets of lessons, teachers are encouraged to select from a wide selection of "Readings" (many of which are primary sources) and "Connections" (activities) that best match the objectives they are responsible to teach as well as the needs and interests of their students.

Two of the very best curricula that this author is familiar with are New York's *Teaching About the Holocaust and Genocide* and *A Holocaust Curriculum: Life Unworthy of Life*, published by The Center for the Study of the Child in Michigan. Although quite different in treatment, the objectives of both programs clearly focus on teaching the *history* of the period. Specifically in the latter case, this multimedia resource package includes lessons that are challenging and engaging, within an historical context that is inclusive and sound. Realizing the constraints that time places on many educators, the curriculum developers have built a great deal of flexibility into it. For those teachers unable to incorporate all of the lessons into their instructional timeframes, two shortened versions involving selected lessons, which in no way compromise the integrity of the unit, are offered for consideration. Another plus of this program is the ease of its implementation. Especially for those who may be new to the field and a bit hesitant, the extremely well-written *Instructor's Manual* makes the unit "teacher friendly."

Teachers do not always agree on what materials are best to use in the classroom. Some will swear to the effectiveness of a particular book, poem, or video, while others may not have the same experience. No doubt it will always come down to knowing what materials are historically accurate and developmentally appropriate for one's students. This course of action can lead to effective teaching. When coupled with the ability to clearly focus on and teach the objectives, this knowledge assists teachers to navigate through the rather cluttered waters of instructional materials.

Methodological/Pedagogical Considerations

Incorporating the Study of the Holocaust into Various Disciplines

Incorporating a study of the Holocaust into existing courses within the school curriculum can be effectively accomplished in a great variety of ways. One of the more common points of inclusion is within courses on United States History. Units on the Great Depression and World War II provide ample opportunities for teachers to introduce the subject by addressing questions such as: Was the Depression a contributing factor to the Nazis' rise to power? Was the Weimar Constitution of 1919 fatally flawed? How did the United States respond to the unfolding events of the Holocaust?

Although most students are not required to take courses in World History, the study of the Holocaust is generally taught within the context of such classes. Teachers frequently incorporate the study of the Holocaust into units of study in European History, such as the *Rise of Dictators* or *The World at War.* Here again, the subject can be introduced by exploring a variety of questions such as: What factors led to the rise of the Nazi dictatorship? What was the nature of Nazi antisemitism, and how was it used by the regime? and Did World War II affect the course of the Holocaust?

Increasingly, government courses, especially at the high school level, include a study of the Holocaust in order to demonstrate how public policy could be directed to genocidal ends. Furthermore, courses under a variety of titles— Contemporary Issues, World Problems, Genocide in the Twentieth Century— allow for students to examine many current world problems. The objectives here focus on having students explore possible solutions to problems. In this context, it is not uncommon to find lessons on the Holocaust being taught, usually as part of a more general investigation of genocide.

Inclusion of Holocaust studies in literature/English classes across grade levels has not only become a popular way to address the subject but clearly demonstrates the multidisciplinary nature of this content. Through the use of a variety of genres, including memoirs, diaries, short stories, poetry, novels, and drama, classes of this type not only satisfy objectives particular to English curricula but also strengthen and enhance the efforts being made by teachers in social studies courses.

Personalizing the History through the Study of Holocaust Literature

It is difficult to convey to students the magnitude and/or significance of the Holocaust. The raw material of history deals with facts, dates, and statistics that seem cold and distant. Events and places are remote with names that often appear to be indecipherable. Yet, that rough edge seems to be made a bit smoother through the use of literature in the classroom. Literature has a way of illuminating historical content. Well-written literary works have a way of engaging students in ways that traditional histories do not. The history becomes more personalized and thought-provoking. Thus, by reading a first-person account, memoir, or short story, the history of the Holocaust could become more than simply learning a series of facts. It could touch students in ways that may cause them to reflect more meaningfully on the significance of this history. Utilizing powerful pieces of literature can assist teachers in their attempts to convey the complexities of a subject that has been called "unthinkable," "inaccessible," and even "unimaginable." If one of our objectives is for our students to "personalize" the tragedy of these horrendous events, then perhaps one of the best means to this end might be found in works of literature, whether read in our English or social studies courses.

One of the more effective ways to begin this literary approach to teaching the Holocaust is to choose a short story or novel whose main character is close in age to the students' own ages. It has been this author's experience that students identify quickly with such characters and they become thoroughly caught up in the story. In the best works, students are led through the complex historic realities of the period through the actions of characters their own age. *Stolen Years* (Zyskind,

1981), *Upon the Head of a Goat* (Siegal, 1994), and *Friedrich* (Richter, 1987) are good examples of books that could be utilized for such an approach. If time permits, the scope of the study could be expanded with another work about young people's lives in one of the ghettos.

Wrestling with the rationale for using Holocaust literature allows a teacher to more clearly select appropriate material. That said, whatever works are chosen need to be engaging and *historically accurate.* It is the teachers' responsibility to provide their students with the most informed and accurate history, not to misinform or distort. That the literature used needs to be developmentally appropriate should go without saying. Teachers need to avoid graphic content that can easily grasp students' attention but may have little to do with the objective of a lesson. Furthermore, books selected should not focus on the unique or the uncommon (e.g., medical experimentation, resistance, the role of Righteous Gentiles) but on the broad events of this history. Failure to avoid the former could very well convey the misconception to students that such events were rather commonplace, thus blurring the distinction between what is essential and what in fact is ancillary.

One point relative to using Holocaust literature in the classroom cannot be overemphasized enough. As Samuel Totten (1996) suggests,

> In order for students to come to a clear understanding of the Holocaust, they *must understand the history of the Holocaust.* In light of that, it is imperative that teachers undergird their use of literature on the Holocaust with a substantial amount of history and that students have a solid sense of the "whos," "whens," "hows," and "whys" of the Holocaust. (p. 23)

This advice is particularly germane for teachers of English. Traditionally, their curricular objectives have dealt with such components as character development, allusions, symbol, images, and metaphor. A typical objective they routinely address might read, "Describe relationships between the author's style, literary form (e.g., short stories, novels, drama, fables, biographies, documentaries, poetry, essays) and intended effect on the reader." Clearly the focus here is quite distinct from what their colleagues in history courses are dealing with, that is, explaining historical continuity and change, analyzing cause-and-effect relationships, marshaling evidence of antecedent circumstances, just to mention a few. Professor Totten's (1996) admonition would seem to challenge, if not require, those who utilize literature as a means to teaching the Holocaust, to venture into the realm of history in order to provide at the very least the historical context students need to grasp the "true understanding" of the period. Furthermore, as Margaret Drew (1991) states:

> . . . literature without history is only a story. Young people have little sense of time, in historical terms. Unless they have studied the history of the period about which they are reading, they have no framework within which to put it. Rarely do they make the connections between what they have read and actual historical events unless they have had some formal study of the historical period in question. They have read an exciting, perhaps moving, story that may have a lasting impression on them, but adds nothing to their understanding of history, as they do not have the knowledge necessary to put it into historical context.

. . . Without that context, the reader sees only the story of one human tragedy, difficult to distinguish from tragic events that can be found in any daily newspaper.

Literature . . . makes the connection between the overwhelming statistics and the human beings represented by those statistics. History provides the perspective that enables the individual story to become, not just one person's experience, but a microcosm representing a much larger truth. The integration of history and literature, by placing the individual story within its historical framework, can further the understanding of the difficult concepts involved in the study of atrocity. (pp. 128–129)

The Selection of Appropriate Learning Activities

Selecting appropriate learning activities for students is one of the more challenging aspects of teaching any subject. Activities should not only be engaging but also challenging and thought-provoking. One particular activity associated with the study of the Holocaust that has caused ample concern over "appropriateness" is the use of role playing and/or simulations. Where these activities are employed, students typically play the roles of murderers or victims. In other cases, students may be singled out because of their eye or hair color and serve as targets for the rest of the class as they "act out" some rather nasty prejudiced behavior against them. The justification for such lessons is that, on conclusion, the students will have a "feel" for "what it was like" during the Holocaust.

This author finds these "activities" frivolous and pedagogically unsound. Survivor testimony is clear as to the tremendous difficulty of finding the right words to describe what they went through. Playing *Gestapo, Concentration Camp,* and *Nuremberg Trial,* or having students teased and ridiculed during the school day, could leave them with the impression that they really do know "what it was like." This oversimplified approach not only leads to a distorted view of events but also to a trivialization of this history. (For a more detailed discussion of this issue, see Samuel Totten's "Diminishing the Complexity and Horror of the Holocaust: Using Simulations in an Attempt to Convey Historical Experiences.")

Teachers need to focus their objectives and not lose sight of the fact that they are dealing with impressionable young people. Role playing/simulations ". . . have been known to produce unprecedented emotional tensions in the classroom, among some students arousing fear, panic and overidentification with Jewish victims and among others, releasing sadomasochistic urges, violent responses, and overidentification with the murderers" (Dawidowicz, 1992, p. 71).

There are many eyewitness accounts and much photographic evidence that teachers can draw on if they want their students to assess this tragedy. This material will provide teachers with sufficient sources to describe the cruel dilemmas and the almost impossible decisions about life and death that victims faced on a daily basis. Furthermore, it does so in an authentic—and not a frivolous—manner.

As mentioned earlier in this chapter, one of the biggest thorns in the side of educators is the time constraints placed on them by institutions. Seldom does the concern over whether or not to teach the Holocaust focus on rationale or the value of the subject matter; rather, it is simply a practical question of, "Where do I find the time to fit it in?" *It is not possible to teach the Holocaust in a single class period.* But given the real pressures teachers face over the time issue, are there any courses of action that might be solutions or at least partial solutions to this problem?

A starting point might be to consider using the five topics mentioned above as a focus for a five-day mini unit. Whereas teaching the history of antisemitism, post-World War I (1918–1933), toward the Final Solution (1933–1939), the Final Solution (1941–1945), and the role of the bystanders in the course of a week would be a challenge for the most experienced of teachers, it would at least provide students with a basic understanding of key elements of the Holocaust. Teachers "blessed" with more time would have the flexibility to elaborate on and add to these suggested topics, making their lessons even more engaging and meaningful.

English and history teachers planning simultaneous lessons is an effective strategy that not only expands coverage within a limited timeframe, but also reaps the benefits associated with the integration of history and literature. Depending on the extent of cooperation among the teaching staff (art and music teachers could certainly make contributions as well), students could spend a considerable portion of their day dealing with varying aspects of the Holocaust, taught from the perspectives of several disciplines.

Since a long-term study is not possible for most educators, involving students in particular academic programs/contests is one way of extending the study well after the classroom content/focus has moved on to another topic. For this author, the National History Day Program, an academic competition in which students research a topic relative to a yearly theme and display their findings in historical papers, documentaries, dramatic performances, or exhibits, was the answer, for it allowed his students to become immersed in a thorough study of the Holocaust, which lasted a full academic year as they prepared their entries. (To obtain information about National History Day, contact National History Day, 0119 Cecil Hall, University of Maryland, College Park, MD 20742.) It no doubt will always come down to the creative solutions of teachers to "find some room" on that proverbially "full plate." For those who are truly committed and care enough to be innovative, and/or for those who always seem "to find a way," the benefit to their students could very well be a lifelong appreciation of the importance of this horrific event, and lessons that simply will not leave them.

Key Ethical Issues

Finally, one has to be aware of ethical issues relative to the teaching of this history that have become concerns among educators. The issue focuses on particular content and teaching methods that may, in fact, hinder the effective teaching of the Holocaust. Could antisemitism, for example, actually be a product of poor teaching? The answer could very well be "yes" if teachers do not pay close enough attention to the emphasis they give to the content they are presenting. If a teacher's view of Jewish history was an unending succession of persecution and suffering, it could mislead students into believing that the Jews must surely be guilty of something and that they deserved their fate. Reinforcing this wayward way of thinking is the long-standing conviction that the Jews were the authors of their own misfortune.

To allow history to be taught in such a manner is not only unethical but simply bad history. The Jewish past is not synonymous with disaster. Although teachers need to emphasize the historical roots of antisemitism and put the Holocaust into perspective, students also need to learn something about the triumphs of the Jewish people as well as the tragedies (Short, 1994). Failure to do so could very well result in antisemitism becoming a product of classroom lessons, taught by well-meaning teachers who are only trying to present an accurate understanding of the period.

Acquainting students with Nazi antisemitic propaganda and stereotypes is another example of how teaching about the Holocaust could give rise to antisemitism. No doubt for most students this will be the first time they are exposed to a study of antisemitism. When they learn that many well-educated and influential people in Germany actually subscribed to such stereotypes, the danger is that a certain credibility through association may develop in students' minds. In a Germany that was viewed as sophisticated and advanced, one which saw Jews as "unpatriotic," a "virus" or as "parasites," a sympathy for the perpetrators rather than for its victims might actually occur.

Is there a strategy that teachers might employ to avoid this troublesome outcome? Students need to be taught about the nature and process of stereotyping. At the very least, students' attention should be drawn to the irrational basis of the stereotyping process; its inherent tendency to generalize in the absence of valid evidence. Unfortunately, teachers seldom have enough time to devote to lessons on antiracism or moral education. Ideally, lessons of this type would/should be taught prior to those dealing with the Holocaust. Furthermore, antisemitism needs to be exposed for what it is—a fraud.

One final consideration: one that arises not necessarily from what teachers do incorrectly but what they inadvertently overlook. Before starting lessons on the Holocaust, it could prove most helpful if teachers explore and challenge any misconceptions their students might have about Jews or Judaism (Short, 1994). Students who hold the impression that Jews are "bad" or that Judaism is "alien" or "threatening" could very well come away with the perception that Nazism was not an unmitigated evil. Through their ignorance, students who possess antisemitic stereotypes may very well view the Holocaust as a story of good triumphing over evil. Unless educators take into account the way in which their students conceptualize Jewish culture and identity, we have no guarantee that our students will appreciate the abject injustice and horror of what they learn about the Holocaust.

Parent and Community Considerations

Given the nature of the content and the sensitive issues that students are exposed to and deal with while studying the Holocaust, there may be a need for teachers to make parents aware of what they are undertaking. It may, in some cases, necessitate the involvement of the community as well.

One particular concern is over the question of the infliction of pain. Although there are valuable lessons derived from a study of the Holocaust, it no doubt could be, for some, a rather painful experience. The question then becomes, How far are teachers entitled to go in making their students aware of the horrors of the Holocaust?

Certainly teachers do not deliberately inflict pain on their students. Nevertheless, the Holocaust *is* about suffering. Furthermore, it is not simply another human rights violation. To skirt this issue or to somehow downplay the horror is to ultimately misinform students and distort the history. The question for teachers then becomes one of achieving a balance. How do teachers satisfy the objectives of the unit while at the same time subjecting students to no more pain than the minimum necessary?

Again, this is why it is imperative for educators to establish, well in advance, a clear rationale as to why they are teaching this subject. Clearly written and well-thought-out objectives keep the lessons focused and go a long way toward insuring that the desired effect is achieved. It is these objectives that teachers need to share with parents and other concerned parties, not only to inform but also to alleviate concerns before they become contentious.

Educators should appreciate the pedagogic implications of using painful material in their lessons (Parsons and Totten, 1993, p. 3). Here again, the concern over role-playing techniques and the tensions that sometimes result is something that warrants serious reservations. Teachers also need to be sensitive to the fact that they may be dealing with students who identify very closely with groups singled out for persecution by the Nazis. Do parents of these particularly vulnerable students have the right to withdraw their children from this part of the curriculum? In the same vein, there may be educators who find the teaching of this material especially troubling. School boards, parents, community members, and teachers oftentimes find themselves wrestling with answers to these questions, questions perhaps best addressed in preparatory discussions over rationale and not left until well into the implementation and teaching of the material.

One final consideration that involves parents and the community with Holocaust education has to do with material that brings to light Christianity's role in fanning the flames of antisemitism. If this topic is essential to any basic understanding of the subject, as this author has already argued, it then raises some rather sensitive issues. How do teachers, who themselves may be Christians, present this history to students who come from homes of practicing Christians? Teachers certainly do not desire to offend, yet fidelity to the history could cause some rather anxious moments. It is not easy for students (as well as some adults) to accept the injustices that have occurred if their religion is singled out as being somehow responsible. Simply avoiding this subject is not an option. Confronting this problem with intelligent discussion in the classroom, and with parents and the community, if necessary, is no doubt the best route to take. If all the concerned parties are made to realize that there occasionally is a degree of discomfort with new knowledge, especially when it challenges things we hold dear, this would seem to provide a basis for an exploration of and response to the charge that organized Christianity played a major role in the historic mistreatment of the Jews (Dawidowicz, 1992, p. 71).

Strategies/Activities for Teaching
Various Aspects of Holocaust History

There are innumerable ways that teachers can be effective and countless activities that can be used successfully to teach about the Holocaust. What follows is a succinct discussion of several of these strategies and activities.

The question of how to have students gain an appreciation of the growing seriousness of the year-by-year attack on the Jews of Germany led this author to develop a lesson that focused students' attention on the barrage of Nazi laws and decrees. This lesson also examines the impact these measures had on various groups (Jew and non-Jews alike) in Germany from 1933–1942 (Wieser, 1995b, pp. C4–C6). In an attempt to personalize the lesson, the measures chosen to be examined were those laws that had a particular impact on the lives of young people of the time. Thus, many of these laws and decrees (prohibition on pets, radios, bicycles, etc.) were included along with some of the more widely known, that is, the boycott of 1933, the Nuremberg Laws (1935), and so on. Arranging the decrees by the year issued, students were asked to rate (1–5) the impact of these laws and decrees on various segments of the population. Here, the teacher had the flexibility to choose from as many groups as he/she wished. Typically, "Jewish student," "Jewish adult," "Jewish businessman," as well as their non-Jewish counterparts, were listed. As students totaled the scores by year, they could clearly see which groups had been most affected and what patterns, if any, developed. The activity requires students to carefully evaluate and reflect on the impact on the selected populations. What on the surface appeared to be outright attack on the Jewish community also resulted in serious ramifications for Gentiles. Thus, students will often come to the realization that although Jews could not sell their newspapers on German streets after September 6, 1935, the non-Jewish businessman who relied on advertising in those papers might feel the sting of this measure as much as the Jewish publishers. (For additional Holocaust lessons by the author, see Wieser, 1995a, pp. C1–C2 ; Wieser, 1995c, pp. 374–376.)

Teachers, especially those in social studies, are always looking for ways to incorporate primary source material into their lessons. Such a strategy adds a certain "connectedness" to the past and can help to create an atmosphere for learning that is quite distinct from the typical classroom. One particular lesson that thoroughly engages students involves an examination of the Nazis' use of euphemisms and the role bureaucrats played in the Final Solution (Kalfus, 1990, pp. 87–93). This activity, which English teachers would find particularly useful, uses what appears to be a business memorandum, outlining specific technical problems with the performance of a van, and suggested solutions. Students are asked to read the document and to see if they can determine what the subject matter is. When asked if they noticed anything odd about the wording, students generally note that the "merchandise" or "load" that the van is designed to transport seems to possess the human abilities to "press," "rush," and "scream." When a student rereads the memo aloud, after the teacher has replaced the euphemisms with their intended meaning, it results in hearing ". . . this Nazi voice of death without its euphemistic cover-up resonate grotesquely in the classroom" (Kalfus, 1990, p. 89). It is at this point that the rest of the document, a brief introduction, is given to the students. They learn that the memo refers to specially designed gas vans used at Chelmno, and that since December 1941, ninety-seven thousand had been "processed."

Prior to reading literary works, Grace Caporino, an English teacher at Carmel High School in Carmel, New York, has her students read Chapter 1 (Precedents) from the student edition of Raul Hilberg's *The Destruction of the European Jews* (1985). This chapter presents key historical and religious policies that helped paved the way for the events of the Holocaust. Not only does this help to answer the question "Why the Jews?"; Hilberg's historical perspective provides Caporino's students with the historical context needed to more fully appreciate the literary works with which they will be dealing.

The question of an individual's responsibility to act and the moral dilemmas associated with these decisions are issues that Rebecca Lawson's high school English students in Sullivan, Illinois, struggle with, as she prepares them for a unit of study that has as its focus literature of the Holocaust. Her students read Maurice Ogden's poem *Hangman*, followed by a short reading, "Do You Take the Oath?" (*Resource Book: Facing History and Ourselves: Holocaust and Human Behavior*, 1994, p. 198), both of which deal with the issues bystanders confronted and the often torturous decision-making process they would endure.

To contextualize events for his students, Stephen Feinberg, a former middle school teacher in Wayland, Massachusetts, had his students create a chronology of events associated with the Holocaust, which literally covers the walls of his classroom. After students read various works, view a video, or hear a speaker, they are encouraged to add to the chronology. Students are asked, "Where does it belong?" Feinberg then enters that bit of information in the appropriate place, and the list grows. As all his classes built their own chronology, it generated animated discussions between classes over the merits of particular details that have been included or excluded. In addition to being an effective strategy for having students come to an understanding of the order in which events happened, it also causes students to note the significance of particular events within the historical context.

The creativity of teachers is a constant source of amazement to this author. Meaningful lessons and engaging activities have our students involved with this history as never before. It is to be hoped that it will cause them to become more reflective about about our world in which man's inhumanity toward his fellow human is far too common.

Conclusion

What has been presented here could be intimidating. The Holocaust is a complex topic. When one deals with human behavior, there are no simple answers. Yet, teachers—in increasing numbers—are taking up the challenge as the study of the Holocaust expands across grade levels, curricula, and the nation. In our enthusiasm as educators to teach this history, we would be well reminded to stay focused on the goals and reasons why we embarked on this journey. Our students must come to an understanding that the Holocaust was not an accident; that this mass murder occurred because individuals and groups made choices that allowed it to happen. A study of the Holocaust provides teachers with the opportunity and means to engage students in powerful lessons, in which self-questioning can lead to the development of thoughtful and caring individuals, and in which students can examine what it means to be a responsible citizen. A structured inquiry, with a well-written curriculum, where objectives are clearly stated, is essential if these goals are to be met and if students are to arrive at any meaningful understanding of this history.

REFERENCES

Bolkosky, Sidney M., Ellisa, Betty Rutgers, & Harris David. (1987). *A Holocaust Curriculum: Life Unworthy of Life.* Farmington Hills, MI: The Center for the Study of the Child.

Bracher, Karl Dietrich. (1970). *The German Dictatorship.* New York: Praeger.

Dawidowicz, Lucy. (1992). "How They Teach the Holocaust." In Lucy Dawidowicz (Ed.), *What Is the Use of Jewish History* (pp. 65–83). New York: Schocken Books.

Drew, Margaret A. (1991, February). "Merging History and Literature in Teaching About Genocide." *Social Education,* 55(2):128–129.

Facing History and Ourselves National Foundation, Inc. (1994). *Resource Book: Facing History and Ourselves: Holocaust and Human Behavior* (p. xx). Brookline, MA: Author.

Friedlander, Henry. (1979, February). "Toward a Methodology of Teaching about the Holocaust." *Teachers College Record 80*(3):519–542.

Garraty, John A. (1998). *Exploring America's Past.* Austin, TX: Holt, Rinehart and Winston.

Hakim, Joy. (1995). "War, Peace, and All That Jazz." *A History of U.S.* Volume 9. New York: Oxford University Press.

Hilberg, Raul. (1985). *The Destruction of the European Jews.* 3 volumes. New York: Holmes & Meier.

Kalfus, Richard. (1990, February). "Euphemisms of Death: Interpreting a Primary Source Document of the Holocaust." *The History Teacher 23*(2):87–93.

Landau, Ronnie. (1994). Letter in *Jewish Chronicle* (August 25, 1989). Quoted in Geoffrey Short (1994a), "Teaching About the Holocaust: A Consideration of Some Ethical and Pedagogic Issues." *Educational Studies 20*(1):53–68.

Parsons, William S., & Totten, Samuel. (1993). *Guidelines for Teaching About the Holocaust.* Washington, DC: United States Holocaust Memorial Museum.

Richter, Hans. (1987). *Friedrich.* New York: Puffin Books.

Rogasky, Barbara. (1988). *Smoke and Ashes: The Story of the Holocaust.* New York: Holiday House.

Short, Geoffrey. (1994). "Teaching the Holocaust: The Relevance of Children's Perceptions of Jewish Culture and Identity." *British Educational Research Journal 20*(3):393–406.

Siegal, Aranka. (1994). *Upon the Head of a Goat: A Childhood in Hungary, 1939–1944.* New York: Puffin Books.

Totten, Samuel. (Summer 1996). "Using Literature to Teach About the Holocaust." *Journal of Holocaust Education 5*(1):14–48.

Totten, Samuel. (January/February 1998). "Using Reader-Response Theory to Study Poetry About the Holocaust with High School Students." *The Social Studies 89*(1):30–34.

Totten, Samuel (April 2000). "Diminishing the Complexity and Horror of the Holocaust: Using Simulations in an Attempt to Convey Historical Experiences." *Social Education 64*(3):165–171.

The University of the State of New York & the State Education Department of Curriculum Development. (1985–1986). *Teaching About the Holocaust and Genocide: The Human Rights Series.* 3 volumes. Albany, NY: Author.

Wieser, Paul. (1995a). "The American Press," *Social Education* 59(6):C1–C2.

Wieser, Paul. (1995b). "Anti-Semitism: A Warrant for Genocide," *Social Education* 59(6):C4–C6.

Wieser, Paul. (1995c). "Hitler's Death Camps," *Social Education* 59(6):374–376.

Wisse, Ruth R. (Winter 1998/1999). "Seeing Jews as Victims Invites New Attacks." *Holocaust and Jewish Resistance Teachers Training Program Alumni Newsletter 21:* 5–6.

Zyskind, Sara. (1981). *Stolen Years.* Minneapolis, MN: Lerner Publications.

Using Primary Documents in a Study of the Holocaust

4

SAMUEL TOTTEN

ROBERT HINES

> *The questions arose for us: what about women and children? I decided here, too, to find a clear-cut solution. I did not believe myself justified to root out the men—say also, to kill them, or to have them killed—and to allow avengers in the form of their children to grow up for our sons and grandsons [to confront]. The hard decision had to be made for this people to disappear from the earth.*
>
> —Speech given by Heinrich Himmler, Reichsführer-SS and Chief of German Police, on October 4, 1943 (cited in International Military Tribunal, 1947–1949).

Not only does the above excerpt from a speech by Himmler provide powerful insights into the goals and objectives of the Nazis, but, like many primary documents of the Holocaust, it provides readers with a unique perspective into a particular aspect of the history. Indeed, such documents provide a "close-up" view of the history in that they are revealing and informative in ways that many other forms of information are not.

Incorporating such documents into a study of the history is capable of providing students with a host of unique insights into the thinking, motives, and actions of the individuals involved in the issues and events at the time. More specifically, through the use of such documents, teachers and students may be able to glean insights into such concerns as when certain decisions were made by the Nazis, the euphemistic language that the perpetrators used to mask their true intentions, the attitude of the perpetrators toward their victims, the victims' response to the flood of Nazi directives, the Judenräte's directives, and so on.

Documents also provide a unique opportunity for students to broaden their reasoning skills. By analyzing the nature or evidence—whether written or photographic—students gain insights into key concepts, issues, and significant aspects of the history. Using original documents is a necessary element in any thorough study of the past. Such resources provide both teachers and students with an opportunity to wrestle with the events as they unfolded and to take on the mantle of historical "detective." Setting a proper context—in relation to the actual time period, the relationship of the incident or event or action under study to other events, the major personalities involved, and so on—leads to the development of a much greater depth of knowledge and understanding. Indeed, analyzing documents, both written and photographic, leads to a special literacy, allowing students to begin to learn and appreciate the craft of historians. In part, this technique is based on an ability to posit penetrating questions about the documents, to search for the answers, and to come to the understanding and appreciation that not all questions can be answered.

Types of Primary Documents Available on the Holocaust

Primary documents on the Holocaust take many shapes and forms. There are primary documents available that were issued by the perpetrators, the victims (including such disparate groups as the leaders of the *Judenrat*, the Resistance, and individual citizens), the churches and church people, the Allied governments, Jewish groups outside of Europe, and others. The most valuable documents for pedagogical purposes are those that provide unique and powerful insights into a particular aspect of the history, address a specific aspect of the history in a good amount of detail, are highly informative, are highly readable, are thought-provoking, and, ideally, are relatively short so that they are able to be read during a single night of homework and/or discussed during a single class period.

Among the many types of primary documents available are: manifestos, appeals, and "calls to arms" issued by the Jewish resistance; transcripts of speeches, decrees, directives, declarations, rulings, regulations, proclamations, proposals, guidelines, minutes of meetings, protocols, memoranda, reports, telegrams, and orders by the Nazis; Nazi-promulgated laws; proclamations by the leaders of the *Judenrat;* and excerpts from diaries and letters by perpetrators, victims, and others.

Also available are contemporaneous photographs and political cartoons. Cartoons that are especially useful address (and frequently satirize) various facets of the Nazis' policies and actions.

Locating Primary Documents

Excellent institutional resources for locating primary documents on the Holocaust are: the libraries and archives of major universities; the United States National Archives; the United States Holocaust Memorial Museum in Washington, DC; Yad Vashem, The Holocaust Martyrs' and Heroes' Remembrance Authority in Jerusalem; and the Simon Wiesenthal Center in Los Angeles.

Among the more reliable published sources for locating primary documents on the Holocaust are: Yitzhak Arad, Israel Gutman, and Abraham Margaliot (Eds.), *Documents on the Holocaust* (Jerusalem: Yad Vashem, 1996); Michael Berenbaum (Ed.), *Witness to the Holocaust: An Illustrated Documentary History of the Holocaust in the Words of Its Victims, Perpetrators and Bystanders* (New York: HarperCollins, 1997); Lucy Dawidowicz (Ed.), *A Holocaust Reader* (West Orange, NJ: Behrman House, Inc., 1976); Martyn Housden, *Resistance and Conformity in the Third Reich* (London and New York: Routledge, 1997); Michael R. Marrus, *The Nuremberg War Crimes Trial 1945–46: A Documentary History* (Boston: Bedford Books, 1997); George Mosse *Nazi Culture: A Documentary History* (New York: Schocken Books, 1981); J. Noakes and G. Pridham, *Nazism 1919–1945: A Documentary Reader.* Three Volumes (Exeter, England: University of Exeter, 1983); and Joachim Remak (Ed.), *The Nazi Years: A Documentary History* (Prospect Heights, IL: Waveland Press, 1990). (Each of these works, as well as others, are included in the annotated bibliography that accompanies this chapter.)

Issues/Subjects Addressed in Primary Documents

The subject matter addressed in primary documents available for use in secondary classrooms is extremely eclectic. It is only possible to highlight a small number of the more instructive and significant issues that are addressed in such documents. (In this chapter, we address primary documents other than personal diaries, personal letters, and contemporaneous first-person accounts. For a discussion of the latter, see Chapter 5, "Incorporating First-Person Accounts into a Study of the Holocaust.")

To provide a sense of the vast array of topics addressed in primary documents on the Holocaust, we have chosen to cite various documents under the following headings: The Rise of the Nazi Party and Early Anti-Jewish Actions/Legislation; The Beginning of the Concentration of Jews into Large Ghettos through the Beginning of the Destruction of Such Ghettos, plus the Warsaw Ghetto Uprising; The Period of Extermination; Jewish Resistance; The United States' Reaction to Events in Nazi-Occupied Europe; and Investigations and Trials. By citing the documents in this way, the reader is provided with a ready-made list of a number of highly significant documents germane to key periods. Although many of these can be located online, the best single source is Yitzhak Arad, Yisrael Gutman, and Abraham Margaliot (Eds.), *Documents on the Holocaust* (1996) (see Box 4.1).

Following the aforementioned listing, we have included a more detailed discussion of those documents issued by churches and church people. Due to most people's unfamiliarity with the issues raised in these documents, we felt the focus of these documents merited a more detailed—and, thus, separate—discussion. The latter is also true due to the fact that many of the documents relating to the churches and church people are found in a variety of books other than those mentioned above.

BOX **4.1**

I. The Rise of the Nazi Party and Early Anti-Jewish Actions/Legislation

The Program of the National-Socialist (Nazi) German Workers' Party (February 24, 1920)

Various Extracts from *Mein Kampf* by Hitler

Organization of the Anti-Jewish Boycott of April 1, 1933—Instructions Given by the Nationalist Socialist Party

First Regulation for the Implementation of the Law for the Restoration of the Professional Civil Service (April 11, 1933)

Nuremberg Laws on Reich Citizenship (September 15, 1935)

Nuremberg Law for the Protection of German Blood and German Honor (September 15, 1935)

First Regulation to the Reich Citizenship Law (November 14, 1935)

Regulation Requiring Jews to Change Their Names (August 17, 1938)

Riots of Kristallnacht—Heydrich's Instructions (November 10, 1938)

Regulation for the Payment of an Expiation Fine by Jews Who Are German Subjects (November 12, 1938)

Extract from the Speech by Hitler (January 30, 1939)

II. The Beginning of the Concentration of Jews into Large Ghettos through the Beginning of the Destruction of Such Ghettos, Plus the Warsaw Ghetto Uprising

Instructions by Heydrich on Policy and Operations Concerning Jews in the Occupied Territories (September 21, 1939)

Establishment of Judenräte (Jewish Councils) in the Occupied Territories (November 28, 1939)

Extracts from Warsaw Ghetto of Chaim A. Kaplan (1940)

Extracts from the Warsaw Ghetto Diary of Avraham Levin (1942)

From the *Diary of Adam Czerniakow* on the Eve of the Deportation from the Warsaw Ghetto (July 22, 1942)

Rumkowski's Address at the Time of the Deportation of the Children from the Lodz Ghetto (September 4, 1942)

Himmler Orders the Destruction of the Warsaw Ghetto (February 16, 1943)

The Last Letter from Mordecai Anielewicz, Warsaw Ghetto Revolt Commander (April 23, 1943)

SS General Stroop on the Battles in the Warsaw Ghetto Revolt—Final Report from the German Battle Diary (April–May 1943)

III. The Period of Extermination

Göring Orders Heydrich to Prepare a Plan for the "Final Solution of the Jewish Problem" (July 31, 1941)

Exchange of Letters Between Reichskommissar Loshse and the Ministry for the Eastern Territories, Concerning the "Final Solution" (November 15, 1941)

(continued)

BOX **4.1**   Continued

Extract from a Report by Karl Jäger, Commander of Einsatzkommando 3, on the Extermination of Lithuanian Jews (December 1, 1941)

Protocol of the Wannsee Conference (January 20, 1942)

From a Report by Einsatzgruppen on the Extermination of the Jews in the Ukraine (October 1941)

Pohl Report on Garment Shipments from Lublin and Auschwitz (February 6, 1943)

Hitler's Testament: Berlin (April 29, 1945)

IV. Jewish Resistance

The Proclamation of the Vilna Ghetto Resistance Organization (January 1, 1942)

Call to Resistance by the Jewish Fighting Organization in the Warsaw Ghetto (January 1943)

The Discussion on Fighting Aims by the Activists of the Bialystok Members of the Dror Movement (February 27, 1943)

An Appeal—Bialystok Ghetto Resistance Organization (August 15, 1943)

Battle Orders of the FPO (Fareinikte Partizaner Organizatzie) (April 4, 1943)

The Last Letter from Mordecai Anielewicz, Warsaw Ghetto Revolt Commander (April 23, 1943)

The Manifesto of the Command of the Jewish United Partisans Organization, FPO, in the Vilna Ghetto (September 1, 1943)

For Your Freedom and Ours, Warsaw Ghetto (April 23, 1943)

Operations Diary of a Jewish Partisan Unit in Rudniki Forest (1943–1944)

"Leaflets of the White Rose—The First Leaflet, The Second Leaflet, The Third Leaflet, The

Fourth Leaflet, Leaflet of the Resistance, and the Last Leaflet" (in Inge Scholl, *The White Rose, Munich 1942–1943* [1983], pp. 73–93).

Note: Among the questions teachers may wish to raise with their students after they have examined documents related to resistance are: How would you define resistance, and why would you define it in that manner? Were there different types of resistance? If so, what were they? Give specific examples from the history to illustrate each type of resistance you note. Provide an explanation as to why each constitutes resistance. What arguments were used to call people to action in the various ghettos in the various ghettos mentioned? What mitigated against individuals answering such calls? Again, give specific examples from the history to support your points. What arguments were used to justify resistance, whether in Germany or the occupied countries? What were the obstacles to armed resistance in Germany? In the occupied countries? Give specific examples from the history to support your answers: How would you compare and contrast the resistance shown by Germans to the resistance shown by non-German victims?

V. The United States' Reaction to Events in Nazi-Occupied Europe

Decisions Taken at the Evian Conference on Jewish Refugee (July 1938)

Assistant Secretary of State Breckinridge: Long, Internal Memo Outlining Ways to Obstruct the Granting of U.S. Visas (June 26, 1940)

(continued)

BOX **4.1**   Continued

U.S. State Department "Do Not Send Documents" on the Riegner Telegram (August 8, 1942)

Rabbi Stephen Wise et al. Requests to U.S. State Department for Action on Rescue of European Jewry (September 1942)

Bermuda Conference Minutes (April 19–30, 1943)

Memorandum "For Secretary Morgenthau's Information Only" on The Deliberate Concealment of Facts for the Treasury Department by the State Department (December 23, 1943)

Secretary Morgenthau's Personal Report to President Roosevelt, John Pehle's Memo (January 1944)

Federal Register, Executive Order No. 9417, Creating the War Refugee Board (January 22, 1944)

War Department Memo Regarding Concern Over the Involvement in Rescue Operations (February 8, 1944)

Bombing Requests to the War Department by the War Refugee Board and Jewish Organizations (June to November 1944)

Aerial Photos of Bombing Buchenwald Munitions Factory: August 24, 1944, and Auschwtiz III-Buna Synthetic Fuels and IG Farben Plants (August 20 and September 13, 1944)

The New York Times: Sunday, October 29, 1944, Section I, Page 7, Columns 1–3, "Bombing Frees Doomed French Prisoners at Amiens, France" (February 18, 1944)

Evaluation Report of George C. McDonald, U.S. Strategic Airforces on Assessing the Polish Relief Supply Mission (October 14, 1944)

VI. Investigations and Trials

Transcripts of Interrogations of Oswald Pohl, Chief of SS Economic and Administrative Main Office, Concerning Concentration Camps and Profiteering from the Possession and Labor of Inmates (June 3–7, 1946)

Excerpts from the Judgment of the United States Military Tribunal Adjudicating the

"Medical Case" on Karl Brandt et al. (August 19, 1947)

Prosecution Brief Against Defendant Ernst Biberstein, Former Mobile killing Squad Commander and Protestant Minister (January 15, 1948)

Documents/Statements Issued by the Churches (Catholic, Protestant, Orthodox Christians) and Church People

The German bishops have long ago said Yes to the new state, and have not only promised to recognize its authority but are serving the state with burning love and all our strength

—Bishop Berning, September 21, 1933 (cited in Remak, 1990, p. 93)

> *In agreement with the judgment of all truly Christian people in Germany, I must state that we Christians feel this policy of destroying the Jews to be a grave wrong and one which will have fearful consequences for the German people. To kill without the necessity of war, and without legal judgment, contravenes God's commands even when it has been ordered by authority, and like every conscious violation of God's law, will be avenged, sooner or later*
>
> —Bishop Wurm to the Head of Hitler's Chancellery, December 20, 1943 (cited in Remak, 1990, p. 93)

Another rich source of documents about the Holocaust are those statements/documents issued by religious organizations and church people. As one might expect, statements were issued both by some who supported the Nazis and by those who protested the Nazis' philosophy and actions. It is significant to note that over the course of the Nazi reign (1933–1945), some church people altered their stance; for example, some initially supported the Nazi state but later questioned its actions, if not its legitimacy. And, in certain cases, some eventually went so far as to call for the Nazis' demise. As with most human endeavors, people's motivations and actions were driven by complex situations, all of which were in constant flux. Teachers need to help students understand that. Indeed, as the authors of the United States Holocaust Memorial Museum's *Guidelines for Teaching About the Holocaust* note: "Because of the complexity of the history, there is a temptation to overgeneralize and thus to distort the facts. . . . A study of the Holocaust raises difficult questions about human behavior, and it often involves complicated answers as to why events occurred [and why people acted the way they did]. Be wary of oversimplifications" (Parsons and Totten, 1993, p. 3). For these reasons, it is imperative that students be made aware of the full complexity of issues involving the stances, statements, and actions of religious organizations and church people during the Holocaust period. (Two short but solid overviews of the complexity of the situation regarding that of the churches and church people are provided in *Nazism 1919–1945: Volume 2, State, Economy and Society 1933–1939: A Documentary Reader*, edited by J. Noakes and G. Pridham. Exeter: University of Exeter, 1986, pp. 582–589, and "Christian Churches" by John S. Conway in Israel Gutman [Ed.], *Encyclopedia of the Holocaust* [1995]: pp. 291–295. New York: Macmillan Publishers.)

There are numerous pastoral statements available of church people's derogatory and insidious assertions about the Jews. Speaking of such statements, Irving Greenberg (1989), in his powerful and disturbing essay "Cloud of Smoke, Pillar of Fire," observed that

> There are literally hundreds of . . . anti-Semitic statements by individual people [and many of these are by Church people] reported in the Holocaust literature. As late as March 1941—admittedly still before the full destruction was unleashed—Archbishop Grober (Germany), in a pastoral letter, blamed the Jews for the death of Christ and added that "the self-imposed curse of the Jews, 'His blood be upon us and upon our children' had come true terribly, until the present time, until today." Similarly the Vatican responded to an inquiry from the Vichy government about the law of June 2, 1941, which isolated and deprived Jews of rights: "In principle, there is nothing in these measures which the Holy See would find to criticize." (p. 308)

In his essay "Christian Churches," Conway (1995) states that ". . . the prevalence of dogmatic Christian attitudes, coupled with xenophobia and heightened ethnocentricity, prevented the growth of . . . [a] positive stance toward Judaism and the Jews. Christian theology provided no adequate defense against the escalating violence and mass murders of the Holocaust" (p. 292). As Conway further notes: *Above all, the absence of any widespread public protest against the 'Final Solution' indicated the success of the Nazi attempt to invalidate the Jews as an object of concern for the German churches"* [italics added] (p. 294).

Also, as Greenberg (1989) observes, "Even some Christians who resisted Hitler failed on the Jewish Question. Even the great Christians—who recognized the danger of idolatry, and resisted the Nazi governments' takeover of the German Evangelical Church at great personal sacrifice and risk—did not speak out of the Jewish question" (p. 309). In this vein, Conway (1995) comments that despite their "refusal to accept the tenets of Nazi ideology or to abandon the Jewish scriptures as a source of revelation, leading figures [of the Confessing Church, a rival of the German Christian movement which supported the Nazi ideological campaign against the Jewish people], such as Martin Niemöller and Otto Dibelius, still maintained the traditional Lutheran antipathy to the Jews on theological and social grounds" (p. 294).

At one and the same time, students need to be made aware of the fact that some, *though miserably few,* church leaders did, in fact, speak out about in regard to the Nazis' actions. *Drawing attention to these documents/statements is not to minimize the collusion and silence of the vast majority of church leaders and Christians, but it will provide unique and important insights into this history and to highlight the fact that courageous and ethical behavior was practiced by some.*

Among the many documents available for use in the classroom vis-à-vis statements of protest against the Nazis' philosophy and their various actions are the following: the March 14, 1937 anti-Nazi encyclical of Pope Pius XI, *Mit Brennender sorge* ("With Burning Concern") (included in Peter Matheson's *The Third Reich and the Christian Churches* [1981]: pp. 67–70. Edinburgh, Scotland: T & T Clark, 1981); the July 1941 sermon delivered by Clemens Count von Galen, Bishop of Münster decrying the "imprisonment of fellow Germans in concentration camps" (cited in Joachim Remak's *The Nazi Years: A Documentary History* [1990]: p. 99); the August 1941 sermon by Clemens Count von Galen, Bishop of Münster, protesting the T-4 killings (cited in Michael Burleigh and Wolfgang Wipperman, *The Racial State: Germany, 1933–1945* [1991]; pp. 152–153); the August 1942 pastoral letter of Jules-Gerard Saliege, Archbishop of Toulouse, which became known as the "Saliege Bomb," demanding compassion for Jews and which had a profound impact on French public opinion (an excerpt is cited in Susan Zuccotti's *The Holocaust, The French, and the Jews*, p. 271. New York: Basic Books, 1993. Also see Paul Webster's *Petain's Crime: The Full Story of French Collaboration in the Holocaust.* Chicago, IL: Ivan R. Dee, 1991); Bishop Wurm's statement to the Head of Hitler's Chancellery, December 20, 1943 (cited in Joachim Remak, *The Nazi Years: A Documentary History*, p. 93); the October 1943 joint pastoral letter that was read in all Danish churches exhorting all Danes to aid Jews (cited, in part, in Leo Goldberger's *The Rescue of Danish Jews: Moral Courage Under Stress.* New York: New

York University Press, 1987, pp. 6–7); and various statements from the Dutch Catholic and Protestant Churches.

Among the questions teachers may wish to raise with their students in regard to these and related issues and documents are: Why were there so few public statements against the Nazis and/or on the behalf of the Jews by the Churches and church people? What impeded or encouraged the Churches—Catholic, Protestant, and Orthodox—to speak out or to remain silent? As for those church people who supported the Nazis, what were their various motivations? Is it the role of the churches and church people to protest unjust laws, the deprivation of civil and human rights, and the mass killing of innocent people? If so, why? If not, why not?

Valuable sources for statements and documents by church organizations and church people that supported or protested the Nazis are: *Third Reich and the Christian Churches,* ed. Peter Matheson (Edinburgh, Scotland: T & T Clark Limited, 1981); *The Nazi Years: A Documentary History,* edited by Joachim Remak (Prospect Heights, IL: Waveland Press, Inc. 1990); *For the Soul of the People: Protestant Protest Against Hitler,* by Victoria Barnett (New York: Oxford University Press, 1992); *Theologians Under Hitler,* by Robert P. Ericksen (New Haven, CT: Yale University Press, 1985); *The German Churches Under Hitler: Background Struggle and Epilogue,* by Ernst Christian Helmreich (Detroit, MI: Wayne State University Press, 1979); *The Church's Confession Under Hitler,* by Arthur C. Cochrane (Philadelphia, PA: Westminster Press, 1962); *The Nazi Persecution of the Churches, 1933–1945* by J. S. Conway (London: Weidenfeld & Nicolson, 1968); and "Cloud of Smoke, Pillar of Fire," by Irving Greenberg. In John K. Roth and Michael Berenbaum (Eds.) *Holocaust: Religious and Philosophical Implications,* pp. 305- 345 (New York: Paragon House, 1989).

General Pedagogical Strategies

There are innumerable strategies that teachers can use to help their students examine and use primary documents. What will be delineated here are some "generic" approaches that are ideal for use with virtually any primary or secondary document in the classroom; that is, strategies that encourage and enable students to carefully examine the unique nature of primary documents and the type of information they contain. Such approaches only constitute the first step in examining such documents. More crucially, such documents need to be placed in their historical context and need to be examined for their historical significance. Bereft of historical context, the study of the documents is sorely inadequate, if not pointless. Indeed, only by thoroughly preparing and then guiding students in their examination of such documents is it likely that students will begin to gain an adequate and accurate understanding of the focus and meaning of the documents.

What follows are *general guidelines that need to be considered prior to developing procedures for specific types of documents:*

- Documents should be chosen with care, taking into consideration the ability of the students in the class, the amount of time allocated for the examination of the documents, and the amount of background information required;

- Documents should be selected that are germane to the specific aspects of the history under study;
- Documents selected for study should be, in and of themselves, thought-provoking;
- Teachers need to help students to differentiate between different kinds of documents, both primary and secondary;
- Teachers should provide (or have students locate) pertinent background information on pertinent individuals, organizations, and places mentioned in the document(s). In other words, it is imperative to place the document(s) in a historical context. At one and the same time, the students should be encouraged and assisted in searching for key information about the documents;
- In written documents, there may be words and allusions to individuals, places, and events that students are not familiar with; thus, it will be incumbent on teachers to devise interesting and pedagogically sound ways to assist their students to gain an understanding of such items;
- At some point during the examination of a document, it is useful and important to assist students to locate the geographical location of the events being addressed or alluded to in a document. This is particularly crucial when studying a subject like the Holocaust, which impacted not only all of Europe but beyond (including the United States, Shanghai, Cuba, and various locations in Central and South America). On a map of the world of that period, colored pins or string can be used to highlight key locations and/or connections between places;
- Students need to be taught that when examining primary documents, it is essential to posit and tackle such questions as: "Who wrote the document? When was it written? Where was it written? Why was it written? For whom was it written? Are there any distinguishing marks on the document?" (West and Schamel, 1997, p. 110).
- Students need to be informed that at the outset of an examination of a primary document "educated guessing" is acceptable, but that eventually such guesses need to be supported with corroborating evidence;
- Teachers should begin with a single document or photo for the express purpose of assisting students to become good observers of detail. It is useful to begin with some or all of the following questions: "How do we know something is true?" "Can we always tell something is true by simply reading something or observing a photo?" "If not, what else is needed to assist us in making such a decision?" "What do you see?" "Is there anything particularly unique about the document? If so, what might its significance be?";
- In certain instances, teachers may wish to have their students brainstorm their initial responses to and/or posit questions they have about the document;
- It is imperative to obtain primary documents from reliable sources and with adequate citations;
- Teachers need to prepare students to appreciate the fact that the most useful sources for classroom use will include some of the following: footnotes,

archival abstracts, and dates. Each of these components are likely to assist one to place the document in historical context and/or to evaluate its authenticity;

- *Teachers need to avoid sending students on vague hunts on the Internet for documents on the Holocaust, for this can and often does lead them to Holocaust denial sites. The latter includes documents that sound and look official but are rife with lies, half-truths, and obfuscations.*

On a related note, students have a tendency to obtain documents from the Internet that provide few or no citations regarding the original source of the document or its creator. For these reasons, as well as others, students should be encouraged to use reliable online archives and resources such as those of the United States Holocaust Memorial Museum and Yad Vashem in Jerusalem. Such archives provide contextual information about each document.

A good rule of thumb is to also to encourage students to visit Web sites ending in edu, org, or gov. (That said, the Simon Wiesenthal Center is a good source to obtain materials, and its online site ends in com.)

Finally, teachers should consider designing a document analysis sheet, which is helpful to students as they first undertake the examination of primary documents. Such sheets should posit questions regarding the type of information, mentioned above, that is needed to assess the focus and value of a document.

Strategies for Examining
Reports, Directives, Petitions

After distributing copies of the document to each student, teachers can initiate an analysis by positing the following questions: (1) What type of document is this?; (2) What is the date of issue, if any, of the document?; (3) What information in the report places it in a particular time period?; (4) Who created the document? What is the evidence for that?; (5) Who was the audience for the document? What is the evidence for that?; and (6) What factual information is in the report? (Alexander and Beyers, 1979, p. 198).

Next, each student could be asked to respond to the following question in writing: What are the key facts/points in the document? How did you make that determination? Or, they could be asked to carefully read the report and then write a short response, paraphrasing it. Next, the students could be asked: What is the purpose of the report? Cite evidence to support your answer.

Still other questions that could be posited for the students to consider are: (1) What inferences, generalizations, and conclusions might be drawn from the report?; (2) What is the tone of the report? Is the tone important? Why or why not? (Alexander and Byers, 1979, p. 198); (3) What is not clear to you in the document?; and (4) "What else do you need to know about the document" in order to be clear as to its purpose and/or significance? (Schamel, 1996, p. 375). (Many of these same questions could be used to assist students to examine the content, style, tone, and significance of contemporaneous letters.)

Strategies for Examining Letters

At the outset of examining a letter, students could be asked to answer the following questions in writing as they examine their copies of the document: What type of document is this? Who created it? (How is he/she significant in regard to the history being studied?) (To whom is it addressed? How is he/she significant in regard to the history being studied?) What is its date? (What significant events were taking place at this time in regard to the history being studied?) (This is an excellent point to have the students refer to a historical timeline regarding the subject under study.) What is the tone of the letter? "Why was this document written? What evidence in the document helped you to know why it was written?" (Mueller and Schamel, 1990b, p. 366).

Other questions that could be asked are: Is the letter an official letter or a personal letter? How can you tell? "Are there any unique physical qualities of the document such as letterhead, seals, or other markings" (Mueller and Schamel, 1990b, p. 366); If so, what are some possibilities regarding the significance of such qualities? Does the author of the letter expect an answer? What is the evidence? What new information about the subject matter/historical period did you learn from this letter? Do you consider this new knowledge as being valuable in helping you to better understand the Holocaust? If so how so? If not, why not? Finally, Is there anything you do not understand in the document? If so, what?

In order to assist students to identify the main ideas in a letter, Mary Alexander and Marilyn Childress (1981) suggest the following activity: "Number each paragraph in the letter. Direct students to number their papers according to the number of paragraphs in the letter. Ask them to write next to each number a sentence that describes the main idea of each of the paragraphs" (p. 136). At the conclusion of this activity, the students can compare and contrast their answers and discuss their rationales regarding the latter.

Strategies for Examining Contemporaneous Political Cartoons

Political cartoons (as well as other types) often present a unique—frequently biting, satirical, wry—perspective on a topic, thus allowing its readers to gain a "new take" or perspective on a topic. Political cartoons created outside Nazi Germany are extremely interesting for students to examine and discuss. Early on, many political cartoonists were quite scathing in their depiction of Hitler and his cronies. Some were even prophetic, in that they suggested Hitler was leading the world and those he hated toward a disaster.

John Harper, Wynell Schamel, and Beth Haverkamp (1996) suggest the following as a way, if time allows, to prepare students to examine political cartoons: "Assist your students to define the following techniques: symbolism, ridicule, caricature, metaphor, satire, and puns" (p. 234). Ultimately, students should be asked to identify any of these conventions in the cartoons they examine.

They also suggest that teachers might wish to "invite an art teacher to join in a class discussion on the elements that make a cartoon effective" (Harper, Schamel and Haverkamp, 1996, p. 234). In doing so, the art teacher could provide examples of how the aforementioned conventions are conveyed in pictorial form.

Next, students could be asked to list the objects or people in the cartoon. Further, they should note whether any of the objects are symbols, metaphors, and if so, of what. Subsequently, the students should discuss what they perceive the symbols or metaphors to mean. Finally, the students should be asked to "describe the action taking place in the cartoon, and describe in their own words" the message of the cartoon (Harper, Schamel, and Haverkamp, 1996, p. 234).

Continuing, the students could respond, in writing, to the following question: "From whose point of view is the cartoon drawn? What evidence do you see of the cartoonist's viewpoint? [What is that viewpoint, and what evidence suggests such a viewpoint?] What traits make you feel sympathetic or unsympathetic to the cartoon's point of view?" (Harper, Schamel, and Haverkamp, 1996, p. 234).

Among the many other activities that teachers can use to engage their students in an examination of a political cartoon are the following: (1) Initially, without any prediscussion, have each student write a brief statement regarding the meaning of the cartoon. An alternative is to ask the students to provide a caption for the cartoon and to provide a written explanation as to how they arrived at such a caption (if the cartoon includes a caption, it should be hidden prior to the activity); (2) "With the class, list on the chalkboard all the images included in the cartoon" (Mueller and Schamel, 1990a, p. 20); (3) Ask the students if any of the images are symbols and what each means. Follow up by asking them "what emotions are conveyed by the symbols" (Mueller and Schamel, 1990a, p. 20); (4) "Assign each student or pair of students one of the topics/images" (more than one student or pair of students will have the same topic) and have them conduct a brief amount of research on the topic/image (Mueller and Schamel, 1990a, p. 20), collecting the most significant information they are able to on the topic, and follow that up with a class discussion; (5) Conclude, once again, by asking the student to provide a caption for the photo. Again, they should provide an explanation for their caption, noting in some detail what led them to such a caption. In small groups of three to four, the students should share their captions and their rationale for the latter; (6) A discussion should ensue as to the significance the cartoon has for the exact piece of history the students are studying (e.g., the early years of Hitler's rise to power, the imposition of the Nuremberg Laws, the 1936 Olympics in Berlin, Kristallnacht, the Anschluss, the beginning of World War II, the ghettoization or deportation of the Jews, etc.); and (7) Finally—this could precede, depending on the teacher's desire—the cartoonist's own caption should be shared with the students and discussed in some detail. Both the meaning of the caption and its significance vis-à-vis the history should be discussed.

Strategies for Examining Photographs

Teachers and students need to keep in mind that photographs can be mistaken for simple factual documents, when, in reality, they represent a specified photographer's point of view. Often a purpose can be extrapolated from a series of photographs that deal with the same topic or a related context when they are compared and contrasted with each other. Such a series should be studied, like written documents, in an evolving chronological order, so that their relationship may be ascertained.

Photographs, of course, can create an overly simplistic view of very complicated events. For example, numerous photographs from the Warsaw Ghetto include many children. Does this mean that children made up a large portion of the four hundred thousand-plus people in the ghetto? Does it mean the photographers were simply keen on taking pictures of children, or found the children's suffering most poignant? Or was such a situation due to the fact that most adults were at work during the daylight hours in order to earn rations to ward off starvation, and thus were not available to be photographed. The answer is probably somewhere in between (Campana, 1999).

It is also important to keep in mind that "Photography does more than reflect reality; it also interprets" (Levin and Uziel, 1999, p. 1). Because of this, using photographs requires extra care on the part of the teacher, with careful attention paid not only to what is in the photograph but also what is missing or has been removed by cropping. Consideration must be given to how the photograph came into existence, how it was preserved, and whether the photographer was a victim, perpetrator, or bystander.

It is not always noted (but should be) that the very presence of the photographer often disrupts and changes the scene. Furthermore, situations and images can be manipulated. As the camera is never free of bias, it is important to understand the interaction of photographers and events (Milton, 1986, p. 27). (For a fascinating and instructive discussion of such issues, see Milton [1986].)

In regard to examining photographs in the classroom, Beth Haverkamp and Wynell Schamel (1994) suggest that at the outset teachers do the following: "Distribute a copy of each photograph to your students. Ask the students to study each photograph for 2 minutes. Then ask them to create a chart listing the people, objects, and actions in the photograph" (p. 304).

Once the students have completed the initial task, teachers can posit various questions (all of which could be placed on a worksheet) that encourage the students to examine the photograph in more detail. Among such questions might be: (1) "What details in the photograph provide clues about what is happening?" (Alexander, 1979, p. 30); (2) Do any details in the photograph suggest a specific time period or date? If so, what are they?; (3) What time of year is it? Is that significant or not? Why?; (4) "Is there evidence in the photograph to place it in a particular location?" If so, what are they? (Alexander, 1979, p. 30); (5) What can you infer about the people in the photographs (Haverkamp and Schamel, 1994, p. 304); (6) What socioeconomic background do you think they represent? (Haverkamp and Schamel, 1994, p. 304); (7) What do the countenances of each individual suggest?; and (8) Do any of the objects in the photograph seem particularly significant or ominous? Explain your answer.

Mary Alexander (1983) also suggests that "It is useful to divide a photograph into quadrants and to look at each in turn, noting striking details" (p. 128).

A Specific Strategy

Highlighted here is an example of a lesson around a specific document on the Holocaust. Many of the generic strategies discussed above are used here in combination with additional strategies that establish the historical context of the document.

As previously mentioned, there are innumerable ways to design such a lesson. Some teachers may engage their students in conducting research, while others may establish the historical context by using films, guest speakers, the reading of key historical essays, or first-person accounts. There is no one correct way. *The key, though, is that teachers are thorough and accurate in their presentation of the history.*

For specific documents on specific aspects of the history, teachers need to develop questions germane to the focus of the document and the specific events, personages, and issues that the document addresses. In doing so, they should make an effort to assure that such questions span the various levels of Bloom's (or another's) Taxonomy (knowledge, comprehension, application, analysis, synthesis, evaluation) in order to assist students to probe as deeply as they are able into the significance of the document. The document, shown in Box 4.2, is entitled "Riots of Kristallnacht—Heydrich's Instructions, November 10, 1938."

Examination of Heydrich's Instructions Regarding Kristallnacht

1. Prior to examining this document students will have, at a minimum, studied about the Nazis' rise to power, including the Germany loss in World War I, the adverse impact of the Versailles Treaty on Germany, and the impact of the economic depression on Germany and elsewhere. Also, prior to examining the above document, the students will have read about Kristallnacht (in an essay entitled "Kristallnacht" by Leni Yahil [1990] in the *Encyclopedia of the Holocaust* and/or the section entitled "Night of the Broken Glass" [pp. 54–56] in Michael Berenbaum's *The World Must Know: The History of the Holocaust as Told in the United States Holocaust Memorial Museum* [1993]).

2. Provide each of the students with a copy of Heydrich's directive.

3. Have the students read the telegram and have them call out any names or terms they may *not* be familiar with (e.g., vom Rath, Gauleiter, Kreisleiter, Order Police, Reichsfuhrer SS, SD, Heydrich, SS Gruppenführer). Such terms should be listed on the board or sheets of butcher paper. Next, the class should arrive at an accurate definition of these terms. The latter can be accomplished in several different ways: Students familiar with the terms could define them. Conversely, the teacher could define them. Or, better yet, small groups of students could be assigned to immediately look up a small number of the terms in the Holocaust resources they have in class. After each group's report, the entire class could develop a chart with the correct definitions. This chart could be used as a reference guide during the examination of the document.

BOX **4.2** Riots in Kristallnacht—Heydrich's Instructions

Secret
Copy of Most Urgent Telegram from Munich of November 10, 1938, 1:20 a.m.

To

All Headquarters and Stations of the State Police

All Districts and Subdistricts of the SD

Urgent! For immediate attention of Chief or his deputy!

Re: Measures against Jews tonight

Following the attempt on the life of Secretary of the Legation vom Rath in Paris, demonstrations against the Jews are to be expected in all parts of the Reich in the course of the coming night 9/10, 1938. The instructions below are to be applied in dealing with these events:

1. The Chiefs of the State Police, or their deputies, must immediately, upon receipt of this telegram, contact, by telephone, the political leaders in their areas—Gauleiter or Kreisleiter—who have jurisdiction in their districts and arrange a joint meeting with the inspector or commander of the Order Police to discuss the arrangements for the demonstrations. At these discussions the political leaders will be informed that the German Police has received instructions, detailed below, from the Reichsfuhrer SS and the Chief of the German Police, with which the political leadership is requested to coordinate its own measures:

a) Only such measures are to be taken as do not endanger German lives or property (i.e. synagogues are to be burned down only where there is no danger of fire in the neighboring buildings).
b) Places of business and apartments belonging to Jews may be destroyed but not looted. The Police is instructed to supervise the observance of this order and to arrest looters.
c) In commercial streets particular care is to be taken that non-Jewish businesses are completely protected against damage.

d) Foreign citizens—even if they are Jews—are not to be molested.

2. On the assumption that the guidelines detailed under para. 1 are observed, the demonstrations are not to be prevented by the Police, which is only to supervise the observance of the guidelines.

3. On receipt of this telegram Police will seize all archives to be found in all synagogues and offices of the Jewish communities so as to prevent their destruction during the demonstrations. This refers only to material of historical value, not to contemporary tax records, etc. The archives are to be handed over to the locally responsible officers of the SD.

4. The control of the measures of the Security Police concerning the demonstrations against the Jews is vested in the organs of the State Police, unless inspectors of the Security Police have given their own instructions. Officials of the Criminal Police, members of the SD, of the Reserves and the SD in general may be used to carry out the measures taken by the Security Police.

5. As soon as the course of events during the night permits the release of the officials required, as many Jews in all districts—especially the rich—as can be accommodated in existing prisons are to be arrested. For the time being only healthy male Jews, who are not too old, are to be detained. After the detentions have been carried out the appropriate concentration camps are to be contacted immediately for the prompt accommodation of the Jews in the camps. Special care is to be taken that the Jews arrested in accordance with these instructions are not ill-treated.

signed Heydrich
SS Gruppenführer

From *Documents on the Holocaust: Selected Sources on the Destruction of the Jews of Germany and Austria, Poland, and the Soviet Union.* Ed. Yitzhak Arad, Israel Gutman, and Abraham Margaliot. Jerusalem: Yad Vashem, 1996.

4. Each student should read the directive, and, as they do so, they should note the following (in writing): (1) The date of the document; (2) The intended recipient(s) of the document; (3) The author of the document; (4) The type of document; (5) Words or phrases that seem particularly significant; (6) The main topic of the document; (7) Three of the most significant points made in the document, and why you deem them the most significant; and (8) Any questions you have about the document.

5. Once the students have completed the above assignment, conduct a brainstorming session in which the students address the following: What larger questions of German-Jewish relations does this document reveal? What is the evidence for that? How does it relate to the earlier documents on racial laws (e.g., the Nuremberg Laws)? Again, what is the evidence for that?

6. At this point, show the section of film in *Genocide* that focuses on Kristallnacht. A short discussion and question-and-answer period should follow this short but powerful clip. (*Genocide* is available from Arts and Entertainment Home Video, P.O. Box 2284, South Burlington, VT 05407.)

7. Return to the questions that the students answered in writing (4). Place the students in groups of three to four students and have them discuss each of their answers. Prior to having the students proceed with the discussion, ask a student in each group to volunteer (or assign one) to serve as a reporter who will write down the most salient points addressed in the group discussion. Emphasize that it is imperative that the groups engage in true discussion (versus a situation where each simply shares his/her answers). That is, a discussion/debate should center around the different perspectives that arise during the course of the small group work.

8. A whole class discussion should follow the small group discussion. This is the point where the teacher needs to act as a moderator as well as the "point person" for assisting the students to challenge one another, to debate one another, and to bring to bear their newfound knowledge of the Nazis' rise to power and their efforts to "define, isolate, exclude, segregate and impoverish German Jews" (Berenbaum, 1993, p. 22). It is also the point at which the teacher must play devil's advocate with regard to prodding the students to dig deeply and probe the information in the document under examination, to place it within its historical context, and to extract—to their best of their ability—the most significant aspects of the document.

Here, too, the teacher should expand on key points the students have made, and also raise new questions and add new points for the students to consider. Among the many issues/questions that teachers might posit are: What is the significance in the fact that this telegram was sent personally by Heydrich? What is the significance of the fact that the telegram was sent to *all headquarters and stations of the state police and to all districts and subdistricts of the SD*? Why is the telegram labeled urgent and what is the significance of that? Why is the measure aimed just at the Jews? What do you think the telegram was marked "secret"? What is the significance of that? Why do you think the recipients of the telegram were told to *telephone* (versus send a copy of the telegram or send a new telegram) to the political leaders in their areas—Gauleiter or Kreisleiter—to arrange a joint meeting with the inspector or commander of the Order Police to discuss the arrangements for the demonstrations? Whose property was to be protected? What is the significance of this? Why were foreign citizens, including Jews from other nations, not to be harassed or molested? What is the significance of this? What is the importance of the statement that "the demonstrations are not to be prevented by the Police"? Why do you think "especially the rich [male] Jews" and those who were not too old or unhealthy were targeted for arrest? How did this situation later change dramatically as the "Final Solution" was implemented?

9. Finally, as a concluding activity, have the students respond to the following questions in writing: (1) "What evidence is there that Kristallnacht was not, as the Nazis asserted, a spontaneous action by the citizenry at large?" and (2) "What impact do you think Kristallnacht had on the Jews who were still residing in Germany and the larger Reich?" Students should support their assertions with solid rationales.

Extension Activities

As a voluntary extension activity, students could:

1. Conduct research into the developing crisis as Jews tried to flee form Germany and the Reich in the post-Kristallnacht period.
2. Conduct research into how the governments and citizens in such countries as the United States and/or England, Holland, Denmark, France, Japan, and so on responded to Kristallnacht.
3. Conduct research into how the major newspapers in the United States and/or Great Britain covered Kristallnacht in their regular news and editorial pages.
4. Locate and analyze at least four to five first-person accounts by Jews that provide different perspectives (e.g., that of an elderly person, a young adult, a child, a man who was incarcerated, a woman whose husband was incarcerated, a rabbi) of what people experienced during Kristallnacht. In the analysis, delineate what each person experienced and what his/her experiences tell us about that devastating forty-eight-hour period.

Conclusion

Those teachers who wish to provide their students with unique and powerful insights into the history of the Holocaust as well as engage them in a fascinating instructional activity, seriously need to consider incorporating the use of primary documents into their lessons and units on the Holocaust.

The pursuit of historical knowledge is not frozen in the past but an ongoing process. When teachers and students struggle with primary documents, they begin to probe past motives, thoughts, and intentions of the authors of the documents. In doing so, preconceived ideas may be challenged. This can be unsettling but well worth the anxiety and the questions that may surface. Furthermore, by carefully selecting a document that complements one's study, one can avail students of information that is capable of illuminating complex or difficult to understand issues. The latter is bound to enhance their understanding and/or appreciation of the period. Teachers have the power in the classroom to open or close young minds. A "documents approach," it is hoped, will assist students to look at the history they are studying in new and powerful ways and, thus, open their minds to the complexity and significance of this history.

REFERENCES

Alexander, Mary. (1979, January). "Photograph of a Land Auction." *Social Education, 43*(1):30–31.

Alexander, Mary. (1983, February). "The Unfinished Lincoln Memorial." *Social Education 47*(2):126–128.

Alexander, Mary, & CeCe Beyers. (1979, March). "Document of the Month: Writing a Letter of Appeal." *Social Education 43*(3):198–199.

Alexander, Mary, & Marilyn Childress. (1981, February). "A Letter on Employment of Married Women." *Social Education 45*(2):134–136.

Arad, Yitzhak, Israel Gutman, & Abraham Margaliot, (Eds.). (1996). *Documents on the Holocaust: Selected Sources on the Destruction of the Jews of Germany and Austria, Poland, and the Soviet Union.* Jerusalem: Yad Vashem.

Berenbaum, Michael. (1993). *The World Must Know: The History of the Holocaust as Told in the United States Holocaust Memorial Museum.* Boston, MA: Little, Brown.

Campana, Andrew. (1999, August 2). Lecture on Photographs and the Holocaust at the Mandel Conference, United States Holocaust Memorial Museum.

Conway, John S. (1995). "Christian Churches." In Israel Gutman (Ed.), *Encyclopedia of the Holocaust* (pp. 291–295). New York: Macmillan.

Freeman, Elsie, T., Walter Bodle & Wynell Burroughs. (1984, November/December). "Eleanor Roosevelt Resigns from the DAR: A Study in Conscience." *Social Education 48*(7):536–541.

Greenberg, Irving. (1989). "Cloud of Smoke, Pillar of Fire." In John K. Roth & Michael Berenbaum (Eds.), *Holocaust: Religious and Philosophical Implications* (pp. 305–345). New York: Paragon House.

Harper, John, Wynell Schamel & Beth Haverkamp. (1996, April/May). "'The Alternative of Williamsburg': A British Cartoon on Colonial American Violence." *Social Education 60*(4):233–235.

Haverkamp, Beth, & Wynell Schamel. (1994, September). "Photographs of Ellis Island: The High Tide of Immigration." *Social Education 58*(5):303–307.

International Military Tribunal (1947–1949). "Document PS 1919" [Himmler Speech]. *Trial of the Major War Criminals.* Nuremberg: Author.

Levin, Daniel & Judith Uziel. (1999). "Ordinary Men, Extraordinary Photos." 18 pages. <www.yadvashem.org.il/holoca . . . erpts/studies/studies/levepri.html>.

Milton, Sybil. (1986). "Images of the Holocaust—Part I. *Holocaust and Genocide Studies 1*(1):27–61.

Mueller, Jean West, & Wynell Burroughs Schamel. (1990a, January). "A Cartoonist's View of the Eisenhower Years." *Social Education 54*(1):20–21.

Mueller, Jean West, & Wynell Burroughs Schamel. (1990b, October). "The First Amendment: The Finished Mystery Case and World War I." *Social Education 54*(6):366–368.

Parsons, William S., & Samuel Totten. (1993). *Guidelines for Teaching About the Holocaust.* Washington, DC: United States Holocaust Memorial Museum.

Remak, Joachim. (Ed.). (1990). *The Nazi Years: A Documentary History.* Prospect Heights, IL: Waveland Press.

Schamel, Wynell. (1996, October). "The 26th Amendment and Youth Voting Rights?" *Social Education 60*(6):374–375.

Schamel, Wynell, & Richard A. Blondo. (1994, February). "Correspondence Concerning Women and the Army Air Forces in World War II." *Social Education 58*(2): 104–107.

West, Jean M., & Wynell Schamel. (1997, February). "Robert E. Lee's Resignation from the U.S. Army." *Social Education 6*(12):108–111.

Yahil, Leni. (1990). "Kristallnacht." In Israel Gutman (Ed.) *Encyclopedia of the Holocaust* (pp. 836–840). New York: Macmillan.

DOCUMENTS: A SELECT ANNOTATED BIBLIOGRAPHY

Note: Readers should consult Chapter 5 for resources on documents such as personal letters and diaries written during the Holocaust period. They should also consult Chapter 11 for suggestions on how to assist students to examine posters, drawings, and so on, germane to the Holocaust.

Aly, Gotz. (1999). *Final Solution: Nazi Population Policy and the Murder of the European Jews.* New York: Arnold Publishers and Oxford University Press. 301 pp. Using extensive primary source documents, Aly delineates the close connection between the Nazis' view of the "new Order" in Europe and the extermination of the Jews.

Arad, Yitzhak (Ed.). (1990). *The Pictorial History of the Holocaust.* New York: Macmillan. An excellent source of photographs on the Holocaust. Among the topics addressed in the photos are: Nazism and its origins, persecution of Jews 1933–1939, European Jews under Nazi rule 1939–1941, the ghettos, mass murder, deportations, death camps, Jewish armed resistance, partisans, end of the war, and attempts to enter Israel. Using the number listed for the photographs in this volume, prints can be ordered online <www.yadvashem.org.il> from Yad Vashem.

Arad, Yitzhak, Yisrael Gutman, & Abraham Margaliot (Eds.). (1981). *Documents on the Holocaust: Selected Sources on the Destruction of the Jews of Germany and Austria, Poland, and the Soviet Union.* Jerusalem: Yad Vashem. 504 pp. A rich and extremely valuable selection of 213 primary source documents on the destruction of the Jews of Germany, Austria, Poland, and the Soviet Union.

It includes a massive number of documents produced by the Nazis, individual Jewish leaders and Jewish groups. Just a fraction of the many important documents included in this book are as follows: "Anti-Jewish Plans of the Nazis Published Before Their Rise to Power"; "Organization of the Anti-Jewish Boycott of April 1, 1933—Instructions Given by the Nationalist-Socialist Party"; "Law for the Restoration of the Professional Civil Service, April 7, 1933"; "Nuremberg Laws on Reich Citizenship, September 15, 1935"; "Nuremberg Law for the Protection of German Blood and German Honor, September 15, 1935"; "First Regulation to the Reich Citizenship Law, November 14, 1935"; "Extracts from Hitler's Speech in the Reichstag on the Nuremberg Laws, September 1935"; "Abolition of the Legal Status of the Jewish Communities, March 1938"; "Decisions Taken at the Evian Conference on Jewish Refugees, July 1938"; "Riots of Kristallnacht—Heydrich's Instructions, November 1938"; "Regulation for the Elimination of the Jews from the Economic Life of Germany, November 12, 1938"; "Deportation of Jews from Austria to Nisko (Lublin), October 1939"; "Eichmann Informs the Jews on Deportations from Austria and on the Theresienstadt Ghetto"; "Identifying Marks for Jews in the Government-

General, November 23, 1939"; "Bans on the Use of Railroads by Jews in the Government General, January 26, 1940"; "Establishment of the Judenräte (Jewish Councils) in the Occupied Territories, November 28, 1939"; "Himmler on the Treatment of Ethnic Groups and Jews in the East, in a Secret Memorandum to Hitler, May 25, 1940"; "The Madagascar Plan, July 1940"; "Official Definition of the Term 'Jew' in the Government-General, July 24, 1941"; "Göring Orders Heydrich to Prepare a Plan for the 'Final Solution' of the 'Jewish Problem,' July 31, 1941"; "Letters from the Jewish Underground Movement"; "Protocol of the Wannsee Conference, January 20, 1942"; "Order by Himmler on July 19, 1942, for the Completion of the 'Final Solution' in the Government-General"; "Proposal for the Sterilization of 2–3 Million Jewish Workers, June 23, 1942"; "Signed Obligation by SS Men Taking Part in an Extermination Operation to Observe Secrecy, July 18, 1942"; "Himmler Orders the Destruction of the Warsaw Ghetto, February 16, 1943"; and "Call to Resistance by the Jewish Fighting Organization in the Warsaw Ghetto, January 1943."

This book is a must for those educators who are serious about incorporating Holocaust documents into their lessons and units.

Arad, Yitzhak, Shmuel Krakowski, & Shmuel Spector (Eds.). (1989). *The Einsatzgruppen Reports: Selections from the Dispatches of the Nazi Death Squads' Campaign Against the Jews, July 1941–January 1943.* New York: Holocaust Library. This volume contains the chilling document record of the activities of the Nazis' mobile killing squads.

Berenbaum, Michael (Ed.). (1997). *Witness to the Holocaust: An Illustrated Documentary History of the Holocaust in the Words of Its Victims, Perpetrators and Bystanders.* New York: HarperCollins. 364 pp. Highly useful for the classroom, this volume includes documents related to the topics listed in the chapter titles: (1) The Boycott; (2) The First Regulatory Assault Against the Jews; (3) Early Efforts at Spiritual Resistance; (4) The Nuremberg Laws; (5) The Conference at Evian; (6) The November Pogroms—Kristallnacht and Its Aftermath; (7) The Beginning of Ghettoization; (8) The Judenrat; (9) A Mosaic of Victims: Non-Jewish Victims of Nazism; (10) The Einsatzgruppen; (11) Babi Yar; (12) The Call to Arms; (13) Hitler's Plan to Exterminate the Jews; (14) The Killers: A Speech, A Memoir, and an Interview; (15) Choiceless Choices; (16) The End of a Ghetto: Deportation from Warsaw; (17) The Warsaw Ghetto Uprising; (18) What Was Known in the West; (19) Why Auschwitz Was Not Bombed; (20) Liberation and Its Aftermath; and (21) The Nuremberg Trials.

Botwinick, Rita Steinhardt. (1998). *A Holocaust Reader: From Ideology to Annihilation.* Upper Saddle River, NJ: Prentice Hall. 207 pp. This book includes several key documents on the Holocaust, including but not limited to: "Speech of the German Delegation" by Count Ulrich von Brockdorff-Rantzau, Versailles, May 7, 1919; "Wear It With Pride, the Yellow Badge" by Robert Weltsch, April 4, 1933; "Organization of the Anti-Jewish Boycott of April 1, 1933—Instructions Given by the National-Socialist Party"; "Nuremberg Laws on Reich Citizenship September 15, 1935"; "Nuremberg Law for the Protection of German Blood and German Honor, September 15, 1935; "Establishment of Judenräte (Jewish Councils) in the Occupied Territories, November 28, 1939"; "Report by Uebelhoer on the Establishment of the Ghetto in Lodz, December 10, 1939"; "Rumkowski's Address at the Time of the Deportation of the Children from the Lodz Ghetto, September 4, 1942"; "Notes by a Jewish Observer in the Lodz Ghetto following the Deportation of the Children"; "Call to Resistance by the Jewish Fighting Organization in the Warsaw Ghetto, January 1943"; and

"Protocol of the Wannsee Conference, January 20, 1942." Many of these 1981 documents are from Yitzhak Arad, Israel Gutman, and Abraham Margaliot (Eds), *Documents on the Holocaust: Selected Sources on the Destruction of the Jews of Germany and Austria, Poland, and the Soviet Union.*

Dawidowicz, Lucy (Ed.). (1976). *A Holocaust Reader.* West Orange, NJ: Behrman House. 397 pp. A collection of documents about various facets of the Holocaust, this book is comprised of the following parts and chapters: Part I. The Final Solution: 1. Preconditions: Conventional Anti-Semitism and Adolf Hitler; 2. The First Stage: Anti-Jewish Legislation; 3. The Interim Stage: "All Necessary Preparations"; 4. The Final Stage: Mass Killings, "Resettlement," Death Camps; Part II. The Holocaust: 5. The First Ordeal: The Jews in Germany 1933–1938; 6. The Ordeals of the Ghettos in Eastern Europe; 7. The Ordeals of the Judenräte; 8. Confronting Death: The Ordeals of Deportation; and 9. Resistance: The Ordeal of Desperation.

Gutman, Israel. (1994). *Resistance: The Warsaw Ghetto Uprising.* Boston, MA: Houghton Mifflin Company. Includes excerpts from key documents (manifestos and proclamations from the resistance, scripts from contemporary radio broadcasts, articles from underground papers, and reports by the Nazis) issued by various individuals and organizations about various facets of the resistance.

Housden, Martyn. (1997). *Resistance and Conformity in the Third Reich.* London and New York: Routledge. 199 pp. This book, which was designed for use with students, examines the complex relationship between ordinary Germans and the Nazi government. It includes key primary sources, including but not limited to: first-person accounts by survivors, former kapos, former Hitler Youth members, a member of the Luftwaffe, a Nazi bureaucrat; leaflets by resistance members; statements and speeches by various Nazis; sections of a report by Reinhard Heydrich; police reports and summaries of interrogation sessions; declarations by opponents of the Nazis; and copies of school curricula designed and implemented by the National Socialists. In the preface, it is stated that "[A] distinctive feature of [this series] is the manner in which the content, style and significance of documents is analyzed. The commentary and the source are not discrete, but rather merge to become part of a continuous and integrated narrative."

Kovner, Abba. (1981). "A First Attempt to Tell." In Yehuda Bauer and Nathan Rotenstreich (Eds.), *The Holocaust as Historical Experience: Essays and a Discussion* (pp. 77–93). New York: Holmes & Meier. This memoir by Abba Kovner, who was a leader of the resistance of the Vilna Ghetto, includes the powerful and vivid manifesto issued by the Jewish Resistance Fighters of the Vilna Ghetto.

Marrus, Michael R. (1997). *The Nuremberg War Crimes Trial 1945–46: A Documentary History.* Boston: Bedford Books. 276 pp. A superb collection of over seventy primary documents about various facets of the Nuremberg Trials. The book is divided into nine chapters and a set of appendices: (1) Historical Precedents; (2) Background; (3) Preparations; (4) The Court; (5) Crimes Against Peace; (6) War Crimes; (7) Crimes Against Humanity; (8) Last Words; and (9) Assessment. The appendices include: Chronology of Events Related to the Nuremberg Trial (1919–1946), The Defendants and Their Fate; Charges, Verdicts, and Sentences; and Selected Bibliography. Among the documents are such pieces as "Winston S. Churchill, Franklin D. Roosevelt, and Joseph Stalin, Moscow Declaration, November 1, 1943"; "Robert H.

Jackson, Opening Address for the United States, November 21, 1945"; "Robert Jackson, Cross-Examination of Hermann Goring, March 18, 1946"; "Marie Claude Vaillant-Couturier, Testimony on the Gassing at Auschwitz, January 28, 1946"; "Robert H. Jackson, Cross-Examination of Albert Speer, June 21, 1946"; and "Rudolf Höss, Testimony on Auschwitz, April 15, 1946."

Mendelsohn, John (Ed.). (1982). *The Holocaust: Planning and Preparation: The Killing of the Jews, Rescue Attempts and Punishment.* New York: Garland. This eighteen-volume collection contains a treasure trove of valuable and significant documents on key aspects of the Holocaust. The volumes are divided as follows: Volumes 1–7, Planning and Deportation; Volumes 8–13, The Killing of the Jews; Volumes 14–16, Rescue Attempts; and Volumes 17–18, Punishment and Trials of the Perpetrators.

Milton, Sybil (Trans. and Ann.). (1979). *The Stroop Report.* New York: Pantheon Books. n.p. *The Stroop Report* is the SS leader Juergen Stroop's actual record of the battle against the Jews during the Warsaw Ghetto Uprising. It includes his summary record and daily reports of German actions, as well as over fifty photographs taken by the Germans forces at the time.

Mosse, George. (1981). *Nazi Culture: A Documentary History.* New York: Schocken Books. 386 pp. This anthology of original source material includes pieces taken from contemporary literature, diaries, newspapers, and speeches. Mosse, a noted scholar of the Holocaust, provides useful introductions to each section and selection.

Noakes, J., & G. Pridham. (1983, 1986, 1987, respectively). *Nazism 1919–1945: A Documentary Reader.* Three Volumes. Exeter, England: University of Exeter. The three volumes of this set (Volume 1: "The Rise to Power, 1919–1934"; Volume 2: "State, Economy and Society, 1933–1939," and Volume 3: "Foreign Policy, War and Racial Extermination") contain a collection of documents on Nazism. All of the volumes "contain material from a wide range of sources both published and unpublished: State and Party Documents, newspapers, speeches, memoirs, letters, and diaries."

Office of the U.S. Chief Counsel for the Prosecution of Axis Criminality. (1946, 1947–1948). *Nazi Conspiracy and Aggression.* 10 volumes. Washington, DC: U.S. Government Printing Office.

Remak, Joachim (Ed.). (1990). *The Nazi Years: A Documentary History.* Prospect Heights, IL: Waveland Press. 178 pp. The editor reports that in this book the ideology of and practices of National Socialism "are described by way of documents nearly all of which were written by the actors, victims, or simple witnesses of the time and at the time." Remak goes on to assert that the point of this book is "to tell the whole essential story of National Socialism, from its obscure ideological beginnings to its seizure of power; to show the uses to which the power was put, at home and abroad, until the bitter end of the Third Reich" (p. vii). The eleven chapters in the book are: The Roots, The Soil, The Program, Power, The Attractions, Propaganda, The Churches, War, Eugenics, The Jews, and Resistance.

Scholl, Inge. (1983). *The White Rose, Munich 1942–1943.* Middletown, CT: Wesleyan University Press. Includes original documents relating to the White Rose Movement, including the six protest leaflets issued by the young group members, the Nazis' indictment of the group members, transcripts of the sentence received by the group members, and moving testaments about their actions and fate.

Trial of Major War Criminals Before the International Military Tribunal. Forty-two volumes. Washington, DC: U.S. Government Printing Office. This set includes the testimony and cross-examination of the major Nazi war criminals tried by the Allies following the conclusion of World War II.

Wolfe, Robert. (1993). *Holocaust: The Documentary Evidence.* Washington, DC: National Archives and Records Administration. 37 pp. This pamphlet includes an introduction that highlights key aspects of the Nazis' ideology and exterminatory policies, as well as a set of "facsimiles" of key Nazi documents dealing with various aspects of the Holocaust years, including: a report by Reinhard Heydrich, Chief of Security Police, to Hermann Göring about the destruction that took place during Kristallnacht; a telegram from Reinhard Heydrich to chiefs of all operation commands of the Security Police regarding the "concentration of Jews from the countryside into the larger cites"; an invoice regarding the shipment of 390 canisters of Zyklon B cyanide gas to be used for "disinfection and extermination" at Auschwitz; a "Statistical Report Regarding the Final Solution of the Jewish Question in Europe"; and a speech by Heinrich Himmler on October 4, 1943. Unfortunately, none of the documents are translated in their entirety. Furthermore, most of the documents are poorly copied and thus difficult to read. Still, this is a valuable booklet for teachers and students, for it includes key documents that illuminate key aspects of the history.

Pedagogical Resources

Alexander, Mary. (1983, October). "Man of the Hour . . . A Comparison of Leadership." *Social Education, 47*(6):435–438. This article and teaching activity compares and contrasts the first one hundred days of President Franklin Delano Roosevelt's leadership with that of Adolf Hitler's first one hundred days of leadership, for the purpose of "ascertaining how each sought to handle the severe economic political distress in his nation" (p. 435). The document highlighted in this teaching activity is a telegram from U.S. Ambassador Frederic M. Sackett to Secretary of State Cordell Hull reporting on Hitler's actions to consolidate his power on March 23, 1933. In addition to providing the historical context regarding the message of the telegram, Alexander—an education specialist at the U.S. National Archives—also includes two timelines that compare major events in the United States and Germany in 1933. The document is from the U.S. National Archives.

Blondo, Richard A., & Wynell Burroughs Schamel. (1993, April/May). "Correspondence Urging Bombing of Auschwitz During World War II." *Social Education* 57(4):150–155. In their article, the authors state that: "In 1944, John W. Pehle, Executive Director of the U.S. War Refugee Board, sent a forceful appeal to Assistant Secretary of War John J. McCloy urging the bombing of railroads and buildings in the Auschwitz-Birkenau complex. McCloy's response presented the arguments for the War Department's decision not to bomb the camps. That correspondence is featured in this article" (p. 150). After setting the historical context, the authors provide a series of teaching suggestions.

Burroughs, Wynell, & Jean Mueller. (1985, September). "A Letter of Appeal on Behalf of Raoul Wallenberg." *Social Education* 49(6):539–543. The document highlighted in this article is a letter by Guy von Dardel to Harry Truman, in which he urges the president to do all he possibly can to convince the Soviet government to divulge the whereabouts of Raoul Wallenberg, a Swedish national who saved tens of thousands of Hungarian Jews from extermination at the hands of the Nazis. von Dardel, Wallenberg's half-brother, notes in the letter that Wallenberg had gone to "Hungary in July, 1944 as the representative of President Roosevelt's War Refugee Board and has been missing since the Soviet Foreign Office early in 1946 declared him to be under Russian protection" (p. 540). In addition to the aforementioned letter, the authors provide a historical context for the letter, as well as numerous teaching activities.

Kalfus, Richard. (1990, February). "Euphemisms of Death: Interpreting a Primary Source Document on the Holocaust." *The History Teacher* 23(2):87–93. This is a fascinating essay about a highly engaging method to assist students to begin to understand "the all-pervasive, destructive force that was National Socialism." More specifically, the author states that "the insidious, administrative language used here [in the document that addresses the exact specifications desired for gas vans to be used for the mass murder of groups of Jews] is a concrete, dramatic example of how an entire caste of civil servants could become active participants in the extermination process."

Medoff, Rafael. (1996). "Teaching About International Responses to News of the Holocaust: *The Columbus Dispatch* Project at Ohio State University." In Rochelle L. Millen, et al. (Eds.), *New Perspectives on the Holocaust: A Guide for Teachers and Scholars* (pp. 166–173). New York: New York University Press. Medoff discusses an interesting and thought-provoking assignment that involves students in a team research project that examines how their local daily newspaper covered a number of major events related to the Holocaust.

National Archives. (1993). *Holocaust: The Documentary Evidence.* (Available from the National Archive Trust Fund, NEDC, P.O. Box 100793, Atlanta, GA 30384; 1-800-788-6282). "In all, 21 original documents—including German-language texts, transcripts, and photographs—have been reproduced along with brief captions that explain the significance of each. The package has been designed to enable schools, libraries, historical societies and other groups to adapt the material to their own audiences and educational goals." The posters, which are printed on heavy paper, measure 22 x 28 inches.

Schamel, Wynell, & Beth Haverkamp. (1995, October). "Nazi Medical Experiment Report: Evidence from the Nuremberg Medical Trial." *Social Education* 59(6):367–373. This teaching activity features a document regarding a medical experiment that Dr. Joachim Mrugowsky, the Designated Reich-Surgeon of the SS and Police, and the Nazi government's "Supreme Hygienist," authorized. The document highlighted here is part of the collection at the United States National Archives.

Totten, Samuel. (1998). "Incorporating Contemporaneous Newspaper Articles About the Holocaust into a Study of the Holocaust." In Robert Hauptman and Susan Hubbs Motin (Eds.), *The Holocaust: Memories, Research, Reference* (pp. 59–81). New York: The Haworth Press. Totten discusses the purpose of using contemporaneous newspaper accounts of various aspects of the Holocaust in the secondary classroom, and highlights methods for doing so.

United States Holocaust Memorial Museum. (1993). *Artifact Poster Set.* Washington, DC: Author. The artifacts highlighted in this poster series are from among the hundreds of artifacts in the United States Holocaust Memorial Museum's Permanent Exhibit.

As the authors of the accompanying *Teacher's Guide* note, the poster set and teacher guide introduce representative aspects of Holocaust history but are not intended as a comprehensive narrative of the Holocaust. Among the topics addressed in individual posters are: "Lost Childhoods," "Ideology of Racial Hygiene," "Locating the Victims: Hollerith Machine," "Isolating the Victims: Stars, Triangles, and Markings," "Spiritual Resistance: Theresienstadt Butterfly Toy," "Deportation and Abandonment: Auschwitz Suitcases," "Rescue: The Danish Boat," "Resistance," and "Loss of Identity: Auschwitz Shoes." Some of the posters include primary documents. A *Teacher's Guide* accompanies the poster set. (The Poster Set can be ordered from the USHMM Shop at Box 92420, Washington, DC 20090.)

Adjunct Information/Services

Bradsher, Greg. (1999). *Holocaust-Era Assets: A Finding Aid to Records at the National Archives at College Park, Maryland.* College Park, MD: National Archives and Records Administration. General inquiries can be sent to: <inquire@arch2.nara.gov> or, for information on particular record groups, call 1-301-713-6800.

Note: Document finder services and photo/microfilm reproductions are available through private agencies, which the National Archives can recommend to the researcher. For example, a large portion of the *Nuremberg War Crimes Trials: Interrogations, 1946–1949* is on microfilm. Scholarly Resources at 104 Greenhill Avenue, Wilmington, Delaware 19805 reproduce these records at a reasonable cost (call 1-800-772-8937).

5 Incorporating First-Person Accounts into a Study of the Holocaust

SAMUEL TOTTEN

The stories finally told by the survivors made others comprehend what could and did happen to communities that were besieged, isolated and destroyed. The stories describe the ghetto, the effect of prolonged starvation, the illusion that all would pass, the Nazi deceptions, the close family ties that weakened the wish to resist, and the belief that here it would not happen, together with, finally, the awareness that gripped the victims when it was too late, when the unbelievable had come about.

—Gouri, 1994, p. 156

Without understanding the private, the human and the individual cost of this tragedy, the significance of the Shoah history cannot be grasped. As much as objective interpretations may succeed in providing us with analytical insights into the barbarism of Nazi politics, they cannot convey the subjective and emotional dimension.

—Lixl-Purcell, 1994, p. 237

As an ever-increasing number of teachers at various levels develop and implement teaching units on the Holocaust, a primary resource worthy of serious consideration is that of first-person accounts by the survivors of the Holocaust, rescuers, the liberators of the concentration and death camps, and other eyewitnesses. As Holocaust survivor and eminent historian Philip Friedman has noted, by using oral testimony, Holocaust history can be written "from the inside." Indeed, the experiences reported in first-person accounts is a history that was "lived," not something that was read about in a book or related to the eyewitnesses by someone else.

As William Parsons and Samuel Totten (1993) have noted: "In any study of the Holocaust, the sheer number of victims challenges easy comprehension. Teachers need to show that individual people are behind the statistics, comprised of families of grandparents, parents and children. First-person accounts and memoir literature provide students with a way of making meaning out of collective numbers" (p. 6).

First and foremost, they serve as testimony to what happened to the individual person and his/her family members, friends, and community during the genocidal assault of the Nazis.

In this chapter—which examines the educational value of utilizing first-person accounts to convey the significance and magnitude of the Holocaust to students—the term "first-person accounts" refers to any written, oral, or videotaped account by survivors and other individuals (with the exception of perpetrators) who witnessed any aspect of the Holocaust. Such accounts take the form of letters, diaries, interviews, testimony at trials and other official and unofficial hearings; memoirs, autobiographies, and oral histories; and statements (of any length) in texts, journals, and other periodicals.

The issues and topics that will be examined herein are the following: the general value of first-person accounts; the educational value of first-person accounts by Holocaust survivors and others; the unique aspects of videotaped accounts and the distinction between written and video accounts; limitations of first-person accounts; issues and concerns to consider when using first-person accounts in classrooms; educational uses of first-person accounts; and methods for incorporating first-person accounts in the classroom.

The General Value of First-Person Accounts

Henry Friedlander (1991) has convincingly argued that contemporaneous documents—both government records and private agency records—or "the written record created at the time the crimes were committed—are the most valuable sources" (p. 91) vis-à-vis first-person accounts. As for the availability of such records and testimony, Friedlander (1991) noted that

> These documents, however, are dispersed in widely scattered archives. . . . Usually only brief excerpts from such documents are used in the classroom, and these obviously fail to convey the immediacy of those events. Better collections, however, are available. The published Nuremberg trial proceedings, available in many libraries, reprinted numerous documents. Recently newer methods of publishing facsimiles of documents have made it possible to present to students authentic documents in their original forms. Garland Publishing has produced *Archives of the Holocaust,* a multi-volume series of such facsimile documents from archives around the world. (p. 91)

Noting the importance of eyewitness accounts as a source for the study of genocide, Friedlander (1991) asserts, "Obviously, the most valuable of these are diaries, notes, and letters composed at the time. Such personal observations as contemporaneous records are unquestionably authentic and thus extraordinarily valuable. . . . Contemporaneous documents possess an authenticity lacking in documents generated after the events they describe" (p. 91). As he points out, however:

The majority of eyewitness accounts were composed after the end of the war. It is obvious that those written almost immediately after the war were more authentic and accurate than those composed many years later. Those composed immediately presented the undiluted memory of recent experience, whereas those produced much later have often only reflected popular views of the experience. Although such later accounts are often engrossing stories, they are the least reliable source for an accurate history of the events. . . . There is, however, one exception to this generalization about eyewitness accounts. This exception involves those accounts that form a part of judicial proceedings. Eyewitness testimonies have been used in all trials of Nazi crimes, starting at Nuremberg and continuing with the . . . American proceedings. Thousands of such testimonies can be found in the trial records. Their value cannot be overestimated. They focus on specific persons and events observed by the witness, and they were tested through cross examination and corroborating evidence. Unlike eyewitness accounts elicited by enthusiastic amateurs with a video camera, trial testimonies obtained by prosecutors during discovery and presented thereafter in open court possess the authenticity and accuracy that make them an important source for the study of genocide." (p. 91)[1]

The clear and significant message here is that teachers need to make a real effort to obtain such documents for use with their students. Fortunately, as scholars and others continue to edit volumes about the Holocaust that contain excerpts from diaries, notes, and letters composed during the Holocaust period, it is becoming much easier for teachers to locate such pieces.[2]

Friedlander is right to warn that not all such material on the Holocaust is of equal merit. Other scholars, archivists, and educators also have stressed that first-person accounts used in the classroom (written, audio, and video) should be rigorously *prepared and verified* for use in the classroom (Johnson, 1989, pp. 288–290; Langer, 1989b, pp. 291–297; Langer, 1989a, pp. 310–316; Langer, 1991; Levin, 1989, pp. 278–284; Totten, 1991a, pp. 321–335). (This issue will be discussed in more detail under the section entitled "Limitations of First-Person Accounts.") Effective skill in analyzing and interpreting survivor testimony thus becomes an additional requisite for the educator. What this means, in part, is having a solid command of the subject matter and "being properly trained to analyze and interpret survivor testimony" (Johnson, 1989, p. 291).

First-person accounts provide a means to penetrate deeper into the dark depths of the Holocaust. Indeed, it seems that the testimony of survivors comes as close as anything possibly can to assisting the rest of humanity in what Holocaust scholar Harry Cargas (1981) has referred to as "understanding the ununderstandable" (p. 203) (Totten, 1991a, p. 322). As Yehuda Bauer (1975), a noted Holocaust historian, also has observed, "These [eye-witness] accounts contain information not to be found in an official document. They recount entire chapters of Jewish internal history under the Nazi occupation (how people lived, their cultural life . . .)" (p. 27).

Brana Gurewitsch (1989), formerly a librarian and archivist at the Center for Holocaust Studies in Brooklyn, New York, basically corroborates the latter point:

The military, civil, and economic records of the period are indeed of primary importance, and no serious historical inquiry will proceed without them. However, these records, produced with specific political and ideological goals, leave gaps which can now be filled only by oral history. The Nazi ideology of the Jew as *Untermensch* [subhuman] does not portray Jews reacting and responding to the events which overtook them. Indeed, the Nazi-Deutsche language of euphemism and subterfuge was deliberately designed to disguise what was really happening, rather than to record events objectively for the future. . . . [I]t is clear that while Nazi records may be useful, they fail to completely describe what was happening. . . . Similarly, because concentration camps were not military objectives, the records of their liberation are extremely scanty in American military reports, where they appear at all. (p. 285)

On another note, the very act of relating one's story in whatever form (e.g., in a diary, a memoir, an oral history, or on videotape) constitutes a "counterstory" to the Nazi degradation, brutality, and genocidal fury that they perpetrated.

And as scholar Geoffrey Hartman (1996b) notes: "Survivor testimonies can be a source for historical information or confirmation, yet their real strength lies in recording the psychological and emotional milieu of the struggle for survival, not only then but also now" (p. 142).

Whereas accounts by other witnesses (e.g., foreign diplomats, journalists, relief workers, liberators) are in an altogether different class from those of the survivors, they are exceptionally valuable as well. Not only do they provide another perspective; they also provide additional evidence about various facets of the Holocaust.

Educational Value of First-Person Accounts by Holocaust Survivors and Others

Experience by this author as well as others indicates that first-person accounts are an effective and powerful tool in teaching the Holocaust to students. More specifically, "by supplementing the study of the Holocaust with such accounts, it moves the study from what is often a welter of statistics, remote places and events, to one that is immersed in the 'particular'" (Totten, 1987, p. 63). At the very least, the use of first-person accounts by a teacher with his/her students "places" a human face on the facts and events that led up to and culminated in genocide.

Many accounts contain powerful images, observations, and thoughts that one cannot shake loose from one's mind. For example, who could ever forget Elie Wiesel's (1969) description of his arrival at Auschwitz:

Not far from us, flames were leaping up from a ditch, gigantic flames. They were burning something. A lorry drew up at the pit and delivered its load—little children. Babies! Yes, I saw it—saw it with my own eyes . . . those children in the flames. (p. 42)

This passage about the "coal miners" in the Lodz Ghetto by Leon Hurwitz (1989) creates an indelible image of a different sort:

> There are no coal mines in the ghetto. But there are coal miners. . . . In the east, the ghetto is enclosed by desolate plots where the city's garbage was dumped before the war. . . . These unfriendly fields, which for years had seen only garbage haulers . . . are suddenly alive with crowds of people. Hundreds of adults and even more children sit there from dawn to dusk and dig into the ground, or rather the waste, using bent iron hooks, small spades and other primitive tools. From a distance you can see only their backs, bent and crooked.
>
> What are they looking for? They are coal mining, and their labor constitutes yet another "branch of industry" in the ghetto. . . . They dig in the garbage so that they can buy their soup, their ration card.
>
> Where did this coal come from? Well, there were normal times before the war, when households kept reserves of coal for the winter. The maids in the better-off homes used to throw the small pieces of coal and the coal dust out with the garbage, which traveled to the dumping fields and accumulated over many years. (pp. 132–133)

These are just two prime examples of the thousands upon thousands of images that students will confront when reading first-person accounts by victims and survivors of the Holocaust.

The power of the individual human story within a persecutive or genocidal situation may thus engage students in a way no other type of information can, in part because of the deeply human aspects—including the passions and emotions—that are communicated. Such accounts are also capable of providing the student with information, insights, and feelings that no textbook can, and that is because the eyewitnesses have lived the experience and/or observed events up close. The stories, then, help the student to gain a unique and fresh perspective on past events, helping them move from solely a cognitive approach to one imbued with an affective component (e.g., feelings, emotions, and values). In certain cases, such stories are capable of gripping the reader in a way that causes him/her to reflect on events with different eyes, sometimes even from a new and even radically different perspective. Ultimately, students are enabled to see the Holocaust ". . . as a human drama [that they] can [possibly begin] to understand" (Bauman, 1992, p. 21).

As Robert Coles (1989), the noted psychiatrist and author, has written: "Stories . . . have a way of working themselves deep within the thinking of many students" (p. 144). Coles further notes: "The whole point of stories is not 'solutions' or 'resolutions' but a broadening and even a heightening of our struggles—with new protagonists and antagonists introduced, with new sources of concern or apprehension or hope, as one's mental life accommodates itself to a series of arrivals: guests who have a way of staying, but not necessarily staying put" (p. 129).

There is, however, a wider purpose to incorporating first-person accounts into a study of the Holocaust. By engaging students on a more personal level, there is the added benefit that students may begin experience the "awakening of [a] moral sensibility" (Coles, 1989, p. 151). In this regard, the study of the Holocaust may actually help students and others to plumb issues of fairness, prejudice, discrimination, antisemitism, racism, injustice, stereotyping, intolerance, and totalitarianism, not merely in history but also in the contemporary world.

Videotaped Accounts

A unique Holocaust video project that has been underway for several years is Facing History and Ourselves' "Elements of Time" project. Using the videotaped interviews of Holocaust survivors conducted by the Fortunoff Video Archive at Yale University, Facing History has developed what it calls video portraits and video montages.

Speaking of the video project (Survivors Film Project) that preceded and eventually became the Yale Fortunoff Video Archive, Geoffrey Hartman (1996b), cofounder of the archive and a survivor of the Holocaust, has remarked that

> It [the establishment of the Survivors Film Project and the collection of video interviews) was a way of compensating for the fact that most visual documentation of that period comes from Nazi sources. Our Holocaust museums are full of photos drawn from the picturebook of the murderers. The mind is exposed to images magnifying the Nazis and degrading their victims. The witness accounts are a view from the other side: they restore the sympathy and humanity systematically denied by Nazi footage. . . . The video project does not impinge on the province of historians, who sift and compare sources, but seeks to open the hearts and minds of both high school students and adult audiences. They see the testimony of a thinking and feeling person rather than of a victim. (Hartman, 1996b, p. 22)

As for the video portraits, themselves, they basically constitute

> chronological studies of individuals who lived through the era of the Third Reich, capturing their important moments of decision making as well as the moments when fate helped in their survival. In most cases the portraits cover several years of a survivor's life so that audiences can get a sense of the accumulation of humiliations, threats, and physical suffering that survivors endured. [Most of the] portraits [are] between twenty and thirty minutes in length so that a class has an opportunity to discuss the tape immediately after viewing it. (Hartman, 1996b, p. xx)

The video montages

> focus on certain themes of Holocaust history using excerpts from several survivors and witnesses who represent different perspectives on the themes under consideration. The montage "Stories of Separation," for example, highlights the moment in which survivors were separated from their families, showing the variety of separation experiences ranging from brief separation in the ghetto to the permanent severing of family ties. (Hartman, 1996b, pp. xx–xxi)

Facing History and Ourselves (1989) notes that the video portraits and montages have been developed ". . . to enable educators to incorporate selected tapes into curricula for various age levels and subject areas, in courses that are not necessarily courses about the Holocaust. Thus, a secondary school teacher able to devote only a few class sessions to the Holocaust as part of a course on European history might select part of the montage 'Childhood Memories'" (pp. xiii–xiv).

Speaking to the power of and value of such videotapes, literary critic and Holocaust specialist Lawrence Langer (1989a) has observed that

When the witness in an oral testimony leans forward toward the camera, apparently addressing the interviewer(s), but also speaking to the potential audience of the future (and this happens frequently in the tapes), asking: "Do you understand what I'm trying to tell you?"—that witness confirms the vast imaginative space separating his or her ordeal from our capacity to comprehend it. Written memoirs, by the very strategies available to the author—style, analogy, chronology, imagery, dialogue, a coherently organized and developed moral vision—strive to narrow this space, easing us into their unfamiliar world through recognizable literary devices.

. . . For the moment, I will argue no more than that videotaped testimonies provide the student of the Holocaust with an unexplored archive of "texts" that solicit from us original forms of interpretation. Reading a book that tries to carry us "back there" is an order of experience entirely different from witnessing someone like Barbara T. [a survivor on a videotape] vanishing from contact with us even as she speaks, momentarily returning to the world she is trying to evoke instead of recreating it for us in the present. Her presence before us dramatically illustrates a merging of the time senses . . . that is virtually impossible to capture in the pages of a book. Yet this is one of the seminal responses of survivors of the Holocaust ordeal. A different kind of "continuity" seems to establish itself in many of these testimonies, one alien to the chronological sequence that governs most written memoirs. (pp. 315–316)

Also commenting on the value and the power of the aforementioned montages, Facing History and Ourselves (1989) explains that

. . . it is possible that students, with limited factual information about the history of the Holocaust, might react to unedited or lightly edited tapes of individual narratives with stress, confusion, and perhaps even boredom. . . . [These potential problems] led us to the concept of the montage. The montages can partially correct against common misconceptions and the naive assumption that every survivor's experience is like every other survivor's, especially when readings and testimonies on parallel themes are selected for study. (p. xiv)

Still, when all is said and done, even though students are able to gain a unique sense of historical immediacy from first-person accounts recorded on video more than from the written word, such video material should, ideally, be used in conjunction with other resources and fully integrated into reading and discussion exercises. This is particularly true when it comes to the critical need to provide students with a strong historical context—and that is the case, no matter which aspect of the Holocaust they are studying.

Limitations of First-Person Accounts

Given the complex nature of the Holocaust, no single telling can ever hope to provide its complete story. That is understood if one keeps in mind that the Holocaust period (from the Nazi takeover in 1933 to the demise of the Third Reich in 1945) lasted twelve agonizing years, and that the genocide—which involved a complex mix of antisemitism, racism, social Darwinism, extreme nationalism, industrial-ism, and totalitarianism—ultimately engulfed millions of people from all across Continental Europe. The point, then, is that no individual or even group of people could provide a comprehensive picture of a genocidal situation based on personal experiences and observations, because it is not humanly possible do so. By their very nature, first-person accounts provide uniquely personal views of specific aspects of the larger genocidal crime. Consequently, teachers and students "should be careful about overgeneralizing from first-person accounts such as those from survivors, journalists, relief workers, bystanders, and liberators" (Parsons and Totten, 1993, p. 6). Concomitantly, when students are initially introduced to first-person accounts, they need to be informed that victim experience "depended on many variables such as their country of origin, how early or late . . . they were apprehended, what work camp or death camp they found themselves in, and what opportunities they had to gain tiny advantages that helped them to preserve their strength" (Facing History and Ourselves, 1989, p. xiv).

Teachers and students also need to keep in mind Friedlander's (1991) point concerning the greater accuracy of accounts recorded during the event as compared with those recorded later. Further, as survivor and acclaimed author Primo Levi (1986) wrote, "Human memory is a marvelous but fallacious instrument. . . . The memories which lie within us are not carved in stone" (p. 23). Continuing, he says, ". . . even under normal conditions a slow degradation is at work, an obfuscation of outlines, a so to speak physiological oblivion, which few memories resists" (Levi, 1986, p. 24).

There are several factors that come into play here: First, as memory fades, general as well as fine details may become garbled or irretrievably lost. Second, certain perceptions may be influenced by later experiences, ideas, rumors, or even popular conceptions of what occurred during a particular event. Whereas some may confuse rumors with reality, others may inadvertently embellish certain details and then over the years accept them as facts. Third, most of the survivors and other witnesses were under extraordinary duress during the genocidal period. This naturally influenced their perceptions at the time and, perhaps, even the accuracy of their later recall (Totten, 1991b).

Linked to such difficulties is the point that—and this is something that students need to be informed of and keep in mind—"Holocaust survivors and eye-witnesses are among the first to indicate the grave difficulty of finding words to describe their experiences" (Parsons and Totten, 1993, p. 8). In fact, many of the survivors who lived through the horrors of the Holocaust have spoken of the impossibility of fully conveying the depths of what they experienced and witnessed. The horror, they assert (and understandably so) was of such magnitude that it cannot be described or explained in a manner that fully elucidates it.

On another note, teachers also need to keep in mind that, more often than not, first-person accounts by survivors and others (e.g., rescuers, liberators, bystanders, etc.) "often lack information on the more general historical framework of the Third Reich since the witnesses convey their own personal experiences" (Facing History and Ourselves, 1989, p. 277). Abraham Edelheit (1988) corroborates this point: "Most [Holocaust] survivors reconstruct their experiences into very narrow terms, usually without reference to any larger historical contexts and with little attention to the larger events around them" (p. 2). Most were and/or are not professional historians. Although that does not diminish the importance of their stories, it does underscore, once again, the crucial nature of the teacher's role in assisting his/her students to gain at least a rudimentary understanding of the events that led up to and culminated in the Holocaust.[3]

Issues/Concerns to Consider When Using First-Person Accounts in Class

There are a number of concerns that teachers need to consider when using first-person accounts. Among these are the need to contextualize the history that is being taught; make distinctions among various types of sources and situations; prepare students to read, view, and discuss first-person accounts in order to avoid stereotyping individuals and/or groups; consider the traumatic impact that accounts can have on anyone (especially young people) who read or view them; and avoid creating cynicism in students.

By contextualizing the history when using first-person accounts and striving for precision of definition and language, teachers can assist students to avoid reliance on preconceived myths and stereotypes about the Jews, Gypsies, Nazis, and any other aspect of the Holocaust period. As Parsons and Totten (1993) have noted, skillful use of first-person accounts by the experienced teacher can assist the student to gain a deeper understanding and appreciation of the complexities and nuances of the wider historical events being discussed. That includes avoiding generalizations such as "all concentration camps were killing centers" (Parsons and Totten, 1993, p. 3), or "all Germans were collaborators" (Parsons and Totten, 1993, p. 3), or the Jews went like sheep to their deaths.

In doing this, teachers should strive to help students to "distinguish between categories of behavior; and clarify the differences between prejudice and discrimination; collaborators and bystanders; armed and spiritual resistance; direct orders and assumed orders; concentration camps and killing centers; and guilt and responsibility" (Parsons and Totten, 1993, p. 3). Contextualizing the Holocaust helps students to begin to understand that particular circumstances at specific times "encouraged or discouraged particular acts" on the part of governments or individual citizens. The point is, "changing events and circumstances" at different times determined individual and collective behavior for all concerned in the Holocaust" (Parsons and Totten, 1993, p. 5).

Related to this is the fact that when reading, listening, or viewing accounts by survivors, it is critical that students make distinctions between fact and opinion, various types of sources, and the range of situations described. As Parsons and Totten (1993) state:

> Students need practice in distinguishing between fact, opinion, and fiction; between primary and secondary sources, and between types of evidence such as

court testimonies, oral histories, and other written documents. . . . [They] should be encouraged to consider why a particular text was written, who the intended audience was, whether there were any biases inherent in the information, any gaps in discussion, whether gaps in certain passages were inadvertent or not, and how the information has been used to interpret various events. (p. 4)

A key task for teachers is to assist their students to differentiate and distinguish—and, therefore, understand—particular words, concepts, and situations employed in the accounts. For example, Primo Levi (1986) noted, "Just as our [those interned in the Nazi concentration and death camps] hunger is not that feeling of missing a meal, so our way of being cold has need of a new word" (p. 115). The same would be true of such concepts as fear, horror, helpless, trapped, isolated, threatened, suffering, tragedy, unbelievable, unthinkable. As Langer (1989a) also has pointed out, even the word "killed" "requires a new word, if it is to be properly understood" (p. 314). So does something ostensibly as simple as the word "liberation." Langer (1994) argues that for some, if not many, "liberation [brought] not rejoicing, but a recognition, an epiphany: 'at this moment I realize that I am alive and I have nobody and I am living'" (p. 73). By emphasizing these distinctions and the need for accuracy of definition at all times, teachers help students to gain a better grasp of what it was the victims and others had to undergo.

All of this also speaks to the crucial need for teachers to avoid *and* to ward off clichés, stereotypes, and false notions as to how and why people acted and reacted during the Holocaust years. For example, in regard to the absolutely false notion that the Jews went to their deaths like sheep to slaughter, teachers need to teach the students both about the devious methods, the horrifying brutality, and abject terror that the Nazis used in order to subdue Jews. At the same time, the students need to learn about and gain an understanding of the various types of resistance the Jews practiced in the face of the Nazi juggernaut. One way of doing this, of course, is to purposely select first-person accounts that address such issues.

Not to address such concerns likely will result in a study bereft of accuracy and intellectual rigor. As Langer (1989b) further asserts, "As the interest grows around the country in disseminating videotaped survivor or witness accounts, we need to recognize the liability of showing them to audiences who are merely curious or well-intentioned or enthusiastic but not informed—or prepared. . . . [Students] need to be [p]repared to hear details they will be unable to believe. [They also need to be] minimally aware of the vocabulary so many testifiers use as if the words had been absorbed into English: Appel (roll call), Lager (camp) . . . Kapo (prisoner unit-leader), and so forth" (p. 296). Over and above that, it is critical to keep in mind that "[u]nderstanding victim behavior requires a clear perception of the role time and place played in responses to potential atrocity" (Langer, 1989a, p. 310). The upshot is, "written text and oral testimony can be largely meaningless without responsible readers" (Langer, 1989a, p. 311).

On a different note, it is imperative that teachers avoid assaulting students with unremitting horror. Parsons and Totten (1993) suggest that

> Graphic material should be used in a judicious manner and only to the extent necessary to achieve the objective of the lesson. Teachers should remind themselves that each student and each class is different, and that what seems appropriate for one may not be for all. . . . [S]tudents are essentially a "captive audience." When we assault them with images [and words] of horror for which they are unprepared, we violate a basic trust: the obligations of a teacher to provide a "safe" learning environment. (p. 6)

If students are assaulted with one horrific story and/or image after another, they may feel so overwhelmed by the events, incidents, and images that they simply "turn off" or "shut down."

It should go without saying that first-person accounts should never "be used as a shock treatment to arouse interest" (Friedlander, 1979, p. 542). Such use constitutes both poor and unconscionable pedagogy.

It also is important that images and texts used in the classroom "do not exploit either the victims' memories or the students' emotional vulnerability" (Parsons and Totten, 1993, p. 6). Teachers need to keep in mind that "[m]any events and deeds that occurred within the context of the Holocaust do not rely for their depiction directly on the graphic horror of mass killings or other barbarisms" (Parsons and Totten, 1993, p. 6).

Furthermore, it is recommended that teachers inform their students in advance as to what they are going to see and/or hear in a video or from a survivor, and allow the students to opt out if they feel the need. This is a practice that many teachers have implemented in order to avoid traumatizing their students.

This, of course, is not to say that horror does not have a place in teaching about the Holocaust. How could it not? It is to say only that students should not be bombarded with the horror.

Still, given that a degree of horror and revulsion is bound to be present in some student reactions to parts of the Holocaust, it is vital that teachers provide ample time for in-depth discussion, so that students can express their innermost thoughts and feelings about the information presented to them. Not to do so is likely to leave the students without an outlet. Ultimately, such a situation could result in the students becoming numb to what they have read, heard, or viewed; or it may simply result in their rejecting both the reality as well as the significance of what they are studying. Opportunities to discuss and vent their thoughts and feelings should be interwoven throughout the study.

Finally, although teachers should present an accurate view of the capability of governments to commit genocide, they should try to avoid fostering a sense of cynicism in their students (Parsons and Totten, 1993, p. 5). This is not to say that a teacher should avoid the hard and terrible facts. That would be pedagogically unsound. What it does mean, though, is that teachers can, for example, focus—at least to a certain extent—on the individuals who risked their lives in order to assist those who were being persecuted. At the same time, though, it is imperative to keep in mind that "at best, less than one-half of one percent of the total population [of non-Jews] under Nazi occupation helped to rescue Jews" (Oliner and Oliner, 1991, p. 363).

Incorporating First-Person Accounts into the Classroom: Suggestions and Methods

There are many ways in which teachers can use first-person accounts during a study of the Holocaust. Those highlighted here are some of the more successful ones that the author has used or are otherwise familiar to him.

At the outset, it should be noted that when using first-person accounts in the classroom, teachers need to carefully *select* such materials; and in doing so, they need to *thoroughly preview* (read, listen to, or view) *the accounts prior to using them* with their students. The materials need to be assessed for their appropriateness for the age group being taught, especially with regard to language, graphic depiction of carnage, the match with the content being taught in the lesson, and the complexity of the account.

I. Educational Uses of First-Person Accounts

A. To Undergird and Add Depth to the Study of the Holocaust

The use of first-person accounts helps to provide students with unique and often diverse perspectives on the issues that most concern them. For example, did the Jews do anything to resist? Did the victims know about the death camps? How did the survivors manage to go on with their lives after suffering such devastation? As previously mentioned, the accounts always should be used to supplement other key resources—essays, films, governmental records, transcripts of court trials, fiction, poetry, artwork, and newspaper articles from the time period. Doing so will assist in providing a more comprehensive picture of an extremely complex subject.

B. To Help Delineate the Complexity of Choices Made during the Holocaust Period and to "Complicate" the Study of the Holocaust

The use of first-person accounts, especially those of survivors, are useful for illuminating how different people acted in various circumstances throughout the Holocaust. For example, first-person accounts also can be used to highlight and illuminate the daily struggle and moral dilemmas faced by ordinary people under Nazism. Accounts could also be used to delineate the differences between those non-Jews who stood by and allowed the events to unfold as innocent people were victimized and those who acted in various ways and capacities to assist the victims and/or attempted to staunch the brutality.

In this regard, Parsons and Totten (1993) stress that

> Teachers need to send a clear message to students that studying complex human behavior usually defies simple answers. To help students resolve questions about genocide, teachers need to guard against "packaging simple answers." [In that regard,] teachers need to encourage students to consider multiple explanations.

[Thus,] units of study should include examples of individuals, groups, and nations making choices that result in a range of consequences." (p. 87)

Oral accounts help to delineate such choices and consequences.

C. To Personalize the Study, to Put a Face on the Statistics

It is imperative to place a "human face" on the Holocaust. This will prevent students from losing sight of the fact that human beings—women, men, children, brothers and sisters, grandpas and grandmas, aunts and uncles, and babies—were deprived of their basic rights and made to suffer at the hands of an unrelenting and brutal enemy throughout the Holocaust years. Put another way, "[f]irst-person accounts provide students with a way of making meaning out of collective numbers" (Parsons and Totten, 1993, p. 6).

Likewise, it helps to prevent a situation in which the perpetrators are simply and simplistically portrayed as monsters. Although many of the perpetrators' actions were monstrous, students need to clearly understand and appreciate that the perpetrators were humans who acted in various ways and for various reasons (none of which are excusable). *In absolutely no way is this to diminish what the perpetrators did*; rather, it is to avoid a situation where the students can dismiss the actions of these individuals as an aberration that has no bearing on greater humanity.

D. To Illuminate Various Periods of the Holocaust Years

First-person accounts are eminently useful for illuminating the uniquely individual aspects of European history prior to, during and beyond the 1930s and 1940s, that is, the pre-Holocaust years, the rise of the Nazi party, the incipient and ever-increasing and punitive discrimination directed against the Jews, the implementation and impact of the Nuremberg Laws, Kristallnacht, the establishment of the ghettos, the roundups, the deportations, acts of resistance, rescue efforts, the concentration and death camps, the liberation, life in the displaced persons (d.p.) camps, and life in the post-Holocaust years. Again, the accounts can strengthen the study by supplementing other resources.

II. Suggestions/Methods for Incorporating First-Person Accounts in the Classroom

A. Using Different Types of Accounts in the Classroom

When incorporating first-person accounts into a study, it is always a good idea to use more than one or two accounts. This will enable students to gain a clearer understanding of the complexity of the Holocaust. It also will provide them with an opportunity to compare the political and social developments and individual experiences in different countries that occurred at the same and/or different times.

It also is wise for teachers to use more than one *type* of account (e.g., written, audio, or video; eyewitness accounts—diaries, letters written during the Holocaust period, etc.; trial testimony; and oral histories) with students. By doing so, the students will be introduced to the various ways in which victims and survivors have related their story and documented the events they experienced and/or witnessed. This approach also will provide the students with opportunities to draw distinctions between the different types of information found in different types of accounts (for example, diaries, notes, and letters that were written during the unfolding of events, and/or oral histories collected shortly after 1945, versus those oral histories that were conducted years after the actual events took place). It also will provide them with an opportunity to discuss such issues as memory, the historical value of different types of accounts, the use of language, and so on.

The wider the range of sources presented to the students, the more they will be able to ". . . look at the Holocaust from a multidisciplinary perspective, since the witnesses touch on geography, sociology, psychology, economic history, politics, art, and literature in their accounts" (Facing History and Ourselves, 1989, p. 277). Again, and this cannot be stressed too strongly, by using different types of accounts students will learn that ". . . we cannot generalize about survivors' experiences since each survivor has a unique story" (Facing History and Ourselves, 1989, p. 277).

B. Avoiding the Trivialization of the Study

As teachers know only too well, many students are rather blasé about the various conflicts and/or tragedies that they come across in various parts of their curriculum. Many, of course, have become inured to violence because of what they see on their television or computer screens and/or experience in their daily lives.

What, then, can teachers do to avoid trivialization of the tragedy of the Holocaust and the various trials and tribulations by those who fell victims to the Nazis? One teacher, Robin Jones, has tried to confront this problem by getting her students to understand the dilemma of discussing, *objectively and rationally,* the brutality visited on a people by another group, as well as the very real need not to ignore or minimize in anyway the anxiety, terror, and horror suffered by the victims. Put another way, she asks: How is it possible to deal with the subject in a way that prevents the historical source material from becoming "just texts" rather than the real experiences of real people? She has found that "by constantly pointing out the distance between the text and reader, the knowledge needed to understand the work and the knowledge lacking, then some sense of perspective is achieved which situates reader and text/event in relation to each other" (Jones, 1996, p. 150).

C. Prepare Students to Read, Listen to, and/or View First-Person Accounts

Teachers need to prepare their students, intellectually as well as emotionally, to read, listen to, and/or view first-person accounts. One way of doing this is to provide the students with, *at the very least,* an overview of the Holocaust (an overall chronology of the events that led up to and culminated in the Holocaust, the "whys" behind the Holocaust, who the perpetrators were as well as their aims, and who the victims were and some of their various fates). This provides students with a context in which to locate the source's testimony, and a means of achieving a deeper understanding of its content. This is vital, as so many people (especially the young) know so little about the Holocaust period. It may also stave off a situation in which the students facilely hold on to their preconceived notions and misconceptions of the Jews, the Nazis, and the Holocaust throughout the study. (Preferably, the students should be well versed in the history and have a solid notion of the whys, whats, wheres, whens, and hows of the key aspects of the Holocaust.)

At the outset of the study, it is also important that the teacher and students address the question why people even recount their stories in first-person accounts. Among the many reasons for doing so are: (1) to relate one's story because one perceives it to be unique or important; (2) to explore one's life, as a whole or in part; (3) to bear witness; (4) to serve as a means of remembrance; (5) to serve as a means of resistance; or, put another way, to assert one's "personhood" against a world that denigrated his/her very humanity; (6) to counter the lies of "revisionists," deniers, falsifiers, and others; and (7) to offer a rationale for one's actions or inaction. (This aspect of the study could be incorporated as an anticipatory set. See "D. Develop and Implement Effective Anticipatory Sets," below.)

Another question that needs to be posed at the beginning of any study of the Holocaust is: Why should we even learn about something like the Holocaust? As one teacher, Leigh Davis of Tuscola High School in North Carolina, related to this author: "When I ask my students why they think I am teaching the Holocaust to them, I get responses that sometimes surprise me. I get reasons that I had not even thought of, and where I find myself responding, 'Yes, that is one of my reasons.'"

On another note, students need to be prepared for the horror that they are likely to confront in first-person accounts of the Holocaust. As previously mentioned, Langer suggests that teachers should "[p]repare [their students] to hear details they will be unable to believe" (1989b, p. 296). This is to "create historically—and emotionally—informed audiences" (Langer, 1989b, p. 296). Such "details" might include the types of actions, the words, the images, and the type of pain that they will learn about. Naturally, such preparation needs to be handled with care and sensitivity. Furthermore, it cannot be accomplished in a perfunctory manner.

In order to consciously and conscientiously address the vital need to prepare their students for what they are going to experience, teachers may wish to develop "briefing sessions," along the lines of Langer's suggestions. They can begin by discussing the fact that the students are going to come into contact with information that is vastly "different" from what they are accustomed to seeing or hearing about. Concomitantly, teachers should address the magnitude of the horror that the students are about to confront (Benz, 1996, p. 20). This provides the students with an opportunity, for lack of a better term, to "acclimate" and/or prepare themselves for the shock that they may experience. Such briefing sessions can and should be used throughout the lesson on the Holocaust, for example, whenever any new information of this sort is to be introduced.

On another note, if students are not prepared in advance to *really listen to and think about* those details that, at first blush, seem unbelievable, they may simply dismiss the stories and events as untrue. That is, they may find the information so strange that they simply will not have a context in which to place it.

Laura Marasco-Walton, a teacher at Cache la Pondre Junior High in LaPorte, Colorado, informed this author that she makes a point of also preparing the students to hear a survivor by discussing beforehand the geographic locations—the location of the survivor's original home, the ghettos and/or camps he/she may have been incarcerated in, and so on—which the survivor may mention during his/her talk, among other key points of information. Marasco-Walton notes that this process makes the survivor's talk both more meaningful and understandable to her students. Marasco-Walton also believes it is imperative that a teacher meet with the survivor prior to his/her appearance in the classroom, not only to obtain this information but also to ascertain anything that the survivor may not wish to discuss or be questioned about by the students.

Ken Elkins, a teacher at Parkview High School in Springfield, Missouri, has also informed this author that he deems it imperative to prepare his students to listen to a survivor by emphasizing the absolute need for them to be sensitive to the speakers. By this, he means the students should avoid adopting the judgmental or confrontational attitude they are accustomed to viewing on certain television talk programs. Elkins also discusses with his students the acceptability of being emotionally moved by a survivor's story or other accounts, relating his own experience in this connection.

In a similar vein, Shannon Lampton, a teacher at School of the Good Shepherd, in Winchester, Tennessee, points out that she prepares her students for a visit by a survivor by discussing appropriate responses to the material. As some of her students tend to laugh or joke out of nervousness or a sense of horror, she tells them that it is both natural and fine to cry.

It is also useful for teachers to conduct "debriefing" sessions following the use of first-person accounts or after listening to a survivor's story. Such debriefing sessions provide the teacher with an opportunity to ascertain what the students have learned as well as discuss questions, concerns, misconceptions, or any confusion that needs to be cleared up. Equally significant, such sessions provide students with the opportunity to discuss their own feelings about the subjects examined. Students need both the opportunity and the structure to share their thoughts and vent their feelings. Not providing such opportunities can result in their feeling depressed and/or a sense of withering despair. It is pedagogically unsound and unconscionable to ignore this need by students.

On a related note, Sarah Stringfellow, a teacher at Fulton Junior High School in Indianapolis, Indiana, told this author that she feels that "teachers really need to drive home the fact that this is *real*—*non*fiction. They need to understand the difference between fiction and nonfiction. Real people, real places, real death. This is not a TV show!"

D. Develop and Implement Effective Anticipatory Sets

At the outset of a study on the Holocaust that utilizes first-person accounts, a teacher can ask his/her students to list individually all of the reasons why a person may wish to "share" or relate his/her experiences of a traumatic event. Following this, the students can be divided into small groups to share and discuss their points, agreeing on a list of ideas to share with the larger class.

Another effective and engaging method of preparing students to read, listen to, and/or view first-person accounts is to divide the class into small groups and provide each group with the same set of "artifacts" or "photos" to examine and discuss. Such artifacts/photos should, of course, be germane to the focus of the study. One excellent resource for such an activity is the "Poster Series" of artifacts designed by and available from the United States Holocaust Memorial Museum in Washington, DC. Students could be assigned the same set of questions to discuss and answer. Each group should be assigned a recorder, who takes down the salient points discussed. A key rule during the small group work is that every student in the group must be alloted time to have his/her say with regard to each photo or artifact. After ample discussion has taken place, the class could come back together in order to discuss each group's insights, comments, and questions.

As an alternative (or in addition) to the aforementioned exercise, another useful group exercise is to use a set of photographs depicting an overview of the Holocaust, or special aspects of it, for example, the pre-Holocaust period, the increasing evidence of the denial of basic rights of the Jews, the roundups, life in the ghettos, the deportations, the concentration camps, the death camps, liberation, and the d.p. camps.

Yet another effective anticipatory set (and this is related to one related in "C. Prepare Students to Read, Listen to, and/or View First-Person Accounts"), teachers can show their students an outstanding documentary on the Holocaust, which clearly delineates the events that led up to and culminated in the Holocaust. This assists the students in situating the history and events of the Holocaust prior to reading, listening to, or viewing accounts about different individuals' experiences. (A particularly useful documentary to use for this purpose is "Genocide, 1941–1945," which is part of the World at War Series. Contact: Arts and Entertainment, 800-423-1212 or write to A & E Home Video, P.O. Box 2284, South Burlington, VT 05407.)

Ultimately, sessions like these provide the students (prior to their reading or hearing the accounts) with a feel for the people involved in the tragedy of the Holocaust.

E. Posit Questions/Problems for the Students to Ponder and Respond to in Writing

An effective pedagogical device for teachers to use when incorporating first-person accounts into their curriculum is to posit key questions to the students, and then have them respond to them in writing. This can be done on scrap sheets of paper, but even more effective is to have them compose their responses in a writing log or journal (see "G" below.) By following the latter method, the teacher can encourage the students to keep a record of their evolving understanding of the complexity of the Holocaust. After they have recorded their answers, small group and/or large group discussions can follow, keying in on the students' perceptions and insights.

Among the questions that teachers might want to pose to their students are the following: "What did you learn from these accounts that you did not know before? Did any of the information/insights you gleaned contradict or challenge previous information and ideas that you had about the Holocaust? What were they, and why they did have that effect? How did this/these account(s) alter your understanding or perspective of the Holocaust and/or the people involved? What lessons did you learn from this/these accounts? What lessons are inherent in such accounts for humanity? "How can the act of telling a story assert authority . . . or militate against" lies by revisionists who attempt to alter the facts (Collins and Varas, 1996, p. 137)?

If using two or more accounts by different people about the same event/incident, a teacher might ask, "How do are these accounts similar? Different? What do these similarities and/or differences tell us? Why is that important to know?" Here, Langer's (1989a) point that "Understanding victim behavior requires a clear perception of the role time and place played in responses to potential atrocity" (p. 310) is particularly relevant.

F. Have Students Maintain Lists of Key Issues, Concerns, Ideas

In order to keep students' attention focused on key issues or concerns that run through many accounts, students could be required to keep a running list of what they discover in their readings and research. For example, they could keep a list of all the "choiceless choices" (e.g., "whatever you choose, somebody loses," Langer, 1994, p. 45) that the speaker in the accounts and/or others were faced with. (For a discussion of "choiceless choices," see Langer's *Versions of Survival: The Holocaust and the Human Spirit* [1982].)

Alternatively, the students could keep a list of how certain conventional (or "everyday" or "normal") language (e.g., train, hunger, ghetto, heroic, even death) had an entirely different connotation during the period of the Holocaust. The latter has been appropriately deemed the "language of atrocity" by Langer (1995). Such an assignment may assist the students to begin to recognize "the poverty of traditional . . . vocabulary" when studying various facets of Holocaust history and/or addressing "the subject of human conduct during the destruction of European Jewry" (Langer, 1995, p. 32).

Students could also keep running lists of the euphemisms that the Nazis used to deceive the Jews, and the rest of the world, as to their real intentions. Such an assignment can assist the students to begin to understand how and why the Jews and other victims of the Nazis were purposely led to believe in false hopes.

To assist the students to be more reflective, they could be required to include a brief comment about each of their findings in regard to choiceless choices and/or the conventional versus the language of atrocity in which they discuss their own insights, conclusions, questions, and so on. Periodically, the students should come together as a group to discuss their findings and insights. Instead of maintaining lists on separate sheets of paper, such assignments could be incorporated into journal or learning log assignments.

G. Have Students Keep Journals or Learning Logs throughout the Study

An excellent method of assisting students to reflect on their study of the Holocaust is to have them maintain learning logs or journals. This can lead to several positive effects—it may assist them to read more closely; it can provide a structured method for getting them to reflect on what they are reading, discussing, and studying; it provides a means for keeping a record of their evolution of understanding; it can prompt them to raise and wrestle with questions about the subject; and it will enable them to carry on a "dialogue" of sorts with the teacher.

One interesting and worthwhile "journaling" method that a teacher uses with her students is as follows:

> Since I want students to relate directly to their reading, they keep reader response journals in which they quote and respond to passages that stand out for them. I ask them to note what the [speaker's] learn [from their experiences], what they want, what they are challenged by, how they react to those challenges, who/what support them, who/what challenges them, and what makes them different from those who surround them. (Kuzmeskus, 1996, p. 124)

Teachers can also, of course, periodically provide their students with key questions to respond to in their journals or learning logs. Among the questions they might posit are: What overt as well as subtle changes did the speaker in the account experience as the Holocaust period progressed? Why is the author telling his/her story? Provide evidence to support your answer; what do you perceive as the most significant aspect of the speaker's story, and why?

Finally, as a concluding assignment, students can write a letter to the speaker of the account. Among the scores of issues/concerns that the student might address are the following: how the speaker's story touched him/her, and why; the most important idea(s), fact(s), or point(s) that he/she learned about the Holocaust via the narrator's story; and, what he/she (the student) wants to share with others in regard to the speaker's story, and why.

H. Combine First-Person Accounts with the Study of Essays, Articles, or a Textbook on the Holocaust

This method, perhaps as much as anything, helps to contextualize the Holocaust for students. Above all, it lends depth to the study. The key reason as to why this is such an effective method is that the accounts: (1) help to bring the study "alive"; (2) provide the students with human-interest stories, which they generally find compelling and moving; (3) avail the students of unique perspectives (each of which are capable of enriching and adding to other perspectives); and (4) add corroborating information/evidence.

In order to "capitalize" on the strength of this method, teachers should attempt to locate first-person accounts that address exactly the same concerns, events, and issues (e.g., roundups, deportations, life and death in the ghettos; Kristallnacht, incarceration in Auschwitz) that the students are studying about.   This direct correlation will help to make the study more engaging for the students, as well as provide additional depth to the study.

I. Combine the Study of First-Person Accounts with the Study of Fictional Works on the Holocaust

The use of fiction is another useful way of engaging students in the study of the Holocaust. Here again, first-person accounts have an important role to play, especially if they recount similar events to those portrayed in a short story, poem, novel, or play.

When using first-person accounts in conjunction with fiction, teachers can assist students in examining such issues as how each medium portrays similar information in different ways, the type of language that is used in each, and so on.

J. Use First-Person Accounts in a Chronological Approach

A powerful use of first-person accounts (especially for those teachers who do not have much time to teach about the Holocaust) is to select the strongest excerpts from diaries, letters, and other types of accounts that address various facets of the Holocaust (e.g., incipient discrimination against the Jews, the implementation of the Nuremberg Laws, the roundups, ghettoization, deportation to the concentration and death camps, life and death in the concentration and death camps, the liberation of the camps, the aftermath of the Holocaust). Once the teacher (or the students) have collected the various pieces, he/she could have the students read, discuss, and study the accounts in chronological order. Again, such material could be examined and discussed in conjunction with a range of other sources.

K. Have the Students Compare and Contrast the Same Type of Information Found in Different Types of Accounts

One of the more informative and instructive exercises that students can conduct is to examine one particular topic from the Holocaust, and note how different sources—contemporary accounts or documents, court testimony, oral history, or video accounts—treat that same episode. If different groups are given individual topics to pursue in this manner, and the results are discussed in class, everybody can be encouraged to ascertain the qualitative differences found in the range of sources used.

L. Use First-Person Accounts to Highlight or Focus on Key Themes, Time Periods, Events, or Individuals

Some teachers have found that a particularly powerful way to incorporate first-person accounts into a study of the Holocaust is to select three or four accounts that address the same theme (e.g., resistance), time period (e.g., the mid- to late-1930s), event (e.g., Kristallnacht) or group of individuals (e.g., the fate of Jewish children). In this way, students are allowed to examine an issue in some depth and are provided with a number of different perspectives.

M. Incorporate the Use of Videotape Accounts into the Curriculum

Videotape accounts can be particularly engaging and instructive, as students are able to see and hear witnesses relive their experiences, anger, sorrow, pain, and loss of the Holocaust years. Many gain a deeper sense of understanding and empathy as they watch and listen as the speaker struggles to explain the horror he/she witnessed, the excruciatingly difficult decisions that were forced on him/her, and/or speak of the absence of loved ones. Indeed, many viewers end up feeling a greater empathy for a speaker on a videotape than they often do if they only read the words or listened to the voice on an audiotape.

N. Invite Survivors and Liberators to Attend Class Sessions

Undoubtedly, one of the most powerful experiences young people can have when studying the Holocaust is to meet, listen to, and engage in discussion with a Holocaust survivor or a liberator of one of the Nazi concentration camps. Unfortunately, as both the survivors and the liberators age, such visits are becoming increasingly difficult to arrange. Be that as it may, a good source in regard to the availability of such individuals are local synagogues, local or national Jewish organizations, Holocaust memorial organizations, and possibly some colleges and universities (especially departments of history and political science).

When inviting a survivor or liberator to class, it is imperative to prepare the students for such a visit. More specifically, in preparation for a classroom visit by a survivor or liberator, a teacher needs to provide students with a sound grounding in the history, prepare them to hear gruesome stories, provide them with some basic background information on the speaker, and establish a clear understanding as to what constitutes appropriate behavior, including the types of questions that are appropriate *and* inappropriate to ask.

O. Student-Conducted Interviews/Oral Histories

CAVEAT: Of all the suggestions herein, the author is most tentative about including this one. The simple reason is that many survivors and others who have lived through or witnessed various aspects of the Holocaust live with horrific memories, and to recall such memories often results in a flood of painful images and a terrible sense of loss.

On yet another note, even those with a fairly decent sense of the history of the Holocaust have blind spots vis-à-vis many situations and events; and, thus, it is difficult even for them to conduct an interview or oral history in a satisfactory manner. To ask or expect a student to conduct a satisfactory interview/oral history is asking a lot. The point is, most students simply will not have the knowledge base needed to develop a sound set of interview questions, let alone the knowledge base to ask intelligent follow-up questions.

There is a danger, then, in requiring all students or even a single student to conduct an oral history of a survivor. Unless a student ardently wishes to conduct such an interview and is willing to put in the requisite amount of time and effort to thoroughly prepare him/herself to do so, such projects should be avoided. It is imperative, of course, that teachers avoid "the danger of destroying the subject [of the Holocaust] through dilettantism . . . , sensationalism and/or exploitation" (Friedlander, 1979, pp. 520, 521).

If such interviews do take place, it is imperative that the student-interviewer be thoroughly prepared by the teacher. It is a simple but significant fact that no one can conduct a decent interview or oral history if he/she is bereft of a knowledge base concerning the subject at hand. Not only should the student be as informed as possible regarding the general subject encompassed by the interviewee's experiences, but the student will require assistance in formulating relevant questions for conducting such an interview.

That being the case, it would be wise for both the teacher and the student to consult key works on interviewing procedures, and to examine other student oral history projects (especially those whose focus was the Holocaust) in order to ascertain how others have undertaken such a project.

After thorough preparation (studying the history, and learning proper interviewing techniques—including how to design an interview instrument, phrase initial questions as well as follow-up questions)—the student-interviewer should prepare an interview instrument, and practice interviewing a classmate or the teacher (ideally, the teacher will have already modeled and discussed effective interviewing techniques) using a tape recorder. The mock interview should be critiqued by fellow class members and the teacher. Following the critique, the student can revise, delete, and add questions. Not only will this help refine the student-interviewer's technique but also will help to highlight—and therefore to eliminate—awkward or confusing questions.

Prior to conducting an interview or oral history, the student needs "to be sensitized in regard to honoring the wishes of the interviewee. That is, if an interviewee states that he or she does not wish to or cannot (for whatever reason) discuss certain information then the student should respect that wish. [Put another way,] from the outset the student should fully understand that he/she is not an investigative reporter, and should not act like one (Totten, 1987, p. 63).

Once such an interview has taken place, the student should transcribe the interview, annotate it where necessary, write an introduction, place the date and location of the interview on the manuscript, and submit it to the school library.

(For a more detailed discussion of such issues, see Samuel Totten's "The Personal Face of Genocide: Words of Witnesses in the Classroom [1987].")

Conclusion

Indubitably, first-person accounts about the Holocaust are excellent resources for use in a classroom. Nevertheless, prior to using such resources, teachers need to be absolutely clear in their own minds why they feel it necessary or useful to employ them. By their very nature, such accounts are capable of providing students with unique insights into human behavior, history, and both the uniqueness and universality of the tragedy of the Holocaust. They also are capable of placing a human face on a tragedy that engulfed millions.

NOTES

1. Speaking of certain historians' criticism of oral history conducted many years after the Holocaust, Hartman (1996b) has written: "[Historians have commented that] "oral history is even less reliable than letters and diaries. [They have said] your belated testimonies seem to be spontaneous but are highly mediated: at such distance from the event memory fades or plays tricks or is contaminated by what the survivor has heard or read. . . ." He then says, "Obversely, can we be sure that the discourse of written history, so revised and contradictory, sometimes in matters of fact but always when it comes to interpretation, is any less mediated? Because 'history' is written by one person, however well-informed, does not mean it has a truth-value transcending the heterogeneous chorus of voices, the being made of many beings, that is so present and alive in literary memoirs or oral documentation" (pp. 134, 135).

2. For an extensive listing and description of such works, see Totten (1991a), *First-Person Accounts of Genocidal Acts Committed in the Twentieth Century: An Annotated Bibliography.* New York: Garland Publishing, 1991; for eyewitness testimony presented at trials see the International Military Tribunal (1947–1949), *Trial of the Major War Criminals Before the International Military Tribunal, Nuremberg, 14 November 1945–October 1946.* Nuremberg: Author. Forty-two vols. [Referred as the *Blue Series*], and Nuremberg Military Tribunals (1947–1953) *Trial of War Criminals Before the Nuremberg Military Tribunals Under Control Council Law No. 10.* Washington, DC: U.S. Government Printing Office, 15 vols. [Referred to as the *Green Series*].

3. For a more detailed discussion of the limitations of first-person accounts, see Totten (1991a), *First-Person Accounts of Genocidal Acts Committed in the Twentieth Century: An Annotated Bibliography.* For a thought-provoking discussion of the value and limitations of video accounts, see Hartman (1996), "Learning from Survivors: The Yale Testimony Project" in Hartman's *The Longest Shadow: In the Aftermath of the Holocaust.*

REFERENCES

Bauer, Yehuda. (1976, October). "Contemporary History—Some Methodological Problems." *History: The Journal of the Historical Association* 61(203):333–343.

Bauer, Yehuda. (Ed.). (1975). *Guide to Unpublished Materials of the Holocaust Period* (Vol. III). Jerusalem: Yad Vashem.

Bauman, Janine. (Summer 1992). "Entering the World of a Holocaust Victim: Schoolchildren Discuss a Memoir." *The British Journal of Holocaust Education* 1(1):14–24.

Baumel, J. T. (Winter 1993). "Through a Child's Eyes: Teaching the Holocaust Through Children's Holocaust Experiences." *The British Journal of Holocaust Education* 2(2):189–208.

Benz, Stephen. (1996). "Culture Shock and I. Rigoberta Menchu." In Allen Carey-Webb and Stephen Benz (Eds.), *Teaching and Testimony: Rigoberta Menchú and the North American Classroom* (pp. 19–26). Albany: State University of New York Press.

Cargas, Harry James. (1981). *A Christian Response to the Holocaust.* Denver, CO: Stonehenge.

Coles, Robert. (1989). *The Call of Stories: Teaching and the Moral Imagination.* Boston: Houghton Mifflin.

Collins, Catherine Ann, & Patricia Varas. (1996). "The Freshman Experience at Willamette University: Teaching and Learning with Rigoberta Menchú." In Allen Carey-Webb & Stephen Benz (Eds.), *Teaching and Testimony: Rigoberta Menchú and the North American Classroom* (pp. 133–147). Albany: State University of New York Press.

Edelheit, Abraham J. (1988, May–June). Review of "I Shall Not." *Martyrdom and Resistance* 14(5):2.

Facing History and Ourselves. (1989). *Facing History and Ourselves: Elements of Time.* Brookline, MA: Author.

Feig, K. (1990). "Non-Jewish Victims in the Concentration Camps." In Michael Berenbaum (Ed.), *A Mosaic of Victims: Non-Jews Persecuted and Murdered by the Nazis* (pp. 161–178). New York: New York University Press.

Friedlander, Henry. (1979). "Toward a Methodology of Teaching about the Holocaust." *Teachers College Record* 80(5):519–542.

Friedlander, Henry. (1991, February). "Nature of Sources for the Study of Genocide." *Social Education* 55(2):91. [Special Issue on "Teaching About Genocide," ed. Samuel Totten and William Parsons.]

Gouri, Haim. (1994). "Facing the Glass Booth." In Geoffrey H. Hartman (Ed.) *Holocaust Remembrance: The Shapes of Memory* (pp. 153–160). Cambridge, MA: Blackwell Publishers.

Gurewitsch, Brana. (1989). "Transforming Oral History: From Tape to Document." In *Facing History and Ourselves: Elements of Time* (pp. 284–288). Brookline, MA: Facing History and Ourselves Foundation.

Hartman, Geoffrey H. (1991, February). "The Fortunoff Video Archive for Holocaust Testimonies: Yale University." *Social Education* 55(2):120. [Special Issue on "Teaching About Genocide," ed. Samuel Totten and William Parsons.]

Hartman, Geoffrey H. (1996a). "Learning from Survivors: The Yale Testimony Project." In Geoffrey H. Hartman, *The Longest Shadow: In the Aftermath of the Holocaust* (pp. 133–150). Bloomington: Indiana University Press.

Hartman, Geoffrey H. (1996b). *The Longest Shadow: In the Aftermath of the Holocaust.* Bloomington: Indiana University Press.

Hurwitz, Leon. (1989). "Life in the Ghetto." Alan Adelson and Robert Lapides (Eds.), *Lodz Ghetto: Inside a Community Under Siege* (pp. 129–133). New York: Viking.

Johnson, Mary. (1989). "Perspectives on Oral History by the Historian Martin Gilbert." In Facing History and Ourselves (Eds.), *Facing History and Ourselves: Elements of Time* (pp. 288–290). Brookline, MA: Facing History and Ourselves.

Jones, Robin. (1996). "Having to Read a Book about Oppression: Encountering Rigoberta Menchu's Testimony in Boulder, Colorado." In Allen Carey-Webb and Stephen Benz (Eds.), *Teaching and Testimony: Rigoberta Menchú and the North American Classroom* (pp. 149–162). Albany: State University of New York Press.

Kuzmeskus, June. (1996). "Writing Their Way to Compassionate Citizenship: Rigoberta Menchú and Activating High School Learners." In Allen Carey-Webb and Stephen Benz (Eds.), *Teaching and Testimony: Rigoberta Menchú and the North American Classroom* (pp. 123–131). Albany: State University of New York Press.

Langer, Lawrence. (1991). *Holocaust Testimonies: The Ruins of Memory.* New Haven, CT: Yale University Press.

Langer, Lawrence. (1989a). "Interpreting Oral and Written Holocaust Texts." In Facing History and Ourselves (Eds.), *Facing History and Ourselves: Elements of Time* (pp. 310–316). Brookline, MA: Facing History and Ourselves Foundation.

Langer, Lawrence. (1989b). "Preliminary Reflections on Using Videotaped Interviews in Holocaust Education." In Facing History and Ourselves (Eds.), *Facing History and Ourselves: Elements of Time* (pp. 291–297). Brookline, MA: Facing History and Ourselves Foundation.

Langer, Lawrence. (1994). "Remembering Survival." In Geoffrey H. Hartman (Ed.), *Holocaust Remembrance: The Shapes of Memory* (pp. 70–80). Cambridge, MA: Blackwell Publishers.

Langer, Lawrence. (1982). *Versions of Survival: The Holocaust and the Human Spirit*. Albany: State University of New York.

Levi, Primo. (1986). *The Drowned and the Saved*. New York: Summit Books.

Levin, N. (1989). "The Importance of Survivor Testimony." In Facing History and Ourselves (Eds.), *Facing History and Ourselves: Elements of Time* (pp. 278–284). Brookline, MA: Facing History and Ourselves Foundation.

Lixl-Purcell, Andreas. (1994). "Memoirs as History." *Leo Baeck Institute Yearbook, 1994*. London: Secker and Warburg.

Niewyk, Donald. (1996). "Holocaust: The Genocide of the Jews." In Samuel Totten, William S. Parsons, & Israel W. Charny (Eds.), *Genocide in the Twentieth Century: Critical Essays and Eyewitness Accounts* (pp. 167–207). New York: Garland Publishing, Inc.

Oliner, Pearl, & Oliner, Samuel. (1991). "Righteous People in the Holocaust." In Israel W. Charny (Ed.) *Genocide: A Critical Bibliographic Review: Volume 2* (pp. 363–385). London: Mansell.

Parsons, William S., & Samuel Totten. (1993). *Guidelines for Teaching about the Holocaust*. Washington, DC: United States Holocaust Memorial Museum.

Rittner, Carol. (1990). "Foreword: The Triumph of Memory." In Michael Berenbaum (Ed.), *A Mosaic of Victims: Non-Jews Persecuted and Murdered by the Nazis* (pp. xi–xv). New York: New York University Press.

Totten, Samuel. (1991a). "First-Person Accounts of Genocidal Acts Committed in the Twentieth Century." In Israel Charny (Ed.), *Genocide: A Critical Bibliographic Review: Volume 2* (pp. 321–362). London and New York: Mansell Publishers and Facts on File.

Totten, Samuel. (Fall 1987). "The Personal Face of Genocide: Words of Witnesses in the Classroom." *Social Science Record: The Journal of the New York State Council for the Social Studies* 24(2):63–67. [Special Issue on "Genocide: Issues Approaches, Resources," ed. by Samuel Totten.]

Totten, Samuel. (1991b). "Introduction." In Samuel Totten (Ed.), *First-Person Accounts of Genocidal Acts Committed in the Twentieth Century: An Annotated Bibliography* (pp. xi–lxxv). Westport, CT: Greenwood Press.

Wiesel, Elie. (1979). "Letter to President Jimmy Carter." *Report to the President*. Washington, DC: President's Commission on the Holocaust.

Wiesel, Elie. (1969). *Night*. New York: Discus Books.

Wieviorka, Annette. (1994). "On Testimony." In Geoffrey H. Hartman (Ed.). *Holocaust Remembrance: The Shapes of Memory*, pp. 23–32. Cambridge, MA: Blackwell Publishers.

FIRST-PERSON ACCOUNTS AND THEIR USE IN TEACHING ABOUT THE HOLOCAUST: SELECT RESOURCES

Accounts/Testimony

Adelson, Alan, & Robert Lapides (Eds.). (1989). *Lodz Ghetto: Inside a Community under Siege*. New York: Viking. 526 pp. A remarkably powerful volume that presents a comprehensive, day-by-day account of events of the second largest ghetto of Nazi-occupied Europe through the voices of the victims and survivors as expressed in memoirs, diaries, notebooks, sketches of the ghetto, announcements, etc.

Adelson, Alan (Ed.). (1996). *The Diary of Dawid Sierakowiak: Five Notebooks from the Lodz Ghetto*. New York: Oxford University Press. 271 pp. A major diary that "faithfully reflects the ghetto reality and is one of the few existing authentic documents related to such issues as the underground resistance of ghetto youths." In unrelenting and harrowing detail, Dawid Sierakowiak chronicles the myriad hardships to which the Jewish inhabitants of the Lodz ghetto were subjected. This constitutes a major and significant resource for teachers and students of the Holocaust.

Adler, Stanislaw. (1981). *In the Warsaw Ghetto: 1940–1943—An Account of a Witness: The Memoirs of Stanislaw Adler.* Jerusalem: Yad Vashem. 334 pp. From 1940 to 1943, Adler was a member of the Jewish Council in Warsaw, initially in the legal department of the Jewish Police Auxiliary and then as the director of the Housing Office. To avoid the deportations, he escaped and hid in the "Aryan" section of Warsaw. His diary describes the many different facets of life and death in the Warsaw Ghetto.

Aroneanu, Eugene (Comp.). (1996). *Inside the Concentration Camps: Eyewitness Accounts of Life in Hitler's Death Camps.* Westport, CT: Praeger Publishers. 174 pp. "This book is a translation of an oral history of the concentration camp experience recorded immediately after World War II as told by men and women who endured it and lived to tell about it. . . . The testimonies are arranged to reflect the chronology of camp experience (from deportation to liberation), the living conditions of camp life (from malnutrition to forced labor), and the various methods of abuse and extermination (from castration to gassing and cremation). The unusual format, which is comprised of various individual's comments (ranging in length from one line to several paragraphs), results in an accumulation of data that, ultimately, provides the reader with an ever-larger and ever-increasing view into the nightmare world of the victims."

Barkai, Meyer (Ed.). (1962). *The Fighting Ghettos.* Philadelphia, PA: Lippincott. 407 pp. Included in this text are excerpts from scores of memoirs by both those ghetto fighters who did and did not survive. They were culled from the over two thousand memoirs and other primary documents in the archives of the Ghetto Fighters House in Israel.

Berenbaum, Michael. (1993). *The World Must Know: The History of the Holocaust as Told in the United States Holocaust Memorial Museum.* Boston: Little, Brown. 240 pp. This volume is packed with short excerpts from first-person accounts (diaries, memoirs, poetry, oral accounts, testimony) by survivors and victims of the Holocaust. These excerpts are ideal for use in the secondary classroom.

Cargas, Harry James (Ed.). (1993). *Voices from the Holocaust.* Lexington: The University of Kentucky Press. 164 pp. This volume contains interviews with notables such as Simon Wiesenthal, Jan Karski, Yitzhak Arad, Leon Wells, Emil Fackenheim, Elie Wiesel, Dorothee Soelle, and others.

Chamberlain, Brewster, & Marcia Feldman (Eds.). (1987). *The Liberation of the Nazi Concentration Camps 1945: Eyewitness Accounts of the Liberators.* Washington, DC: United States Holocaust Memorial Council. 214 pp. In this volume, the United States Holocaust Memorial Council has gathered extraordinarily powerful eyewitness accounts and testimonies of the individuals who were "variously involved in the horrors of the Holocaust and the physical, if not emotional or mental, release of the liberation." It includes accounts by survivors, war correspondents, medical personnel, the military, chaplains, and others.

Dafni, Reuven, & Yehudi Kleiman (Eds.). (1991). *Final Letters: From Victims of the Holocaust.* New York: Paragon House. 128 pp. Selected from the Yad Vashem Holocaust

Archive in Jerusalem, this book is comprised of a collection of letters Jews wrote during the Holocaust. Written on anything they could find and often left in hiding places or dropped from deportation trains, some of the letters "are final farewells, last signs of life, [while] others show hope mixed with dreadful uncertainty." Certain of these letters are ideal for use in the classroom in that they are short, extremely informative, and quite powerful.

Friedman, Ina R. (1990). *The Other Victims: First-Person Stories of Non-Jews Persecuted by the Nazis.* Boston, MA: Houghton Mifflin. 176 pp. This volume (which was especially developed for a readership comprised of fifth through ninth grade students) presents first-person accounts by individuals other than Jews who suffered at the hands of the Nazis during the Holocaust years. The stories of a young Gypsy, a homosexual, a Jehovah Witness, a black, a Czech schoolboy, a physically handicapped person, a civil disobedient, and others are highlighted. Many of the stories included herein also would be ideal for use at the upper secondary level.

Gutman, Israel. (1994). *Resistance: The Warsaw Ghetto Uprising.* Boston: Houghton Mifflin. 277 pp. An important work that "draws on diaries, letters, and other sources in an account of the April 1943 Jewish revolt against Nazi forces."

Hilberg, Raul, Stanislaw Staron, & Josef Kermisz (Eds.). (1979). *The Warsaw Diary of Adam Czerniakow.* New York: Stein and Day. 420 pp. This diary, by the extremely controversial chairman of the Warsaw Ghetto *Judenrat* (the Nazi appointed organization that administered every aspect of life in the ghetto), was initiated on September 6, 1939 and halted on July 23, 1942. Not only did Czerniakow see to the daily running of the ghetto, but he was often forced by the Nazis to make decisions as to which Jews would be slated for deportation to the death camps. He committed suicide when he was ordered to round up children for the death camps. Historian Nora Levin has called this "one of the most powerful documents of its kind in all of Holocaust literature."

Holliday, Laurel. (1995). *Children in the Holocaust and World War II: The Secret Diaries.* New York: Pocket Books. 409 pp. Comprised of diaries and memoirs of children who experienced various events during World War II. A vast number deal with the Holocaust. The children range from ten to eighteen years old, and resided in such countries as Austria, Belgium, Czechoslovakia, Denmark, England, Germany, Holland, Hungary, Israel, Lithuania, and Poland. Many of the accounts are ideal for use in the secondary level classroom.

International Military Tribunal. (1947–1949). *Trial of the Major War Criminals Before the International Military Tribunal, Nuremberg, 14 November 1945–October 1946.* Nuremberg: Author. Forty-two vols. [Known as the *Blue Series.*] Included herein is the official transcript of the proceedings of the International Military Tribunal, which was formed in order to try the major Axis war criminals at the end of World War II. The forty-two volumes in the set constitute the official text of the proceedings in the English, French, and German languages. This is a major and invaluable source for early and detailed first-person testimony.

Kahn, Leora & Rachel Hager. (1996). *When They Came to Take My Father: Voices of the Holocaust.* New York: Arcade Publishing. 176 pp. Photographs by Mark Seliger. Contains the powerful accounts of fifty survivors, along with recent photographs. The accounts come from individuals who survived a number of different circumstances during the war: incarceration in Auschwitz; hiding under the guise of being a Polish Gentile; spending time as a refugee in Shanghai, Switzerland, or the Dominican Republic; incarceration in Theresienstadt; being a "Mengele twin"; hiding in a convent and with a peasant couple in southern France; incarceration in labor camps; being saved by Raoul Wallenberg; and being saved by Oskar Schindler.

Klein, Gerda Weissmann. (1996). *All But My Life: A Memoir.* New York: Hill and Wang. 261 pp. A moving memoir that relates Klein's three years as a slave laborer of the Nazis, three months on a forced winter march from Germany to Czechoslovakia, and her liberation. Highly popular with students, this memoir served as the basis for the HBO Academy Award-winning best documentary short "One Survivor Remembers."

Klemperer, Victor. (1998). *I Will Bear Witness: A Diary of the Nazi Years 1933–1941.* New York: Random House. 519 pp. This is one of the most remarkable and valuable diaries to document daily life in Nazi Germany. Kept by a Dresden "Jew"—a veteran of World War I, a man of letters and a historian, the husband of a non-Jew, who had converted to Protestantism in his youth—it provides a unique, vivid, and invaluable account of the ever-increasing deprivation of civil and human rights of Jews under the Nazi regime. The collective entries slowly but inexorably draw the reader into the claustrophobic, increasingly threatening, and all-pervasive fear that the Nazi terror and their promulgations, regulations, and restrictions had on the life of each and every Jew living in Germany.

Klemperer, Victor. (2000). *I Will Bear Witness: A Diary of the Nazi Years 1941–1945.* New York: Random House. This volume constitutes the second half of Klemperer's diary. The first half, *I Will Bear Witness: A Diary of the Nazi Years 1933–1941,* was published in 1998.

Langer, Lawrence (Ed.). (1995). *Art from the Ashes: A Holocaust Anthology.* New York: Oxford: 694 pp. Comprised of a section entitled "Journals and Diaries" (pp. 153–233). Included therein are the following: Abraham Lewin's "Diary of the Great Deportation" (about the Warsaw Ghetto); Jozef Zelkowicz' "Days of Nightmare" (about the Lodz Ghetto in Poland); and Avraham Tory's "Memoir" (about the Kovno Ghetto in Lithuania). Under a section entitled "The Way It Was," there are first-person accounts by survivors Elie Wiesel, Primo Levi, Charlotte Delbo, and others.

Mendelsohn, John (Ed.). (1982). *The Holocaust: Selected Documents in Eighteen Volumes.* New York: Garland Publishing. This series is comprised of eighteen volumes that contain primary documents on various facets of the Holocaust. The series is divided into four main sections: Planning and Preparation, The Killing of the Jews, Rescue Attempts, and Punishment.

Niewyk, Donald. (1998). *Fresh Wounds: Early Narratives of Holocaust Survival.* Chapel Hill: University of North Carolina. 414 pp. This book is unique in that it is comprised of interviews of Holocaust survivors recorded in 1946 while the interviewees were still in d.p. camps in Europe. Shortly after the war, American psychologist David P. Boder interviewed 109 victims of Nazi persecution—most were Jewish survivors of the Holocaust. Thirty-six of the interviews are included in this volume. Ranging in age from their early teens through their seventies, the interviewees are men and women from Poland, Lithuania, Germany, France, Slovakia, and Hungary. The interviews are particularly valuable in that they were recorded so soon after the events, which were still fresh in the minds of the individuals.

Rittner, Carol, & John K. Roth (Eds.). (1993). *Different Voices: Women and the Holocaust.* New York: Paragon House. 435 pp. *Different Voices* "gathers together—for the first time in a single volume—the latest insights of scholars, the powerful testimony of survivors, and the eloquent reflections of writers, theologians and philosophers" regarding women's experiences during the Holocaust. "Part One, 'Voices of Experience,' recounts the painful and poignant stories of survivors, stories of resistance, compliance, medical experiments, all kinds of horror, and total vulnerability. Part Two, 'Voices of Interpretation,' offers the new insights of women scholars of the Holocaust, including evidence that the Nazis specifically preyed on women as the propagators of the Jewish race. In part Three, 'Voices of Reflection' women artists and intellectuals contemplate the Holocaust."

Rothchild, Sylvia (Ed.). (1981). *Voices from the Holocaust.* New York: New American Library. 456 pp. Culled from 250 people living in the United States who were willing to tape their memories of the Holocaust for the William E. Wiener Oral History Library of the American Jewish Committee, these accounts tell of life before the Holocaust, life during the Holocaust, and life in the United States in the aftermath of the Holocaust. The individuals, whose stories are told herein, were from all across Europe, and represent every "social level and shade of belief in Jewish life."

Wiesel, Elie. (1969). *Night.* New York: Bantam. 127 pp. In this now-famous memoir, the reader is presented with a stark and graphic first-hand account of the destruction of the Jewish community of Sighet in Transylvania, the establishment of two ghettos in Sighet in 1944, the nightmarish deportation to Auschwitz, and the brutally degrading treatment and horrific slaughter of the Jews by the Nazis. It is told by Eliezer, a fifteen-year-old survivor, who is ripped from his family home and orthodox way of life, and transported to Auschwitz, where he loses his mother, younger sister, father, and his faith in God. It also relates Wiesel's experiences in Birkenau, Buna, and Buchenwald. It presents an extremely powerful examination of the ramifications of the Holocaust: "The relationship between man and God, man and man, and man and himself." One of the most powerful works readily available for use in the secondary school.

Bibliographies

Cargas, Harry James (Ed.). (1985). *The Holocaust: An Annotated Bibliography.* Chicago: American Library Association. 196 pp. This text includes four sections of interest vis-à-vis personal accounts: "Memoirs of the Victims" (pp. 50–70); "Survivors and the Second Generation" (pp. 124–129); "Jewish Resistance" (pp. 71–79); and "Oral History" (p. 164).

Edelheit, Abraham, & Hershel Edelheit. (1986). *Bibliography on Holocaust Literature.* Boulder, CO: Westview Press. 842 pp. In part, this bibliography lists almost four hundred personal accounts (diaries, memoirs testimonies, autobiographies, magazine articles, and journal articles) of various individual's experiences in regard to the Holocaust. Less than thirty citations, however, are annotated.

Totten, Samuel. (1991). *First-Person Accounts of Genocidal Acts in the Twentieth Century: An Annotated Bibliography.* Westport, CT: Greenwood Press. 351 pp. Two chapters in this volume ("Holocaust," pp. 91–260, and "Fate of the Gypsies During the Holocaust Years," pp. 261–273) are comprised of several hundred annotations of first-person accounts by survivors, rescuers, liberators, and others.

Tyrnauer, Gabrielle. (1989). *Gypsies and the Holocaust: A Bibliography and Introductory Essay*. Montreal: Interuniversity Centre for European Studies and Montreal Institute for Genocide Studies. 51 pp. This landmark bibliography contains several citations (in English, French, and German) of first-person accounts by Gypsies concerning their experiences during the Holocaust years.

Critical Analysis/Commentary

Ball-Kaduri, K. Y. (1975). "Evidence of Witnesses, Its Value and Limitations." *Yad Vashem Studies on the European Jewish Catastrophe and Resistance* 3(79):79–90. In this outstanding essay, Ball-Kaduri examines the value and limitations of evidence by witnesses of "the period of Nazi-rule and the Holocaust." Among the issues he addresses are: "Is Evidence Given by Witnesses Valid Material for the Historian?"; "Relative Value of Different Parts of the Same Testimony"; "Institutions Dealing with Witnesses' Evidence"; Classifications and Publication of Evidence for the Use of the Historian"; and "Limitation of Testimony."

Hartman, Geoffrey H. (Ed.). (1994). *Holocaust Remembrance: The Shapes of Memory*. Cambridge, MA: Blackwell Publishers. 306 pp. This volume includes several scholarly essays—all of which are thought-provoking—on various aspects of first-person accounts. Among the titles of some of the essays are: "On Testimony," "The Library of Jewish Catastrophe," "Voices from the Killing Ground," "Remembering Survival," "Christian Witness and the Shoah," and "Film as Witness: Claude Lanzmann's *Shoah*." A chapter that teachers may find particularly valuable is Lawrence Langer's "Remembering Survival," as it includes an enlightening discussion of the use of language in first-person accounts.

Hartman, Geoffrey H. (1996). *The Longest Shadow: In the Aftermath of the Holocaust*. Bloomington and Indianapolis: Indiana University Press. 179 pp. In various chapters throughout this book, Hartman, a survivor of the Holocaust and cofounder of the Fortunoff Video Archive for Holocaust Testimonies at Yale University, discusses the purpose, value, and limitations of video accounts of Holocaust survivors. Particularly fascinating and instructive are the chapters entitled "The Longest Shadow," "Learning from Survivors: The Yale Testimony Project," and "Holocaust Testimony, Art, and Trauma."

Langer, Lawrence L. (1995). *Admitting the Holocaust: Collected Essays*. New York: Oxford University Press. 201 pp. Langer examines the impact of literature and first-person accounts to convey "the rupture in human values" that constituted the Holocaust. His discussion of such key issues as memory ("normal" versus "tainted memory"), language ("normal language" and the "language of atrocity"), the poverty of language to describe certain horrors of the Holocaust, and ways to read and attempt to understand testimony, are extremely valuable for those educators who plan to use first-person accounts in their classrooms.

Langer, Lawrence. (1991). *Holocaust Testimonies: The Ruins of Memory*. New Haven, CT: Yale University Press. "[A]n analysis of the unique ways in which oral testimony of survivors contributes to our understanding of the Holocaust. It also sheds light on the forms and functions of memory as victims relive devastating experiences of pain, humiliation, and loss. Drawing on the Fortunoff Video Archives for Holocaust Testimonies at Yale University, Langer shows how oral Holocaust testimonies complement historical studies by enabling us to confront the human dimensions of the catastrophe."

Langer, Lawrence L. (1998). *Preempting the Holocaust.* New Haven, CT: Yale University Press. 207 pp. This is yet another thought-provoking book by Langer, in which he examines, in part, various types of accounts as well their value. Among the many essays in this collection are: "Legacy in Gray: The Ordeal of Primo Levi"; "Gendered Suffering: Women in Holocaust Testimonies"; "The Alarmed Vision: Social Suffering and Holocaust Atrocity"; "The Stage of Memory: Parents and Children in Holocaust Texts and Testimonies"; and "The Inner Life of the Kovno Ghetto."

Langer, Lawrence. (1982). *Versions of Survival: The Holocaust and the Human Spirit.* Albany: State University of New York Press. 267 pp. A detailed examination of survivors' responses (both autobiographical and literary) to the Holocaust.

Laqueur, Walter. (Winter 1996). "Three Witnesses: The Legacy of Viktor Klemperer, Willy Cohn, and Richard Koch." *Holocaust and Genocide Studies* 10(3):252–266. This is a fascinating and highly informative essay in which Laqueur cogently argues that diaries provide an invaluable source for understanding life in the Third Reich. In the body of the essay Laqueur discusses three diaries that document life in Germany under the Nazis.

Pedagogical Pieces

Bauman, Janina. (Summer 1992). "Entering the World of a Holocaust Victim: Schoolchildren Discuss a Memoir." *The British Journal of Holocaust Education* 1(1):14–24. An interesting qualitative study of how one teacher in England used a "ghetto memoir" (*Winter in the Morning: A Young Girl's Life in the Warsaw Ghetto and Beyond, 1939–1945,* by Janina Bauman) in her classroom. It examines the students' (fourth form, or tenth graders') responses to the book as well as the pedagogical strategies the teacher used to teach the book.

Baumel, Judith Tydor. (Winter 1993). " 'Through a Child's Eyes': Teaching the Holocaust through Children's Holocaust Experiences." *The British Journal of Holocaust Education* 2(2):189–208. This piece describes an interesting teaching unit that U.S. teachers may wish to consider adapting in their own classrooms.

Byer, Lisa & Lauren Cohen (Eds.). (1986). *Journal of Testimony, Volume III: The Legacy.* Cleveland Heights, OH: Cleveland Heights High School. 64 pp. (To obtain information about this booklet, write to: 13263 Cedar Road, Cleveland Heights, OH 44118. Contact person: Dr. Leatrice B. Rabinsky). This booklet, designed by high school students who were enrolled in a course entitled "Literature of the Holocaust," contains interviews of Holocaust survivors, biographical pieces about Holocaust survivors, and poetry about the Holocaust, which was written by the students.

Facing History and Ourselves. (1989). *Facing History and Ourselves: Elements of Time: Holocaust Testimonies.* Brookline, MA: Author. 402 pp. This resource text is a companion manual to the Facing History videotape collection of Holocaust testimonies. It includes transcriptions of the videos in the collection (integrated with descriptions of the speakers), as well as background information and guidelines for using them in a classroom. It also includes a number of outstanding essays on various aspects of Holocaust video testimonies and their use in the classroom.

Totten, Samuel. (forthcoming). "First Person Accounts of the Holocaust." In Walter Laqueur and Judith Tydor Baumel (Eds.), *The Yale University Holocaust Encyclopedia*. New Haven, CT: Yale University Press. This essay presents a succinct overview of key issues vis-à-vis first-person accounts of the Holocaust.

Totten, Samuel. (Summer 1994). "The Use of First-Person Accounts in Teaching About the Holocaust." *The British Journal of Holocaust Education* 3(2):160–183. This piece includes a discussion of the value, limitations, and various classroom uses of first-person accounts of the Holocaust.

Organizations

Facing History and Ourselves National Foundation (16 Hurd Road, Brookline, MA 02146-6919). This educational organization has collaborated with the Fortunoff Video Archives for Holocaust Testimonies at Yale to develop video testimony appropriate for use in high school, college, and university settings. Of particular value is its *Facing History and Ourselves: Elements of Time—Holocaust Testimonies* volume, which is a "resource text that serves as a companion manual to the Facing History videotape collection of Holocaust testimonies."

Fortunoff Video Archive for Holocaust Testimonies at Yale University (Sterling Memorial Library, Room 331C Yale University, New Haven, CT 06520). The Archive has "short documentaries made from its video testimonies . . . available [for use by] schools and communities; and, it has analyzed and "entered into RLIN (Research Libraries Information Network) over two thousand hours of testimony, so that major museums and educational institutions will have access to a computerized index summarizing the testimonies" (p. xxvi).

Gratz College Holocaust Oral History Archives (10th Street and Tabor Rd., Philadelphia, PA 19141). The accounts that have been transcribed in the holdings of the Gratz collection have been entered onto the OCLC, a computerized online network, so that they can be accessed by students and scholars in more than three hundred libraries across the United States.

U.S. Holocaust Memorial Museum (100 Raoul Wallenberg Place SW, Washington, DC 20024-2150). The museum features a Holocaust oral history project. Thus far, the museum has produced two excellent films, which feature the words, memoirs, and insights of Holocaust survivors: "The Courage to Care" and "To Bear Witness." The museum is also in the process of developing oral accounts for use in classrooms.

6

Choosing Holocaust Literature for Early Adolescents

KAREN SHAWN

In the literature of the Holocaust, there is conveyed that which cannot be transmitted by a thousand facts and figures.

—Albert H. Friedlander

The Shoah (Holocaust) was the attempt to annihilate every Jewish man, woman, and child in Europe, and also the actual annihilation of six million Jews, carried out by Germany and its collaborators under Adolf Hitler, largely unopposed by the rest of the entire free world.

It is difficult to teach about such a tragedy to early adolescents (ten- to fifteen-year-olds). Young people today, however, already know something about the Holocaust. Indeed, the media preclude their innocence. Furthermore, the documentation attesting to the rising tide of racism and antisemitism grows; writings and Web sites denying the Holocaust proliferate; and, thus, the need to teach grows. We can decide only how, and not whether, to explore its significant impact on our lives.

Implicit in the question of "how" to teach this history is the question of context; that is, where within the educational framework of a public middle or junior high school does such an introductory course of study most appropriately belong?

This author believes it is best suited to a response-centered English Language Arts class, where the subject can be explored and personalized through literature. This chapter offers a rationale for that context, and proposes eight guidelines, each with illustrative examples, for choosing appropriate literature.

Across the United States, education about the Holocaust—when officially offered in the public schools—is most often found in the history and/or the social studies curriculum. Dawidowicz (1990) reported that the Holocaust is "studied in the context of totalitarianism in Europe (Nazism, fascism, and Communism) and of World War II, and sometimes also as part of the American history curriculum for the period" (p. 26). The problem with this placement is twofold. First, in the history/social studies class, it is usually taught only as an addendum to World War II. Second, the focus more often has been on transmitting information about the event rather than on the students' capacities to make meaning of that event. Generally, it has been the case that knowledge is objectively disseminated, and examined in a detached and academic manner. Put another way, the traditional history classroom is neither literature-rich nor process-oriented.

Research suggests that literature should be an integral part of the history/ social studies curriculum (Guzzetti, Kowalinski, & McGowan, 1992; Sanacore, 1990; Wilson, 1988). Guzzetti et al. (1992) notes, even if tentatively, "It appears that students can acquire more concepts and a greater understanding of those concepts through literature and literature-based instruction than through a traditional approach" (p. 121).

Although some districts have incorporated trade books and historical fiction as adjuncts to standard social studies texts, all too often the typical middle/junior high school history/social studies curriculum provides room for neither the introduction of historical literature and related affective discussion nor an overview of Holocaust history. Adherence to the traditional discipline continues, in part because of teacher reluctance and lack of formal education about the Holocaust, and additionally, because of departmental time constraints and curricular requirements, as well as because there is not enough empirical evidence to support the consistent inclusion of literature in the history curriculum.

That said, I believe that an ideal setting for an introductory unit about the Shoah is the response-centered English Language Arts classroom. Learning about the Shoah in a response-centered English class provides a particularly appropriate synthesis of content and process. To begin to understand the Holocaust, students must read and examine a discrete body of knowledge. To shape this knowledge, they must humanize the facts and figures. As they begin to ponder the personal, social, philosophical, and theological implications of the event, they need to share with a community of learners, through speaking and writing, their tentative reflections and conclusions.

Literature, in its exploration of universal themes and concerns, and in its presentation of the individual story to illustrate generalities of the human condition, is a cornerstone of both English and Holocaust education. Such an emphasis results from the value of literature, both cognitive and affective, and from the recognition that "children are seekers of meaning." Many are curious "about the dilemmas of human existence that have perplexed philosophers and theologians from the dawn of time . . . [and they] are intensely interested in exploring questions of values, feelings, meaning, and the relationship of self to others" (American Federation of Teachers, 1992, p. 19).

When adolescents begin to consider their place in, and transformations of, society, they can find in Holocaust literature opportunities to question decisions, to judge good and evil, and to rehearse different responses to life's infinite possibilities.

Once agreement is reached to teach the Holocaust in an English class, an essential question must be confronted: On what basis do we select readings from the myriad available?

Eight principles for selecting books—for library acquisition, whole-class or small group reading, and/or independent reading—appropriate for students in grade five through nine should govern our choices:

1. Good books and stories are developmentally appropriate, presenting the truth without unduly traumatizing young readers. The subject of the mechanics of the death camps is suitable only for older high school students. Where concentration and death camp experiences are included in books otherwise appropriate for middle/junior high school, graphic description, while accurate, is minimal. For the vast majority of children, perhaps with the exception of grandchildren of survivors, or others growing up in homes directly touched by the cataclysm, the subject need not be broached at all in a school literature curriculum before grade five.

2. Accompanying illustrations, art, and photographs are appropriate in content and tone. They are accurate in their reflections of the time, mood, and place, and are respectful of the people whom they portray.

3. Good books are rooted in historical context and reflect historical reality. Diaries, memoirs, testimonies, autobiographical and biographical stories, and fictionalized accounts of true stories are the mainstay of an effective use of Holocaust literature for children in grades five through nine. Even as fiction, good Holocaust literature depicts the truth with the highest degree of accuracy, presenting authentic feelings, dilemmas, and experiences using language realistic to the period.

4. Good books personalize the statistics, fostering empathy, compassion, involvement, and identification with victims and survivors. They speak of one particular person, family, event, time period, and place. They engage and affect students through the quality of the writing, appeal of the characters, excitement and poignancy of the plot, and power of the theme.

5. Good books feature—rather than marginalize—the Jewish experience and particular Jewish responses during the Shoah, rather than such other aspects as, for example, the actions of the perpetrators. They feature Jewish life in all its diversity, and include specifics of the ordinary, daily prewar community, detailing *what was* as a prelude to the depiction of *what no longer is.* The focus is on Jews as they lived rather than as they died.

6. Good books bring students from the Holocaust era into the reassuring present, giving hope to young readers.

7. Good books have the potential to motivate students to examine their own lives and behaviors and effect change where possible, providing a bridge from the world of the Holocaust to the present. They promote exploration of universal issues and themes evoked by the unique stories of the Holocaust.

8. Good books offer flexibility in the classroom:
   a. They are relatively easy to read and discuss.
   b. They do not require unreasonable preparation by a teacher unfamiliar with Holocaust history.
   c. They lay the groundwork for subsequent teaching of Holocaust history.
   d. They provide an active learning experience for students, offering opportunities for dramatic reading, listening, discussion, cooperative learning, distance learning through e-mail, writing, and individualized research.

We know that the more we learn about the Shoah, the more questions we have. The same seems true about teaching the subject. No sooner do we formulate guidelines for text selection then related questions arise. For example, how do we judge a book's developmental appropriateness? When early adolescents ask questions, how do we balance the necessity for honest answers with our need/desire/ responsibility to temper the harsh realities of an adult world gone terribly wrong? Is it possible to individualize readings to meet the educational and emotional needs of a heterogeneous class? How do we choose and use literature to balance the uniqueness of the Shoah with the ongoing demand to universalize? How do we understand and explore through literature the "lessons" of the Shoah?

It is worth returning to the guiding principles to try to answer these questions.

1. *Literature must be developmentally appropriate.*

It is clear from any publisher's catalogue, as well as from speaking with teachers, that the term "developmentally appropriate," when used in conjunction with Holocaust literature, has a meaning all its own.

The 1999 Social Studies School Service Holocaust Resources and Materials catalogue, for example, offers a host of books well suited only for middle/junior high school students, but it recommends them for children far younger.

For example, for primary graders, including those still in kindergarten, the catalogue recommends the book *Star of Fear, Star of Hope* (Hoestlandt, 1995), described as "directly and gently show[ing] the dangers confronting Jews in Nazi-occupied France" (p. 43).

For students in grade two, a recommended book is *The Shadow Children* (Schnur, 1994), a "coming-of-age tale convey[ing] the terror of ordinary people under the Nazi regime and the postwar guilt felt by individuals of conscience" (p. 44).

For readers in grades five and up, the catalogue recommends *A Nightmare in History: The Holocaust 1933–1945* (Chaikin, 1992), a book that is "illustrated with striking photographs" and that "traces the step-by-step process the Nazis devised for moving Jewish citizens from their homes to annihilation in death camps such as Auschwitz-Birkenau" (p. 42).

The Holocaust, as one of the above titles indicates, is often described as a "nightmare." What do we adults do when we have a nightmare? We might wake our spouse and recount the ordeal, reach for a bedside pad and write it down, go into the kitchen for a glass of milk, or turn on the radio. Who among us would wake our children and share the experience with them? Yet many of us seem willing to tell the nightmare of the Holocaust to even the very youngest students. *When did we teachers become collaborators in the crime of robbing our children of their innocence?*

In *The Hurried Child: Growing Up Too Fast, Too Soon,* Elkind (1988) believes that the trend toward teaching young children "the wrong things at the wrong time for no purpose" (p. xi) is an outgrowth of the "superkid" phenomenon. Parents insist that their children are precociously competent and can be "hurried" into learning and doing. Elkind attributes this inclination to adults' need to accommodate changes in society and alleviate their concomitant guilt and anxiety.

Television reflects this trend, offering facts and factoids all the time to anyone who can see and hear. There are no built-in roadblocks, such as gaining admission, or learning to read.

Publishers, too, have found a way to reach an ever-younger audience. Twenty years ago, books were scaled to the emotional, linguistic, and syntactical abilities of the reader, guaranteeing that children had to be literate and somewhat conceptual and analytical before they could be exposed to certain topics. Today, the industry attempts to bypass the literacy roadblock by publishing picture books for primary graders on topics that were in the past taught, if at all, as nonfiction or news stories to junior high and high school students.

Book reviewers collude. In David Adler's *Hilde and Eli: Children of the Holocaust* (1994), Hilde and her mother, along with a trainload of prisoners, are gassed. Eli and his family are chased with clubs and gassed in the showers; their bodies are burned. The *Booklist* endorsement reads: "This picture book . . . will bring home to grade-schoolers what the Holocaust meant to kids like them."

In reviewing Adler's *A Picture Book of Anne Frank* (1993), the *Bulletin of the Center for Children's Books* presents as an observation—rather than as an outraged call to arms—the following statement: "As Holocaust history enters elementary school curricula for younger age groups, teachers and librarians are faced with the formidable task of finding titles that present a *complex, horrifying subject* for *primary graders' listening or independent reading [italics mine]*" (dust jacket).

Some teachers, too, have accepted the concept of "superkid," introducing subjects previously considered taboo. *The "superkid" paradigm allows them to rationalize what is more their "need to teach" than students' "need to know."*

"Of course, children need to know what happened during the Holocaust so they can make sure it never happens again," a kindergarten teacher told me emphatically during a workshop in an Ohio school. "I understand that I have to water it down for my children, so I teach them only two vocabulary words: 'showers' and 'camps.'"

In *Four Perfect Pebbles: A Holocaust Story* (Perl & Lazan, 1996), a book marketed for elementary school students, we read in the first three paragraphs the following words and phrases:

> concentration camp . . . muffled noises . . . gasps and moans, rattling coughs and short, piercing cries . . . ever-present stench of unwashed bodies disease, and death . . . prisoners . . . died . . . tumbled from their bunks . . . bodies taken away to be burned or buried in mass graves. (pp. 1–2)

Why is it necessary to give such information to our five- to ten-year-olds?

In this vein, essayist Charles Krauthammer (1995) laments, "Teaching the most wrenching social history to the very young assaults their innocence by deliberately disturbing their cozy, rosy view of the world. . . . They live only once, and for a very short time, in a tooth-fairy world. Why shorten that time further?" (p. 80).

Will introducing children to these images and ideas without relevance to their experiences or regard for their sensibilities help them to prevent such a thing from happening again, or will it only "ratchet up [their] tolerance" (Cardwell, 1998, p. 26) for what they can read and watch? And if it does the latter, is it not possible that children may become cynical, indifferent, and thus less, not more, moved to empathy and action by the real-life violence they learn about in the classroom?

We fail our young people when we give them more information or sensations than they can process. We fail our children when we don't make classrooms an emotional haven. We fail our children when we invite them to enter, unsuspecting, a world filled with inexplicable, painful, harsh and terrifying realities: great violence, utter powerlessness, loss of control, xenophobia, betrayal, isolation, indignity, dehumanization, torture, murder.

We may not be able to shield them from the realities of the television news, or the escapist violence of movies, or the perversities of some Internet sites, but our classroom is still under our control. There, we can still offer our children stories that will help them to grow into trusting, secure, confident young people. But first we have to believe that certain subjects should remain taboo for young children.

In discussing the price of the openness and candor of today's society, Neil Postman (1982) reminds us that "certain facets of life—its mysteries, its contradictions, its violence, its tragedies—. . . are not considered suitable for children to know; [and] are, indeed, shameful to reveal to them indiscriminately" (p. 15). He adds, "It is clear that if we turn over to children a vast store of powerful adult material, childhood cannot survive. By definition adulthood means mysteries solved and secrets uncovered" (Postman, 1982, p. 88). How have we forgotten this?

The Holocaust literally eliminated the childhood of millions. We stain, we diminish, we end the childhood of the next generation when we showcase the agonies of Primo Levi and Elie Wiesel for our sixth graders, or introduce Anne Frank, now a character in glossy picture books, to primary school students, or explain death camps, no matter how gently, to kindergartners.

More than they need to know about the Shoah, youngsters need to believe that adults know the difference between right and wrong, that they are rational and can control their violent impulses. They need to believe that their parents or other trusted adults can and will protect them when they are threatened. They need to believe that good will prevail, that evil will be punished. The Holocaust teaches them the opposite, introducing them to an upside-down world where every moral precept they have learned is violated with impunity. Unlike a happily-ever-after fairy tale told by a reassuring mother, the Holocaust is real. Its relentless telling in American primary schools seems to be governed not by theories of child development but by market research and state mandates.

All that said, there is no compelling reason to introduce this subject as a unit of class study before grade five. Individual children, however, who may have heard at a much younger age frank discussions of the Holocaust at home, in houses of worship, or on the television, may ask specific and difficult questions. Simple, brief, straightforward answers are more appropriate than any reading.

2. In our increasingly visual culture, the second guideline is essential: *Illustrations, art, and photographs in children's books must be appropriate in content, tone, and relation to text. They should accurately reflect the time, mood, and place, and be respectful of the people whom they portray.*

The photographs in the essay *The Children We Remember* (Abells, 1983) are authentic and respectful. Culled from the archives of Yad Vashem, the pictures help the reader to visualize the events told in simple, spare prose. Unfortunately, the one-sentence-per-page, large-print format is not consonant with the stark visual content; it makes the book appear to be a rudimentary read-aloud, and is thus mistakenly marketed to primary grades.

Flowers on the Wall (Nerlove, 1996) suffers from a different dissonance. Its beautiful, gentle watercolors attract the youngest readers, and indeed the book is marketed for children as young as five. But the text is grim: Rachel is sick, her parents lack money for food and heat, her brother is forced to drop out of school to work, Jews are beaten and deported. The final paragraph is even more appalling: Rachel and her family are deported to Treblinka, "a concentration camp. Rachel's dreams, along with those of thousands of other Warsaw Jews, faded like the flowers on her apartment wall. And then they were gone forever" (unpaginated).

In contrast, Lloyd Bloom's luminous, almost three-dimensional illustrations of *One Yellow Daffodil* (Adler, 1995) enhance each page of this gentle story of Morris Kaplan, the lonely survivor who finds himself enfolded in the affections of a neighborhood family. Morris is drawn as aged but attractive. His longing for his lost family is made clear by the sepia-colored memories he calls forth; loneliness is etched in his warm, expressive face. But his quiet pleasure in his new friends is illustrated as well. The pictures allow readers to glimpse his tragic past, while finding comfort in the strength of his present.

In *Memories of My Life in a Polish Village 1930–1949,* (Fluek, 1990), each page of this beautifully told memoir, appropriate for students in grades five and up, boasts a miniature, jewellike painting by the author/artist, survivor Toby Knobel Fluek. In scenes of family, neighborhood, and preparations for the Sabbath and the holidays, Fluek, in vibrant hues, intimately portrays pre-Holocaust Jewish life. Two haunting chapters, each with detailed paintings, describe the Russian and the subsequent German occupation of her village and her experiences in hiding and on the run. With paintings of her liberation, marriage, and children, she brings us back to her fully realized present.

3. A good book is rooted in historical context and reflects historical reality.

It's odd to have to make such a statement. One rarely worries about the historicity of *Uncle Tom's Cabin, Red Badge of Courage,* or *All Quiet on the Western Front.* Teachers take their verisimilitude for granted. But then, the authors of the aforementioned works are not trying to relativize the slavery; they are not denying the occurrence of the Civil War or World War I. Unfortunately, that is not the case with the Holocaust.

Then, too, authors of those classics were careful to get their facts as well as their feelings right. Unfortunately, that is not the case with some authors writing today about the Shoah, especially, it seems, when they write for children.

Take, for example, Karen Ackerman's *The Night Crossing* (1994), a simple, fifty-six-page novel that tells the story of Clara and her family, forced by the Nazi occupation of Austria to leave their Innsbruck home and make a hazardous journey across the foothills of the Swiss Alps to the safety of Switzerland. The tone is gentle and appropriate for elementary readers, and Elizabeth Sayles' black-and-white illustrations are softly reassuring.

But Ackerman doesn't attend to historical facts. Rather, she describes a nonexistent war between Germany and Austria in 1938, which supposedly ruined

Austrian neighborhoods and forced Clara's family to sell their piano for firewood. "Unlike the city, the Austrian countryside seemed untouched by the war" (p. 27). She misuses the symbol of the Jewish star, planting it on Clara's coat in 1938, when such marking was not mandated in Austria until 1941. Furthermore, "slight shadows remained on each of their coats in the places where Mama had removed the yellow stars" (p. 24), indicating they had been there for some time. And if they had been there, and they did leave "shadows," wouldn't Mama try to cover them in some way, since the family was about to embark on a journey where they must not be identified as Jews? And why are the Jews being persecuted? Why do "Jews get branded like animals" (p. 4)? Why are "terrible things" happening "especially [to] Jewish Austrians" [p. 5]? Ackerman never tells us.

Precision and reliability are especially important criteria for Language Arts teachers, who often don't have the background to know every historical fact and, thus, depend on the accuracy of reputable literature. Although the purpose of Holocaust fiction is not to teach facts, when dates and events are mentioned, authors are obligated to get them right.

In omitting a historical context for antisemitism, Ackerman is not alone. Abells, in *The Children We Remember* (1983), writes only, "The Nazis hated the children because they were Jews" (unpaginated). Rachel, in Nerlove's *Flowers on the Wall* (1996), "knew that the local police would beat a Jew for no reason" (unpaginated). David Adler's *The Number on My Grandfather's Arm* (1978) is a bit better; after he writes that Hitler blamed the many problems in Germany on the Jews, he adds, "Of course that was nonsense." But he continues, "In other countries, too, in Italy, Hungary, Austria, Yugoslavia, and in my Poland, people all talked about how they hated the Jews" (p. 14). No explanation follows.

"What in the world must the Jews have done," many students must wonder, "to have so many people hate them?"

Worse are those books that attempt an explanation and err, introducing readers to old canards about Jews. In *Four Perfect Pebbles: A Holocaust Story* (Perl & Lazan, 1996), there is no discussion of centuries-old Christian antisemitism or Nazi ideology and its racial antisemitism. Instead, the reader is told,

> True, Jews didn't run the giant industries of Germany . . . but they were involved in business and professions . . . In . . . Berlin . . . the major department stores were Jewish-owned. . . . Whatever abilities, talents, influence, or wealth the Jews of Germany possessed were seen as a threat by the Nazis. (p. 14)

When we explore literature written for middle and junior high schoolers, we find historical honesty included in a variety of appropriate ways. The novels *Uncle Misha's Partisans*, by Yuri Suhl (1973), and *The Man from the Other Side*, by Uri Orlev (1991), serve as exemplars. The former is based on the true story of the Jewish partisan experience in family camps in the forests near a Ukrainian village and was inspired by an actual episode. The partisans' discussions and reminiscences help the reader to understand the actions and motivations of the young fighters.

Orlev's novel, too, uses conversation to contextualize antisemitism in this story of a Polish boy who joins his stepfather in helping Jews in the Warsaw Ghetto.

Also contextually grounded is Olga Levy Drucker's *Kindertransport* (1992), an engaging autobiography that begins in the winter of 1932 when Olga, "Ollie," is five. Her life in Stuttgart, Germany, reflects a typical childhood. She moves to a new home, travels, attends school and camp, and enjoys loving relationships with family and friends. Rich descriptions of Jewish life before the war are a necessary context for readers to understand what was lost; Drucker provides this. The gradual nature of the restrictions on Jews after Hitler comes to power are also crucial for understanding the complex situation of the Jews who remained in Germany from 1933 through 1938; Drucker offers this as well. As Hitler rises to power, intimations of danger hover over the Jewish community. Ollie is aware of the parades of Brown Shirts, of flags flying, of signs in shop windows forbidding Jews to enter.

4. The fourth guideline, requiring books to present limited, *recognizable human experiences, fostering empathy, compassion, involvement, and identification with the victims and survivors of the Holocaust and personalizing the statistics,* is reflected in the majority of literature for students in grades five and above.

Of particular note is Lillian Boraks-Nemetz' beautifully written autobiography, *The Old Brown Suitcase: A Teenager's Story of War and Peace* (1994). In chapters that alternate between 1947 and 1949 in Canada and 1938 and 1945 in Poland, Boraks-Nemetz offers us a vivid account of the difficulties of refugee life made more painful by flashbacks of her wartime life, first in the Warsaw Ghetto and then in hiding in Zalesie, Poland.

No young reader will forget twelve-year-old Motele, the well-drawn hero of Suhl's *Uncle Misha's Partisans* (1973). Another notable character is thirteen-year-old Inge Dornenwald, in Doris Orgel's novel *The Devil in Vienna* (1978), a strong young woman who, living in Vienna in 1938, confronts dilemmas faced by Jews not yet swept up in the Nazi net of death. Memorable too, is, Alex, the eleven-year-old protagonist in Uri Orlev's novel *Island on Bird Street* (1984)—witty, courageous, ingenious, and, above all, hopeful—as he struggles to survive in an abandoned ghetto hideout, while he awaits his father's return.

Each of these main characters humanizes the statistics of the Holocaust. Each acts as a careful guide for pre- or early adolescent readers, orienting them to the complex world they are entering with a simple yet clear historical framework: through the rise of Nazism in Germany and Austria, the partisan experience, life in hiding, on the run, in the ghetto, but not beyond: up to the gates of the death camps, but not inside. While such literary works may not serve a cathartic purpose for students, moving them to tears of rage, impotence, or despair, they do act, more appropriately, as a catalyst, encouraging them to read and learn more, to think, question, reflect, at their own pace, in their own time.

Virtually hundreds of books fit the last component of this fourth guideline, *engaging and affecting students through the quality of the writing, appeal of the characters, excitement and poignancy of the plot, and power of the theme.* Orlev's *The Man from the Other Side* (1991), for example, is a well-written, fast-paced novel that raises provocative questions about the phenomenon of rescue. Fourteen-year-old Marek is a boy with whom most adolescents will identify. When he becomes involved with neighborhood boys who intimidate and rob Jews trying to pass as Christians in the Polish section of Warsaw, he feels guilty, but stops only when his mother tells him that his own father was a Jew. Questions of people's moral stance during the Holocaust abound. Marek's stepfather, Antony, a sewer worker, is a professed antisemite. Yet he helps Jews escape the ghetto through the sewers at great risk to himself. He profits handsomely from his efforts. But he refuses payment when he saves Jewish babies, saying, "I may not like Jews, but I have nothing against human beings" (p. 21). In this vividly drawn portrayal of wartime Warsaw, Marek himself becomes a rescuer, and leaves the reader wanting to learn more about this complex time and place.

A notable exception to the generally good writing is Carol Matas's *After the War* (1996), a simplistic, superficial narrative with comic book dialogue, plot, and characters. More like a cops-and-robbers after-school special than a serious attempt to explore the Shoah, Matas includes gratuitous and unrealistic descriptions of hand-to-hand fighting ("The crowd is beating some of the occupants of the house, using bricks, sticks, or stabbing them over and over with knives, all the time screaming" [p. 16]); grisly details about bayonets and bodies in pits ("I lay on a mound of dead bodies in the camp at Buchenwald and the Nazis began to stick their bayonets into everyone to make sure they were all dead" [p. 89]); and an obligatory love interest ("Slowly he leans over and kisses me, full on the mouth" [p. 89]). The book is ahistorical, using the Holocaust as a plot device.

5. The fifth guideline focuses on the Jewish experience of, and the Jewish response to, the catastrophe. I make the assumption that all study of this subject in the middle/junior high years is introductory and brief, with a typical unit including only one or two books and a few related readings. Therefore, I encourage teachers to choose literature that *highlights, rather than marginalizes, the Jewish experience and particular Jewish responses during the Shoah; that features Jewish life in all its diversity, including specifics of ordinary, daily pre-war life.*

Teachers need to introduce students to protagonists clearly identified as Jews both before and after they are met as victims. They need to offer books that illustrate the vibrancy and contributions of the prewar European Jewish community as well as of the survivors in today's thriving, multifaceted communities in America and in Israel. Books must be chosen that show that Hitler did not defeat the Jewish people.

A novella illustrative of this guideline is *The Grey Striped Shirt* (1993), by Jacqueline Jules, a very simple but powerful book appropriate for a fifth or sixth grader. In gradually recounting the story of their Holocaust experiences for granddaughter Frannie, Grandma Trudie and Grandpa Herman talk about the strength, courage, and faith of the Jews. "A Jew believes in the future," Frannie's grandmother explains. "No matter how bad it was, we kept the faith that one day the war would be over . . . we would lead a normal life—get married, have children and grandchildren" (p. 57). They speak of alternatives when armed resistance was impossible: "We fought the Nazis by staying alive" (p. 54). Finally, they tell the story in the context of a present-day Jewishly observant lifestyle. Frannie goes to synagogue regularly with her grandparents and celebrates the Jewish Sabbath.

Understanding the Jewish perspective is important for all students, but particularly for those who know nothing about Jewish culture, history, institutions, contributions, or the people themselves except those they come to meet through this study. *How tragic the irony if such study were to lead only to further stereotyping and misunderstanding, or to the impression that the most important facet to be learned about the Jewish people is their victimization.*

A book such as Mary Baylis-White's *Sheltering Rebecca* (1989), set in Australia, may inadvertently give the above message. It is the story of Sally Simpkins, a Christian girl who befriends a Jewish refugee, Rebecca. Sally marries Rebecca's brother, Helmut. Helmut's Jewish identity is never mentioned even when his grandchild, at twelve, asks about the war years.

There were many thousands of fully assimilated German Jews just like Rebecca and Helmut, and it's important for children to understand that they were persecuted solely because they were born Jews and not because they were actively practicing, or even acknowledging, their religion. The degree of acculturation and assimilation was without relevance in determining the ultimate fate of Jews during the Holocaust; this is a crucial concept in teaching the event.

But if it is a student's sole introduction to the story of the Nazis' attempt to destroy the Jews, this book seems an ironic choice. Although it is a story of survival, it is not a story of the survival of Jewish life.

Another dimension of this problem is illustrated by certain books about resistance fighters, rescuers, or bystanders, which detail their story but exclude the Jewish experience.

In Carol Matas's *Code Name Kris* (1990), for example, a fictional, action-packed account of young people in the Danish Underground, the Jewish Danes have little relevance to the story. So, too, in Robert Elmer's *A Way Through the Sea* (1994) and *Into the Flames* (1995), two of a series of action-adventure novels set in Denmark.

Yet, stories of the rescue and resistance can easily show the relationship between the rescuing family and the Jews they saved, as is beautifully done in Lois Lowry's novel, *Number the Stars* (1989). Stories told from the perspective of a bystander can include his or her view of the Jewish experience as well, as is powerfully done in the works of Hans Peter Richter, *I Was There* (1962) and *Friedrich* (1970).

6. The sixth stricture suggests that *good books bring students back from the Holocaust era into the reassuring present. They are hopeful and life-affirming, and include acts of religious, spiritual, and armed resistance, illustrating the indomitable will to survive and the strength of the human spirit.*

One such book is Erwin and Agnes Herman's *The Yanov Torah* (1985), a story recounting the efforts of inmates in a work camp in Yanov, Poland, who, at grave risk, smuggled into the camp tiny pieces of a Torah scroll. Painstakingly, inmates collected and pieced together the segments so that even there they could have the central religious symbol of the Jewish people and their tradition. This story of faith, resistance, and hope was written for a Jewish audience, but every reader can feel the triumph of the inmates' spiritual victory.

To affirm the strength of the human spirit, we also look for stories recounted by survivors who have found at least a surface peace and happiness in their lives since the war. When we meet "whole human beings, however inwardly scarred they are," writes James Young (1988) in discussing survivor testimony, we "rehumanize the survivors" and "might return just a fraction of the dignity and humanity the Nazis attempted to destroy" (p. 163).

In this regard, Lena Kuchler-Silberman (1987) tells an uplifting story in her memoir *My Hundred Children*. She recounts her experiences passing as an Aryan and working as a governess, even as she knows her parents have been murdered. In early 1945, she returns to a devastated Warsaw to discover that her sister, too, had been killed. Utterly depressed, she questions the purpose of living. But when she discovers a roomful of children orphaned by the Holocaust, she sets herself the task of caring for the sickly and despairing youngsters, whose numbers ultimately grow to 170. In 1946, she smuggles one hundred of her charges into France and, then, in triumph, into Israel. Winner of the citation "Mother of Israel," Kuchler-Silberman exemplifies the indomitable survivor.

Saving the Fragments: From Auschwitz to New York (1985), Isabella Leitner's sequel to her memoir *Fragments of Isabella* (1978), is another compassionate story with a positive message: The Nazis are evil and must be remembered as such, but the rest of humanity must offer each other a healing and life-affirming kindness and acceptance. In New York in 1945, Leitner struggles to regain some semblance of normalcy after the agony of Auschwitz; when bitterness and anguish threaten to overcome her, she admonishes herself to look ahead with an optimistic spirit, thinking, "I must keep walking into the future" (p. 38).

In stark contrast is *Nightfather: A Novel* by Carl Friedman (1994), brilliant but utterly depressing. Teachers find this book appealing because it is engaging, well written, and easy to read, and opens many possibilities for discussion. It is an important addition to survivor literature. But one must be wary of sharing this book with students below high school age, and of making this the only depiction of survivors students have. It is one story of a damaged soul, an individual not representative of the vast majority of those who survived the camps.

In this brief, tersely told narrative, two generations of victims haunt us. Ephraim, the father, is a survivor who still has night terrors and daily morbid memories. His wife tries to protect the children, Simon, Max, and the narrator, an unnamed girl, from the consequences of his depression. But Ephraim's experiences become theirs, shaping their every encounter. In school, the child-narrator draws a man hanging. "See, he's dead, his tongue is blue" (p. 5), she tells the teacher. At dinner, the children hear about a camp guard who bashed in the brains of anyone who "dared to complain about the quality of the soup" (p. 10). Ephraim tells his own version of children's stories. In his "Little Red Riding Hood," grandmother is in the hospital block with typhus. Ephraim's obsessive connection to the past both sensitizes and traumatizes his children, and the narrator offers a vividly painful picture of one survivor's—her father's—inability to heal.

The tragic stories of the countless survivors who still suffer the anguishes of the Holocaust experience must be told. Depressed, bitter, lonely, unable to take comfort in family or friends, they, too, need their experiences recounted and remembered. But if our teaching time is limited, and if our goals include helping students to empathize with, and learn more about, survivors, one must choose for the initial offerings literature that focuses on the positive aspects of the saved remnant.

7. Guideline seven lauds books that have *the potential to motivate students to examine their own lives and behaviors, providing a bridge from the world of the Holocaust to the present, and promoting opportunities to explore universal issues and themes evoked by the unique stories of the Holocaust.*

Good literature, by definition, conveys the complexities of morality, ethical attitudes, and individual and social responsibility. Good Holocaust literature helps readers to make their own connections between the uniqueness of the event and its universal implications, and to define for themselves the "lessons" of the Holocaust. Teachers, therefore, are relieved of the task of trying to suggest to students artificial, superficial connections and comparisons to the Holocaust in an attempt to make the subject "relevant" and "inclusive." They are relieved, too, of the task of trying to find stories that, like Aesop's fables, draw one fully formulated, universally identifiable conclusion from a particular event: The Holocaust does not allow that, so neither should good Holocaust literature.

Some students may find lessons and universal implications in Judy Hoffman's *Joseph and Me in the Days of the Holocaust* (1979) as they discover the selflessness of Judy's Dutch Christian hiding family. Others may find them in the sacrifices made by Alex and Mela Roslan and their children, a Polish Catholic family who risked their lives to save eight-year-old Jacob Gutgeld and his two brothers. This true story of a rescue from the Warsaw Ghetto is told in Malka Drucker and Michael Halperin's inspiring novel called *Jacob's Rescue: A Holocaust Story* (1993).

Such stories raise any number of questions: What are the short- and long-term emotional consequences of having to hide your religion, beliefs, name, identity? What makes people get involved and even risk their lives to help someone in danger? How can we encourage such helping behavior today? What are appropriate responses today to newly identified rescuers? What can we learn from the rescuers? How does the plight of the Jews move us to consider the potential consequences of persecution and racism in today's America?

In Bernard Gotfryd's short story "A Chicken for the Holidays" (1990), lessons may come from the young narrator, who breaks curfew and risks his life leaving the ghetto to secure a chicken for his family's Jewish holiday meal. Or the lesson may come from the boy's mother, who, while touched and grateful to her son, refuses to serve an unkosher chicken. When the boy asks, "Won't God forgive us?" the mother responds, "In wartime or peacetime, we're a people who must abide by the laws, or else we'll cease to be a people" (p. 47). Questions of theodicy may include, "Where was God during the Holocaust? Why does God let such terrible things happen? How can we still have faith after the Holocaust?"

Different lessons and questions may come from the novels of Hans Peter Richter, who writes frankly of his participation as a Nazi Youth in *I Was There* (1962), and, in the sequel, *Friedrich* (1970), of the friendship between a Jewish boy and his German neighbor, and its tragic conclusion. "How do I respond to peer pressure? Is there potential for evil in all of us?" our students might wonder. "Has humanity changed as a result of this event? In what ways do we still live in the shadow of this watershed event? Why should students learn about the Holocaust? What does it mean for us today? How can we work to prevent ongoing genocides? How do we respond to those who deny the Holocaust? How can we integrate our knowledge of this event into our daily life in a positive way?"

Personal lessons and universal implications may come from discussing the musings and choices of any of the characters caught up in the madness that was the Holocaust. Alex, in the aforementioned *Island on Bird Street*, wonders whether it's right to kill someone who wants to kill him. Marek, in *The Man from the Other Side*, struggles with the knowledge that although his stepfather is saving the lives of Jewish infants, he is destroying their identification papers so they can be adopted without the "burden" of their Jewish identity. Alex Roslan, the Polish rescuer in *Jacob's Rescue*, risks his own children's lives to help Jacob and his brothers.

8. The final guideline speaks to form as well as function: *Literature must offer flexibility in the classroom.*

The best books are not helpful if we cannot use them in class. Those reviewed positively above are all teacher-friendly. High interest, relatively easy to read when used with the appropriate developmental level, and focusing on individuals, they lend themselves well to class discussion. Anthologies such as Gotfryd's *Anton the Dove Fancier and Other Tales of the Holocaust* (1990) are excellent for cooperative learning groups, with each group reading a different story and preparing a response to it. Anthologies generally contain selections from before, during, and after the Shoah, more and less specific in their discussion of humiliation, isolation, hunger, despair, and loss, allowing the teacher to individualize assignments to meet not just the varied educational needs but also the differing emotional demands students present.

Any of the recommendations herein can be made into Reader's Theater pieces or dramatic readings by teachers or students, offering opportunities for active learning and listening. The books provide countless topics for Internet research and e-mail discussions with students in other schools. *The Island on Bird Street*, for example, has served as the centerpiece of an international reading project sponsored by the Ghetto Fighters House in Israel in which American middle school classes are paired with comparable Israeli classes. Children read the book in their native language, chose passages that were particularly meaningful to them, and then discussed the passages and related their ideas through e-mail.

Because they are historically contextualized and include accurate and authentic details, the books recommended here do not require unreasonable study on the part of the English teacher. Of course, teachers should have a basic knowledge of the events of 1933–1945, as well as an overview of the preceding and following years. But, in general, Language Arts teachers will feel comfortable assigning and discussing these books without having had a formal course of study in Holocaust history.

At the same time, because the selections are powerful and engaging, history teachers should find them appealing as research assignments, or as outside readings which complement material studied in history class. Ideally, literature benefits both disciplines. Louise Rosenblatt (1976) affirms the complementary relationship of literature with the social sciences, noting the immediate, personal impact of the former and the objective, analytic experience of the latter. She asks,

> Will the history of the Depression impress [the student] as much as will Steinbeck's *The Grapes of Wrath*? . . . Obviously, the analytic approach needs no defense. But may not literary materials contribute powerfully to the student's images of the world, himself, and the human condition? (p. 8)

"The teacher of literature," she notes, "will have made a valuable contribution if the student leaves his experience of the literary work eager to learn what the . . . historian [has] to offer" (Rosenblatt, 1976, p. 121).

Literary narrative provides a human face for historical abstractions, as teachers address the mandate of Holocaust education set forth by Richard Libowitz (1988): "The student must confront history and its contemporary questions or the course is a fraud; the student must wrestle with his/her own soul or the course is a failure" (p. 71).

Stories make individual and concrete the general and abstract. Stories help students make the complex ideas and events of the Holocaust personally meaningful. They neither replace nor conflict with history; instead, they help us to understand it more fully.

Thus, we turn to literature to help us enter what Elie Wiesel (1990) has called "the kingdom of fire and ashes" to help us explore this event that has forever altered human sensibilities. Literature helps us to speak of the one and not just the six million, to portray the Jews as vital and vibrant people and not just as victims, to provide an alternative to despair by offering vivid examples of heroism, courage, and righteous acts. Sharing personal stories of those who endured the Holocaust helps teachers move away from "reporting" to their students and toward helping them establish a "rapport" with those they meet through diaries, memoirs, testimony, fictionalized accounts of true experiences, essays, and poetry.

And, so, why does the story of the Shoah belong in the English classroom? Filmmaker Arnost Lustig (1979) answers wisely:

> Ultimately, it will most probably be literature which will give us the most faithful picture of the Jewish catastrophe in Europe, thanks to the qualities and attributes which exist only in literature and which have secured for literature its place in human culture and civilization, where it can never be replaced. Aristotle was wise when he gave priority to poets over historians in the effort to find the truth. (p. 312)

REFERENCES

Abells, C. B. (1983). *The Children We Remember*. Rockville, MD: Kar-Ben Copies, Inc.

Ackerman, K. (1994). *The Night Crossing*. New York: Alfred A. Knopf.

Adler, D. A. (1995). *One Yellow Daffodil: A Hanukkah Story*. San Diego, CA: Gulliver Books.

Adler, D. A. (1994). *Hilde and Eli: Children of the Holocaust*. New York: Holiday House.

Adler, D. A. (1993). *A Picture Book of Anne Frank*. New York: Holiday House.

Adler, D. A. (1978). *The Number on My Grandfather's Arm*. New York: UAHC Press.

American Federation of Teachers. (Fall 1992). "What Should Elementary Students Be Doing? Outlines of a 'Thinking Curriculum.'" *American Educator 16*(3):18–22.

Baylis-White, Mary. (1989). *Sheltering Rebecca*. New York: Lodestar Books.

Boraks-Nemetz, L. (1994). *The Old Brown Suitcase: A Teenager's Story of War and Peace*. Port Angeles, WA: Ben-Simon Publications.

Cardwell, D. (1998, October 11). "Cheap Thrills, Seriously." *The New York Times Magazine*, p. 26.

Chaikin, M. (1992). *A Nightmare in History: The Holocaust 1933–1945*. New York: Clarion Books.

Dawidowicz, L. S. (1990, December). "How They Teach the Holocaust." *Commentary 9*(6):25–32.

Drucker, M., & M. Halperin. (1993). *Jacob's Rescue: A Holocaust Story*. New York: Bantam Skylark.

Drucker, O. L. (1992). *Kindertransport*. New York: Henry Holt.

Elkind, D. (1988). *The Hurried Child: Growing Up Too Fast, Too Soon*. Reading, PA: Addison-Wesley.

Elmer, R. (1995). *Into the Flames*. Minneapolis, MN: Bethany House.

Elmer, R. (1994). *A Way Through the Sea*. Minneapolis, MN: Bethany House.

Fluek, T. K. (1990). *Memories of My Life in a Polish Village 1930–1949*. New York: Alfred A. Knopf.

Friedlander, A. H. (1968). *Out of the Whirlwind: A Reader of Holocaust Literature*. New York: Union of American Hebrew Congregations.

Friedman, C. (1994). *Nightfather: A Novel*. New York: Persea Books.

Gotfryd,. B. (1990). "A Chicken for the Holidays." In B. Gotfryd, *Anton the Dove Fancier and Other Tales of the Holocaust* (pp. 40–47). New York: Washington Square Press.

Guzzetti, B. J., Kowalinski, & T. McGowan. (1992). "Using a Literature-based Approach to Teaching Social Studies. *Journal of Reading 36*(2):114–122.

Herman, E. & A. Herman. (1985). *The Yanov Torah*. Rockville, MD: Kar-Ben Copies.

Hoestlandt, J. (1995). *Star of Fear, Star of Hope*. New York: Walker and Company.

Hoffman, J. (1979). *Joseph and Me in the Days of the Holocaust*. Hoboken, NJ: KTAV Publishing.

Jules, J. (1993). *The Grey Striped Shirt*. Los Angeles, CA: Alef Design Group.

Krauthammer, C. (1995, March 27). "Hiroshima, Mon Petit." *Time*, p. 80.

Kuchler-Silberman, L. (1987). *My Hundred Children*. New York: Dell.

Leitner, I. (1985). *Saving the Fragments: From Auschwitz to New York*. New York: New American Library.

Leitner, I. (1978). *Fragments of Isabella*. New York: Dell.

Libowitz, R. L. (1988). "Asking the Questions: Background and Recommendations for Holocaust Study." In Z. Garber (Ed.), *Methodology in the Academic Teaching of the Holocaust* (pp. 57–73). Lanham, MD: University Press of America.

Lowry, L. (1989). *Number the Stars*. Boston, MA: Houghton Mifflin.

Lustig, A. (1979). "Holocaust Literature II: Novels and Short Stories." In B. L. Sherwin & S. G. Ament (Eds.), *Encountering the Holocaust: An Interdisciplinary Survey*. New York: Impact Press.

Matas, C. (1996). *After the War*. New York: Simon & Schuster.

Matas, C. (1990). *Code Name Kris*. New York: Charles Scribner's Sons.

Nerlove, M. (1996). *Flowers on the Wall*. New York: Margaret K. McElderry Books.

Orgel, D. (1978). *The Devil in Vienna*. New York: Dial Press.

Orlev, U. (1991). *The Man from the Other Side*. Boston, MA: Houghton Mifflin.

Orlev, U. (1984). *Island on Bird Street*. Boston, MA: Houghton Mifflin.

Perl, L. & M. B. Lazan. (1996). *Four Perfect Pebbles: A Holocaust Story*. New York: Greenwillow Books.

Postman, N. (1982). *The Disappearance of Childhood*. New York: Delacorte Press.

Richter, H. P. (1970). *Friedrich*. New York: Holt, Rinehart and Winston.

Richter, H. P. (1962). *I Was There*. New York: Holt.

Rosenblatt, L. M. (1976). *Literature as Exploration* (3rd. ed.). New York: Noble and Noble.

Sanacore, J. (1990). "Creating the Lifetime Reading Habit in Social Studies." *Journal of Reading* 33(6):414–418.

Schnur, S. (1994). *The Shadow Children*. New York: Morrow Junior Books.

Social Studies School Service. (1999). *Holocaust Resources and Materials*. Culver City, CA: Author.

Suhl, Y. (1973). *Uncle Misha's Partisans*. New York: Four Winds Press.

Wiesel, E. (1990, February 11). Speech to The American Gathering of Jewish Holocaust Survivors. Washington, DC.

Wilson, M. (1988). "How Can We Teach Reading in the Content Areas?" In C. Weaver (Ed.), *Reading Process and Practice: From Socio-Psycholinguistics to Whole Language* (pp. 280–320). Portsmouth, NH: Heinemann.

Young, J. E. (1988). *Writing and Rewriting the Holocaust: Narrative and the Consequences of Interpretation*. Bloomington: Indiana University Press.

Incorporating Fiction and Poetry into a Study of the Holocaust at the Secondary Level

SAMUEL TOTTEN

Most people have a difficult time comprehending a million of anything, let alone the murder of eleven million people—the murder of six million Jews, plus the murder of approximately five million others (including but not limited to Gypsies, the mentally and physically handicapped, political prisoners, Slavs). Those who wish to attempt to understand what happened and why are faced with a enormous and complex task, one that leads into a tangle of historical, political, social, religious, and moral issues and conundrums. Compounding this is our increasing distance from the events; added to this is the fact that for many, if not most, young people today, all history seems like "ancient history." In light of these factors, incorporating literature into a study of the Holocaust may be one of the most powerful and effective entry points into this complex history.

It is through stories that human beings come to ponder myriad facets of the human condition—the beauty and the horror, the hope and the despair, the thoughtfulness and thoughtlessness, and the kindness and cruelty of which humans are capable. Fortunately, a great quantity of outstanding Holocaust literature—including novels, short stories, poetry, and plays—exists that is ideal for use by teachers and students who choose to wrestle with this unique—and, often, overwhelming—aspect of history.

Value of the Incorporation of Literature into a Study of the Holocaust

Literature has the power to affect people in ways that many other pieces of writing often do not. In addition to impacting one's thoughts, literature has the ability to impact one's beliefs and feelings. In other words, literature is capable of affecting both the cognitive *and* affective levels of one's being. Outstanding literature is also capable of "personalizing" this history, placing a "face" on horrendous facts and events. In a real sense, the incorporation of high quality literature into a study of the Holocaust is often capable of "moving the study from a welter of statistics, remote places and events, to one that is immersed in the 'personal' and the 'particular'" (Totten, 1987, p. 63). By combining the study of literature with the study of history, students are often more apt to contemplate and reflect on the significance of the history of the Holocaust.

Milton Teichman (1976) argues that "[T]he Holocaust cannot remain an abstraction to those who read the literature. It becomes infinitely more than historical facts, theories, speculations—important as these may be. It becomes the experience of individuals-of victims, perpetrators, bystanders. It becomes a crushing personal event in individual lives. . . . One *feels* the tragedy; one is moved to anger, indignation, compassion. And one is often led to confront one's own values and to reflect on the meaning the Holocaust offers for one's own life" (p. 615). He concludes by stating that Holocaust literature "is a literature which shows how precarious our being human is, how easily humans can forfeit their humanity. . . . In short, it is a literature with a massive human weight and generates intense self-questioning and self-searching. It can touch students on deeply personal levels . . . [Indeed,] it gives students unique opportunities for self-confrontation, self-understanding, and the enlargement of sensibility" (Teichman, 1976, p. 613). If students are going to benefit from reading this literature, then they will need the guidance of an instructor who encourages the examination of penetrating questions. Likewise, it will require a teacher who embraces a pedagogy that is not satisfied with simple answers to complex questions.

In *The Call of Stories: Teaching and the Moral Imagination,* Robert Coles (1989) clearly delineates the power that stories (both fiction and people's personal stories) can have on the reader/listener. At one point he says, "We all remember in our own lives times when a book has become for us a signpost, a continuing presence in our lives. Novels [as well as other types of literature] lend themselves to such purposes; their plots offer a psychological or moral journey, with impasses and breakthroughs, with decisions made and destinations achieved" (Coles, 1989, p. 10). Indeed, not only do certain works of literature induce one to become "involved" with the stories of others, but they also provide a means to journey into one's self—one's own mind, heart, and soul. By reading, studying, and discussing literature, one can begin to make connections between one's lived life and those of others. That is not to say that one will even come close to completely understanding what a person experienced during something so overwhelming as the Holocaust, but literature is a powerful *entry point* for attempting to appreciate another's experiences, insights, sorrows, pain, and hope. In that sense, literature provides a unique and powerful lens with which to view and examine the world.

The eminent poet William Carlos Williams suggested to Coles that while ". . . novels or short stories aren't meant to save the world, [a] story *can* engage a reader—not every reader, and some readers only somewhat, but plenty of readers a lot, a whole lot. I mean, art reaches the mind and the heart, and in a way that it doesn't easily get shaken off" (Coles, 1989, p. 120). Isn't this exactly what most educators would hope would happen during a study of the Holocaust—that is, that the students experience such an awakening to this earth-shattering event that its import and ramifications would *never leave them?*

The best literature about the Holocaust is also capable of assisting students to come to an understanding of "deep truths" (Drew, 1991, p. 128). Such truths may include truths about the motivations of the perpetrators, the cataclysmic impact of the daily incidents during the Holocaust years upon the victims, the varied reactions of the victims, and the motivations of the bystanders and rescuers.

Directly related to the above point, Holocaust survivor and scholar Henry Friedlander (1979) suggests that, . . . a study of the literature of the Holocaust could serve as a springboard for analysis [of the whys, hows, whens and whats of the Holocaust]" (p. 541). He goes on to state, "Using various readings—memoirs, novels, plays, essays—students can engage in a semistructured discussion of the issues raised by the Holocaust" (Friedlander, 1979, p. 541).

Ultimately, studying literary responses to the Holocaust can assist students to: (1) confront the extent of the injustices and murderous actions of the Nazis; (2) recognize the deeds of resistance and heroism in ghettos and concentration camps; (3) explore the spiritual resistance manifested by the various responses—including the literary—which portray the dignity of an individual or a people whose spirits transcended the evil of their murderers; (4) recognize the different roles—such as victim, oppressor, bystander, and rescuer—which were assumed or thrust on people during the Holocaust and the choices or lack of choices that evolved as a result; (5) analyze the corruption of language cultivated by the Nazis, for example, use of the terms "emigration" for expulsion, "evacuation" for deportation, "deportation" for transportation to a place that often resulted in death, "aktions" for roundups that usually led to mass murder, and "Final Solution" for the systematically planned annihilation of every single Jew; and, (6) make important and unique distinctions regarding the various nuances and shades of gray concerning the actions of individuals and groups. High-quality literature avoids stereotyping individual and group personalities, beliefs, actions, and, in doing so, "complicates"—in the most positive sense of the word—people and situations so that they are portrayed in a way that is "true" to life.

Carefully selected literature also provides the older and more mature students with a glimmer of insight into the devastating reality of the Holocaust; that is, "life lived in extremity," for example, the unbearable and horrific injustice, cruelty and hatred meted out by the perpetrators, the overwhelming fear, anxiety, and loss experienced by the victims, and the degradation and abject horror that permeated all aspects of life and death under the Nazi reign of terror. That said, while it is essential to study the devastation of the Holocaust in order to understand that the Holocaust was not simply another human rights infraction but rather something cataclysmic in the annals of humanity, teachers should not bombard their students with one horror after another to the point where the students descend into a state of hopelessness and abject anger directed at all of humanity.

The best literature on the Holocaust allows students to examine their own lives and to ponder what it means to be "just," to be prejudiced, to discriminate and hate, and to be a bystander, a perpetrator, or a victim. Literature is also capable of assisting students to ponder how some are ill-treated or made to feel "other," to be maligned not because of what they have done or said, but because, for example, of their religion, beliefs, or background. It also assists them in considering serious ethical and moral questions/dilemmas that place them in the "shoes" of the characters in order to gain a sense of their (the characters') predicaments. Literature highlights the complexities and ambiguities inherent in behavior, which far too many prefer to think of strictly in terms of black and white.

With regard to the latter point, James Farnham (1983) asserts that

> The teaching and learning opportunities inherent in the Holocaust are immense. . . . It can be taught from many points of view, those of literary analysis, history, and psychology to name but three, but it has been my experience that dealing with the ethical dimensions of the literature of the Holocaust is a strong invitation to students to confront the values of life in general . . .
>
> Few bodies of literature are so pregnant a source of problematic issues as the literature of the Holocaust. . . . That this thinking is stimulated is, I think, most vital. Teaching students the historical and sociological facts of the Holocaust is of little value unless the ethical implications of the facts are raised. (p. 67)

Be that as it may, in order for students to come to a *clear understanding of the Holocaust, they must understand the history of the Holocaust.* In light of that, it is imperative that teachers undergird their use of literature on the Holocaust with a substantial amount of history. This can be accomplished in a number of ways, and it doesn't matter how it is done; what does matter, however, is that students have a solid sense of the "whos," "whens," "hows," and "whys" of the Holocaust. In this regard, Peggy Drew (1989) has argued that

> The magnitude of the Holocaust is so great that any individual story, if read in isolation, is going to reflect only one aspect of historical truth. Some [literature] deals more directly with the atrocities themselves, but even these, without the historical perspective, only tell one person's [or family or group's] story. They do not differ to any great degree from any story of personal tragedy, because they do not, indeed they cannot, reflect the "disruption of a familiar moral universe." Only when read within an historical context, with some knowledge of the scope and magnitude of the Holocaust, is the reader able to put the individual story into a more universal perspective. (p. 21)

Elsewhere, Drew (1991) astutely observes that

> Young people have little sense of time, in historical terms. Unless they have studied the history of the period about which they are reading, they have no framework within which to put it. Rarely do they make the connections between what they have read and actual historical events unless they have had some formal study of the historical period in question. They have read an exciting, perhaps moving, story that may leave a lasting impression on them, but adds nothing to their understanding of history, as they do not have the knowledge necessary to put it into historical context. (p. 128)

Drew (1991) concludes by asserting that ". . . unless [the history and situations within that history] are made real, there is little point in studying these events. If the study of genocide is not also the study of humanity and inhumanity, if it does not add to our understanding of human behavior, then what is its purpose in the curriculum?" (p. 128). This point suggests the critical need for teachers to establish clear and strong rationales for teaching a piece of Holocaust literature.

Finally, and this is germane to the aforementioned point, what should *never* be forgotten as teachers go about preparing and implementing lessons about this history is the profound fact that *millions on millions of innocent people—mothers, fathers, children, grandmothers, grandfathers, uncles, and aunts—were subjected to horrendous discrimination, cruelty, and horrific deaths at the hands of the Nazis and their collaborators, not because of what they did but because of who they were.* Furthermore, teaching this material should not, *ever,* simply result in another English or history lesson, where stories, for example, are selected only because they are "exciting" (as the author heard one teacher say) or a poem only for the purpose of examining its prosody and structure.

Availability of Literature on the Holocaust

There is a huge amount of literature (novels, novellas, short stories, children's and early adolescent literature, young adult literature, and poetry) that addresses various facets of the Holocaust. It is eclectic in style, and includes, but is not limited to, that which is documentarylike, "realistic," surrealistic, and "lamentative." The storylines address a wide array of situations, incidences, and events, including the ever-increasing prejudice and discrimination against the Jews in Nazi Germany, the roundups and deportations, the abject hardships and death in the ghettos, resistance efforts, the deportations to the concentration and death camps, the selections and killings, the horrific "medical experiments" conducted in some of the camps, the liberation, and life in the post-Holocaust years.

Much of the finest literature was written by those with first-hand experience of the Holocaust. Some of this literature, including a great deal of poetry, was written during the period 1933–1945, in ghettos and camps and by partisans in the woods, but most was written after the conclusion of World War II. Many who did not experience the Holocaust first-hand also have written plays, poetry, novels, short stories, and young adolescent literature about the Holocaust.

Like most bodies of literature, the quality of works that portray some aspect of the Holocaust ranges from the mediocre to the superb. As this author has argued elsewhere:

> The mediocre is that which trivializes the magnitude of the Holocaust or turns it into melodrama. It is also that writing that treats the Holocaust as simply another event in history or another story to be told, without fully acknowledging its specialness. Finally, it is also that writing that uses the tragedy of the Holocaust as a background event or metaphor in order to either heighten the interest of the primary story or to draw historical or personal but flawed analogies between one event and another. (Totten, 1988, p. 211)

The weakest literature also has a tendency to portray the history inaccurately, to stereotype the appearance, ideas, behaviors, and beliefs of people, and to create wooden or unbelievable characters. Two examples of such works are Elisabeth Reuter's *Best Friends* (1993) and Carol Matas's *Daniel's Story* (1993).

The strongest pieces of literature about the Holocaust for young adolescents are those that are well written, engaging, developmentally appropriate, and historically accurate. (For a listing and description of many of the best literary works available for children and young adolescents, see the U.S. Holocaust Memorial Museum's *Annotated Bibliography* and the *Facing History and Ourselves Holocaust and Human Behavior Annotated Bibliography.* Complete citations of these bibliographies are included in the annotated bibliography that accompanies this chapter.)

The strongest literary works for older students meet basically the same criteria, except that they contain a more complex storyline and/or character development. (For a listing and description of these works, readers should consult one or more of the annotated bibliographies that accompany this chapter.)

Selection of Holocaust Literature for Use in the Classroom

As previously mentioned, when selecting any resource or curricular materials for classroom use, teachers need to reflect continuously on their curricular rationale. Ascertaining the "why" will influence the selection of genre (e.g., novel, short story, poetry, drama) as well as the focus of the storyline (e.g., the particular aspect of the Holocaust such as the pre-Holocaust period and beyond; life in the ghettos; the roundups, deportations, and death camps; the resistance; or a combination of these). Selection of the genre and specific works will also be contingent upon student interest as well as the amount of time that can be allocated for such a study. Early on, teachers also need to decide how they are going to use the literature (e.g., the sort of teaching strategies and learning activities that will be most effective in assisting the students to study and learn the literature).

Prior to using a work, teachers must ascertain whether a piece is developmentally appropriate for use with his/her students. The most effective way to accomplish this is by reading the material prior to using it. For the most part, the most conscientious teachers do this. In those situations where teachers have neglected to read a work prior to using it with their students, the results have often been less than positive—and, in certain cases, disastrous. This is due to three main reasons: (1) the work proved too difficult for students to understand; (2) the work included profanity unsuitable for classroom use; and/or (3) the carnage described and depicted was overly graphic and thus unsuitable for use with certain students.

Teachers need to take into consideration a number of other key issues prior to selecting a piece of Holocaust literature for classroom use, as described in the following.

First, the work should be historically accurate, and not convey misconceptions about the history or the people involved. On a simple, but important level, one needs to ascertain the following: Are the dates of actual events correct? Are the names of actual people correct? Is the chronology of actual events correct?

On a more complex level, does the literary work delineate the incidents and events in their varied complexity versus providing a simplistic portrayal that is bereft of the intricacies involved (including the torturously difficult no-win decisions many of the victims faced)?

Furthermore, even though the events are fictionalized, a teacher should ask him/herself such questions as: Could the events have happened in the manner described or are they outlandish? Is the work set in a historical context that conveys the significance of the historical period, events, incidents? Does the literature address or complement those issues that we are examining in the larger study? If a teacher answers "No" to any of these questions, then another piece of literature needs to be selected.

Margaret Drew (1991) also suggests that:

> ... if the literature is to add to the understanding of history, ... teachers should select books that represent the broad events of that history rather than uncommon or unique occurrences. For example, books on the Polish resistance during the Holocaust may be historically accurate; the fact that 85 percent of the Polish Jews died in the Holocaust, however, makes it obvious that this is far from typical of Holocaust experiences in Poland. A story of resistance, like ... [the] Newbery Award winner, *Number the Stars*, by Lois Lowry, represents a larger movement, as 98 percent of the Danish Jews were saved, but even so, the Holocaust is essentially a story, not of resistance, but of atrocity. Used in conjunction with other books, works like this can add to the understanding of the Holocaust, used in isolation, they distort the history. (p. 128)

Second, teachers need to evaluate the readability of the piece.   Is the piece at the right reading level (not too easy, not overly difficult) for his/her particular students? Is the reading level at the right level of sophistication (e.g., not simplistic or too erudite).

Karen Shawn (1994) suggests that in order to provide students with the best learning experience possible, teachers need to consider the "flexibility" of the piece (p. G4). That is: (1) Is the piece "relatively easy for students to read, and for teachers to discuss with students, individually or in groups"?; (2) Would the piece be useful in "laying the groundwork for the teaching of Holocaust history"?; and (3) Do the pieces "offer opportunities to explore a variety of important issues and themes"? (Shawn, 1994, p. G4).

Third, the work must be engaging and thought-provoking to the students.
There is little justification in using a work that students are likely to find boring or bereft of the power to move them to deeper thought. This is not to say that a difficult work or one that challenges their abilities should not be used. It is to say that there is an ample number of works to choose from and teachers should attempt to select a work that will most likely engage their students. When feasible, it is wise to provide the students with an opportunity to select those works that they find most engaging, thus capitalizing on the students' natural curiosity and interests.

Fourth, literary works should be selected that are not so long or so complex that they almost automatically result in there not being adequate time for ample discussion of the work.   A study of the Holocaust demands that there be ample time for the students to wrestle with and discuss the complex and horrific material to which they are being introduced, to raise questions and issues that they are likely to have, and to be allowed to vent their concerns and, in many cases, their horror. Thus, works that almost automatically mitigate against such discussion (either due to their size or complexity) should be avoided for classroom use and replaced by other works. Students should be encouraged to read the longer or more complex works on their own outside of class.

Fifth, literary pieces that romanticize the history of the Holocaust should be avoided.   Some authors use the Holocaust as a "setting" in order to develop a maudlin story or one of unrequited love. Such works need to be totally avoided as they distort the history and draw the reader away from the significance that the Holocaust period has for humanity. On another note, and this is related to the above point by Drew, some authors have a tendency to overemphasize the aspect of rescue, thus distorting the history. Teachers need to keep in mind that "at best, less than one-half of one percent of the total population [of non-Jews] under Nazi occupation helped to rescue Jews" (Oliner and Oliner, 1991, p. 363).

Sixth, the literary work should present "true to life" characters as opposed to caricatures or stereotypes.   In this regard, the works should "offer recognizable human experiences, and foster involvement and identification with the victims of the Holocaust" (Shawn, 1994, p. G4).

Corroborating Shawn's points, Masha Rudman and Susan Rosenberg (1991) sensibly suggest that: "Jewish characters should be portrayed as functioning human beings who have decisions to make, and who, rightly or wrongly, make them. Protagonists should be three-dimensional, neither wholly sweet-natured and generous nor constantly strong and heroic" (p. 163). They go on to argue that the most "[e]ffective stories of the Holocaust refrain from elevating their characters to mythic proportions. Instead, they underscore the common humanity of all the victims as well as the survivors and rescuers" (Rudman and Rosenberg, 1991, p. 170).

Seventh, in light of the fact that many of the literary works on the Holocaust include ghastly and horrifying images, scenes, incidents, and events, a teacher must use the soundest judgment possible when selecting and employing such works in class.   Teachers must absolutely avoid bombarding their students with one horrific image after another. Unfortunately, some teachers believe that only by bombarding students with the most horrific images and stories will they (the teachers) "get through" to their students, that is, "drive home" the horror of Holocaust. Instead of capturing the students' attention or inducing learning, however, such actions may, paradoxically, achieve the opposite effect. Whereas some students may simply turn away from the history, others may become so numb that they cannot focus on it.

It is best to use those "texts that do not exploit . . . the students' emotional vulnerability" (Parsons and Totten, 1993, p. 6). More specifically, "[g]raphic material should be used in a judicious manner and only to the extent necessary to achieve the objective of the lesson" (Parsons and Totten, 1993, p. 6).

Eighth, literature of the Holocaust should "offer sufficient stimulus for readers to draw their own conclusions and avoid didactic sermonizing" (Rudman and Rosenberg, 1991, p. 163).   Literature that presents powerful and historically accurate storylines with believable characters do not need to preach about the horrors of the Holocaust; it will be evident throughout.

Ninth, the literature selected should be capable of challenging students to examine their own lived lives and world.   Ideally, a study of such literature will prod students to examine their own prejudices, including why and how they interact with and treat people whom they may perceive as "different" from themselves. It is to be hoped that it also will make students more conscious and concerned about civil and human rights infractions in their own communities, state, nation, and across the globe.

Tenth, works should be chosen that ". . . enlighten students [and] encourage further study of the Holocaust, thus helping to ensure remembrance" (Shawn, 1994, p. G4).   Teachers need to select works that will "plant a seed" of concern in their students' minds vis-à-vis the significance the Holocaust has for humanity as well as their own lives.

When selecting pieces for children and young adolescents (ten- to fifteen-year-olds), stories that use particularly offensive profanity are better left unused. There are enough outstanding works for use in the classroom that teachers do not need to select pieces whose language will either offend certain students and/or incense parents.

Finally, it is worth noting that both early adolescents and older students often are intrigued with stories and novels whose protagonists are approximately the same age as themselves. Works such as these are likely to engage the students even more than other Holocaust literature due to the fact that many young readers will more readily identify with the characters in the story.

Additional Commentary on Holocaust Poetry

The most finely wrought poetry has the power to penetrate as deeply as anything language has to offer into the mysteries of being and the multifaceted aspects of life. Just as the brutality of the genocide of the Jews, the Gypsies, and others causes one to ponder long and hard the "face" of humanity, the most powerful poetry about the Holocaust also causes one to ponder long and hard about the fact of genocide, including the human and inhuman proportions of it. Furthermore, "poetry encourages us to view the human and natural scene with a fresh eye, uncontaminated by the clichés of customary speech" (Langer, 1995, p. 558). This is particularly important when examining such a shattering event as the Holocaust.

As far as using poetry in the classroom, one of its many advantages over long short stories, novels, and plays is its brevity. Its succinctness is ideal for those facing a packed curriculum and/or serious time constraints.

The subject matter addressed in the poetry of the Holocaust is as rich as that found in fiction. There are poems by those who wrote poetry in the forest, the ghettos, the concentration camps, and even in the death camps; by survivors of the Holocaust who wrote in the aftermath of that tragedy; and by Jews and non-Jews who either did not live in Europe during that period and/or were not even alive. Holocaust survivor Elie Wiesel (1977) has written the following about the first group:

> Poems, litanies, plays: to write them Jews went without sleep, bartered their food for pencils and papers. They gambled with their fate. They risked their lives. No matter. They went on fitting together words and symbols. An instant before perishing in Auschwitz, Bialystok, in Buna, dying men described their agony. . . . There was then a veritable passion to testify for the future, against death and oblivion, a passion conveyed by every possible means of expression. (p. 9)

In the same vein, Aaron (1983) has noted that

> Astonishing as it may be, literary activity was vital and widespread in the ghettos, in hiding, among the partisans, on the "Aryan" side, and even in some of the concentration camps. Indeed, after waves of mass deportations to death centers, those who temporarily hugged life in the various places feverishly turned to writing. Spontaneous literary activity not only continued but actually increased when one would expect language to evaporate, to turn to ashes in the conflagration of gas chambers and crematoria.
>
>   . . . Although the writers availed themselves of the entire spectrum of literary genres, the most popular one was poetry. That this poetry is probably the richest of the Holocaust literature should not be surprising. For poetry—perhaps because it provides, more often than any other literary genre, the most precise correlatives for states of consciousness—was the first vehicle of reaction against Nazi barbarism. Moreover, the poets, writing from "the heart of darkness," reflect an immediacy of experience that is untainted by the remembering process of memory. Nothing but total recall could unveil the truth articulated in this body of literature. (pp. 120–121)

There are poems that are easy to understand, as well as a huge body of poetry that is difficult and complex, many of which are interwoven with erudite allusions and symbols. The latter need not be avoided, but prior to introducing them into the classroom, teachers need to make sure that their students have the cognitive abilities, reading skills, and knowledge bases to analyze and ultimately understand such poetry. (For list of poems appropriate for various students at the secondary level, see Appendix A.)

On a different note, those poems and songs that use the Holocaust as a metaphor for one's personal ills and pains, draw false and simplistic analogies between the Holocaust and certain other human rights infractions or other injustices must be avoided. Pieces such as Sylvia Plath's "Lady Lazarus" and "Daddy," Aaron Kurtz' "Behold the Sea," the Boomtown Rats' "I Never Loved Eva Braun," and Lenny Bruce's "My Name Is Adolf Eichmann," all of which have found their way into various Holocaust curricula, do little to nothing to further student understanding of the Holocaust. Indeed, most of them are more likely to provide students with a skewed view of the Holocaust and pass the Holocaust off as simply another "ailment" among many found in society. Over and above that, their wording (e.g., "cute" rhymes, mocking voices, and flippant tone) can seduce students into thinking that the Holocaust was no more serious than the issues their favorite musicians and bands sing about in their songs today. In light of that, a simple rule of thumb is to avoid them; instead, teachers should use those poems that are truly thought-provoking, well-wrought, and, most important, deal with significant aspects of the Holocaust.

Methods for Incorporating Literature into the Classroom

There are, of course, innumerable ways in which teachers can incorporate literature into their study of the Holocaust. Provided here are selected instructional strategies appropriate for use in grades seven to twelve. They are based on the author's personal teaching experiences and those of other successful educators.

1. *Anticipatory Sets.* At the beginning of a study, it is always worthwhile to obtain a sense of the students' existing knowledge base of the Holocaust. One way is to have students write down everything they know about the Holocaust—basic facts: dates, countries involved, people involved; concepts (totalitarian, fascism, anti-Semitism); focus; and so on. Next, the students should work individually to develop a "cluster" or "mind-map" reflecting their knowledge. Once that is completed, the class as a whole could develop a single "cluster" on the board. Such a preassessment allows teachers to ascertain their students' knowledge base regarding the breadth, depth, and accuracy of their students' knowledge. (For information on using clusters, mind-maps, or webbing in the classroom, see Carol Booth Olson (Ed.), *Practical Ideas for Teaching Writing as a Process at the Elementary School and Middle School Levels.* Sacramento: California State Department of Education, 1996).

2. *Establishing a Basic Understanding of Holocaust History.* When studying a piece of Holocaust literature, it is vital that students gain an understanding *about the history* of the Holocaust. Grace Caporino, an English teacher at Carmel High School in Carmel, New York, helps her students gain key insights into the history of the Holocaust prior to reading literary works by doing the following: "I begin with a brief chronology of the immediate events in Europe which preceded the Holocaust and then I assign Chapter 1 ("Precedents") in the student edition of Raul Hilberg's *The Destruction of the European Jews* (New York: Holmes and Meier, 1985). That chapter illuminates both the historical and religious policies that paved the way for the events of the Holocaust. [More specifically,] Hilberg discusses the cyclical 'trend in the three successive goals of anti-Jewish administrators' (e.g., the conversion, expulsion and exclusion policy from the fourth century through the Middle Ages laid the groundwork for Hitler's Final Solution of annihilation). My students raise questions such as 'Why the Jews?' They do not understand why the Jews have been a target group for persecution throughout history and they know nothing of Christian complicity in this matter. Students examining Holocaust literature for the first time are often confused about the apparent ease with which Hitler implemented the Final Solution. Hilberg's historical perspective explains the present by shedding light on the past. Hilberg notes that in the past, 'The missionaries of Christianity had said in effect: You have no right to live among us as Jews. The secular rulers who followed had proclaimed: You have no right to live among us. The Nazis at last decreed: You have no right to live' (p. 8). Another feature of this chapter is Hilberg's illustration of a side-by-side comparison of the church canonical law and the Nazi anti-Jewish measures. For students seeking a better understanding of the dynamics of both perpetrator and victim in the Holocaust, as well as an understanding of the forerunners of Hitler's policies, Hilberg's 'Precedents' provides satisfactory answers" (Written statement provided to the author by Caporino, 1991). (Another excellent work for assisting students to gain an understanding of the history of the Holocaust is Michael Berenbaum's *The World Must Know: The History of the Holocaust as Told in the United States Holocaust Memorial Museum*. Boston, MA: Little, Brown, 1993. This volume was written for use by high school students; not only is it reader-friendly but it includes numerous and invaluable photographs and excerpts from first-person accounts.)

The same sort of preparation can be done for specific pieces of poetry about various aspects of the Holocaust. For example, if students read poems in ". . . *I Never Saw Another Butterfly": Children's Drawings and Poems from Terezin Concentration Camp, 1942–1944* (New York: Schocken Books, 1993), they could first read, study, and discuss the chapter entitled "A 'Model' Concentration Camp: Theresienstadt" in Bea Stadtler, *The Holocaust: A History of Courage and Resistance* (West Orange, NJ: Behrman House, 1994).

3. *Reader-Response Theory.* An extremely powerful way to engage students in a study of literature is through the use of "reader-response theory." Commenting on the basic difference between a traditional approach to literary study and the reader-response process, Louise Rosenblatt, a pioneer in the field of reader-response theory, argues persuasively that the reader should not be perceived as "a blank tape registering a ready-made message. [Rather, he/she should be] actively involved in [coming to an understanding of a work] out of his/her responses to the text" (quoted in Sheridan, 1991, p. 804). Unlike many traditional methods of literary study, reader response is a process that honors the students' backgrounds, diverse experiences, unique insights, and perspectives as an integral component in the study of literature. Thus, instead of relying on the omniscient thoughts of a critic or the privileged knowledge of the teacher, it recognizes and highly values each individual student's response to a piece of literature.

In an essay entitled "Rewriting the Book on Literature: Changes Sought in How Literature is Taught, What Students Read," John O'Neill (1994) has written that:

> Basically, reader response theory differs most radically from previous theories about teaching literature in the degree of emphasis placed on the reader's response to an interpretation of the text. . . . In reader response theory, the text's meaning is considered to reside in the 'transaction' between the reader and the text, not from the text alone.
>
> . . . In practice, reader response theory considers very carefully how students respond intellectually and emotionally to the text. . . . By validating students' responses, teachers can spark a lively discussion from which a careful literary analysis will flow. . . . Rather than beginning with a discussion of symbolism or metaphor, for example, teachers should allow an exploration of these aspects to develop from students' own observations about the work.
>
> . . . *the emphasis on getting students to respond to the literature doesn't mean that any response is as good as another. Students are continuously urged to return to the text to find validation for their views.* [italics added] (pp. 7, 8)

The key is to provide the students with an opportunity to begin to examine literature from their own unique perspective, without imposing anyone else's interpretation on them. This is a method that avoids that stultifying situation in which students feel compelled to come up with the so-called single correct answer. (For a thorough and enlightening discussion of reader-response theory methodology, see Alan C. Purves, Theresa Rogers and Anna O. Soter, *How Porcupines Make Love III: Readers, Texts, Cultures in the Response-Based Literature Classroom.* White Plains, NY: Longman, 1995. For a discussion of a pedagogical strategy that uses reader-response theory to assist students to examine a Holocaust-related poem, see Samuel Totten's [2000] "Incorporating Poetry into a Study of the Holocaust at the High School Level Via Reader Response Theory.")

4. *Reflective Journals.* Having students keep reflective journals throughout the study is a good method for accomplishing all of the following: to assist them to examine their newfound knowledge of the Holocaust; to raise questions or concerns they have about what they're reading; to ponder the meaning the literature has for their own lives; and to provide the teacher with critical information in regard to the level of the students' understanding or misunderstanding of key facts, concepts, and issues.

Specific journal assignments could require students, for example, to reflect on the meaning that a story or poem has for them, comment on new insights they have gleaned about the Holocaust from a story or poem, discuss whether a literary work is one they will likely remember or not and why, comment on or examine a novelist's or poet's use of inverted symbolism or biblical allusions, or record a line or image in a poem that particularly stood out for them and provide an explanation as to why that was so. There are unlimited ways to use such a journal; and, in that respect, teachers and students are limited only by their imagination.

The journals can also serve as a means of two-way communication for the teacher and student. While reading a student's journal, the teacher could posit questions for the student to address in the next set of entries. Likewise, a student could raise questions/issues for the teacher to address. Writing in the journals could be done in both class and at home.

It is imperative that clear and well-structured guidelines be provided to the students (e.g., how they should go about writing a reflective journal, the need for depth over superficial coverage, the need to avoid simply reiterating what one has read versus the need to comment on one's new insights/perspectives). If the latter is not done, then more often than not the journals will become not much more than a recapitulation of the story and/or what the teacher has said about a work.

5. *Writing Assignments for Reflective Purposes.* Any type of writing assignment that requires students to reflect on what they've read and to analyze and synthesize is an ideal exercise. One worthwhile assignment is to have the students write a letter to a character in a literary work, in which they comment on key insights gained, the most important new ideas/concepts/insights gleaned, what they may never forget after reading the work, what they wish to *always* remember, and what they want to share with someone else about the work. Students need not address all of the questions but rather choose the one or two that really catch their individual interest. Students should be encouraged to let their "own voices" and feelings shine through. They should be reminded (and required) to include a salutation and a closing, just as they would in any letter they write.

Such writing becomes much more personal, powerful, and meaningful than many staid assignments in which students are required to write a typical essay. By writing about something they care deeply about and by connecting the affective and cognitive domains, the assignment becomes less of a school assignment and something that has personal relevance for the student. (This is not to say that essays do not have a place in such a study. They do!)

6. *Using Individual Poems as an Introduction to a Lesson.* Individual poems can be used as an introduction to a lesson on a particular topic (e.g., life in the ghettos, deportations, the mass murder of the Jews), theme (e.g., "bystanding," loss, remembrance), or a unit of study. For example, when focusing on the issue of remembrance and/or the ramifications that the Holocaust has for those living today, a teacher might introduce Yuri Shul's "The Permanent Delegate." Or, if a teacher wishes to focus on the issue of culpability or denial, he/she might introduce William Heyen's "Riddle." By contrast, if a teacher wishes to drive home the point that individuals were behind the statistics (e.g., the six million who perished), he/she may design a learning activity around Herman Taube's "A Single Hair." Discussion of a poem can raise a host of issues that the students can pursue and revisit during their study of the actual history of the Holocaust period.

7. *Outside Reading Assignments.* To both conserve classroom time and to provide a worthwhile homework assignment, Stephen Feinberg, a former middle school teacher in Wayland, Massachusetts, and now an employee at the United States Holocaust Memorial Museum, assigned his students an outside reading assignment in which each student was asked to select a book from the following list: *Friedrich, Devil in Vienna, Night, The Diary of Anne Frank, Upon the Head of the Goat*, and *The Upstairs Room*. Students were allowed to select any other novel/ memoir that deals with the Holocaust as long as it constituted quality literature. The directions he gave his students were as follows: "Two weeks after you begin reading the book, you will be asked to write me a letter in which you will describe what you have read so far. The description should include mention of the main characters in the book and a brief description of the plot and/or theme of the book." This part of the assignment constitutes a check on whether the students are making progress or not on their reading; and, as such, it is not graded.

The rest of the directions were as follows: "After you have finished reading the book, you will be asked to write me another letter. This second letter should indicate how the book increased your understanding and knowledge of the Holocaust or Nazis. This letter should include specific references to the action in your book. This second letter will receive a grade."

8. *Comparing and Contrasting a Fictional Work and a First-Person Account.* Having students read a fictional work and a first-person account by a victim of the Holocaust, a survivor, a liberator, or other eyewitness about a similar event, and then comparing and contrasting (during a classroom discussion, a small group discussion, or in writing) the information and insights gleaned from the two genres provides students with a rich lens to examine the events of the Holocaust. (For other ideas on how to incorporate first-person accounts into a study of the Holocaust, see Chapter 5.)

9. *An In-depth Study of an Author-Survivor's Life and Works.* For those teachers who wish to have their students engage in an in-depth literary study, a powerful assignment is to have the students examine how an author's life influenced the plots, themes, motifs, and symbolic structures of his/her works. Prior to assigning this project (which is most appropriate for tenth, eleventh, and twelfth graders), the teacher needs to ascertain whether enough biographical or autobiographical materials (biographies, autobiographies, oral histories, interviews, biographical essays, etc.) are available on particular authors. Without ample materials available on an author, this project is nearly impossible to undertake. Next, the teacher should develop a list of twenty to thirty authors (novelists, playwrights, short story writers, poets), and then provide his/her students with a quick and concise overview of the author's life, works, and so on. In this way, hopefully, the students will discover an author about whom they wish to learn more. The basic assignment for each student is as follows: Read at least one major biography or autobiography about or by the author; if the author selected is a novelist or playwright, then read at least three major works by the author; if the author selected is a short story writer or poet, then read approximately ten short stories and twenty poems, respectively (the teacher could require that certain stories and poems be read but also allow the student to select a number on his/her own); and read at least three critical essays about the author's work. Finally, in a major paper, analyze how the author's life (formative years, various experiences, beliefs, friendships, religious and political affiliations, etc.) had an impact on his/her plots, symbolic structure, imagery, motifs, and themes. (For a more detailed description of such a project, see Samuel Totten's "Examining the Holocaust Through the Lives and Literary Works of Victims and Survivors" [1998]).

10. *Highlighting Certain Topics and/or Themes.* Select pieces of literature that address certain topics and/or themes that can be used to complement a historical study of the Holocaust. Some of the many themes one might focus on are: the ever-increasing discrimination faced by the Jews from 1933 onward; the bystander syndrome; life and death in the ghettos; the death camps; resistance; the "choiceless choices" people were forced to make; "the other victims" (e.g., Gypsies, the mentally handicapped, physically handicapped of the Holocaust); hope against hope; abject fear; loss; mourning; the aftermath of the Holocaust. Ida Fink's short story "The Key Game," for example, could be used to illuminate issues such as the abject fear Jews experienced at the hands of the Nazis, the plight of children during the Holocaust years, the problematics of attempting to go in hiding, and the fate of the Jews.

The literature can serve as entry points into an examination and discussion of key issues as well as a "springboard for analysis" (Friedlander, 1979, p. 541). Ideally, the literary works and their themes should be interwoven throughout the study in order to assist the students in being more reflective about what they are reading, studying, and discussing.

11. *Comparing and Contrasting Literary Works on the Same Subject and/or Theme.* Select two or more literary pieces (novels, novellas, short stories, poems) on the same or a similar incident or event, and have the students compare and contrast the various perspectives, experiences, and actions of the characters; the similarities and differences of the portrayal of events; the similarities and differences evident in the perspectives of the authors; and the differences in style of the works.

12. *Using Literature to Introduce Students to a Study of the Holocaust.* Stephen Feinberg found that "novels such as Jane Yolen's *The Devil's Arithmetic,* Lois Lowry's *Number the Stars,* and Esther Hautzig's *The Endless Steppe* are good to introduce middle school students (grades six through eight) to the study of the Holocaust. Questions that can be addressed in a three- to five-day study of any these works are: 'What is a Jew?' *(The Devil's Arithmetic);* 'What was the Holocaust?' *(Number the Stars);* 'Who were the Nazis?' *(Number the Stars);* 'Why did the Nazis mistreat some people?' *(The Devil's Arithmetic);* 'What are some of the consequences of war and the mistreatment of people?' *(The Endless Steppe, Number the Stars);* and 'Where did this activity take place?' *(Number the Stars, The Endless Steppe,* and *The Devil's Arithmetic)*" (written statement provided to the author by Feinberg).

Feinberg also found that novels such as Doris Orgel's *The Devil in Vienna* and Hans P. Richter's *Friedrich* appeal to upper-middle level/junior high school students (grades seven through nine) "for they all deal with the emotional and social issues that teenagers grapple with." He adds that "the videotape entitled *Friendship in Vienna,* based on Orgel's novel, deals with issues of courage, survival, friendship, and family dynamics. All of these issues strike a responsive chord in middle school and junior high school students, and serve as the entry way to a fuller examination of the Holocaust as a historical reality. [It should be noted that] with a limited amount of time available, these works can raise meaningful and pertinent questions, moral and philosophical in nature, about the Holocaust. Students can address the issue of personal versus collective responsibility for the actions of nation/states or the sort of power an individual has in dealing with social issues. Encouraging a comparison with our own time, they can wrestle with the possibility of a Holocaust-like tragedy happening in our own society" (personal communication from Stephen Feinberg, July 1992).

13. *Examining "Choiceless Choices."*   During a study of Holocaust literature, the students could focus on what literary critic and Holocaust specialist Lawrence Langer (1982) refers to as the "choiceless choices" that the Nazis' victims were forced to make on a daily basis (e.g., the people "were plunged into a crisis . . . where crucial decisions did not reflect options between life and death, but between one form of abnormal response and another, both imposed by a situation that was in no way of the victim's own choosing," p. 72). Langer (1982) cites several examples of such choiceless choices. In one situation, in a barrack at Auschwitz, "there was a single limited source of water for washing and for draining excrement from the latrine. If the women took the water for washing, the primitive sewage system would be blocked, creating an intolerably offensive (and unhealthy) situation" (p. 74). In another case, a non-Jewish physician/prisoner at Auschwitz "was able to save one woman selected for gassing by reporting to the Political Division that an SS man needed her particular skill in his work. But her success was tainted by the response from that department: 'We'll have to take another in her place'" (p. 75). Holocaust literature is rife with such situations. By examining such "choiceless choices," the students can begin to gain unique insights into the tortuously difficult situations faced by the victims of the Nazis. Likewise, through an examination and discussion of such situations, the students may be more likely to empathize with the horribly difficult dilemmas that confronted the victims.

As students come across such situations in their readings, they could be required to record and comment on them in their learning logs/journals. Or, a large piece of butcher paper could be taped to the class wall during the study, and each time a student or the class as a whole comes across such a situation, it could be noted on the butcher paper. Periodically, the teacher could draw the attention of the class to the list and conduct a discussion or learning activity around it.

14. *Responding to One's Newfound Knowledge about the Holocaust via Poetry.*   Following an in-depth study of the history of the Holocaust (in which students read primary and secondary documents, study various types of literary responses, view films, listen to guest speakers, and/or view tapes of survivors), students could create poetry to express their thoughts, feelings, and new insights.

15. *Using Poetry as an Alternative Means of Reflection and/or Assessment.* Instead of having students keep journals on a daily basis, allow those students who wish to do so to create a poem in regard to their newfound insights and/or feelings concerning the Holocaust. This activity serves to provide powerful and unique closure to a lesson(s) and/or sections of a unit.

16. *Critiquing Holocaust Poems Written by Those Who Did Not Personally Experience the Holocaust through the Lens History.* Students who have engaged in *a fairly thorough study* of the Holocaust can use their newfound knowledge of the history to critically examine the themes, content, and style of the poems written by those who did not personally experience the Holocaust. For example, students could be asked to critique the strengths and weaknesses of a poem like "Yellow Starred" by Sister Mary Philip deCamara, included in Charles Fishman (Ed.), *Blood to Remember: American Poets on the Holocaust* (Lubbock: Texas Tech University Press, 1991). Among the issues that might be raised are: What is the author trying to convey through her use of the literary device of synecdoche? Is this an effective device or not? Explain. What are the strengths and the weaknesses of using synecdoche to "get at" the heart of the Holocaust? Select illustrative lines from the poem, and provide an explanation for each of your points. Why does the author use Anne Frank's name as opposed to that of another victim's? In light of the focus of Anne Frank's diary and the point at which it ends, is there anything problematic in using Anne Frank's name in this poem? What is the "danger" and/or misnomer of using Hitler as the single perpetrator of the Holocaust? Explain your answer. All of these questions should simply be used as "starter" questions in order to examine key issues surrounding the significance of the history of the Holocaust and the ramifications it has for contemporary society.

17. *Examining the Concept of the Shrinking World of the Jews.* In order to explore the idea of the "shrinking universe" of the Jews as the Nazis perpetrated their crimes, teachers could—during a study of the history—use Wladyslaw Szlengel's powerful poem "Things" (which is included in Frieda W. Aaron's *Bearing the Unbearable: Yiddish and Polish Poetry in the Ghettos and Concentration Camps* [Albany: State University of New York Press, 1990] and is a poem that focuses on the "contraction of the history of the Warsaw ghetto") in conjunction with the following statement by Elie Wiesel (1984): "The Nazis' aim was to make the Jewish universe shrink—from town to neighborhood, from neighborhood to street, from street to house, from house to room, from room to garret, from garret to cattle car, from cattle car to gas chamber. And they did the same to the individual—separated from his or her community, then from his or her family, then from his or her identity, eventually becoming a work permit, then a number, until the number itself was turned into ashes" (p. 1). If used with care, the tripartite use of the history, Szlengel's poem, and Wiesel's statement are capable of providing students with a powerful view of what the Jews faced. (Another poem that would be ideal for use with this activity is Abraham Sutzkever's "Teacher Mira," which is a poem about the ever-shrinking number of surviving children in the Vilna Ghetto school.)

18. *Focusing on the Fate of Children via Poetry Written by Children during the Holocaust.* During a study of the Holocaust that draws particular attention to the fate of the approximately one and a half million child victims of the Nazis, the students could study poems that children wrote while incarcerated in Theresien-stadt. Many are included in Hana Volavkova's (Ed.), " . . . *I Never Saw Another Butterfly": Children's Drawings and Poems from Terezin Concentration Camp, 1942–1944* (New York: Schocken Books, 1993). These poems could be used in conjunction with diary excerpts written by children during the period and/or other types of first-person accounts in which individuals relate what they experienced as children during the Holocaust period.

19. *Studying Poems by Victims and/or Survivors.*   A special study could be conducted of the poetry that was written about various facets of the Holocaust *by those who actually experienced the events.* More specifically, the students could be introduced to poetry that was actually written during the Holocaust years as well as that which was written in the aftermath of the Holocaust by survivors. As Henryk Grynberg has written, "the quickest reaction" to the genocide "came in poetry; first of all from the Polish-Jewish poets who wrote while locked in the ghettos and isolated in their hideouts before the annihilation of the ghettos and the so-called final solution" (quoted in Aaron, 1990, p. 1). Information about the poets' lives could be introduced by the teacher or researched by the students in order to gain a greater understanding of the poets and their poetry. (An excellent place to begin a search for biographical information on various poets lives is Lawrence Langer, *Art from the Ashes: A Holocaust Anthology* [New York: Oxford University Press, 1995].) Other useful sources are introductions to a poet's collected works and critical essays on a poet's poetry. Among the poets that might be considered for such a study are Jozef Bau, Paul Celan, Yitzhak Katzenelson, Abba Kovner, Nelly Sachs, Hanna Senesh, Abraham Sutzkever, and Wladyslaw Szlengel.

20. *Exploring and Reacting to Gripping Images and Phrases.*   An engaging way to help students understand how different poets have attempted to illustrate and convey the "reality" of the Holocaust as well as how they, paradoxically, have attempted to address its ineffability is to have students focus on the gripping images and extraordinary phrases that poets have used—many of which are likely to "stick in the mind" long after the study is over.

A thought-provoking activity along this line is to have the students—individually or as a class—keep a running chart (preferably on large sheets of butcher paper, which can be taped to a wall in the classroom) of the various lines, phrases, and images that they come across that stand out for them and/or make them see the Holocaust with "different eyes." Across from the listing, they can briefly comment on their perception of the image or phrase and how it has assisted them to begin to see the Holocaust in a new and unique way. Class discussion could revolve around such information.

21. *Ascertaining Why People Wrote Poetry during the Holocaust.*   People wrote poetry for different reasons during the Holocaust period—to produce art as a form of resistance, to break out of their forced isolation and to assert one's humanity, to commemorate the victims, to serve as a form of remembrance, or to constitute a unique form of testimony. As Elie Wiesel (1977) has asserted: "If the Greeks invented tragedy, the Romans the epistle, and the Renaissance the sonnet, our generation invented a new literature, that of testimony. We have all been witnesses and we all feel we have to bear testimony for the future. And that became an obsession, the single most powerful obsession that permeated all the lives, all the dreams, all the work of those people. One minute before they died they thought that was what they had to do" (p. 9).

Students could read biographical and critical essays about poets who have written poetry about the Holocaust and select quotes by them (the poets) in regard to their reasons for doing so. Students could then design posters or other media, such as murals or poems, to post around the room, including the quotes and their sources. These quotes could be used during the study of the Holocaust to revisit such issues as resistance, remembrance, lamentation, and/or other poetic purposes (e.g., an affirmation of life, a cry for help, testimony, "moral and cultural sustenance" [Aaron, 1983, p. 129], etc.), as well as to delve into why and how people attempted to respond to such an overwhelming catastrophe such as the Holocaust.

22. *Combining a Study of a Poem with the Study of a Poster of a Museum Artifact.* One way for students to begin to understand both the depersonalization as well as the personal nature of the Holocaust is to combine a reading of Abraham Sutzkever's "A Cartload of Shoes" with a photograph or poster of the piles of shoes left behind by the victims of the Nazis. (For a powerful translation of Sutzkever's poem, see Frieda W. Aaron, *Bearing the Unbearable: Yiddish and Polish Poetry in the Ghettos and Concentration Camps.* Albany: State University of New York Press, 1990, pp. 55–56.)

The United States Holocaust Memorial Museum's Education Department has designed a set of posters based on artifacts included in the museum's permanent exhibit, and among these is a poster of victims' shoes. A teaching guide with ideas on how to incorporate the posters into a study of the Holocaust accompanies the poster series. The poster on the shoes and the suggested teaching activities ideally complement the above exercise. For additional information on the Poster Set, write to: Museum Shop, U.S. Holocaust Memorial Museum, 100 Raoul Wallenberg Place SW, Washington, DC 20024.

23. *Combining a Photograph and Poetry on the Same Topic.* After locating the famous photograph of a young boy with his hands up as the Nazis rounded up the people imprisoned in the Warsaw Ghetto, the photograph should be photocopied and made into an overhead. While viewing the overhead, the students should be given the following directions (which could be typed on a handout and given to each student so each can proceed at his/her own pace): (1) Describe in as much detail as you can what you see in the photograph by jotting down phrases or sentences, and (2) Once you have described the photograph in as much detail as possible, explain in a sentence or two what you think is taking place in the photograph. Once all of the students have completed task number two, a small group and/or a class discussion could be conducted. (Sources that include the aforementioned photograph are: Barbara Rogasky, *Smoke and Ashes: The Story of the Holocaust*. New York: Holiday House, 1988, p. 188; and Seymour Rossel, *The Holocaust: The World and the Jews, 1933–1945*. West Orange, New Jersey: Behrman House, 1992, pp. 13 and 15.)

After discussing the photograph, each student should be given a copy of a poem entitled "The Little Boy With His Hands Up" by Yala Korwin. (The poem is available, among other places, in Charles Fishman (Ed.), *Blood to Remember: American Poets on the Holocaust*. Lubbock: Texas Tech University Press, 1991, pp. 54–55.) The teacher or a student should read the poem. On completion of the reading, the students should engage in a reader-response activity; students can then refer back to their initial reaction to the photograph.

Finally, the teacher could give a minilecture on the situation that was captured in the photograph, providing the students with details from historical and first-person accounts that would add to the students' greater understanding of the situation.

24. *Addressing the Issue of Reparations via "Draft of a Reparations Agreement" by Dan Pagis.* Following a reader-response theory activity on Dan Pagis's poem, entitled "Draft of a Reparations Agreement," the class could research/examine (1) the purpose reparations generally serve, and (2) the arguments that have ensued in Israel over accepting reparations from Germany for the crimes against humanity it committed during the Holocaust years. A discussion could then ensue over (3) the students' own positions in regard to reparations vis-à-vis the Holocaust and the reasoning behind such positions; as well as (4) the attitude reflected in the poem with regard to the issue of reparations. (For a thought-provoking discussion of the issue of reparations as well as Pagis's poem, see the chapter entitled "Israel" in Albert H. Friedlander's *Riders Towards the Dawn: From Holocaust to Hope*. New York: Continuum, 1994, pp. 223–253.)

25. *A Chronological Overview of the History via a Combination of Essays, First-Person Accounts, and Fiction/Poetry.* Select a number of literary works that provide a chronological overview of the Holocaust (from pre-Holocaust days through the concentration and death camps to liberation and beyond), and interweave them with a set of essays and first-person accounts that address the same events in the same order.

26. *Incorporating Art into a Literary Study.* After studying the Holocaust or reading a literary work (novel, poem, short story, or play) that particularly moved him/her, a student could create a piece of art (watercolors, oil painting, pen and ink drawing, pastel drawing, charcoal drawing, photographs, collage, sculpture, mobile) that expresses his/her feelings, new insights, and so on.

Alternately, after handing out a particularly powerful poem to each of the students, the teacher or a student could read the poem aloud. Then, without further discussion (although the student could refer to the poem and reread it as many times as he/she wishes), each student could create a piece of art (e.g., a drawing, a painting, a collage, a piece of sculpture, mobile, etc.) in response to the poem. On completion of the artwork, each student could write a short response as to why he/she created what he/she did; and in doing so, he/she should include a statement as to the meaning the poem has for him/her. Students could also address how their work elucidates the poem. Finally, the teacher could conduct a class discussion about the poem and, when appropriate, have the students introduce and discuss their individual pieces of art. As a final activity, the students could create a new piece of artwork based on their new insights. Again, they could write a short response to what they have created, and add an extended response as to how their initial creation differs from their second and why.

Ruth Ann Cooper, a curriculum coordinator for the Tulsa (Oklahoma) Public Schools, has students develop murals that depict their response to the Holocaust literature they have read and studied. "Murals made of individual Holocaust drawings [by each student] and then glued to butcher paper," she suggests, "[can be hung] on a back wall" (Cooper, 1994, p. 16). Alternatively, students could develop a large mural (on butcher paper) around key topics/information they have studied in the literature (reflecting key characters, time period, events, history, etc.)

Another engaging and thought-provoking activity is to provide the students with small (5" x 5") tiles, have them paint their responses to their study of the Holocaust literature on the tiles, glaze and fire the tiles in a kiln, and create an area such as a wall space or countertop where the tiles can be viewed by other students and the general public. Generally, both the artistic as well as the heartfelt responses are indicative of the impact that the study of the Holocaust has had on the hearts *and* minds of the students.

All of these activities are ways to engage students in the use of various multiple intelligences (Armstrong, 1994; Gardner, 1983).

27. *Developing an Anthology of Literary Works on the Holocaust.* Different groups of students could develop their own anthology of literary readings, copying off key works they wish to include, developing their own artwork to accompany the volume (or using copies of the art created during and/or following the Holocaust years), and writing up connecting information (introductions, etc.) between the pieces. The students—along with the teacher—could develop a set of criteria for selecting those works to be included in the anthology. The anthology could be bound and included in a class or school library for use by other students.

28. *Book Reviews.* Students could write book reviews of novels, novellas, plays, short story collections, and poetry collections about the Holocaust for publication in the school newspaper or publications that solicit and publish student work. Prior to having students attempt such a project, they should be informed of what constitutes a quality book review and be provided with exemplary examples.

29. *Studying Inverted Symbolism.* A thought-provoking way to assist students to come to an understanding and "appreciation" of how various authors have attempted to come to come to grips with an event that has often been deemed "unbelievable," "unspeakable," "ineffable," "incomprehensible," "inexpressible," and "beyond imagination" is to have them study the use of inverted symbolism. By drawing the students' attention to the use of inverted symbolism, it may also assist them to begin to understand how the Holocaust "turned the world upside-down." A useful activity in this regard is to have the students, as a class, keep a running chart (preferably on large sheets of butcher paper, which can be taped to a wall in the classroom) of the various instances of inverted symbolism that they come across. Across from the listing of the symbol, they can comment on (1) the traditional or typical use of the symbol, (2) the way in which the author used the symbol, and (3) the purpose for the author's use of the inverted symbol. As the list grows, the students will begin to gain a more holistic view of the use of such literary devices. Periodically, class discussions could focus on the information on the list.

An example of the use of an inverted symbol is Elie Wiesel's use of "night." As Wiesel has stated:

> [W]henever I say "night" I mean the Holocaust, that period. "Night" has become a symbol for the Holocaust for obvious reasons. As we have said, a night has descended upon mankind, not only in Europe, but everywhere. . . . Night enveloped human destiny and human history.
>
> . . . It is strange but night, before that, would have meant different things: dreams, poetry, waiting for the Messiah. . . . Night is a poetic image, a romantic one at that. After all, night preceded day, night induces people to love each other, to give birth and life. Ironically, it has become the opposing symbol, anti-life, anti-man, anti-Messiah. Night had become the opposite of whatever we call creativity and creation. (quoted in Cargas, 1976, p. 54)

30. *Studying Parody.* When used effectively, parody can be illustrative of how "normality" and/or the accepted view of life and beliefs are turned upside down. A classic case in point is Elie Wiesel's parody of Psalm 150 in his work *Night* (1960). As Simon P. Sibelman (1992) notes in his essay, "Chaos into Art: The Holocaust and Literature":

> The ultimate psalm of the Psalter positively enjoins Man to exalt in God's presence, each verse possessing a driving spirit of joy. Wiesel's lugubrious eight-lined parody negates the psalmist's message while openly accusing God of complicity in the creation of the *anus mundi* and in the callous murder of His "Chosen People." The result of this anti-psalm is to press the reader to question the Divine message and the one by which Wiesel negates it. We are uncomfortably compelled to construct an inventory of our beliefs and perceptions of reality and of God. Wiesel's art engages us in a dialogue of re-evaluation of traditional Western moral and religious values. (p. 179)

Students could locate an example of a situation, person, group, or idea that is being parodied and write the passage out on a large sheet of butcher paper. Next, small groups of students could select one parody and then discuss it in relation to the following: (1) how the parody and the original idea differ, listing the differences point by point; (2) the meaning of the parody; (3) whether the parody works for them, and why or why not; and (4) how the parody enhances, neglects to enhance, or detracts from the meaning of the story or poem, and why that is so. Class discussion could serve as a follow-up to this activity.

31. *Examining the Use of Language.* When undertaking a study of the Holocaust, it is useful for students to focus on the issue of language, particularly the need to "strive for precision of language" (Parsons and Totten, 1993, p. 3). An important lesson is how people's use and understanding of language today (including the use of such common terms as "train" or "hunger," for example) does not parallel the reality of what the victims of the Nazis experienced.

For example, when young people think of the term "train," they generally think of a line of coaches with comfortable seats, large windows and a dining car. During the Holocaust period, however, the trains used to transport the Jews to the concentration and death camps were box cars without seats, toilets, air conditioning, or heating, and in which people were stuffed into them and left there until they arrived at their destination (and many of them perished en route due to suffocation, heart attacks, and other physical crises). In speaking of her unit on Jane Yolen's *The Devil's Arithmetic*, Vicki Zack (1991) comments on her young (fifth grade) students' reaction to the Jews deportations: "They [the students] asked why the people did not look out the windows and how people could suffocate in a 'train.' For the children the word train evoked common, everyday images; indeed who would believe that humans would be transported in cattle cars and later branded" (p. 45).

On a related note, Parsons and Totten (1993) point out that

> Words that describe human behavior often have multiple meanings. Resistance, for example, usually refers to a physical act of armed revolt. During the Holocaust, it also meant partisan activism that ranged from smuggling messages, food, and weapons to actual military engagement. But, resistance also embraced willful disobedience: continuing to practice religious and cultural traditions in defiance of the rules; crafting fine art, music and poetry inside ghettos and concentration camps. For many, simply maintaining the will to remain alive in the face of abject brutality was the surest act of spiritual resistance. (p. 4)

Students should be provided with the opportunity to compare and contrast their use of common terms (e.g., "starvation," "trains," "resistance," "camps," and "resettlement") with the way the Nazis used them. An easy and effective way to do this is to have the students (at the outset of the lesson or during the course of the lesson) define—individually—in their own words and in writing terms such as "hunger," "starvation," "evacuation," and "resistance"). As the class moves through the unit, a chart that delineates the vast and radical differences of such usage could be kept and posted at the front of the room.

This is also the ideal place to introduce the concept of "euphemism" (e.g., "resettlement" instead of "deportation"; "emigration" instead of "expulsion"; "evacuation" instead of "deportation"; "special treatment" for the gassing of people; and "Final Solution" for the annihilation of every Jew on the face of the earth), and the distinction between figurative and literal language.

32. *Concluding Activities.* A. As a concluding activity to a lesson or unit, students could examine various perceptions of the term "Holocaust literature" (see examples that follow). Students could select one of the quotes and then write a short piece in which they agree or disagree with the statement, and provide solid rationales for their answers.

> It would seem that a "Holocaust literature" is an impossibility—that, indeed, the phrase itself is a contradiction in terms. The reasons are at least threefold: first, there is no way to link a life-affirming enterprise such as literature with a death-bound phenomenon of such magnitude; second, no gift for literary description, no matter how blessed that gift, could possibly encompass the horror of the Holocaust experience itself; third, since any writing involves some degree of distance, such "detachment" would violate the sanctity of the actual suffering and death undergone by the victims. (Ramras-Rauch, 1985, p. 3)

> Through aesthetic principles or stylization and even through the solemn prayer of the chorus the unimaginable ordeal still appears as if it had some ulterior purpose. It is transfigured and stripped of some of its horror and with this, injustice is already done to the victims. (Words of German refugee philosopher T. W. Adorno, quoted in Ezrachi, 1980, p. 52)

> There is no such thing as Holocaust literature—there cannot be. Auschwitz negates all theories and doctrines, to lock it into a philosophy is to restrict it. To substitute words, any words, for it is to distort it. A Holocaust literature? The term is a contradiction. (Wiesel, 1978, p. 234)

> The opposite of art is not ugliness but indifference. (Wiesel, 1986, EY21)

B. Another useful concluding activity is to provide students with thought-provoking quotes to respond to in writing, with the charge to analyze the meaning of the quote through the prism of the literary works and historical pieces that they have read and studied. One such quote might be Albert Einstein's "The world is too dangerous to live in—not because of the people who do evil, but because of the people who stand by and let them." Another thought-provoking quote that could be used is one by Lawrence Langer (1978): "With the disruption of a familiar moral universe, the individual must find 'new' reasons for living and 'new' ways of confronting the prospect of death introduced into reality by atrocity. Such disruption mars not only an ordered universe, but the identity of one's self, one's conception of where he fits and how (and why) he is to act as a human being in a dehumanized world" (p. 10). These are just two of the scores and scores of quotes by victims and survivors of the Holocaust, literary artists, and others that could be used.

Conclusion

Powerful stories and images found in Holocaust literature and poetry often adhere to the minds and hearts of those who have read and studied them. It is to be hoped that this, in turn, will cause readers to become more reflective about what they have studied, the world they live in, how they treat people, and how they react to civil and human rights infractions committed in their communities and beyond. If educators seek to assist students in gaining deeper insight into the Holocaust, to become more reflective and thoughtful human beings, to ponder and care about man's inhumanity to man, and to examine one's lived life in regard to personal and social responsibility, then the thoughtful use of Holocaust literature is a valuable vehicle for reaching those goals.

REFERENCES

Aaron, Frieda. (1983). "Poetry in the Holocaust Dominion." In Randolph L. Braham (Ed.), *Perspectives on the Holocaust* (pp. 119–131). Boston & London: Kluwer-Nijhoff Publishing.

Aaron, Frieda W. (1990). *Bearing the Unbearable: Yiddish and Polish Poetry in the Ghettos and Concentration Camps.* Albany: State University of New York Press.

Armstrong, Thomas. (1994). *Multiple Intelligences in the Classroom.* Alexandria, VA: Association for Supervision and Curriculum Development.

Cargas, Harry James. (1976). *Harry James Cargas in Conversation with Elie Wiesel.* New York: Paulist Press.

Coles, Robert. (1989). *The Call of Stories: Teaching and the Moral Imagination.* Boston, MA: Houghton Mifflin.

Cooper, Ruth Ann. (March 1994). "From Holocaust to Hope: Teaching the Holocaust in Middle School." *Middle School Journal* 25(3):15–17.

Darsa, Jan. (1991). "Educating about the Holocaust." In Israel W. Charny (Ed.), *Genocide: A Critical Bibliographic Review: Volume Two* (pp. 175–193). London and New York: Mansell Publishers and Facts on File.

Drew, Margaret A. (1991, February). "Merging History and Literature in Teaching About Genocide." *Social Education* 55(2):128–129.

Drew, Peggy. (Fall 1989). "Holocaust Literature and Young People: Another Look." *Facing History and Ourselves News,* pp. 20–21.

Ezrachi, Sidra Dekoven. (1980). *By Words Alone: The Holocaust in Literature.* Chicago, IL: University of Chicago Press.

Farnham, James. (1983, April). "Ethical Ambiguity and the Teaching of the Holocaust." *English Journal* 72(4):63–68.

Felstiner, John. (1986). "Paul Celan's *Todesfuge.*" *Holocaust and Genocide Studies: An International Journal* 1(2):249–264.

Friedlander, Henry. (1979, February). "Toward a Methodology of Teaching About the Holocaust." *Teachers College Record* 80(3):520–542.

Gardner, Howard. (1983). *Frames of Mind: The Theory of Multiple Intelligences.* New York: Basic Books.

Langer, Lawrence L. (1978). *The Age of Atrocity: Death in Modern Literature.* Boston, MA: Beacon Press.

Langer, Lawrence L. (1995). *Art from the Ashes: A Holocaust Anthology.* New York: Oxford University Press.

Langer, Lawrence L. (1982). *Versions of Survival: The Holocaust and the Human Spirit.* Albany: State University of New York Press.

Matas, Carole. (1993). *Daniel's Story.* New York: Scholastic Inc.

Oliner, Pearl, & Samuel Oliner (1991). "Righteous People in the Holocaust." In Israel W. Charny (Ed.), *Genocide: A Critical Bibliographic Review.* Volume 2, pp. 363–385. London: Mansell.

O'Neill, John. (1994, June). "Rewriting the Book on Literature: Changes Sought in How Literature is Taught, What Students Read." *ASCD Curriculum Update,* pp. 1–4, 6–8.

Parsons, William S., & Samuel Totten. (1993). *Guidelines for Teaching About the Holocaust.* Washington, DC: Author.

Ramras-Rauch, Gilas. (1985). "Introduction." In Gila Ramras-Rauch and Joseph Michman-Melkman (Eds.), *Facing the Holocaust: Selected Israeli Fiction.* Philadelphia, PA: The Jewish Publication Society.

Reuter, Elisabeth. (1993). *Best Friends.* New York: Pitsopany Press.

Rudman, Masha Kabakow, & Susan P. Rosenberg. (Summer 1991). "Confronting History: Holocaust Books for Children." *The New Advocate* 4(3):163–176.

Rushforth, Peter. (1994). "'I Even Did a Theme Once on That Anne Frank Who Kept The Diary, and Got an A Plus on It': Reflections on Some Holocaust Books for Young People." *Dimensions: A Journal of Holocaust Studies* 8(2):23–35.

Shawn, Karen. (1994). "'What Should They Read and When Should They Read It?': A Selective Review of Holocaust Literature for Students in Grades Two Through Twelve." *Dimensions: A Journal of Holocaust Studies* 8(2):G1–G16.

Sheridan, Daniel. (1991, November). "Changing Business as Usual: Reader Response Theory in the Classroom." *College English* 53(7):804–814.

Sibelman, Simon P. (1992) "Chaos into Art: The Holocaust and Literature." The *British Journal of Holocaust Education* 1(2):171–184.

Teichman, Milton. (1976, February). "Literature of Agony and Triumph: An Encounter with the Holocaust." *College English* 37(6):613–618.

Totten, Samuel. (1998). "Examining the Holocaust Through the Lives and Literary Works of Victims and Survivors." In Robert Hauptman & Susan Hubbs Motin (Eds.), *The Holocaust: Memories, Research, Reference* (pp. 165–188). New York: The Haworth Press, Inc.

Totten, Samuel. (2000). "Incorporating Poetry into a Study of the Holocaust at the High School Level Via Reader Response Theory." In Samuel Totten (Ed.), *Teaching Holocaust Literature.* Boston: Allyn & Bacon.

Totten, Samuel. (1988). "The Literature, Art, and Film of the Holocaust." In Israel W. Charny (Ed.), *Genocide: A Critical Bibliographic Review* (pp. 209–240). London and New York: Mansell Publishing and Facts on File.

Totten, Samuel. (1987). "The Personal Face of Genocide: Words of Witnesses in the Classroom." *Social Science Record: The Journal of the New York State Council for the Social Studies* 24(2):63–67.

Wiesel, Elie. (1960). *Night.* New York: Hill and Wang.

Wiesel, Elie. (1977). "The Holocaust as Literary Inspiration," pp. 4–19.

Wiesel, Elie. (1978). *A Jew Today.* New York: Random House.

Wiesel, Elie. (1978). "Then and Now: The Experiences of a Teacher." *Social Education* 42(4): 266–271.

Wiesel, Elie. (April 19, 1984). "All Was Lost, Yet Something Was Preserved." *The New York Times Book Review,* 1, 23.

Wiesel, Elie. (1986, January 5). "Welcoming 1986." *The New York Times,* p. EY21.

Young, Gloria. (1993). "The Poetry of the Holocaust." In Saul S. Friedlander (Ed.), *Holocaust Literature: A Handbook of Critical, Historical, and Literary Writings* (pp. 547–574). Westport, CT: Greenwood Press.

Zack, Vicki. (1991, January). "'It Was the Worst of Times': Learning About the Holocaust Through Literature." *Language Arts* 68:42–48.

APPENDIX

With so much poetry available, only those pieces that this author has found particularly useful for classroom at the secondary level will be highlighted. Each poem selected has been chosen for one or more of the following reasons: it is extremely thought-provoking, it highlights a theme that teachers are likely to explore with their students, its focus is such that it is capable of "capturing" both a student's mind and heart, and it is, for one or more reasons (e.g., its language, images, theme), likely to stay with one long after it has been read. Many of the poems contain fairly simple language, allusions that are not arcane, and readily accessible ideas and points. They also contain imagery, for the most part, that is bereft of horrific images and scenes. What follows, of course, is a mere sampling of what is available. There are sure to be dozens—if not scores—of other poems that teachers would find interesting and worthwhile to include in their lesson/units on the Holocaust.

The poems that the author has found to be *readily accessible and of greatest interest to most students* in grades nine to twelve are: "Riddle" by William Heyen, "The Little Boy With His Hands Up" by Yala Korwin, "There Were Those" by Susan Dambroff, "Written in Pencil in the Sealed Railway-Car" by Dan Pagis, and some of the many poems included in ". . . *I Never Saw Another Butterfly": Children's Drawings and Poems from Terezin Concentration Camp, 1942–1944,* edited by Hana Volavkova. Particularly powerful among the latter poems are: "Terezin" by Mif, "The Butterfly," "Fear," "Untitled," "The Garden," and "Homesick."

Prior to reading and studying the Terezin poems in ". . . *I Never Saw Another Butterfly": Children's Drawings and Poems from Terezin Concentration Camp, 1942–1944,* students need to study the facts of life and death in Terezin. Then and only then can they begin to fully appreciate the sense of anxiety, longing, want, sadness, hope against hope, loss, and unintended irony that comes through so clearly in these poems. They need to know, for example, that

> [w]hile at the camp [the children] were forced to work from eighty to one hundred hours per week, with those over fourteen years of age working the same hours and type of work as the adults. From Terezin they were shipped further east to the death camps, usually Auschwitz. Of the fifteen thousand children under the age of fifteen who were sent to the camp, only one hundred survived. (Young, 1993, p. 553).

Without such knowledge, many of the poems may sound like they are about poverty-stricken areas found in many cities (e.g., New York, Detroit, Los Angeles, Cairo, Delhi, Bangkok, Mexico City) throughout the world.

A particularly popular poem with educators who teach the Holocaust is Maurice Ogden's "The Hangman." While not about the Holocaust per se, it is an interesting resource for examining certain issues (e.g., bystanders, choices people make and do not make, individual responsibility, social responsibility) that get to the heart of many concerns vis-à-vis the Holocaust.

The following poems[1] may find an appreciative readership among the more advanced students: "Draft of a Reparations Agreement" by Dan Pagis, "Testimony" by Dan Pagis, "Europe, Late" by Dan Pagis, "Autobiography" by Dan Pagis, "There Were Those"* by Susan Dambroff, "1945"* by Bernard S. Mikofsky, "Babi Yar" by Yevgeny Yevtushenko, "For Our Dead"* by Marilynn Talal, "The Survivor" by Tadeusz Rózewicz, "Pigtail," by Tadeusz Rózewicz, "Why I Write About the Holocaust"* by Gary Pacernick, "Survivors"* by Mary Sarton, "Burnt Pearls" and "Smoke of Jewish Children" by Abraham Sutzkever, "The Permanent Delegate" by Yuri Shul, "A Dead Child Speaks" and "O the Night of the Weeping Children!" by Nelly Sachs, "I Have Never Been Here Before" by Jacob Glatstein, "A Single Hair" by Herman Taube, "Terezin" by Hanus Hachenberg, "Say This City Has Ten Million Souls," by W. H. Auden, "Digging"* by Frank Finale, "AD"* by Kenneth Fearing, "Memories of December"* by Gizela Spunberg, "Shema" by Primo Levi, "Yellow Starred"* by Sister Mary Philip de Camara, "A Few More Things About the Holocaust"* by Leatrice H. Lifshitz, "Terezin" by Hanus Hachenburg, "For Our Dead"* by Marilynn Talal, "Yahrzeit"* by Miriam Kessler, "Tattoo"* by Gregg

Shapiro, "Roses and the Grave"* by Vera Weislitz, "It's High Time"** by Wladyslaw Szlengel, "Hospital"** by Jozef Bau, "A Cartload of Shoes"** by Abraham Sutzkever, "The Teacher Mire"** by Abraham Sutzkever, "Things"** by Wladyslaw Szlengel.

Teachers who teach advanced placement students also may wish to consider Paul Celan's "Todesfuge." Although extremely complex, Celan's poem is powerful and thought-provoking. Other poems that advanced placement students may find interesting and/or challenging are "XXXVIII"* by Derek Walcott, "The Hindenburg"* by Van K. Brock, "There Is One Synagogue Extant in Kiev"* by Yaacov Luria, "Miserere"* by William Pillin, and "The Tailor"* by Patricia Garfinkel.

1.   While most of the poems marked with a single asterisk (*) have appeared in separate collections and/or journals, all are contained in Charles Fishman (Ed.), *Blood to Remember: American Poets on the Holocaust.* Lubbock, TX: Texas Tech University Press, 1991. Those poems marked with a double asterisk (**) all appear in Frieda W. Aaron, *Bearing the Unbearable: Yiddish and Polish Poetry in the Ghettos and Concentration Camps.* Albany: State University Press of New York, 1990.

SELECT ANNOTATED BIBLIOGRAPHY

In light of the vast number of poems, short stories, and novels available on the Holocaust, individual literary works have not been included here. Readers should consult the bibliographies listed below for information regarding individual works.

Bibliographies

Cargas, Harry. (1985). *The Holocaust: An Annotated Bibliography.* Chicago, IL: American Library Association. 196 pp. Includes a large number of annotations of key literary works, including a brief but useful section on poetry (pp. 148–150).

Drew, Margaret. (1988). *Facing History and Ourselves: Holocaust and Human Behavior Annotated Bibliography.* New York: Walker and Company. 124 pp. Especially developed for use by educators who are interested in teaching about the Holocaust, this bibliography is divided into five key parts (I. Children's Books, II. Adult Books, III. German Culture, IV. Genocide of the Armenian People, and V. Choosing to Participate). It also includes five useful appendices (A. Basic Readings Lists, B. Literature as History, C. Legacy of the Holocaust: A Supplementary Reading List; D. Human Behavior: A Supplementary Reading List, and E. Genocide of the Cambodian People).

Edelheit, Abraham J. and Hershel Edelheit (Eds.). (1986). *Bibliography of Holocaust Literature.* Boulder, CO: Westview Press. 842 pp. This massive bibliography contains a section entitled "The Holocaust and the Literary Imagination."

Shawn, Karen. (1994). "'What Should They Read and When Should They Read It?': A Selective Review of Holocaust Literature for Students in Grades Two Through Twelve." *Dimensions: A Journal of Holocaust Studies,* 8(2):G1–G16. Provides an overview of forty-seven works. It also includes a short but thought-provoking introduction that suggests possible criteria to use when selecting Holocaust literature for classroom study. A must read for educators.

Szonyi, David. M. (Ed.). (1985).*The Holocaust: Annotated Bibliography and Resource Guide.* New York: KTAV Publishing House. 396 pp. Includes annotated works of fiction and imaginative literature (novels, short stories, drama, poetry).

Totten, Samuel. (1988). "The Literature, Art, and Film of the Holocaust." In Israel Charny (Ed.), *Genocide: A Critical Bibliographic Review* (pp. 209–231). London and New York: Mansell Publishers and Facts on File. Includes an essay and an accompanying annotated bibliography of novels, short story collections, drama, and collections and volumes of poetry.

United States Holocaust Memorial Museum. (1993). *Annotated Bibliography.* Washington, DC: Author. This bibliography includes sections that highlight fiction ideal for use with middle level and junior high school students, high school students, and adults. It also includes a section for adults entitled "Poetry, Drama and Art" and another entitled "Literary Criticism."

General Anthologies

Brown, Jean E., Elaine C. Stephens, & Janet E. Rubin. (1997). *Images from the Holocaust: A Literature Anthology.* Lincolnwood, IL: NTC Publishing Group. This anthology is ideal for use in the secondary-level classroom, as it includes a rich and valuable array of short historical pieces, first-person accounts, short stories, poetry, and drama on a wide range of key issues vis-à-vis the Holocaust. The titles of the ten chapters are: Rumblings of Danger, In Hiding, Fleeing for Their Lives, Surrounded by Ghetto Walls, Imprisoned in the Camps, Resisting Evil, Liberation, The Days After, A Mosaic of Courage, and Echoing Reflections.

Langer, Lawrence (Ed.). (1995). *Art from the Ashes: A Holocaust Anthology.* New York: Oxford University Press. A massive and superb anthology that is comprised of essays, excerpts from journals, diaries and first-person accounts, fiction, drama, and poetry, and a discussion and examples of the artwork by the "painters of Terezin."

Teichman, Milton, & Sharon Leder. (1994). *Truth and Lamentation: Stories and Poems on the Holocaust.* Urbana: University of Illinois Press. This anthology is divided into two sections ("Transmitting Truths" and "Lamentations"), each of which includes a rich collection of short stories and poetry. Among the many authors whose works are included are: Tadeusz Borowski, Sara Nomberg-Przytyk, Cynthia Ozick, Elie Wiesel, Aharon Appelfeld, Pierre Gascar, Jakov Lind, Charlotte Delbo, Paul Celan, Dan Pagis, William Heyen, Abraham Sutzkever, Abba Kovner, Nelly Sachs, Ida Fink, and Primo Levi.

Literary Criticism/Commentary

Ezrahi, Sidra DeKoven, (1980). *By Words Alone: The Holocaust in Literature.* Chicago: University of Chicago. 262 pp. This volume is comprised of eight chapters: 1. Introduction; 2. Documentation as Art; 3. Concentrationary Realism and the Landscape of Death; 4. Literature of Survival; 5. The Holocaust as a Jewish Tragedy A: The Legacy of Lamentations; 6. The Holocaust as a Jewish Tragedy B: The Covenantal Context; 7. The Holocaust Mythologized; and, 8. History Imagined: The Holocaust in American Literature.

Langer, Lawrence L. (1995). *Admitting the Holocaust: Collected Essays.* New York and Oxford: Oxford University Press. 202 pp. This well written and highly readable collection of essays addresses a wide array of issues vis-à-vis the Holocaust, including—but not limited to—its portrayal in literature. Among the many fine essays in the book are: "Cultural Resistance to Genocide"; "Fictional Facts and Factual Fictions: History in Holocaust Literature"; "The Literature of Auschwitz"; "Aharon Appelfeld and the Language of Sinister Silence"; "Myth and Truth in Cynthia Ozick's 'The Shawl' and 'Rosa'"; and "Malamud's Jews and the Holocaust Experience."

Langer, Lawrence. (1978). *The Age of Atrocity: Death in Modern Literature.* Boston: Beacon Press. 256 pp. In one of the initial chapters ("Dying Voices"), Langer provides a perspicacious examination of various issues germane to the Holocaust as they are depicted in modern literature. The book concludes with a chapter entitled "Charlotte Delbo and a Heart of Ashes."

Langer, Lawrence. (Spring 1987). "Cultural Resistance to Genocide." *Witness* 1(1):82–96. A thought-provoking essay that questions the common assumption that art created during the Holocaust by Jews constituted "cultural resistance."

Langer, Lawrence. (1982). *Versions of Survival: The Holocaust and Human Spirit.* Albany: State University of New York Press. 267 pp. A penetrating examination of how various researchers and survivor/authors/poets view what it means to be human in the aftermath of the Holocaust. A large section of Chapter 2 is dedicated to an examination of Tadeusz Borowski's work; Chapter 3 focuses on the work of Elie Wiesel's writing; and Chapter 5 analyzes the work of Gertrud Kolmar and Nelly Sachs.

Rosen, Norma. (Spring 1987). "The Second Life of Holocaust Imagery." *Witness* 1(1):10–15. [Special issue on The Holocaust] An examination of "the way in which certain images from [Holocaust] literature reverberate . . . at intense moments."

Rosenfeld, Alvin H. (1988). "Holocaust Fictions and the Transformation of Historical Memory." *Holocaust and Genocide Studies: An International Journal* 3(3):323–336. Rosenfeld examines how "[t]he trend in popular Holocaust fiction [that] appeals to the cravings of the tabloid imagination points to a progressive erosion of historical memory of the Nazi crimes against the Jews."

Stadtler, Bea. (1993). "Juvenile and Youth Books About the Holocaust." In Saul S. Friedman (Ed.), *Holocaust Literature: A Handbook of Critical, Historical, and Literary Writings* (pp. 575–58). Westport, CT: Greenwood Press. Stadtler's piece should be of particular use to middle level and junior high teachers.

Essays/Criticism on Poetry

Aaron, Frieda W. (1990). *Bearing the Unbearable: Yiddish and Polish Poetry in the Ghettos and Concentration Camps.* Albany: State University of New York Press. 242 pp. A highly praised pioneering study of Yiddish and Polish Jewish concentration camp and ghetto poetry. It includes numerous poems in Yiddish and Polish as well as their English translations.

Aaron, Frieda W. (1983). "Poetry in the Holocaust Dominion." In Randolph L. Braham (Ed.), *Perspectives on the Holocaust* (pp. 119–131). Boston and London: Kluwer-Nijhoff Publishing. An insightful essay on various aspects of Holocaust poetry. The titles of some of the many sections of the essay provide a sense of its breadth: "Role of the Poet in the Landscape of Death," "Poetics of Confrontation with the Anus

Mundi," "Constriction of Language and Image," "Crisis of Faith in the Trauma of History," and "Poetics of Testimony."

Alexander, Edward. (1979). *The Resonance of Dust: Essays on Holocaust Literature and Jewish Fate.* Columbus: Ohio State University Press. 256 pp. This volume includes a chapter on the poetry of Nelly Sachs and Abba Kovner ("Holocaust and Rebirth: Moshe Flinker, Nelly Sachs, and Abba Kovner"), and a section on Yiddish Holocaust poetry (which primarily focuses on the poetry of Jacob Glatstein and Aaron Zeitlin) in a chapter entitled "The Holocaust and the God of Israel."

Cargas, Harry James. (1993). "The Holocaust in Fiction." In Saul S. Friedman (Ed.), *Holocaust Literature: A Handbook of Critical, Historical, and Literary Writings* (pp. 533–546). Westport, CT: Greenwood Press. This essay includes a brief commentary on the works of Emily Borenstein *(Night of the Broken Glass),* Albrecht Haushofer *(Moabit Sonnets),* William Heyen *(Erika: Poems of the Holocaust),* Charles Reznikoff *(Holocaust),* W. D. Snodgrass *(The Führer Bunker),* and Elie Wiesel *(Ani Maamin),* among others who have produced works on the Holocaust.

Ezrahi, Sidra DeKoven. (1982). *By Words Alone: The Holocaust in Literature.* Chicago: The University of Chicago Press. 262 pp. Although this volume (which basically constitutes a literary history of the Holocaust) primarily focuses on prose works, Ezrahi also addresses the poetry of an eclectic group of poets (Paul Celan, Irving Feldman, Uri Zvi Greenberg, Itzhak Katzenelson, Randall Jarrell, Denise Levertov, Abba Kovner, Dan Pagis, Sylvia Plath, Tadeusz Rózewicz, Nelly Sachs, and Abraham Sutzkever).

Ezrahi, Sidra DeKoven. (1994). "Conversation in the Cemetery: Dan Pagis and the Prosaics of Memory." In Geoffrey H. Hartman (Ed.), *Holocaust Remembrance: The Shapes of Memory* (pp. 121–133). Oxford, UK and Cambridge, MA: Blackwell Publishers. A fascinating and instructive essay in which Ezrahi discusses, analyzes, and wrestles with the question: "How are we to read the poet of undeciphered riddles and uncharted mazes, who in his last writing provides maps and compasses, a whole new syntax to restructure the inscriptions of memory?"

Ezrahi, Sidra DeKoven. (1992). "'The Grave in the Air': Unbound Metaphors in Post-Holocaust Poetry." In Saul Friedlander (Ed.), *Probing the Limits of Representation: Nazism and the "Final Solution"* (pp. 259–276). Cambridge, MA: Harvard University Press. A fascinating essay that primarily addresses various facets of Celan's "Todesfuge." Ezrahi also briefly discusses Pagis' "Written in Pencil in the Sealed Railway-Car."

Felstiner, John. (1986). "Paul Celan's Todesfuge." *Holocaust and Genocide Studies: An International Journal,* 1(2):249–264. A critical and thought-provoking essay about one of the most complex and powerful poems on the Holocaust.

Felstiner, John. (1992). "Translating Paul Celan's 'Todesfuge': Rhythm and Repetition as Metaphor." In Saul Friedlander (Ed.), *Probing the Limits of Representation: Nazism and the "Final Solution"* (pp. 240–258). Cambridge, MA: Harvard University Press. An insightful and informative essay that discusses how Celan's language was a valiant attempt to convey the "rupture" that the Holocaust constituted in the history of humanity, the brouhaha that erupted over his poem when another poet charged Celan with plagiarism, and an analysis of the poem in which Felstiner examines how and why Celan wrote the poem as he did. The essay concludes with the full text of "Todesfuge" in German and English.

Friedlander, Albert H. (1993). *Riders Towards the Dawn: From Holocaust to Hope.* New York: Continuum. 328 pp. In addition to briefly addressing the poetry of Primo Levi, Dan Pagis, Uri Greenberg, Else Lasker-Schueler, Yehuda Amichai, and Abba Kovner, this volume includes a thought-provoking chapter entitled "A Different Language: The World of the Poets," which provides an examination of the poetry of Paul Celan, Nelly Sachs, and Erich Fried.

Langer, Lawrence L. (1975). *The Holocaust and the Literary Imagination.* New Haven and London: Yale University Press. 300 pp. A pioneering and valuable work on the aesthetics of Holocaust literature. Among the poets Langer discusses in this volume are Paul Celan and Nelly Sachs.

Langer, Lawrence. (1982). *Versions of Survival: The Holocaust and Human Spirit.* Albany: State University of New York Press. 267 pp. Chapter 4 focuses, in part, on the work of poetess Nelly Sachs.

Roskies, David G. (1984). *Against the Apocalypse: Responses to Catastrophe in Modern Jewish Culture.* Cambridge, MA: Harvard University Press. 374 pp. This volume includes an informative essay on the life and poetry of Abraham Sutzkever.

Rosenfeld, Alvin H. (1980). *A Double Dying: Reflections on Holocaust Literature.* Bloomington and London: Indiana University Press. 210 pp. A valuable work on Holocaust literature, it includes insightful commentary on the works of such poets as Paul Celan, Jacob Glatstein, Uri Zvi Greenberg, Yitzhak Katznelson, Dan Pagis, Nelly Sachs, and Sylvia Plath.

Young, Gloria. (1993). "The Poetry of the Holocaust." In Saul S. Friedman (Ed.), *Holocaust Literature: A Handbook of Critical, Historical, and Literary Writings* (pp. 547–574). Westport, CT: Greenwood Press. An insightful bibliographic essay that is divided into three major sections: "Poets Who Did Not Survive," "Poets Who Survived," and "Others."

Drama

Skloot, Robert. (1983). *The Theater of the Holocaust.* Madison: University of Wisconsin. 416 pp. This anthology is comprised of several plays that deal with various aspects of the Holocaust. Among the plays are Charlotte Delbo's "Who Will Carry the Word?"; George Tabori's "The Cannibals"; and Simon Wincelberg's "Resort 76."

Steinhorn, Harriet. (1983). *Shadows of the Holocaust.* Rockville, MD: Kar-Ben. This volume, by a survivor of Bergen-Belsen, contains five short plays. In an essay entitled "Juvenile and Youth Books About the Holocaust," Bea Stadtler states that "while some of the dialogue is a bit forced, the book is a very worthwhile classroom tool."

Poetry Collections

Ausubel, Nathan, & Maryann Ausubel (Eds.). (1957). *A Treasury of Jewish Poetry.* New York: Crown. 471 pp. This anthology includes a number of powerful poems on the Holocaust, including those by Ephim Fogel ("Shipment to Maidanek") and Hirsh Glik ("We Survive!").

Borenstein, Emily. (1981). *Night of the Broken Glass: Poems of the Holocaust.* Mason, TX: Timberline Press. 83 pp. Written by a woman whose relatives were murdered in the Holocaust, the poems in this book are categorized under three main headings: 1. I Must Tell the Story, 2. May It Never Be Forgotten, and 3. Psalm of Hope.

Celan, Paul. (1972). *Selected Poems.* Middlesex: Penguin Books. 108 pp. This volume includes Celan's "Todesfuge."

Fishman, Charles (Ed.). (1991). *Blood to Remember: American Poets on the Holocaust.* Lubbock: Texas Tech University Press. 426 pp. This volume contains 256 poems by 191 poets, some of whom are survivors of the Holocaust.

Fishman, Charles (Ed.). (in progress). *On Broken Branches: World Poets on the Holocaust.* By the editor of *Blood to Remember: American Poets on the Holocaust,* this book promises to be a valuable addition to the field.

Heyen, William. (1984). *Erika: Poems of the Holocaust.* New York: The Vanguard Press. 128 pp. This collection, which includes Heyen's "The Swastika Poems," contains a number of haunting poems that would be ideal for use with upper-middle school/junior high and secondary level students. Earlier editions of this volume were published under the title *Swastika Poems.* Heyen's father emigrated to the United States from Germany in 1928, but this two brothers remained in Germany where they fought and died in World War II for Nazi Germany. In addition to addressing the horrific nature of the Holocaust, many of the poems also reflect the anguish that the latter situation caused both Heyen's father and himself.

Howe, Irving, & Eliezer Greenberg (Eds.). (1969). *A Treasury of Yiddish Poetry.* New York: Holt, Rinehart & Winston. 370 pp. This volume of modern Yiddish poetry contains numerous important poems on the Holocaust.

Katzenelson, Yitzhak. (1980). *The Song of the Murdered Jewish People.* Haifa, Israel: Ghetto Fighters' House. 133 pp. A major poem by a man who was murdered at Auschwitz in 1944, this epic chronicle that is comprised of fifteen cantos was composed in an internment camp in France. The poem, which serves as a lament for the murder of the Warsaw Jews, delineates, canto by canto, the ever-increasing terror and brutality (the German invasion of Poland, the aktions, the deportations, the agonizing decisions made by the *Judenrat,* the fate of the children, the revolt of the Warsaw Ghetto) to which the Jews in Poland were subjected. The events described in the poems were well known by Katzenelson, a member of the Warsaw Ghetto.

Kovner, Abba. (1973). *A Canopy in the Desert: Selected Poems.* Pittsburgh, PA: University of Pittsburgh Press. 222 pp. This volume includes poems such as "My Little Sister," "A Parting from the South," and "A Canopy in the Desert." All—in various ways and to different degrees—address the tragedy of the Holocaust by a poet/survivor who was the leader of the Vilna Ghetto resistance group, the United Partisan Organization. The introductory essay by poet/translator Shirley Kaufman is both interesting and informative.

Kovner, Abba. (1986). *My Little Sister and Selected Poems 1965–1985.* Oberlin, Ohio: Oberlin College. 159 pp. This volume contains Kovner's major poem sequence on the Holocaust, "My Little Sister," as well as other pieces that address various aspects of the Holocaust. The short introductory essay by poet/translator Shirley Kaufmann is very informative.

Lefwich, Joseph (Ed.). (1961). *The Golden Peacock: A Worldwide Treasury of Yiddish Poetry.* New York: Thomas Yoseloff. 722 pp. This collection contains much of the best Yiddish poetry about the Holocaust. It includes poems by Itzik Feffer, Mordecai Gebirtig, Hirsh Glick, Binem Heller, Leib Olitzky, and Simcha Shayevicth.

Levi, Primo. (1976). *Shema: Collected Poems of Primo Levi.* London: The Menard Press. 56 pp. These poems by the noted Jewish Italian author who fought with a band of partisans until he was captured by the Nazis present vivid images of life and death in Nazi-occupied Europe. The title, "Shema," means "Hear!" in Hebrew, which is the first word of prayer affirming God's oneness.

Pagis, Dan. (1989). *Variable Directions: The Selected Poetry of Dan Pagis.* San Francisco: North Point Press. 153 pp. This volume includes a number of powerful poems (including "Written in Pencil in the Sealed Railway-Car," "Europe, Late," "Testimony," and "Draft of a Reparations Agreement") about different aspects of the Holocaust.

Rózewicz, Tadeusz. (1991). *They Came to See a Poet.* London: Anvil Press Poetry. This collection contains such poems as "The Survivor," "Pigtail," and others that are either about certain aspects of the Holocaust or informed by it. The volume includes an informative introductory essay about Rósewicz and his poetry.

Sachs, Nelly. (1967). *O The Chimneys.* New York: Farrar, Straus & Giroux. 387 pp. This collection, by a German Jewish survivor of the Holocaust (who fled to Sweden in 1940) and a recipient of the Nobel Prize for Literature, includes a wealth of poetry, whose focus and themes are the Holocaust.

Sachs, Nelly. (1970). *The Seeker and Other Poems.* New York: Farrar, Straus & Giroux. 399 pp. These poems by Nelly Sachs, who fled Germany in 1940 and was later a recipient of the Nobel Prize for Literature, are about various aspects of the Holocaust.

Schiff, Hilda (Ed.). (1995). *Holocaust Poetry.* New York: St. Martin's Press. This collection includes a wide selection of Holocaust poetry by authors from around the globe (including those who perished under Nazi rule, survivors, and those born after the Holocaust). It is divided into eight sections: Alienation; Persecution; Destruction; Rescuers, Bystanders, Perpetrators; Afterwards; Second Generation; Lessons; and God. Among the poets whose work is represented here are Dan Pagis, Abraham Sutzkever, Paul Celan, Nelly Sachs, Mikos Radnoti, William Heyen, Tadeusz Rózewicz, Abba Kovner, Primo Levi, and Jacob Glatstein. Curiously, some of the works included are actually statements by noted figures (e.g., Niemöller and Wiesel, for example) rather than poetry, per se.

Sutzkever, A. (1991). *Selected Poetry and Prose.* Berkeley and Los Angeles: University of California Press. 433 pp. This volume, written by a survivor of the Holocaust and a poet who has been referred to as Israel's foremost Yiddish poet, includes numerous powerful and haunting poems about various aspects of the Holocaust.

Volavkova, Hana (Ed.). (1993). *". . . I Never Saw Another Butterfly": Children's Drawings and Poems from Terezin Concentration Camp, 1942–1944.* New York: Schocken Books. 106 pp. The poems and drawings in this volume were created by children incarcerated at Theresienstadt. A note at the end of the volume reports that of the fifteen thousand children under the age of fifteen who passed through Terezin, "only 100 came back." Prior to reading these poems, students need to have learned about the facts of life and death in Terezin; then and only then will they be able to begin to appreciate fully the sense of anxiety, longing, want, sadness, hope against hope, loss, and unintended irony that clearly comes through in these poems.

Whitman, Ruth. (1986). *The Testing of Hanna Senesh.* Detroit, MI: Wayne State University Press. 115 pp. In this book of poetry, Whitman "explores the last nine months of Hanna's dramatic mission as a British emissary behind enemy lines in Nazi Europe" (p. 13). (A quote from the essay, "Historical Background," by Livia Rothkirchen, serves as the preface to the volume).

Short Story Collections

Borowski, Tadeusz. (1967). *This Way to the Gas, Ladies and Gentlemen.* New York: Viking Press. 180 pp. The haunting short stories in the collection are based on Borowski's experiences in Auschwitz. Each story presents life and death in the concentration camp in all of its "brutal and naked reality."

Fink, Ida. (1996). *A Scrap of Time and Other Stories.* Evanston, IL: Northwestern University Press. A remarkable collection of stories about life and death in Poland during the Holocaust years. Many of the stories are short, powerful, thought-provoking, and, thus, ideal for the classroom.

Lind, Jakov. (1964). *Soul of Wood and Other Stories.* New York: Grove Press. 190 pp. This collection of short stories portrays the evil and insanity so prevalent while the Nazis carried out their atrocities. Many of the stories are surrealistic in tone, while others constitute allegories of sadism.

Lustig, Arnost. (1976). *Night and Home.* New York: Avon. This book of powerful short stories "explores the nightmarish interaction between Jews and the meticulous efficiency of the Nazis' program for extermination."

Ramras-Rauch, Gila, and Joseph Michman-Melkman. (1985). *Facing the Holocaust: Selected Israeli Fiction.* Philadelphia: The Jewish Publication Society. 292 pp. "The [twelve] stories [some of which are excerpts from novels] contained in this volume represent attempts by contemporary Israeli writers to come to terms" with the Holocaust. Among the authors represented herein are Uri Orlev, Aharon Appelfeld, and Yehuda Amichai. The volume also includes an excellent introduction to Holocaust literature by Israeli authors and an outstanding afterword, which addresses the relationship of Hebrew literature to the Holocaust.

Pedagogical Pieces

Danks, Carol. (1995, October). "Using Holocaust Short Stories and Poetry in the Social Studies Classroom." *Social Education* 59(6): 358–361. In this article, Danks succinctly discusses certain caveats and guidelines that need to be taken into consideration when using short stories and poetry in a study of the Holocaust, and then discusses ways to teach Ozick's "The Shawl," the short stories in Borowski's *This Way for the Gas, Ladies and Gentlemen,* and various pieces of poetry.

Drew, Margaret A. (1995, October). "Incorporating Literature into a Study of the Holocaust." *Social Education* 59(6): 354–356. Among the issues Drew discusses in this piece are criteria teachers ought to use in selecting literature for use in the upper elementary and secondary classrooms, key issues that should be addressed in the study of the Holocaust, and various first-person accounts and novels that can be incorporated into such a study.

Drew, Peg. (Fall 1989). "Holocaust Literature and Young People: Another Look." *Facing History and Ourselves News*, pp. 20–21. Drew argues that in addition to reading literature students need a solid grounding vis-à-vis the history of the Holocaust. Only in that way, she argues, will they be able to make sense of the events that led up to and resulted in the Holocaust.

Farnham, James. (1983, April). "Ethical Ambiguity and the Teaching of the Holocaust." *English Journal* 72(4):63–68. A thought-provoking piece that discusses the clash between the value systems of students and actions of victims in the camps, the complexities of ethical behavior, and "ethical problems from the [Holocaust] literature."

Greeley, Kathy. (1997). "Making Plays, Making Meaning, Making Change." In Samuel Totten and Jon E. Pedersen (Eds.), *Social Issues and Service at the Middle Level* (pp. 80–103). Boston, MA: Allyn and Bacon. In this fascinating essay, Greeley discusses and explains how she involved her students in the writing and production of a play that dealt, in part, with key issues germane to the Holocaust.

Kimmel, E. A. (1977, February). "Confronting the Ovens: The Holocaust and Juvenile Fiction." *The Horn Book Magazine*, 84–91. In his examination of juvenile fiction about the Holocaust, Kimmel notes that, as of the late 1970s, no Holocaust fiction written for children had been written about the death camps. After predicting that a novel about the death camps would eventually be written, he raises the issue as to "whether or not that novel [would] come any closer to the question at the core of all this blood and pain" (p. 91).

Meisel, Esther. (1982, September). "I Don't Want to be a Bystander": Literature and the Holocaust." *English Journal* 71(5):40–44. Very briefly discusses the use of two poems: Nelly Sach's "The Chorus of the Rescued" and Ka-Tzetnik's "Wiedergutmahung."

Rudman, Masha Kabakow, and Susan P. Rosenberg. (Summer 1991). "Confronting History: Holocaust Books for Children." *The New Advocate* 4(3):163–176. This article presents and discusses numerous rationales for including literature in a study of the Holocaust, issues several caveats in regard to selecting and using Holocaust literature in the classroom, and provides a critique of various types of Holocaust literature.

Rushforth, Peter. (1994). "'I Even Did a Theme Once on That Anne Frank Who Kept The Diary, and Got an A Plus on It': Reflections on Some Holocaust Books for Young People." *Dimensions: A Journal of Holocaust Studies* 8(2):23–35. Provides a solid overview of ten key books appropriate for use by teachers whose students are in the upper-middle level to junior high levels.

Shimoni, Gideon (Ed.). (1991). *The Holocaust in University Teaching*. New York: Pergamon Press. 278 pp. This volume includes selected syllabi of Holocaust courses. The following pieces focus on literature of the Holocaust: "The Holocaust and Canadian Jewish Literature"; "Literature and Historical Memory: Holocaust Literature"; "Literature of the Holocaust"; and "Analysis of Literature for Children and Young Adults: Books About the Holocaust." Many of the other syllabi also include the use of key literary works.

Totten, Samuel. (1998). "Examining the Holocaust Through the Lives and Literary Works of Victims and Survivors." In Robert Hauptman and Susan Hubbs Motin (Eds.), *The Holocaust: Memories, Research, Reference,* pp. 165–188. New York: The Haworth Press.

Totten, Samuel. (2000). "Incorporating Poetry into a Study of the Holocaust at the High School Level Via Reader Response Theory." In Samuel Totten (Ed.), *Teaching Holocaust Literature.* Boston, MA: Allyn and Bacon. This piece highlights the way the author conducted a reader-response activity around Dan Pagis's poem "Written in Pencil in the Sealed Railway-Car." Student responses are included with succinct comments.

Yolen, Jane. (1989, March). "An Experiential Act." *Language Arts* 66(3):246–251. Discusses the value of the literary device of "time travel," especially as it relates to her novel about the Holocaust, *The Devil's Arithmetic.*

Zack, Vicki. (1991, January). "'It Was the Worst of Times': Learning About the Holocaust Through Literature." *Language Arts* 68:42–48. Zack, a fifth-grade teacher in Canada, discusses a study of the Holocaust that she and several of her students conducted using Jane Yolen's *The Devil's Arithmetic.*

For Better or Worse: Using Film in a Study of the Holocaust

JUDITH DONESON

To use or not to use film in teaching of the Holocaust? The facile reference to Hamlet's quandary is merely rhetorical, as film is rapidly supplanting both litera-ture and academic texts as the main purveyor of historical knowledge for the gen-eral public. In *Mystic Chords of Memory*, Cornell historian Michael Kammen's (1991) superb meditation on how Americans remember the past, Kammen con-cludes that "for better and for worse, the media convey a fair amount of what passes for history and memory" (p. 667). "For better" is the reality that film makes history accessible and meaningful to a public that more often than not remains ignorant of past events. The debates engendered by the highly criticized NBC/TV docudrama *Holocaust* (1978) and Steven Spielberg's *Schindler's List* (1993), both in the United States and Europe, have indeed situated the Holocaust into our collec-tive memory thereby better securing its place for posterity.[1] "For worse" suggests the implicit obstacles in a society that is influenced by film, teachers included, yet is not media-literate. Utilizing film in a classroom situation requires an added degree of sophistication both about the history involved, for our purpose, the Holocaust, and the methodology of "reading" film.

The vast inventory of film relating to the Final Solution consists of film shot by the Nazis to be used for antisemitic propaganda, footage of the concentration camps filmed by the liberating Allied armies, a considerable array of fiction and nonfiction films, propaganda films and newsreels, movies made for television, and survivor testimonies.[2] Can we sift from these a "selective" list—a standard cur-riculum—of those films we deem suitable for educational purposes? That is a rea-sonable question, for there are "model texts" that have been employed in teaching the Holocaust, including the historical studies of Raul Hilberg, Yehuda Bauer, Lucy Dawidowicz, and Christopher Browning, and, for literature—among oth-ers—Elie Wiesel and Primo Levi.

Can we suggest, therefore, a similar representative sample of films to be used by educators? This supposes the possibility of developing a standardized cinematic narrative on the Holocaust, which is a highly questionable proposition. On the one hand, film is subject to time constraints, which means one is generally forced to make film fit the academic hour, thereby negating the integrity of the creation. By necessity, this eliminates the screening of movies like *Schindler's List,* or Claude Lanzmann's *Shoah,* or even Leni Reifenstahl's giant homage to Nazi propaganda, *Triumph of the Will,* forcing us to resort to films of "appropriate" length. All too often, the goal becomes to "use" film because of its easy access to the viewer's attention—a viewer who has generally been weaned on the media and who is less inclined to read written texts. The quality and content of the film becomes negligible, as long as it "fits." We are reminded of the stepsisters in *Cinderella* who force the shoe on their substantial feet, knowing in advance that they are not the intended choices. And, I might add, cynically but perhaps accurately, such films also serve the instructor's purpose—one less lecture to draft, all too often a principal catalyst for determining when to present a film.

On the other hand, I do not intend to suggest that all suitable films that readily accommodate the time constraints of the typical class hour are necessarily of poor or trivial quality. I am, nonetheless, advancing the recommendation that a film be utilized in an informed manner in the same way one selects a textbook. Indeed, the academic rigor generally intrinsic to studying historical texts is all too often absent when examining film. Therefore, an instructor familiar with a written text encompassing a sound history of the material will not necessarily discern the biases of the filmmaker, whose tools are not the requisite documents of history but rather the representation of selected images, real or fictitious, juxtaposed against dialogue, actual or created, and edited to suit the prejudice of the creator. The historian seeks the scholarly approbation of his or her colleagues; the filmmaker, according to myth, entertains, which results in a more subjective critique of the production based on personal preference. In other words, one can rely on the validity of the respected historical text; one must learn to discern the techniques of the film in order to uncover its authentic character.

In order to illuminate the complexity of decoding movies, we will examine three nonfiction films, which have enjoyed favor in the classroom, in Holocaust centers, and commercially: *Anne Frank Remembered* (1995), Jon Blair's Academy Award–winning documentary; *Daniel's Story* (1991), a fourteen-minute film for children produced by the United States Holocaust Memorial Museum; and *Survivors of the Holocaust* (1996), a compilation of survivor testimonies from the archives of Steven Spielberg's Shoah Foundation. Our inquiry will concentrate on the historicity of each interpretation both in terms of accuracy and as potential fodder for Holocaust deniers, a matter we are obligated to be on the watch for, despite the idiosyncratic and contemptible character of their allegations. As for *Anne Frank Remembered,* it suffices, in some respects, as a palliative to questions arising out of the context of Anne's diary. In the example of two of these films, *Daniel's Story* and *Survivors of the Holocaust,* a glaring slight of the past—one that challenges history itself—invades their narratives.

For almost forty years, *The Diary of Anne Frank* has been troubled by allegations of falseness. In fact, the earliest documented attacks on the diary date from November 1957, when a Swedish newspaper decided that the diary owed its final form to the pen of American author Meyer Levin (Barnouw & van der Stroom, 1989, pp. 84–104). Regardless of the attackers' bogus contentions, among them, that Anne and Peter, a resident of the Annex, were not Jewish names, certain factors that beset the diary in the 1950s and continue into the present lend credence to these spurious debates (Doneson, 1987, pp. 59–83). These include the well-publicized battle waged by Meyer Levin for the rights to adapt Anne's diary into a play and film.

Meyer Levin had read a copy of the diary in Paris and contacted Otto Frank, Anne's father, offering to help him find a publisher in the United States. In return, Levin requested that he be allowed to attempt a dramatization of Anne's work. Levin succeeded in introducing the diary to the editors at Doubleday, where, indeed, the American version was published in 1952. His play, however, was rejected, leading to a public battle over the "ownership" of the material in Anne's diary. One side was comprised of Levin and various Jewish groups, claiming that the Pulitzer Prize-winning play adapted by Albert and Frances Hackett de-Judaized Anne's work as well as her intentions. The opposing faction was led by Otto Frank, who found it necessary to expurgate many of Anne's entries, either because they were too personal—such as items of a sexual nature—or because they described the acrimonious relationship between Anne and her mother. Mr. Frank preferred to have the diary exemplify the universal nature of teenage angst. These variances in focus led to a bitter lawsuit filed by Levin against Otto Frank and the play's producer, Kermit Bloomgarden. Levin's lifelong obsession with the diary helped to destroy him.[3]

In the end, Otto Frank's attempts to veil his daughter's thoughts was frustrated with the publication of *The Diary of Anne Frank: The Critical Edition*, prepared by the Netherlands State Institute for War Documentation as an antidote to accusations of the diary's falseness. It contains Anne's original diary, her own edited version, and the popular rendition revised by her father. This was followed by the "definitive" edition of *The Diary of Anne Frank*, which is now dated, thanks to the uncovering of another five pages of Anne's writing, omitted by her father, in which she describes her parents' flimsy marriage.[4]

But Anne, herself, contributed to some of the fictions in the diary. For instance, the Van Pels become the Van Daans, with their first names also transformed, though their son Peter remains Peter in both. Dr. Fritz Pfeffer becomes Mr. Albert Dussel. But whereas in the earlier version of the diary, those who helped Anne are given pseudonyms, in the "definitive" edition, their correct names are used—according to the Foreword of the latest edition—"as they so justly deserve to be" (Frank and Pressler, 1995, p. vii.). One wonders, are not the Van Pels and Dr. Pfeffer entitled to their legitimate status in this history, as there is nothing else to perpetuate their memory? The original Goodrich-Hackett play, their screenplay for the 1959 film, and their script for the 1980 television dramatization, nonetheless, all duplicate Anne's example.

Jon Blair (1995) adds to the mix when he informs us in *Anne Frank Remembered* that Anne had heard via a broadcast from the Dutch Government-in-Exile in London that on the arrival of peace in Europe, there were would be prizes offered for the best diaries written during the war. It is at this juncture that Anne, with a view toward the future, begins to alter her original words and impressions.

All of the concerns mentioned—the rewritten diary, Otto Frank's edited first version, the play, the film, the critical edition, the Meyer Levin affair, Anne's use of pseudonyms in her diary, and so on—simply add to the confused complexion of the history of the diary. The principal ingredient in dealing with all of these issues is knowledge—of the diary, of its history and of its seeming contradictions.[5] Regardless, for an uninformed instructor, or a sick mind, searching for flaws in Holocaust history, the diary remains a breeding ground for controversy. Which version will one read? How often is the 1959 Hollywood film screened? Is the original play still performed? If one is familiar with several renditions, which becomes acceptable? And how do we accord Fritz Pfeffer—alias Mr. Dussel—and the Van Pels—alias the Van Daans—their proper place in history? Jon Blair's film, *Anne Frank Remembered,* helps to clarify many of these issues, including accusations against the diary as being a hoax, and deserves a niche in the cinematic historiography of the Holocaust. Not only does it enlighten the teacher trapped in the malaise of misinformation attached to the diary, but also, when used by an informed instructor in the classroom, it serves as an articulate antidote for the students who have been confused by these issues of accurate history.

By contrast, *Daniel's Story,* a fourteen-minute film for children maintaining the guise of a "documentary" or "nonfiction" work produced by the United States Holocaust Memorial Museum, creates a character cloaked in the attire of history but who, in contrast to Anne, simply never existed. In the "Introduction" to *Daniel's Story Videotape: Teacher Guide,* one reads:

> In any study of the Holocaust, the sheer number of victims challenges easy comprehension. Teachers need to show that individual people are behind the statistics; these individuals formed families with grandparents, parents, and children. First-person accounts and memoirs provide students with a way of identifying with the individuals who, collectively, become numbers. (United States Holocaust Memorial Museum, 1993, p. 1)

Only there never was a Daniel.

The contradiction is obvious when, in the next paragraph, it is explained that Daniel is, truly, a composite portrait culled from the actual experiences of German Jewish families. His is a fictional persona. So who is Anne Frank? Also fictional? What makes one more real than the other to the viewer? Ascribing legitimacy to a fictionalized figure such as Daniel is a historical liberty rife with possibilities for questioning the authenticity of all diaries and testimonies. Additionally, it is logical to assume that when factual film and photographs "verify" the veracity of a tale, which in fact is not singularly true but possibly happened, it is permissible to question all representations that claim authenticity. Some will be reliable. Some will not. And how will we know?

The accuracy of all surviving testimonies comes into question when just one story "poses" as genuine. And this arises not only with marginal figures, such as deniers who are on the prowl for such inconsistencies, but it also opens the forum for any reflective person to wonder what did or did not take place.

Several examples that question the accuracy of specific incidents or memoirs, which have stirred considerable controversy, come to mind. We are reminded of literary critic Alfred Kazin's speculation as to whether Elie Wiesel (1982) invented the image in his memoir *Night* of a young boy hanged at Auschwitz. Wiesel's (1995) scathing response amounted to a crucifixion of Kazin (pp. 335–336). Or let us consider the film *Europa, Europa,* which structures itself on truth, even including the appearance of the real-life central figure at the film's conclusion, yet is rife with impossibility (Doneson, 1998, pp. 140–156, 224–225). And then there is Jerzy Kosinski, whose *The Painted Bird,* thought to be an autobiographical telling of his childhood during the war, turns out to be a fiction written by a poseur (Sloan, 1996, pp. 46–63). And Otto Frank, when trying to convince Broadway producer Kermit Bloomgarden to refer to the authenticity of Anne's diary in the theater program, relates the story of an American woman sitting next to a Dutch woman at the play and telling her she had seen it three times. When the Dutch woman claimed she had known Anne, the American woman feigned surprise that the characters and events in the play were real (Doneson, 1987, pp. 80–81).

That is why a film like *Daniel's Story,* understandably a film for children yet still accountable to its commitment to the past, owes it to all survivors not to jeopardize any testimony by claiming authenticity where it does not reside. This is not Daniel's story. It is a chronicle of events made appetizing for easy consumption while imperiling the validity of personal testimonies whose names are identified with the events they so tragically endured: Anne Frank, Emmanuel Ringelblum, Chaim Kaplan, Adam Czerniakow, and others whose names are truly inscribed in history.

Apart from its historicity, we must take issue with a further ingredient in this brief but popular film, one on which its entire chronicle is structured: the battle between the Nazis and the Jews. Germans perform no function in the persecution of the Jews. As Daniel informs us in his narration: "There were many Jewish families in our town. And everybody got along." But, he tells us a bit later, "People called Nazis were now running Germany." And that is the way it continues: Nazi students burn books, the Nazis keep making new rules, life becomes harder and sadder for the Jewish people, the Nazis burn down synagogues, the Nazis take over Jewish-owned stores, the Nazis take houses and send people away, the Nazis treat Jewish people like criminals, the Nazis take them to a concentration camp and make them wear prison uniforms. Always the Nazis. The film speaks consistently of the Nazis as if they stood outside the German polity, rather than shaping the ideology carried out by the German nation during World War II.

Ultimately, what we see in *Daniel's Story,* along with its simplification of the past, is an ensuing evasion of history. This American film actually corroborates the German revisionist view of its past. In his study on the New German Cinema, *From Hitler to Heimat: The Return of History as Film,* Anton Kaes (1989) examines how German film confronts World War II. Throughout his challenging inquiry, we are left to ponder the role of the Holocaust in German history, an event that is all but absent from this cinematic discourse (Doneson, 1991, pp. 207–213).

Filmmaker Edgar Reitz, as an example, created a fifteen-hour series for German television entitled *Heimat* (1984), in his words, "partly in reaction against the

American soap opera *Holocaust"* (1978) (quoted in Doneson, 1987, p. 208). The film follows the lives of what we have come to label "ordinary Germans" in the mythical village of Shabbach before, during, and after World War II. Neither the Nazis nor the Jews play a significant role in the existence of the villagers who simply try to survive the travails of life and war. Angered by the revisionist narration in the film, German historian Hans Mommsen sees Heimat's message as "this terrible thing, National Socialism . . . done to us by a few brutes called Nazis, a tiny minority who seized power and distorted the peaceful life of ordinary German people" (quoted in Doneson, 1987, p. 208). From a different perspective—that of the Jewish victim—*Daniel's Story* does the same thing for children. It reduces the Holocaust to the actions of "a few brutes called Nazis." And that brings into question history itself.

History as narrated by survivors is the fundamental concern of *Survivors of the Holocaust* (1996), a compilation of testimonies from Steven Spielberg's Shoah Foundation, which was originally televised nationwide and has since been made available to schools across the United States, who no doubt will seize the opportunity to show students a "Spielberg" film in the classroom. Like *Daniel's Story, Survivors of the Holocaust* is a composite picture of the Holocaust, only instead of one voice representing the experiences of German Jewry, there are several voices telling the same tale, a generic narrative of the Holocaust. And, yet, even in an unnamed context—all stories merge into one—there are contradictions in the tale. Early in the film, for instance, one survivor, speaking of a nameless place, says that the Jews were mostly observant. A brief cut later, another, also referring to nowhere, says the Jews were very much assimilated. Of course, it does not take a "denier" to detect the inconsistency, thereby allowing one to question the accuracy of the testimonies.

Further obstacles occur when historical evidence such as dates, events, and military strategy are explained by survivors. One witness, for example, attempts to interpret why the Polish air force could not attack the Germans. Because he is not a historian or military strategist, the margin for error in his clarification spirals. This allows the informed viewers, particularly those less sympathetic to the account, to find the flaws in historical memory and, thus, challenge the veracity of personal remembrance. The survivor's account must reflect only the individual witness to a particular experience. Articulated inaccuracies that are simple to correct lay the groundwork for questioning memory.

We are reminded of the Jerusalem trial of John Demjanjuk, once thought to be Ivan the Terrible, a guard at the Treblinka death camp. At a dramatic juncture in the courtroom, an aged and insistent survivor of Treblinka thrust his body before Mr. Demjanjuk, scrutinized his countenance and spat on him as he cried with certainty that he was Ivan, the vicious watchman at Treblinka. Only the survivor was mistaken. The wrong person had been tried and John Demjanjuk was subsequently allowed to return to the United States. The impression of the witness having erred, however, lingers. Survivors are susceptible to the rigors of history and remembrance, which actually underscores the necessity in their testimonies to adhere only to personal recollections. Otherwise, all can be challenged—even the gruesome truth.

The locale of the interview is also germane if we hope to retain optimal understanding of the Holocaust for future generations. The Fortunoff Survivor

Testimonies, housed at Yale University—among the first eyewitness accounts of the Holocaust to be recorded in a methodological manner—are filmed in the stark environment of a television studio. In direct contrast to the Fortunoff method, the Spielberg interviews are filmed in lovely homes adorned with decorative objects and framed by vases of fresh flowers. Some survivors are enveloped by loving family members and their resurrected lives seem to have erased the bleakness of the past. "It's a Hollywood spin," declares Lawrence Langer (quoted in Shatz and Quart, 1996). The survivors become merely props, much like Daniel in *Daniel's Story*, in the evolving "yarn" of the Final Solution. Or, as a *The Village Voice* article critical of Spielberg's efforts flippantly describes it, "history made palatable" (Shatz and Quart, 1996).

In the testimonies in *Survivors of the Holocaust*, one senses two times—past and present—as if they were disconnected. Perhaps this is possible. When the viewer hears one survivor, encircled by his beaming wife, children, and grandchildren, cheerily acclaim that he "cheated Hitler's henchmen. And this is what I got right here; a lovely family; my wife and my kids," one perceives that the past is behind. The gentleman continues: "And this is the happiest moment of my life because I loaded everything on tape. Maybe I'm not gonna be crazy anymore." The plug for the Shoah Foundation aside, the ease with which he sheds his anguish—as simple as a videotape—challenges the severity of his experience. It does comply, however, with Hollywood's notion of a happy ending. Lawrence L. Langer (1991) opens *Holocaust Testimonies*, his examination of the videotaped Fortunoff oral histories, by recounting an interview in which both a husband and his wife had lost their entire families during the Holocaust. Langer (1991) details: With her children sitting next to her, Mrs. B. confesses: "We are left with loneliness. As long as we live, we are lonely" (p. ix).

One additional segment in *Survivors of the Holocaust* tries the observer's willingness to embrace the testimony. Following the piece on the concentration camps—the film is chronological and divided according to topic—one witness plaintively proclaims: "How can I forget Auschwitz, Maidenek, Treblinka . . ." as he delivers the litany of names and camps. But, then, he looks up from a paper he holds in his hands; he has been reciting from a list. He continues. "How can I forget," and again he reads an inventory of names of friends and family. "So much pain to remember, but it's so hard to forget," he whimpers as he averts his glance from the register in his hand. If it is so hard to forget, one wonders, then why must he refer to a script? This might invalidate, in a reckless manner, the competency of the survivor to remember. Or, perhaps the more hateful among the viewers might postulate, did these events occur, or were they written for the movie?

Apropos of this, Steven Spielberg's *Schindler's List* (1993) once again captured headlines when Emily Schindler scolded him in her memoirs for embellishing Oskar Schindler's role in saving Jews. She, after all, was the one who was attentive to the Jews' welfare (quoted in Kiernan, 1996, p. 2A). To believe or not to believe?

In his essay questioning American Jewry's overemphasis on the Holocaust, Michael Goldberg (1995) recapitulates the following sequence:

> A class of non-Jewish schoolchildren visits the U.S. Holocaust Museum in Washington. They come to a case filled with religious artifacts of the victims. Their teacher points to some of the objects and explains, "There's a prayerbook, and there are some candlesticks, and . . ." hesitating for a moment when his gaze falls upon a talit [a prayer shawl], "there's a tablecloth." (pp. 55–56)

The example is striking. It prompts our awareness that it is compulsory for an instructor to be informed, to be attentive to the subtleties inherent in a text—or movie—he or she employs, and then to confront the material accordingly. For as we have seen in the films examined in this chapter, cinematic records of events like the Holocaust can be orchestrated to serve the filmmaker's vision, which may or may not conflict with the historical reality. To utilize Holocaust films in the classroom requires an effort by the instructor to recognize potential difficulties and teach the material judiciously. That is our commitment, not only to history, but also to those who perished.

NOTES

1. Regarding "Holocaust," see, among others: "Television and the Effects of *Holocaust*," in Judith E. Doneson, *The Holocaust in American Film* (Philadelphia, PA: The Jewish Publication Society, 1987); Siegfried Zielilnski, "History as Entertainment and Provocation: The TV Series 'Holocaust' in West Germany.'" In Anson Rabinbach & Jack Zipes (Eds.), *Germans and Jews Since the Holocaust: The Changing Situation in West Germany* (New York: Holmes and Meir, 1986), pp. 258–283; and Anton Kaes, *From Hitler to Heimat: The Return of History as Film* (Cambridge, MA: Harvard University Press, 1989). "Schindler's List" received massive attention in both print and the media, including the volume *Spielberg's Holocaust: Critical Perspectives on Schindler's List*, edited by Yosefa Loshitsky (Bloomington: Indiana University Press, 1997).

2. See Judith E. Doneson's "The Use of Film in Teaching About the Holocaust." In Gideon Shimoni, *The Holocaust in University Teaching* (Oxford, UK: Pergamon Press, 1991), pp. 15–23, and Judith E. Doneson's "Why Film?" in Donald G. Schilling, *Lessons and Legacies II: Teaching the Holocaust in a Changing World* (Evanston, IL: Northwestern University Press, 1998), pp. 140–156, 224–225.

3. One can read about this in two works by Meyer Levin: his nonfiction account *The Obsession* (New York: Simon and Schuster, 1973) and a fictionalized account of the Anne Frank litigation *The Fanatic* (New York: Simon and Schuster, 1964). Additionally, accounts of the American history of the *Diary* can be found in Judith E. Doneson's "The Diary of Anne Frank in the Context of Post-War America and the 1950s." In *The Holocaust in American Film* (Philadelphia, PA: Jewish Publication Society, 1987), pp. 57–83; Lawrence Graver, *An Obsession with Anne Frank* (Berkeley: University of California Press, 1995); Ralph Melnick's *The Stolen Legacy of Anne Frank* (New Haven, CT: Yale University Press, 1997); and Cynthia Ozick's "Who Owns Anne Frank?" *The New Yorker*, October 6, 1997, pp. 76–87.

4. David Barnouw & Gerrold van der Stroom's *The Diary of Anne Frank: The Critical Edition* (New York: Doubleday, 1989), and Otto Frank & Miriam Pressler *The Diary of a Young Girl: Anne Frank* (New York: Anchor Books, 1995). The five pages became an issue in 1998 as a biography of Anne Frank was appearing and its author was refused permission to include the newly discovered material.

5. In a seminar I taught on American Jewish History in Film at Washington University in St. Louis, two of my students pointed out the contradiction in the *Diary*, in which Anne refers to Charlotte Pfeffer as Dussel's girlfriend, whereas in my book *The Holocaust in American Film*, Charlotte Pfeffer writes to the authors of the play and the film script as Mrs. Pfeffer. Such discoveries lend ammunition to those who would deny the Diary's authenticity.

REFERENCES

Barnouw, David, & Gerrold van der Stroom. (Eds.). (1989). "Attacks on the Authenticity of the Diary." In *The Diary of Anne Frank: The Critical Edition* (pp. 84–101). New York: Doubleday.

Doneson, Judith. (1987). *The Holocaust in American Film.* Philadelphia, PA: The Jewish Publication Society.

Doneson, Judith. (1991) "Review Essay: From Hitler to Heimat: The Return of History as Film." *Holocaust and Genocide Studies* 6(2):207–213.

Doneson, Judith. (1998). "Why Film?" In Donald Schilling (Ed.), *Lessons and Legacies II: Teaching the Holocaust in a Changing World.* Evanston, IL: Northwestern University Press.

Frank, Otto, & Miriam Pressler. (Eds.). (1995). *The Diary of a Young Girl: Anne Frank.* New York: Anchor Books, Doubleday.

Goldberg, Michael. (1995). *Why Should Jews Survive? Looking Past the Holocaust Towards a Jewish Future.* New York: Oxford University Press.

Kaes, Anton. (1989). *From Hitler to Heimat: The Return of History as Film.* Cambridge, MA: Harvard University Press.

Kammen, Michael. (1991). *The Mystic Chords of Memory: The Transformation of Tradition in American Culture.* New York: Alfred A. Knopf.

Kiernan, S. (1996, May 1). "Schindler's Role Overstated," *St. Louis Jewish Light,* p. 2A.

Kozinski, Jerzy. (1965). *The Painted Bird.* New York: Houghton-Mifflin.

Langer, Lawrence L. (1991). *Holocaust Testimonies: The Ruins of Memory.* New Haven, CT: Yale University Press.

Schilling, Donald G. (Ed.). (1998). *Lessons and Legacies II: Teaching the Holocaust in a Changing World* Evanston, IL: Northwestern University Press.

Shatz, Adam & Alissa Quart. (1996, January 9). "Spielberg's List." *The Village Voice* 41(2):31–34.

Sloan, James Park. (1996). *Jerzy Kosinski: A Biography.* New York: Dutton.

Sloan, James Park. (1994, October 10). "Kosinski's War." *The New Yorker* 70(32):46–53.

United States Holocaust Memorial Museum. (1993). *Daniel's Story: Teacher Guide.* Washington, DC: Author.

Wiesel, Elie. (1995). *All Rivers Run to the Sea: Memoir.* New York: Knopf.

Wiesel, Elie. (1982). *Night.* New York: Bantam.

Expressing the Inexpressible through Film

JOHN MICHALCZYK

STEVE COHEN

I. Introduction

Over the past half-century, film has allowed us to revisit vicariously the deeds, the sites, and those involved in the Holocaust. The medium provides access to not only the historical events of the Holocaust, but to the psychology and behavior of both victim and victimizer. With its graphic power, it stands as a cultural, sociopolitical witness to the values of the period which the films depict. Whereas films during the Third Reich were used to manipulate and propagandize, today the power of film is capable of moving, educating, and provoking deep thinking.[1] With a proper integration of the film into the curriculum, it can be an effective educational tool.

II. Critical Issues

Presenting films about the Holocaust in an educational setting is a challenge. Using films to examine the Holocaust brings the instructor to one of the central issues involved in this endeavor: understanding how to express the horrors of the time without disturbing the psychological development of the student.

It is crucial that the teacher first be highly knowledgeable and sensitive to the subject and its use for a specific audience. After having previewed a film, the teacher must use it only if it is appropriate to the emotional and cognitive levels of their students. On a different but related note, in certain instances, some schools will notify parents in case students are troubled after viewing a film.

The general public in America has most often been exposed to the fictional, Hollywood, or televised version of the Holocaust. These features or docudramas often have been criticized for being "sanitized" versions of the events. Indeed, most middle-aged Americans grew up with an image of the Holocaust based on the story of Anne Frank, as portrayed in Anne's diary, as well as on stage and screen. However, following the initial public awareness that the televised Adolf Eichmann trial of 1961 had on the development of understanding of the Holocaust, it was with the NBC prime time eight-hour mini-series *Holocaust* in 1978 that the Holocaust entered many American homes. The larger American audience began to grasp the extent, the complexity, and the tragedy of the Holocaust for the first time. With *Genocide*, in the "World at War" series (1982), then *Shoah* (1986), and, most recently, *Schindler's List* (1993)—each an educational milestone—we have been able to grasp more fully the nuances of the Holocaust on an historical, emotional, and personal level. In all of those films, and in others that will be discussed in this chapter, what the teacher confronts is the filmmaker's struggle to discover a visual language to express or represent moments of the Holocaust. The teacher, therefore, serves as resource person, commentator, and interpreter, in order to assist the student in comprehending the events as seen through the prism of film.

One of the major challenges in utilizing films in the classroom is the time restriction. In a forty-five-minute class period, it is not possible to introduce a feature film, screen it, and discuss it, and it is even a struggle to do this over two periods. Pragmatically, unless it is a short film or documentary, it is more feasible to use film clips or excerpts to illustrate a point. Although a film is designed as an integral whole, it is possible to focus on one aspect for a more coherent presentation. This is especially recommended in the development of units on specific aspects of the Holocaust. Excerpts of the film, *The Courage to Care* (1985), for example, can be shown in conjunction with aspects of rescue in different countries.[2]

A useful series for developing class units of study is *Witness to the Holocaust* (1984), the Anti-Defamation League's two-videocassette film supplemented with a guide. These seven seventeen- to twenty-minute segments cover the evolving stages of the Holocaust: the rise of the Nazis, ghetto life, deportations, the Resistance, the "Final Solution," and the liberation of the camps. In a forty-five-minute period, it would be possible to present the topic briefly, distribute and comment on handouts with details from the study guide, screen the segment, and introduce topics for discussion for the next class.

III. Curriculum Development

There are, increasingly, more collections available, especially on video. Through major resources such as the United States Holocaust Memorial Museum, the Anti-Defamation League, Facing History and Ourselves, and the National Center for Jewish Film, there is the possibility of choosing historically accurate and developmentally appropriate films to illustrate most aspects of the Holocaust. The primary objective in this essay is to serve as a guide through the countless films available, offering suggestions in an organized way to facilitate the incorporation of film into a study of the Holocaust. Each section that chronicles the evolution of the Holocaust can serve as a miniunit, with some commentary and parallel reading.

A. Antisemitism

At the root of the Holocaust is the virulent hatred of Jews, which has religious, political, social, and economic underpinnings. Starting with the polemics in the early centuries of Christianity that developed around the Gospels, most notably those of Matthew and John, antisemitism evolved quickly in Western civilization. In order to confront the history of antisemitism, there must be a willingness to accept the fact that certain early developments of Christian theology first alienated the Jews and then condemned them. From the conflict among Jews, the new sect of Christians, and the Romans emerged a tendency to consider the Jews not only as different and "the Other," but, more seriously, guilty of the death of Jesus in a conspiracy with the Romans. Throughout the Middle Ages, this label of "Christ-killers" aided in the persecution of Jews, destruction by crusading Christians, and at times, expulsion from their own countries, as in Spain in 1492. Antisemitism, both Christian and secular, later reached its peak in the Third Reich.

Several films, oriented more toward high school and general audiences, help to clarify the highly sensitive issues of Christian antisemitism. The PBS special, *The Longest Hatred* (1993), is a hard-hitting documentary that explores the roots of anti-semitism in early Christian times, especially through revealing interviews with theologians. As it is a very long film, certain interviews could be used to show the range of views on antisemitism from some Catholic expressions of antisemitism, based on the New Testament, to acknowledgment of Christianity's unfortunate behavior toward the Jews prior to the Second Vatican Council in the 1960s. *Shadow on the Cross* (1990) focuses on the history of Christian-Jewish relations over the past two millennia, with a section dealing with Christian antisemitism during the Third Reich. The first sequences of *The Cross and the Star: Jews, Christians, and the Holocaust* (1992) provide a basic understanding of the early Christian-Jewish climate in which antisemitism first erupts.

A devout Christian teacher may find it difficult to screen these films about Christian antisemitism, because they appear to attack the early historical bases of Christianity. Furthermore, it is critical for the teacher to lead a discussion of these works in a sensitive manner, which does not undermine the religious faith of the teacher or student. This can be done using history and common sense as guides.

B. The Third Reich—Life in Germany under the Nazis

The Nazi Party came to power in Germany in 1933. Although the era of the Holocaust and World War II has remained a particularly fertile ground for writers and filmmakers in the decades following the end of the war, it is still a period that is "distant" from our current students. Films from the era help connect today's students with the past. Abundant archival footage, recorded by the Nazis, details life in the Third Reich and leaves an indelible image of power and persuasion.

The films in this section, for the most part, may be used with most secondary school students. They provide a glimpse of Germany before large-scale mass murder had taken place in Eastern Europe. These films attempt to humanize and even glorify the nation. At the same time, however, they "complicate" the thinking of those students who start with a picture of a nation of demons.[3] In other words, these films that the Nazis produced themselves—often for propaganda purposes—prevent students from rushing to the judgment that all Germans are monsters. It is critical, however, that the films be properly introduced in order to uncover their intent and subliminal seduction.

Leni Riefenstahl's *Triumph of the Will* (1935), a film of the 1934 Nazi Party Congress in Nuremberg, provides the strongest self-portrait of the Nazi movement. Scenes of youthful boys and girls engaged in trust games, and marches, and songs merge with speeches by members of the Nazi hierarchy. In light of its length and repetition of marching troops, excerpts of this film are suggested, and they are particularly effective in the classroom. The brief speeches, for example, of Propaganda Minister Joseph Goebbels and the highly antisemitic Nazi Party leader Julius Streicher provide a glimpse into the Party politics of the early Reich. *Triumph of the Will* gives the students the chance to see how the Nazis told their own story to themselves and the German people. Today, *Triumph of the Will* is viewed as a masterpiece of documentary work, albeit tainted with an ideology that helped lead Germans down a slippery slope.

Olympia (1937), a lengthy documentary of the 1936 Olympics in Berlin, is another effort by Leni Riefenstahl to record the "glory" of the Germans in the Reich at the beginning of their "Golden Age." Showing excerpts of the film, such as the opening sequence of the link of ancient Greece to the new Germany or the achievements of African American gold medal runner Jesse Owens, can stimulate the class to discuss issues such as Germany's rebirth and nationalism, or, in Owens' case, race and the Reich.

The Hitler Youth movement is usually a particularly intriguing subject for adolescents. Thinking about youths their own age during this era can spark interest and reflection. Teachers often are able to engage students with questions of belonging. They can ask students who or what attracts them to a group and why they join. Seeing the Hitler Youth groups in the first years of Hitler's rule as an organization that attracted students, and not as merely a school for future soldiers, tends to force students to think about the lure of belonging to a group, a gang, a team, or a school. In presenting the Hitler Youth movement, it might be advantageous to indicate especially why it was such an attraction for vulnerable German teenagers. Alfons Heck, a former member of the Hitler Youth, is the subject of *Heil Hitler: Confessions of a Hitler Youth* (1991). The thirty-minute interview with archival footage allows this man to reflect on his own past as part of a collective movement in the Third Reich.

Other documentaries also examine the Nazi era. A PBS video produced by Bill Moyers, *The Democrat and the Dictator* (1984), which was part of his series *A Walk Through the 20th Century,* spans the twelve-year period during which Hitler served as the Chancellor and later Führer of Germany, and Franklin Delano Roosevelt was President of the United States. The film, which plays the two leaders and the two governmental systems against one another, is particularly worthwhile for use at the high school level. The meaning of democracy is a strong theme throughout the program.

Erwin Leiser's *Mein Kampf* (1961) provides an overview of the Third Reich. The prelude of the film offers an insight into using the material in the program as a guide to the future: "As human beings, we are responsible for what he (Hitler) did—for he was one of us. May we be wise enough and strong enough to prevent this from happening again." The film traces the history of Germany from World War I through World War II, using many excerpts from *Triumph of the Will.* Intertwining images of the Holocaust with historical scenes from World War II creates a larger context of the Holocaust for the students. The film concludes with the liberation of the camps.

Another documentary that focuses on Hitler and his ideology also are worth viewing. *Hitler: The Whole Story* (1989) was made in conjunction with Joachim Fest's biography of the Nazi leader. This documentary constructs a strong foundation for the student in the understanding of the sociopolitical rationale of the Third Reich. Given its length, a segment of each of the three parts is recommended for class presentation and discussion.

Kristallnacht was, of course, much more than "a night of broken glass." November 9–10, 1938, was a two-day reign of terror against the Jewish population of Germany. Kristallnacht led to the destruction of thousands of Jewish businesses, homes, and synagogues, as well as the murder of nearly one hundred Jews and the arrest of thirty thousand Jewish men. The events of that evening—seen by some as the beginning of the end of "the Jewish problem" in German-occupied countries and by others as the end of the first stage of Nazi policy against the Jews—have been the subject of a few cinematic treatments. For example, the physical and psychological impact on a family of Kristallnacht is included in the 1991 short film *Camera of My Family: Four Generations in Germany 1845–1945*. The words and photographs of Christine Hanf Noren, born to a Jewish family in 1938, who all were forced to flee Germany, form the basis of this work. *Camera of My Family* is important also for highlighting the fact that the Jewish community was extremely vibrant before it became the victim of Nazi aggression.

A lengthier treatment of Kristallnacht, and one best suited for high school and college students, is *Now . . . After All These Years* (1981). Harald Lueders and Pavel Schnabel's film looks at what happened in the small town of Rhina during Kristallnacht. The filmmakers interviewed the older residents of Rhina in the 1970s, and asked for their reminiscences of life with their Jewish neighbors. They then traveled to Washington Heights in New York City, where many of Rhina's Jews had settled after Kristallnacht. Their memories of Rhina were quite different from those of their former neighbors. In the final segment, the producers showed the taped interviews with the Jewish former residents of Rhina to a town meeting of Rhina's elder citizens and its younger generation. The reaction that ensued reflects the cultural and generational differences of both groups who face the traumatic past.

The 1988 PBS documentary by Peter Chafer, *Kristallnacht: The Journey from 1938–1988,* marks the fiftieth anniversary of the events. The archival footage of the burning of synagogues graphically illustrates the extensive damage to the Jewish community. As reflected in this work, Kristallnacht signals the shift from the destruction of the Jewish businesses seen as an economic threat to the liquidation of religious institutions. Another film, *More Than Broken Glass: Memories of Kristallnacht* (1988), merges interviews of survivors with photographs and historical footage. Both could be used in a high school curriculum.

C. Resistance

Resistance took many forms during the Holocaust period, from less dangerous actions such as a young boy turning his backside to a Nazi parade in the Netherlands or listening clandestinely to the BBC in Nazi-occupied Paris, to the rescue of Jews and, finally, to the most dangerous—armed resistance. The spiritual resistance of Pastors Kaj Munk in Denmark and Andre Trocme in France show another facet of resistance as well. Munk's spiritual support of the Jewish community is finely detailed in the research of Professor Helle Mathiasen and in her interview for *The Cross and the Star* (1992). Pierre Sauvage's shortened classroom version of *Weapons of the Spirit* (1987) chronicles the spiritual resistance of Pastor Trocme and his Huguenot community in France. This film can be used for a discussion of both resistance and rescue.

For the two decades following the end of World War II, there hovered over Europe and America the romantic and mythic narrative of the heroic French Resistance. When Marcel Ophuls's controversial documentary *The Sorrow and the Pity* (1970) appeared, the public was shocked to see their heroes with feet of clay and the inefficacy of the resistance movement. As part of a high school course, shown in individual sequences, this well-documented film poignantly situates political and armed resistance in the larger context of World War II.

A film that enables young students to see a commitment to the truth in the face of death is Michael Verhoeven's *White Rose* (1982). Young German philosophy and medical students, along with their professor, daringly established a resistance network through their anti-Reich publication of newsletters. Their action was seen as treason, and most were condemned to death by guillotine.[4]

Often forgotten in the narrative of the Holocaust is Jewish resistance. Although each occupied country had a form of resistance, some countries had a more significant armed struggle and, specifically, Jewish resistance. The subject of Jewish resistance was more widely discussed following the PBS broadcast of *Partisans of Vilna* (1986).[5] The Vilna resistance fighters chose a more defiant and aggressive stand against Nazi occupation. *Partisans of Vilna* recounts the moral dilemmas facing the Jewish youth who organized an underground resistance in the Vilna ghetto and then fought in the forests. The film's two-hour length prevents it from being seen in its entirely in one class, but short sequences of resistance-building can be presented, especially in upper-level classes. The archival footage and stills, as well as the songs of resistance, make the Jewish resistance come alive for the student. The focus on the commander, Abba Kovner, who wrote the first manifesto for Jewish resistance, which he entitled "Let Us Not Allow Ourselves to be Led Like Sheep to the Slaughter," makes the historical events of 1943 very personal.

Forests of Valor (1989), from Israel Educational Television, also gives an insight into the Eastern European resistance movements, with historical footage and first-hand accounts. Nechama Tec's research into the Bielski partisans offers solid written documentation to the nature and diversity of this type of Jewish resistance, and would be ideal to study with these films.[6] The short documentary *The Warsaw Ghetto Uprising* (1993) chronicles the evolution of the ghetto's organization to its final liquidation and the deportations.

The National Center for Jewish Film distributes *Flames in the Ashes* (1985), the third part of a trilogy on Jewish resistance (the first and second parts are *The Eighty-First Blow* [1975] and *The Last Sea* [1979], respectively). Through the voices of the 120 survivors, we hear first-hand accounts of life in the Sobibor concentration camp and the events of the Warsaw Ghetto Uprising. A selection of the interviewees could be used to show the diversity of personalities, occupations, and motivations of the resisters.

Chuck Olin's *In Our Own Hands* (1998) chronicles the resistance in its powerful portrayal of the Jewish Brigade whose strategies were devised by David Ben-Gurion and Chaim Weizmann. The resisters were five thousand trained soldiers, many of whom came from Palestine's self-defense force, the Haganah. The film is a crucial link between the events of the Holocaust and the establishment of Israel in 1948 and is available through the National Center for Jewish Film.

The above films can be used in a high school curriculum with some introduction. Through the use of these films, the teacher can point out the active resistance of the Jewish community to Nazi oppression, thereby destroying the popular and false stereotype of a passive role of the Jews in the face of likely extermination.

D. Rescue

Closely tied to resistance is the topic of rescue. In the eyes of the Nazis, the rescue of those Jews targeted for elimination was a defiant act of resistance, subject to deportation or immediate death. Until the 1970s rescue was only interpreted through the eyes of readers of Anne Frank's diary "Kitty," or the stage and film version of the events. Jon Blair's Oscar-winning documentary, *Anne Frank Remembered* (1995), brings a detailed historical discussion to today's audiences. The powerful intimacy of the diary itself has led other curious readers and viewers to explore the topic through personal stories in books and films such as *The Hiding Place* (1975).

When Phillip Hallie's (1979) publication *Lest Innocent Blood Be Shed* uncovered the topic of widespread rescue by an entire community of French Huguenots in Le Chambon, the subject fell into the purview of a larger, general audience. Pierre Sauvage's personal involvement with the story, as set in *Weapons of the Spirit* (1988), revealed the importance of a community taking a stand on human rights. In his assessment of the heroics of these individuals, Sauvage shows that they honestly believe that they only followed the basic principle of "Love Thy Neighbor as Thyself" and did nothing extraordinary.[7]

The Italian image of resistance and rescue is presented in a readable, yet well documented text by Susan Zuccotti (1987), *The Italians and the Holocaust*.[8] To parallel this study, the teacher could use two class sessions to show Joseph Rochlitz's lengthy documentary, *The Righteous Enemy* (1987), which interweaves the director's personal story of his interned father with the actions of Italian officials who saved thousands of Jews from deportation.

Swedish diplomat Raoul Wallenberg's efforts at saving approximately one hundred thousand Jews in Hungary in the latter years of the war is considered one of the more heroic, large-scale attempts at rescue. *Raoul Wallenberg: Between the Lines* (1985), could be supplemented by Sharon Linnea's (1993) text *Raoul Wallenberg: The Man Who Stopped Death*.

The release of *Schindler's List* (1993) provided an added interest in the area of rescue. The focus on Oskar Schindler's clever subterfuges in rescuing Jews in the Krakow region of Poland has made a dramatic impact. Historical detail provided by Thomas Keneally's (1982) text and Jon Blair's 1983 BBC program, *Schindler: The Documentary*, can furnish the teacher with useful supplementary material for discussion.

The 1985 half-hour documentary, *The Courage to Care*, nominated for an Academy Award, is a perfect teaching tool about refusal to succumb to Nazi power and oppression. A teacher's guide includes exercises, historical discussion, and photos to spark a discussion on following one's own conscience.

The topic of Christian rescue is provocative, because some critics fear it may overshadow the issue of the horrors of the Holocaust that either were permitted or glossed over by the Christian churches. While the Vatican did not challenge the perpetrators of the genocide with excommunication, an encyclical, or a bold-faced moral confrontation, individual Catholics worked clandestinely by way of issuing false baptismal certificates, sheltering Jews in monasteries, and creating escape routes. Some of this is dramatically depicted in *The Assisi Underground* (1985), which recounts the efforts of a Franciscan friar to save threatened Jews under the eyes of the Gestapo. A sequence or two could be used to reflect the dilemmas that the friars faced in their rescue efforts.

The most educational series to date on rescue has emerged from the work of Documentaries International in Washington, DC. The producer has assembled several educational documentaries that portray moral courage in various European countries. Two films about Poland illustrate the challenges of rescue in Poland. *The Other Side of Faith* (1990) reveals how a young Polish Catholic girl, along with her younger sister, saves the lives of thirteen Jews. The film *Zegota: A Time to Remember* (1991) depicts the clandestine couriers who saved thousands of Jews in Poland through their work with resistance organizations. *Rescue in Scandi-*

navia (1994), narrated by actress Liv Ullman, recounts the intrigue and danger of the Danish rescuers in their escort of Jews to the safe haven of Sweden. Italian rescue of approximately thirty thousand Jews is recalled in *A Debt to Honor* (1995). Greek actress Irene Papas narrates *It Was Nothing—It Was Everything: Reflections on Greek Jews During the Holocaust* (1998) about the heroism of non-Jewish Greeks to help their fellow countrymen during the Holocaust. *Treason or Honor* (1999) uncovers the most dangerous aspects of resistance and rescue in Nazi Germany. This series of films are normally accompanied by study guides for use in junior high and high school curriculum. Nechama Tec's 1986 text of Christian rescue of Jews in Poland, *When Light Pierced the Darkness*, offers a perceptive study that would aptly supplement the above films.

E. Bystanders

On the allegorical level, a film that immediately provokes discussion is the twelve-minute animated work *The Hangman* (1964), based on Maurice Ogden's poem about a mysterious stranger who erects a gallows in a town square. The film offers an indictment of those who do not raise their voice in protest, and has a parallel to the bystander during the Holocaust.

A second allegorical film, lasting only nine minutes, *Ambulance* (1962), depicts the Nazis herding a group of Jewish children and their teacher into a van, which eventually becomes a metaphor for the gas chamber. The teacher's protective character corresponds in part to that of Janusz Korczak, who died with his young orphan charges at Treblinka.

F. Ghettos

Of the many ghettoes created by the Nazis in order to isolate the Jews, Warsaw, Krakow, and Lodz have served as case studies of resistance, rescue, transport, and community. Charles Roland's 1992 text, *Courage under Siege*, featured in the film *In the Shadow of the Reich: Nazi Medicine* (1995), helps one understand the human condition of the Jews in the Warsaw Ghetto. Images of the ghetto from the archives of the National Center for Jewish Film at Brandeis University illustrate in the film the tragic conditions there. A more historical approach is taken in the BBC film *The Warsaw Ghetto* (1969). Gail Stewart's 1995 text *Life in the Warsaw Ghetto* furnishes an excellent parallel to the film. The thirty-minute video *Birthday from Hell* is a photographic picture of the ghetto through the lens of a German soldier who visits the ghetto on his birthday in 1943 and clandestinely photographs it. The pictures only surface at the deathbed of the soldier almost a half-century later.

A powerful, highly stylized film, *Lodz Ghetto* (1989) reconstructs a perceptive view of the Polish ghetto. Alan Adelson and Robert Lapides's text *Lodz Ghetto: Inside a Community under Siege* (1991) illustrates the day-to-day experience of ghetto life. The latter is based on diaries and eyewitness accounts in Lodz from the period of the Occupation. Several excerpts from these accounts would be sufficient for students to grasp the horrid conditions to which the Jewish community was subject.

G. Concentration and Death Camps

The world of the concentration and death camps has been the subject of many treatments on film. As very little, if anything, remains of authentic footage recorded in the camps themselves by the Nazis, much of the material has to be studied from postwar documentation and reenactment. Diverse feature films, such as Arthur Miller's teleplay about musician Fania Fenelon in *Playing for Time* (1980), can be used by selecting representative sequences.

Theresienstadt, also known as Terezin, was a "model camp" set up by the Nazis. Red Cross members visited it during the war and were convinced by the façades and charades of the Nazis that the human rights of the Jewish community were not being violated. The Nazis themselves described Theresienstadt to serve their own purposes in a film made during the war—*The Führer Gives the Jews a City* (1944)—available through the National Center for Jewish Film at Brandeis University. This propagandistic treatment can be contrasted with such realistic documentaries as *Theresienstadt: Gateway to Auschwitz* (1993) and *Terezin Diary* (1990).

The reality of most camps was far different from Theresienstadt. The PBS program *Triumph of Memory* (1972) depicts four non-Jewish survivors of concentration camps, who describe their daily lives in places like Mauthausen and Auschwitz. Peter Cohen's *Architecture of Doom* (1991) uses the aesthetics of the camps as his meditation on their existence. This artistic and complex film relates the cleaning-up of Germany to the racial cleansing in the Reich's plans of genocide.

The concentration camps are, rightly, linked in our minds with the genocide that took place throughout Europe. Although Nazis eliminated Jews all over the continent, the bulk of the mass murder took place in Poland. Much of it, particularly in 1941 and 1942, occurred in innumerable small towns and hamlets. From 1942 until the end of the war, death camps handled the unspeakable task. One site in particular, Auschwitz, has become the burning symbol of the Holocaust. From the "Arbeit Macht Frei" (Work Will Make You Free) slogan over its entrance gates, to its row on row of brick barracks, Auschwitz has become an extraordinary image in our minds made vivid by photographs and documentaries. Resnais' *Night and Fog* was filmed on location at Auschwitz in 1955. One of the first documentaries to uncover the horrors of the genocidal plan of the Nazis, it makes a strong statement about the universal tragedy of the historical events. Still considered one of the most powerful and unsettling depictions of the Holocaust, it is criticized for not making it explicit that the Holocaust was a Jewish-centered genocide.

The short documentary *Auschwitz: If You Cried You Died* (1991) has been distributed widely and used very successfully. Its power lies in the personal accounts of two Holocaust survivors as they return to Auschwitz.

Original images of the liberation of Auschwitz camp in January 1945 can be seen in the Russian footage of *Auschwitz (Osweiecim)*. This twenty-minute film also touches on the medical experiments of the Nazis, to be discussed later in this chapter. In 1985, other footage was added to create a one-hour version about the liberation in a German film, *The Liberation of Auschwitz 1945*.

Auschwitz and the Allies (1980) presents the importance of the camp in international politics. It asks the questions, "When did the Allies know about the existence of the camp?" and "What did they do with that knowledge?"

Mass murder, by definition, can be quite a difficult concept for students to grasp, and the above films furnish an historical understanding of the camps. *Kitty: A Return to Auschwitz* (1980) personalizes the story of mass murder by returning to the site with one survivor—Kitty Felix Hart. Another survivor's story that has worked effectively in the classroom is Gerda Weissman Klein's *One Survivor Remembers* (1995). Klein's (1995) powerful story is also published in *All But My Life*, and is tangentially a part of the American Experience documentary *America and the Holocaust* (1994), which is about Kurt Klein's attempt to get his family out of Nazi Germany and into America while strict immigration laws were in place.

Ideal for its subject of children and its half-hour format, *The Children of Izieu* (1992) draws a tragic picture of Klaus Barbie's orders to the Lyon Gestapo to transport and exterminate at Auschwitz forty-four Jewish children from the orphanage La Maison d'Izieu in France. An important eyewitness to the raid, Leon Reifman, offers details that reinforce the images of antisemitism in France as seen in Louis Malle's feature film *Au Revoir les Enfants* (1987).

Claude Lanzmann's *Shoah* (1986), a nine and one-half-hour documentary, is an extraordinary ten-year undertaking. Unlike other films about the Holocaust, this one has no images from the death camps, the roundups, or the massacres. Interviews with survivors, former Nazis, resistance leaders, and people who owned farms or lived in apartments overlooking the sites of war crimes make up this epic. While it is far too long for use in a secondary classroom, there are innumerable valuable clips that can be used. The supposedly clandestine one of a former SS Nazi camp guard, for example, reveals an authentic, inside view of the camp workings.

The film *Genocide*, from the BBC "World at War" series (1982), is a solid one-hour study of the Final Solution. It provides a strong chronological narration with images of mass murder. This is a valuable film that high school teachers can use with their students. The short twenty-four-minute overview *The Holocaust* (1993) depicts the evolution of the Third Reich from 1933 to 1945, and concludes with a visit to the Yad Vashem Holocaust Memorial in Jerusalem. The graphic nature of some of the footage may limit the audiences to older students.

There are certain films that are so overwhelmingly horrific that teachers should show them with extreme caution, if at all. Among these are Alain Resnais' Night and Fog *(1955), as well as the American government film* Nazi Concentration Camps, *commissioned by General Eisenhower in August 1945. The State Department of the United States Government produced* Death Mills *in 1945. A compilation of many of the British and American films undertaken following the liberation of the camps was produced as a PBS Frontline documentary called* Memory of the Camps *(1985). The liberation of Bergen-Belsen is especially graphic and revealing, and should be shown with caution. These films are more important for the education of teachers.*

Discovering rare and raw footage of the Majdanek camp near Lublin, Poland, in 1986, German directors assembled *Majdanek 1944* to record the first Nazi war crimes trials and uncover the evidence of the Nazi genocide program.

Jews, although the principal targets of the Nazis, were not their only victims. Other persecuted groups included Jehovah Witnesses, Slavs, homosexuals, and Resistance fighters. *Persecuted and Forgotten: The Gypsies of Auschwitz* (1989) explores the Nazi destruction of this community by interviewing survivors of the Nazi era who recount the murderous policies of the Third Reich as well as the difficult years after the war ended.

Several films look at the camps from the perspective of the liberators. Henri-Cartier Bresson's *The Reunion* (1946), developed for the U.S. Information Service, uses a liberator as an entry point into an understanding of genocide. The Russian perspective of the liberation of the camps mentioned earlier can be considered raw documentation of the January 1945 events.

Most of the films on the Holocaust look at the victims of Nazi horrors. *Wannsee Conference* (1984), a reenactment of the January 20, 1942, meeting at which the Final Solution was bureaucratized, presents the Nazi genocide program through the minutes of the meeting held by the fourteen key representatives of the SS and the Nazi administration. Whereas this film has been viewed as useful by some educators, others have criticized it for its inaccurate portrayal of events.

H. Eugenics: The Basis of Racial Theory and Nazi Medicine

Some of the racial theory that served as the foundation of Nazi policies and the basis for genocide stemmed from a longstanding belief in the "betterment" of society. At the turn of the century, more than thirty countries, including the United States, England, France, and Germany, turned to eugenics—the science of well-being—to help create a "pure" and, therefore, "better" society. Social Darwinism was seen as a beacon of hope in a society that had as part of its population poor immigrants, social deviants, and the severely handicapped. Philosophers, biologists, physicians, and philanthropists, among others, met at national and international conferences to help plan a "brave new world." Their principle motivating force was the desire to eliminate those considered inferior elements of society, especially the physical and mentally handicapped. Sterilization, as lobbied for by major eugenic groups, would prevent these "lesser" beings from reproducing and, therefore, contaminating society. Several of the first sequences of the documentary *In the Shadow of the Reich: Nazi Medicine* (1995) deal with eugenics and sterilization as a means of perfecting society.[9] *Selling Murder: The Killing Films of the Third Reich* (1991) reveals the inner workings of the euthanasia policies of the Reich through interviews of eyewitnesses, as well as a compilation of films that dealt with "hereditary" illness.

These films, with some historical introduction, could be used on the high school level, given the clarity of the issues presented. They help pave the way for understanding the Holocaust as a continuation of the racial theory that civilization can be perfected by the elimination of those who are marginalized and declared unfit. From these films, we can understand how American eugenicists like Charles Davenport and Harry Laughlin served as a link between an international movement toward improving society, by denying basic human rights to individuals, and Nazi racial policies. This section can be made even more relevant today by a discussion of genetic engineering, cloning, controversial human experimentation, and the like. Above all, it can serve as a prelude to a serious study of Nazi medicine.

I. Nazi Medicine

There has long been an interest in medicine and ethics during the Third Reich. Doctors, considered to be the healers of society, instead were found to be killers at various stages of the genocide. Doctors were present to help develop racial theory, and diagnose the handicapped first for sterilization, then, later, for "euthanasia." Following the Wannsee Conference of January 1942, seen as the bureaucratic launching of the "Final Solution" program, doctors used their medical knowledge to assist in the elimination of Jews with their understanding of science. At the selection ramps they determined who should live and who should die. In the camps, doctors performed unethical and inhuman experiments on their unwilling subjects. These crimes against humanity were uncovered during the Physicians Trial at Nuremberg in 1946.

A short unit could be taught at the upper levels of high school on human values and medicine during the Third Reich. Using basic research on racial theory from Robert Proctor's (1988) *Racial Hygiene: Medicine Under the Nazis*, as well as from Arthur Caplan's (1992) *When Medicine Went Mad*, and the more complicated *Nazi Doctors: Medical Killing and the Psychology of Genocide* by Robert Jay Lifton (1986), the teacher can begin to lay the groundwork for communicating current values in medicine and biotechnology. The films *Selling Murder: The Killing Fields of the Third Reich* (1991) and *In the Shadow of the Reich: Nazi Medicine* (1995) explore the various ways the doctors aided and abetted the cause of genocide. This material would be best suited for advanced high school classes and could dovetail with studies in science, notably biology.

J. Judgments at Nuremberg and the Aftermath

The criminal and inhuman actions of the perpetrators lead us to the question of judgment. U.S. War Department documentarist Pare Lorenz chronicled the trials of the Nazis in an early postwar history of the Nazi rise to power in *Nuremberg* (1946), which contains graphic scenes of the death camps. With a more contemporary presentation, the History Channel's *Nuremberg: Tyranny on Trial* (1995) marks the relevance of the trial a half-century later. French filmmaker Marcel Ophuls conducted longer investigations of the principles of Nuremberg and the idea of war crimes trials in two films. The first, *Memory of Justice* (1976), forces his viewers to think about Nuremberg in the context of French crimes in Algeria and American policies in Vietnam. The second, *Hotel Terminus* (1988), uses the trial of Klaus Barbie as the vehicle to examine the concept of justice. The lengthy feature film *Judgment at Nuremberg* (1961) sets out the critical issues of war crimes and crimes against humanity.

One post-Nuremberg Trial that still haunts us today is that of a major bureaucratic mastermind of the Final Solution, Adolf Eichmann. Steven Schlow's *Force of Evil* (1989) poignantly documents the career of Eichmann in the context of many key issues of the Holocaust, and serves as a sound historical overview of these topics for the educator. A television production, *The Trial of Adolf Eichmann* (1997), helps provide some perspective to the 1961 trial by the assembling of much of the lost footage of the trial, from which emerges an understanding of Hannah Arendt's observation regarding "the banality of evil."

IV. Instructional Strategies

To use the time effectively in the teaching of the Holocaust, it is recommended to appeal to various learning skills of the student. Some learn quickly through the written word and find a text very helpful to return to over and over again. Others are visually oriented and rapidly grasp data from the visual expression—photography, filmstrips, video/film. Both forms of learning can easily dovetail if the teacher selects issues that have both a written text and a companion film available. *Schindler's List,* for example, can be used to create a unit around the theme of rescue, utilizing Thomas Keneally's (1983) text and Spielberg's film, as well as Jon Blair's 1983 documentary on Oskar Schindler.

Short films, no longer than thirty minutes, are rewarding, because there is time to introduce the work briefly with some time following the film to underline certain themes for discussion and assignments in the subsequent class. The level of presentation and discussion with each film differs according to the content. Each should be previewed and selected with the film's complexity and graphic nature in mind.

Documentaries are normally easier and more useful to integrate into the curriculum than are feature films. An advantage of documentary film is the possibility of breaking up the work into segments and developing each, perhaps following the organization of the filmmaker in the script. Full feature films, or even certain sequences, however, often necessitate introducing plot, characterization, historical situations, and so on, in order to situate the student in the film. There are certain exceptions, however, as in the case of a sequence from *The Pawnbroker* (1965) or *Schindler's List* (1993) that could be isolated for discussion.

Film is, of course, a visual medium. Often, however, when teachers use a film, they start to discuss it with students as they would a history book. Our advice is to use the medium to its best advantage. Begin the discussion by talking about what images from the film stayed with the students. What was the general and then specific picture left in their mind? What did they see? Did the music affect the way they felt about a situation?

Another starting point would be to take a major character in the film who is a crucial link to the historical content. In this case, documentaries work better than feature excerpts, although the latter should not be dismissed. Students could be asked to recount how this person thought, felt, and behaved.

Starting from there, it is easier to get students to engage in a discussion of the content of the film. Once they have talked about what they saw, heard, and felt, the teacher can continue the discussion with observations about the content and, ultimately, the meaning of the material.

To prepare to use Holocaust films sensitively and practically in a curriculum, the teacher could take several steps. Concretely, the teacher could obtain resource information and/or materials such as books or films that could be used in the preparation of teaching with Holocaust films from the United States Holocaust Memorial Museum or a Holocaust resource center. These video resources could provide an annotated filmography with suggestions for units and age groups. (For additional resource information on films, see Appendix B.)

Educators could establish or work closely with a History Club to study World War II as an extracurricular activity in high school. The topics of the Holocaust, military, resistance, rescue, and so on would be a thematic way to organize screenings. Films could be shown regularly, inviting a teacher or a local survivor/witness to introduce the film.

Prior to screening a film, teachers should provide the students with a handout dealing with the key historical dates, names of participants, and several questions that might be used in the subsequent discussion. Listing the books that the library has on the topic, or the Web sites dealing with the Holocaust, might be useful if the students are working on essays or reflection papers on specific topics.

Reading through filmographies of specialized books on Holocaust film for suggested topics and films is also helpful. Although they do not include materials from the 1990s, the following works are very substantial in their filmographies:

Avaisar, Ilan. *Screening the Holocaust: Cinema's Images of the Unimaginable.* Bloomington, IN: Indiana University Press, 1988.

Doneson, Judith. *The Holocaust in American Film.* Philadelphia, PA: The Jewish Publication Society, 1987.

Insdorf, Annette. *Indelible Shadows: Film and the Holocaust.* 2nd ed. New York: Cambridge University Press, 1989.

A valuable filmography developed specifically for use by teachers that was published in the mid-1990s is the United States Holocaust Memorial Museum's (USHMM) *Annotated Videography.* It is available in the USHMM's *Teaching About the Holocaust* (Washington, DC: Author, 1994, pp. 63–83).

In short, the teacher should use the strength of the medium to engage students in the study of history. The final step should be to utilize the film to help trigger thoughts about "applied history," or how this material impacts on the present or future lives of the students.

V. Conclusion

In teaching a generation of students who are more than a half-century removed from the events of the Holocaust, but who have a strong visual orientation, film is a highly educational vehicle. A challenge that may now arise could be the plethora of materials available. Wise choices early on in the establishment of the curriculum in general and a specific syllabus with chronological or thematic units will further the developmental process of students at various levels of education.

NOTES

1. For a discussion of Third Reich films, see Erwin Leiser, *Nazi Cinema* (New York: Collier Books, 1974), and David Stewart Hull, *Film in the Third Reich* (New York: Simon & Schuster, 1973).

2. An illustrated text would be helpful to use in conjunction with a specific country: Carol Rittner & Sondra Meyers (Eds.),*The Courage to Care* (New York: New York University Press, 1986).

3. For a controversial view of German complicity in the Holocaust, read Daniel Goldhagen's text, *Hitler's Willing Executioners: Ordinary Germans and the Holocaust* (New York: Alfred Knopf, 1996).

4. Franz Mueller of Munich, a member of the White Rose Movement, currently lectures on the international scene with an accompanying exhibit and the *White Rose* film.

5. For a discussion of this documentary, see Annette Insdorf, *Indelible Shadows: Film and the Holocaust,* 2nd ed. (New York: Cambridge University Press, 1989, pp. 164–166).

6. For a basic understanding, see sections on Jewish Resistance in John Michalczyk's (Ed.), *Resisters, Rescuers, and Refugees* (Kansas City, MO: Sheed & Ward, 1997, pp. 107–133).

7. For a discussion of this film, see Annette Insdorf's *Indelible Shadows*.

8. See Susan Zuccotti's *The Italians and the Holocaust: Persecution, Rescue, and Survival* (New York: Basic Books, 1987).

9. A companion piece to the film *In the Shadow of the Reich: Nazi Medicine* can be found in John Michalczyk's "Euthanasia in Nazi Propaganda Films: Selling Murder." In John Michalczyk, *Medicine, Ethics, and the Third Reich* (pp. 64–70). (Kansas City, MO: Sheed & Ward, 1994).

REFERENCES

Adelson, Alan & Robert Lapides. (Eds.). (1991). *Lodz Ghetto: Inside a Community Under Siege.* New York: Viking Penguin.

Avisar, Ilan. (1988). *Screening the Holocaust: Cinema's Images of the Unimaginable.* Bloomington: Indiana University Press.

Caplan, Arthur. (Ed.). (1992). *When Medicine Went Mad: Bioethics and the Holocaust.* Totowa, NJ: Humana Press.

Doneson, Judith. (1987). *The Holocaust in American Film.* Philadelphia, PA: The Jewish Publication Society.

Frank, Anne. (1953). *The Diary of a Young Girl.* New York: Pocket Books.

Goldhagen, Daniel. (1996). *Hitler's Willing Executioners: Ordinary Germans and the Holocaust.* New York: Knopf.

Hallie, Philip. (1979). *Lest Innocent Blood Be Shed: The Story of the Village of Le Chambon and How Goodness Happened There.* New York: Harper & Row.

Hull, David Stewart. (1973). *Film in the Third Reich.* New York: Simon & Schuster.

Insdorf, Annette. (1989). *Indelible Shadows: Film and the Holocaust,* 2nd ed. New York: Cambridge University Press.

Keneally, Thomas. (1982). *Schindler' s List.* New York: Simon & Schuster.

Klein, Gerda Weissman. (1995). *All But My Life.* New York: Hill and Wang.

Lanzmann, Claude. (1987). *Shoah: An Oral History of the Holocaust.* New York: Pantheon.

Leiser, Erwin. (1974). *Nazi Cinema.* New York: Collier Books.

Lifton, Robert J. (1986). *Nazi Doctors: Medical Killing and the Psychology of Genocide.* New York: Basic Books.

Linnea, Sharon. (1993). *Raoul Wallenberg: The Man Who Stopped Death.* Philadelphia, PA: Jewish Publication Society.

Michalczyk, John (Ed.). (1994). *Medicine, Ethics, and the Third Reich: Historical and Contemporary Issues.* Kansas City, MO: Sheed & Ward.

Michalczyk, John (Ed.). (1997). *Resisters, Rescuers, and Refugees: Historical and Ethical Issues.* Kansas City, MO: Sheed & Ward.

Proctor, Robert. (1988). *Racial Hygiene: Medicine Under the Nazis.* Cambridge, MA: Harvard University Press.

Rittner, Carol & Sondra Meyers. (Eds.). (1986). *The Courage to Care: Rescuers of Jews During the Holocaust.* New York: New York University Press.

Roland, Charles. (1992). *Courage Under Siege: Starvation, Disease and Death in the Warsaw Ghetto.* New York: Oxford University Press.

Tec, Nechama. (1986). *When Light Pierced the Darkness: Christian Rescue of Jews in Nazi-Occupied Poland.* New York: Oxford University Press.

Stewart, Gail. (1995). *Life in the Warsaw Ghetto.* San Diego, CA: Lucent Books.

Szner, Zvi & Alexander Sened. (Eds.). (1987). *With a Camera in the Ghetto.* New York: Schocken.

Zuccotti, Susan. (1987). *The Italians and the Holocaust: Persecution, Rescue, and Survival.* New York: Basic Books.

APPENDIX A

Select Filmography

Note: The address for each of the rental agencies is listed in Appendix B

General

America and the Holocaust: Deceit and Indifference (1994). PBS Video

Genocide (1982) from "World at War" Series, National Center for Jewish Film/Social Studies School Service/PBS

Holocaust (1993, 24-minute documentary), Ergo Media

Holocaust (1978, TV series), Movies Unlimited, Social Studies School Service

Witness to the Holocaust (1984), Anti-Defamation League, Social Studies School Service (with guide)

Antisemitism

The Cross and the Star: Jews, Christians, and the Holocaust (1992), First Run Features

The Longest Hatred: The History of Anti-Semitism (1993), Ergo Media, PBS Video, Films for the Humanities

Shadow on the Cross (1990), Landmark Films

The Third Reich (1933–1945)

Architecture of Doom (1991), First Run Features

The Camera of My Family—Four Generations in Germany 1845–1945 (1991), Social Studies School Service

Daniel's Story (1993), U.S. Holocaust Museum

The Democrat and the Dictator, in "A Walk Through the 20th Century" Series (1984), PBS

Force of Evil (1989), National Center for Jewish film

Heil Hitler: Confessions of a Hitler Youth (1991), Social Studies School Service

Hitler: The Whole Story (1989), NDR International

In the Shadow of the Reich: Nazi Medicine (1995), First Run Features

Kristallnacht: The Journey in 1938–1988 (1988), PBS Video

Mein Kampf (1961), FACETS

More Than Broken Glass: Memories of Kristallnacht (1988), Ergo Media, FACETS

Now . . . After All These Years (1981), Alfred Cantor, Inc.

Olympia (1937), FACETS, Amazon.com

Selling Murder: The Killing Films of the Third Reich (1991), British Channel 4

Triumph of the Will (1935), Movies Unlimited, FACETS, Amazon.com

Wannsee Conference (1984), FACETS, National Center for Jewish Film

Resistance

Eighty-First Blow (1975), National Center for Jewish Film

Flames in the Ashes (1985), National Center for Jewish Film, Ergo Media

Forests of Valor (1989), Social Studies School Service, Ergo Media

In Our Own Hands (1998), National Center for Jewish Film

The Last Sea (1979), National Center for Jewish Film

Partisans of Vilna (1986), National Center for Jewish Film

The Sorrow and the Pity (1970), FACETS

Warsaw Ghetto Uprising (1993), Ergo Media

White Rose (1982), National Center for Jewish Film

Rescue

A Debt to Honor (1995), Documentaries International

Anne Frank Remembered (1995), FACETS

Assisi Underground (1985), Social Studies School Service

The Courage to Care (1985), Social Studies School Service

Diary of Anne Frank (1959), National Center for Jewish Film

The Hiding Place (1975), Movies Unlimited, Amazon.com

It Was Nothing—It Was Everything: Reflections on Greek Jews during the Holocaust (1998), Documentaries International

The Other Side of Faith (1990), Documentaries International

Raoul Wallenberg: Between the Lines (1985), Social Studies School Service, FACETS

Rescue in Scandinavia (1994), Documentaries International

The Righteous Enemy (1987), National Center for Jewish Film

Schindler's List (1993), Social Studies School Service (and available at most video stores)

Schindler: The Documentary (1983), FACETS

Treason or Honor (1999), Documentaries International

Weapons of the Spirit (1988), Social Studies School Service, National Center for Jewish Film

Zegota: A Time to Remember (1991), Documentaries International

Bystanders

Ambulance (1962), National Center for Jewish Film

The Hangman (1964), National Center for Jewish Film

Ghetto

Lodz Ghetto (1989), Jewish Heritage Project

The Warsaw Ghetto (1969), Social Studies School Service, FACETS

Birthday from Hell (not available)

Warsaw Ghetto Uprising (1993), Ergo Media

Transport and Camps

Architecture of Doom (1991), First Run Features

Au Revoir les Enfants (1987), Orion Home Video

Auschwitz (Osweiecim) (not available)

Auschwitz: If You Cried You Died (1991), Impact America Foundation

Auschwitz and the Allies (1980), Distributor unavailable

The Children of Izieu (1992), National Center for Jewish Film

Death Mills (1945), National Center for Jewish Films

The Führer Gives the Jews a City (1944), National Center for Jewish Film

Kitty: A Return to Auschwitz (1980), Social Studies School Service

The Liberation of Auschwitz 1945 (1985), National Center for Jewish Film

Majdanek 1944 (1986), National Center for Jewish Film

Memory of the Camps (1985), PBS/Frontline

Nazi Concentration Camps (not available)

Night and Fog (1955), Social Studies School Services, National Center for Jewish Film

One Survivor Remembers (1995), U.S. Holocaust Museum

Persecuted and Forgotten: The Gypsies of Auschwitz (1989), EBS Productions

Playing for Time (1980), No current distributor

Shoah (1986), Simon Wiesenthal Center, FACETS, and video stores

Terezin Diary (1990), Ergo Media

Theresienstadt: Gateway to Auschwitz (1993), Ergo Media, FACETS

Triumph of Memory (1972), PBS Video

Wannsee Conference (1984), National Center for Jewish Film, Social Studies School Service

Nuremberg/War Criminals

Force of Evil (1989), National Center for Jewish Film

Hotel Terminus: The Life and Times of Klaus Barbie (1988), FACETS

Judgment at Nuremberg (1961), National Center for Jewish Film, Social Studies School Service

Memory of the Camps (1985), PBS Video

Memory of Justice (1976) (not available)

Nuremberg (1946), National Center for Jewish Film

Nuremberg: Tyranny on Trial (1995), Social Studies School Service

The Trial of Adolf Eichmann (1997), PBS Video

Post World War II

The Pawnbroker (1965), National Center for Jewish Film

The Reunion (1946), National Center for Jewish Film

APPENDIX B

Audio-Visual Resources

Anti-Defamation League: 823 United Nations Plaza, New York, NY 10017. Film Library, 22-D Hollywood Ave., Ho-Ho-Kus, NJ 07423.

Documentaries International: 1880 K St., NW Suite 1120, Washington, DC 20006

EBS Productions: 330 Ritch St., San Francisco, CA 94107. Phone: (415) 495-2327.

Ergo Media: P.O. Box 2037, Teaneck, NJ 07666. Web site: <www.jewishvideo.com>.

FACETS: 1517 West Fullerton, Chicago, IL 60614.

Facing History and Ourselves: 16 Hurd Rd., Brookline, MA 02146.

Films for the Humanities: Box 2053, Princeton, NJ 08543.

First Run Features: 153 Waverly Place, New York, NY 10014.

Impact America Foundation: 9100 Keystone at the Crossing, Suite 390, Indianapolis, IN 46240-2158.

Jewish Heritage Project: 150 Franklin St., No. 1 W, New York, NY 10003.

Landmark Films: 3450 Slade Run Dr., Falls Church, VA 22042.

M.C.E.G./Sterling: 2121 Ave. of the Stars, Suite 2630, Los Angeles, CA 90067.

Movies Unlimited: 6736 Castor Ave., Philadelphia, PA 19149.

National Center for Jewish Film: Brandeis University, Lown #102, Waltham, MA 02254. Web site: <www.brandeis.edu/jewishfilm/index.html>.

NDR International: Rudower Chaussee 3, Berlin 12489, Germany.

Orion Home Video: 1888 Century Park East, Los Angeles, CA, 90067.

PBS Video, 13220 Braddock Place, Alexandria, VA 22314.

Simon Wiesenthal Center: 9760 West Pico Blvd., Yeshiva University of Los Angeles, Los Angeles, CA 90035.

Social Studies School Service: 10200 Jefferson Blvd., Room J4, P.O. Box 802, Culver City, CA 90232-0802.

U.S. Holocaust Memorial Museum: 100 Raoul Wallenburg Place SW, Washington, DC 20024-2150.

Annotations on many of these films can be found in the United States Holocaust Museums' *Teaching About the Holocaust* (Washington, DC: Author, 1994, pp. 63–83). Many of these films can be purchased through Amazon.com or Movies Unlimited.

10 The Internet and the Study of the Holocaust

DEREK S. SYMER

I. General Introduction to New Computer Technologies: Challenges and Opportunities

During the 1990s, the Holocaust emerged as an integral and vital subject of historical exploration throughout the United States and the world. A pair of parallel forces drove this process, namely the introduction of Holocaust studies courses at the college and university levels and the development, funding, and construction of culturally transcendent Holocaust memorials and museums. Also contributing to the urgency of Holocaust studies was the acute recognition that an aging generation of Holocaust survivors needed to record their stories for the benefit of future generations. Now, at the start of the next decade, there remains little doubt that the combination of these forces has successfully planted the Holocaust into the mainstream American consciousness. Perhaps the best signal of this phenomenon is the dramatic rise of teaching about the Holocaust at the secondary school level.

The recent period has also witnessed the rapid and widespread influx of computer technology in our nation's schools. Once perceived as being slow and costly, yet somehow vaguely desirable, computers are now affordable, requisite components of many classrooms. Driven by faster processors, expanded memory, higher speed modems with lightning-fast access to the Internet and World Wide Web, and CD-ROM drives, today's computers provide educators access to a broad array of resources unavailable only a few years ago. Indeed, many schools throughout the United States have invested substantially in computer hardware, software, and the construction of networks linking schools to the Internet. In general, there are two important explanations for the permeation of computer technology into the classroom. First, it is widely believed that the economic security of today's generation of American students rests on educating them in basic computer competency and technology. Second, youth are attracted to computers and enjoy using them, so computers are seen to be naturally beneficial teaching tools. These arguments, however, do not necessarily mean that computers themselves are effective teachers. The best scenario features teachers who are adept at using computers as strong and effective adjuncts to quality classroom learning.

The rise of computers and computer-assisted learning offers great opportunities for teachers who include the Holocaust in their curriculum, or who intend to in the future.[1] There are many diverse and compelling reasons to consider implementing computer-based technology to assist in teaching the Holocaust. An important consideration is the abundance and diversity of information available through new technology sources at a relatively small cost to the school. With a computer terminal and connection to the Internet, teachers and students can explore immense amounts of primary and secondary source material on the World Wide Web that would, for the most part, be unavailable to them otherwise. Used productively, this technology can empower students to locate resources that answer fundamental questions and address significant issues. To cite just a few examples, students can view or listen to oral histories of Holocaust survivors; examine photographs; read scholarly texts; locate reference materials such as glossaries, bibliographies, or chronologies; study maps; and read original primary source documents. In addition, it is quite likely that the diversity of interactive and multimedia material will stimulate students to explore topics beyond what is taught in the classroom. A classroom teaching segment on *The Diary of Anne Frank* may motivate some students to learn more about the fate of children during the Holocaust, while others may wish to learn more about the fate of Jews in Eastern Europe.

Computers can facilitate boundless educational and research opportunities for all levels of students. They can then explore the history inside or outside of the traditional classroom setting. Although computers should not make studying the Holocaust "fun" per se, they can assist in making this topic more tangible, more immediate, and more accessible for many students. Another important benefit is that geographic barriers can be broken down in cyberspace. Students can learn about the Holocaust from international Web sites published in countries outside of the United States, including Israel, Germany, Austria, Poland, and elsewhere. They can communicate with expert scholars, survivors, or other students from around the world. They can even visit Holocaust museums and memorials in cyberspace, taking "virtual tours" of these museums and learning more about actual places where the Holocaust occurred. Most important, for many teachers, a broad array of resources are available that may help them in teaching the Holocaust. These materials include teaching guidelines, lesson plans/units, and related projects from a variety of different Web sites. These materials can be used in conjunction with existing plans or used to mold new teaching initiatives.

While many of these benefits seem almost self-evident, educators should confront the pedagogical challenges that new computer technologies present before launching headfirst into cyberspace. A popular yet prescient song by The Police proclaimed back in the 1980s: "Too much information, running through my brain . . . Too much information, driving me insane." These lyrics aptly anticipated the overabundance of cyber-information in the 1990s and 2000s. The amount of material available on the World Wide Web is staggering and can intimidate even veteran Web users. Moreover, as anyone who has spent more than a few minutes on the Internet can attest, retrieving relevant and reliable information on any topic requires patience, focus, experience, and good judgement. Navigating your search, most frequently performed with the assistance of Internet search engines such as Northern Light or AltaVista, can be a frustrating and tedious process. Whatever the intended search—be it a topic in world history, a biography of a famous person, or a product review—users will encounter many competing Web site options. Multitudes of diversions, such as Web advertising and hyperlinks, are ever-present and have the potential to distract users, especially younger ones. It is no secret that attention spans are significantly reduced on the World Wide Web, and this may present a challenge in some teaching settings. Once users think they have located seemingly pertinent information, they may encounter well-intentioned but erroneous information, or, worse, hateful and deliberately false information. The daily proliferation of new Web sites means that alongside the many rewarding places to visit on the Web, there are certainly an equal number of Web sites to avoid because they are irrelevant, outdated, or unreliable. The reason is simply that the World Wide Web gives anyone with a computer and basic Web publishing skills the opportunity to publish anything they wish. Holocaust deniers, hate groups, and others can publish a slick Web page that can look authoritative or benign, when in fact they are neither.

The combination of immense information resources on the Internet, the complexity of using new computer technology, and differentiating between useful and irrelevant information, may leave many teachers feeling overwhelmed or intimidated. Some experts contend that disproportionate resources have been allocated for computer infrastructure, including hardware and computer networking. They argue that school spending on computer infrastructure vastly outweighs teacher training. Others suggest that there is simply not enough time for teachers to learn how to use new technologies effectively.[2] These obstacles should not discourage teachers from experimenting, if not embracing new technologies. Clearly, overcoming obstacles such as inadequate training, insufficient resources, or lack of time depends in large part on teachers taking the initiative to learn more about available computer resources and learning how to engage their students with these new resources. With a limited amount of time, planning, and research, any teacher can prepare an engaging and stimulating lesson plan that integrates new computer technologies.

II. New Technologies: Availability and Access

The primary purpose of this section is to list and briefly examine specific types of computer technologies including the World Wide Web, interactive CD-ROMs, e-mail, Listservs, or bulletin boards. Although this chapter assumes basic operating knowledge of computers, including fundamental capabilities in accessing the Internet and using the CD-ROM drive of your computer, some suggestions are provided for those with less experience to expand their understanding of this field. Ideally, one should be in a professional situation where the latest technology is available. If this is not the case, perhaps this chapter will provide some suggestions for redressing the situation. If one is truly computer illiterate, then this chapter should be used in conjunction with a simple reference guidebook that can explain how to use a computer and access resources on the Internet. Another possibility would be to enlist the technical support of someone with computer expertise. Another possible solution might be to use the expertise of a student to help train one in the fundamentals of computer use. In fact, a teacher could work together with a student to evaluate various Internet resources, while learning how to use the computer.

Over the past fifteen years or so, computer technology has undergone a tremendous rate of change. For example, within two short years a top-of-the-line computer can revert from being the "latest sports car model" to a Model-T. The upshot is, if one has a very slow computer or outdated Internet connection, it will frustrate everyone involved, thereby significantly reducing the effectiveness of this technology. And if students have faster machines at home, they may be similarly discouraged in the classroom. As a result, one might consider not employing computer technology at all unless sufficient speed and access is available.

Among the new computer resources educators should consider to assist in teaching about the Holocaust, clearly the World Wide Web will be the most useful tool and will continue to be so for the foreseeable future.[3] The World Wide Web is essentially the multimedia component of the Internet, and it allows text, graphic images such as photographs and maps, as well as audio and video, to be transmitted from a Web server to a Web browser in a language that both can understand.[4]

Although the focus here is on the World Wide Web, CD-ROMs are still an attractive option that educators might consider.[5] Most CD-ROMs are simple to install and use on computers. CD-ROMs offer nearly 640 MB of information on a single disk, and among the benefits are increased speed of information retrieval, better video, graphic, and audio capabilities, and, most important, "interactivity." Interactivity is the primary difference between a CD-ROM and a book. In a book, one reads material in a linear fashion that is consciously laid out by the author; an interactive CD-ROM allows the computer user to explore material according to his or her specific interests and pace. Links and buttons allow the users to jump around in the material. A well-designed CD-ROM will allow the user to explore many different paths but still find an understandable and coherent story at the end.

E-mail, Listservs, and bulletin board news groups are additional resources that can be utilized. These are also very easy to use with any standard Internet access package. E-mail, or electronic mail, allows students and teachers to correspond one-on-one with scholars, Holocaust survivors, or other students around the world. Classes can use e-mail to pose questions to authorities in any number of fields. Sometimes in a matter of hours or days, a response will be forthcoming. Often times, Web sites will have e-mail capability to allow users to ask questions of the person or organization that created the Web site. Listservs, also called discussion groups or bulletin boards, are an electronic forum in which members of an online community can post questions, responses, and opinions on any given subject. People usually join a Listserv because they have a specific common interest with other members of the group.[6] There are several important Listservs that have the Holocaust as their focus. The United States Holocaust Memorial Museum's

Discussion List for Holocaust Teachers, the H-Net List for History of the Holocaust, and the Association of Holocaust Organizations Information List are three one might consider examining. Most of these are targeted to a more scholarly or academic audience but can be audited by teachers and advanced students. Some also provide a fully searchable history, so specific postings can be obtained months or years after a topic is discussed.

III. Pedagogical Uses of the Technology

There are five essential elements of successfully using and integrating the World Wide Web in the classroom.[7] These elements should be similar to planning and executing any successful project: conceptualizing, planning, researching, implementing, and evaluating.

First, one must conceptualize the project. A decision must be made as to whether or not computers need to be used at all. Many may feel that teaching the Holocaust is complex enough without adding the complexity of the World Wide Web to the equation. But one must keep in mind that the emergence and existence of new technological resources requires educators to stay informed about topical cyberspace issues. Whether or not educators decide to use the Internet, CD-ROMs, or other resources, there is no question that students will utilize these resources on their own. Therefore, even if educators never move beyond step one, thinking about these issues will help them to guide students if they work with computer resources independently. One must also think of the role the computer should play in developing a plan. Perhaps a teacher wants students to research a specific place or event in Holocaust history, view oral histories, or write a report based on certain Web sites. The best approach is to conceive of a discreet assignment using the Web. This will better focus the students' efforts and help them locate specific resources without getting lost in cyberspace.

Second, one must establish a plan for the project. This involves determining exactly what types of resources one will need and how computers can aid one in locating them. A key question is: Do we have adequate computer resources at our school to use the Web for teaching the Holocaust? Teachers might have to work with the technical department of their school system to allocate sufficient resources to purchase a computer. A well-conceived plan that is not rushed will work much better than a hastily thrown together one. One needs to decide how much time should be devoted to the project. Perhaps teachers will allocate one hour per week to learn how to use computers better. Over the course of an entire school year this can result in the attainment of significant expertise.

The third phase—researching—involves locating and evaluating Web-based resources. Teachers need to learn to navigate the World Wide Web and to locate information in a swift and efficient manner. In doing so, they need to become familiar with Web search engines and subject specific directories. When beginning to explore the World Wide Web, it is helpful to have navigational assistance. One option is to use Internet search engines such as MetaCrawler, InfoSeek, or

AltaVista. These can be quite effective when trying to locate very specific Web sites. Other resources worth familiarizing oneself with are so-called hotlists or directories. With hotlists, an individual has gone to the trouble of compiling and annotating Web sites on a specific topic. Hotlists frequently provide hypertext links to many pages as well. For the Holocaust, there are several hotlists that offer various amounts of annotated guidance. David Dickerson's Homepage located at <http://www.igc.apc.org/ddickerson> is a fine example of a thorough hotlist. This homepage is the most comprehensive annotated list of Holocaust-related Web sites that this author has found. This homepage also includes lists of sites dealing with antisemitism and Jewish history and culture.

Next, teachers need to find a series of Web pages that provide information that complements their in-class lesson. Then they need to become experts at evaluating Web sites once they reach their destination. By doing this, they learn how to tell a good Web site from a poor one. There are important considerations, or criteria, one should keep in mind when evaluating electronic material for quality and content.[8] It may be a helpful exercise for teachers to define exactly what constitutes an authoritative and legitimate source of educational materials concerning the Holocaust. Most educators probably purchase textbooks or other resources from reputable publishers, and may seek out specific authors when purchasing historical books. In the world of print publishing, discerning readers can usually rely on a publishers' imprimatur to distinguish quality works from less reliable works. One needs to apply these same standards to the use of Web sites, CD-ROMS, and other forms of electronic media. It bears repeating: with the expansion of these types of media, it is much easier for anyone to publish. This is especially true of information on the Internet, where all it takes is a computer, scanner, Web server, and basic HTML programming skills to become an instant "expert" or "authority" on any subject. As we will see shortly, some Web sites look reputable, but may be published by Internet design companies or by those lacking academic or other relevant credentials, and may be bereft of desired accuracy. It may be useful to start with Web sites of established and reputable organizations or institutions. An example would be a Holocaust organization in your area, or the United States Holocaust Memorial Museum in Washington, DC.

At the same time, there are a number of high-quality Web sites and other types of electronic media published by profit-making companies, passionate individuals, and others who may be unfamiliar to one. By becoming an astute Internet user, one can quickly identify the credibility and source of a Web site. First, it is imperative to make sure to examine the domain name of the site. There are several different types of domain names, so being able to identify them is important: .org is a noncommercial, nonprofit entity; .com is a commercial, for-profit entity; .gov is a U.S. government site; .mil is a U.S. military site; .edu is an accredited postsecondary educational institution; .net is a computer network; .int is an international organization; .il (Israel), .de (Germany), .at (Austria), .ca (Canada), and .au (Australia) are important country identifiers—these are frequently preceded by .co. Knowing what each of these domain identifiers means will provide insight into the possible agenda behind a particular Web site.

It is also necessary to consider issues such as authorship, accuracy, credentials, objectivity, and presentation. Users should ask themselves the following series of questions: Is it possible to identify who created or authored the Web page and their reasons for doing so? This type of information should be easy to find from the Web site's main homepage. Are the creators of the Web site open to your feedback and questions? A good Web site will solicit and encourage feedback from visitors in order to make corrections and improvements in the future. Do they provide an address and phone number where one can contact them? Is it clear who has authored various pieces of information contained in the Web page? Sometimes a site may have an impressive sounding name or sponsoring information but not provide any clues as to its actual mission, intentions, or authorship. One should be looking for factual accuracy. Any repetitive or excessive errors in spelling or grammar signal that something is amiss. Does the individual or organizational author of material on that Web site possess any special expertise, knowledge, or academic credentials that allow them to be an authority on the subject matter? This applies to any Web site you visit, not just Holocaust-related ones. Does the author have any academic or advanced degrees, or do they work at a Holocaust research institution with which one is familiar? Even if the author is a professional scholar or academician, does his or her field of expertise allow him or her to write on the Holocaust? Perhaps the author is not a trained academic but rather a Holocaust survivor; the latter will undoubtedly provide a different perspective on the Holocaust. Does the author provide source information for documents and photographs that they use? It is worthwhile checking to make sure that the Web site has been revised recently. Web sites that change or are updated every few months suggest an attempt to improve the quality. By examining these fundamental aspects of Web sites, educators should be able to make some critical conclusions about the material.

One must remember that technology should augment classroom learning. Teachers should consider all types of resources when teaching the Holocaust. In some cases, it may not be necessary or even effective for a teacher to use a computer to assist in teaching the Holocaust.[9] Utilizing the resources of a local public or university library is also helpful. Often times, printed materials are more concise, understandable, and comprehensive than materials online. Perhaps there are Holocaust survivors or educators in one's area who would be willing to visit the classroom. The interactivity and impression of a "real person" far exceeds talking to the same person via computer connection.

Fourth, the World Wide Web should be used to complement an existing segment on the Holocaust, but it should not replace or act in lieu of teacher-student interaction. It is important to stress that computer-based technologies should serve as an adjunct in the overall process of teaching the Holocaust in the classroom. By no means should the use of technology supplant a teacher's role in teaching this subject, nor should a teacher defer to the Internet or other new technologies. Once one has located information, using it to augment students' comprehension of sensitive subjects such as the Holocaust is tougher still. Students should be made aware of the gravity and importance of the historical issues at stake. This is a topic that requires human interaction and discussion for proper understanding, and will certainly raise issues or emotions that require a teacher's guidance. Therefore, it is recommended that classroom sessions on the Holocaust take place before students utilize the Internet or other technological resources.

Fifth, it is important to evaluate the success of the project. Questions such as the following should be considered: Did students learn more about the Holocaust by using the Web? What were the drawbacks to using the Web and are there ways it can be improved next time? This information should be used to inform how the Holocaust is to be taught next time. This should be an evolving and dynamic process. Once educators have successfully mastered these skills, working with new technologies can effectively complement Holocaust teaching. Finally, it is valuable to share such lessons with students. The students may not only learn something about the Holocaust but may begin to become more critical thinkers as well as savvy, discerning Internet users. The benefits should be mutual, as students will undoubtedly explore and identify Web sites that can be used in later lessons or in later years.

IV. Holocaust Resources on the World Wide Web

The following section will identify and provide comments on some of the more prominent Web sites concerning the Holocaust. These comments are not meant as a definitive appraisal of all Holocaust-related Web sites. There are now such a large number of Holocaust-specific resources for educators available on the World Wide Web that a comprehensive evaluation is nearly impossible.[10] Moreover, the rate at which Web pages are updated and changed makes any definitive statement unwise. The Web is dynamic and ever-changing; indeed, this is one of its greatest strengths.

The Southern Institute for Education and Research, located at Tulane University, sponsors a site for teachers that seeks to promote tolerance through education and training. This Web page can be found at <http://www.tulane.edu/~soinst/>. Initially, this site violates some fundamental rules including clashing fonts and annoying sounds. Moving beyond these problems, however, the user can click on a section for "Anti-Bias Teacher Education Project," which currently offers three lesson plans on the Holocaust and the Civil Rights movement. A notice on the Web page states that "these events can be used as case studies to help young people understand the need to oppose intolerance by actively promoting a more diverse and just society." One of these "events," called "Deathly Silence: Everyday People in the Holocaust," is a detailed resource for teachers. The Deathly Silence Guide "provides instructional resources for teaching the history of the Holocaust and ethnic conflict. . . . The workshop and manual prepare teachers to develop lessons that address: (1) the meaning of the term 'Holocaust,' (2) the role of everyday people—the 'innocent bystanders'—in systematic murder, and (3) why the Holocaust is important in understanding today's world."

Most major Holocaust museums and memorials now offer Web sites on the Internet and succeed to varying degrees in offering material for teachers and students. The Web site of the United States Holocaust Memorial Museum can be found at <http://www.ushmm.org>. The United States Holocaust Memorial Museum (USHMM), located adjacent to the National Mall in Washington, DC, is the leading American institution for Holocaust research and documentation, and is also a memorial to the millions of Jewish and other victims of the Holocaust. *Logically, this is one of the first sites educators and students should consult when searching for Holocaust-related information on the Web.* The Web site of the USHMM serves a multitude of purposes and interests, both inside and outside the museum. Its first priority is to provide general information to assist visitors to the museum. It contains practical information about museum exhibitions, outreach programs, workshops, lectures, and other special events. It offers "online" exhibitions, which are essentially electronic versions of museum exhibitions. It is a place where researchers and scholars can begin to explore the museum's vast archival, photograph, film, and library holdings; this is especially useful for students and scholars with access or proximity to the museum, as the initial search for materials can be initiated online. In short, a user can spend hours exploring this site, and it should be expected that this site will only continue to expand its offerings to the public.

Despite this wealth of information, however, this site (at the current time) presents a mixed picture for students and teachers at the secondary school level. On the positive side, teachers can locate online teaching guidelines concerning the Holocaust. These offer an excellent point of departure for teachers who wish to integrate the study of the Holocaust into their existing curriculum. It includes a rationale for teaching the Holocaust as well as methodological considerations. It should be noted that teachers also can obtain this type of information by simply calling or writing the museum's education department. There also are transcripts of museum lectures and publications that teachers can access.

For students, the possibility to download photographs from the museum's photo archives or to explore a museum exhibition in cyberspace are two strong features. Here, the Holocaust Museum's Web site offers something to those who cannot visit the museum in Washington, DC. Breaking down geographical barriers, Web site users can engage in a virtual tour of the museum's traveling exhibitions. At the same time, the section of the Web site called "Learning About the Holocaust" contains disappointingly little information. One brief essay describes the history of the Holocaust from 1933 to 1945. Another essay details the fate of children during the Holocaust. Anyone seeking more detailed information, or reference material such as glossaries, bibliographies, timelines, definitions of key events, and so on, would be disappointed by the meager offerings. In addition, students may find the site somewhat visually boring and graphically inconsistent. This site needs to compete for students' attention with other sites, and content alone will not hold students' attention. This is one of the challenges for creators of Holocaust Web pages: balancing a stimulating visual and interactive environment with the seriousness of the subject matter. As institutions such as the USHMM struggle with issues such as adapting their holdings and institutional mission to the Web, their Web sites will be constant works-in-progress. In addition, it almost seems as if the museum's many departments are competing to have their individual needs met on the Web site, as opposed to having an overarching Web concept that unites all museum departments in one organized "cyber" mission.

A second important museum-based Web site is that of the Simon Wiesenthal Center and its associated Museum of Tolerance based in Los Angeles, California. There are really two key Web addresses to access: <http://www.wiesenthal.com> (Homepage of the Simon Wiesenthal Center and Museum of Tolerance, Los Angeles, CA) and <http://motlc.wiesenthal.com> (Museum of Tolerance Online Multimedia Learning Center). The Simon Wiesenthal Center, based in Los Angeles and named for an Austrian Holocaust survivor and famed Nazi hunter, exists to combat prejudice and hatred, to promote tolerance and human rights, and to remember the victims of the Holocaust. As a result, the Wiesenthal Center Web site contains information about the Holocaust but is not solely concerned with that topic, and includes information on promoting tolerance and combating hatred. Both Web sites offer an attractive interface that students will find immediately engaging and understandable. Another success is in the area of interactivity. Visitors may pose a question to a Holocaust survivor via the Web site and receive an e-mailed response. Unfortunately, the turnaround time for this is quite slow. Additional online educational resources include answers to thirty-six questions about the Holocaust, a brief and rather incomplete Holocaust glossary, a timeline, and a section devoted to Black-Jewish relations. One can also find biographies of children who died in or survived the Holocaust. Perhaps the most useful online resource for students is an extensive bibliography that will help users locate books on specific themes and topics, such as antisemitism, racial hatred, women and the Holocaust, and much more. Finally, this Web site is a good departure point for understanding more about how and where hate groups operate on the World Wide Web. This section, called "On Alert: Cyber Watch," offers a glimpse at the operations of hate groups.

The Museum of Tolerance Online Multimedia Learning Center (<http:// motlc.wiesenthal.com>) is one of the largest "learning center" resources available in cyberspace. It is not an understatement to call this one of the largest bodies of Holocaust material on the Web, and teachers and students can utilize much of it. Teachers will find the curricular resources useful, while students can find answers to many questions including an extensive glossary, interactive timeline, and bibliographies. The multimedia learning center resource includes over three thousand texts and ten thousand photographs. There is also an online exhibition that details the history of the Holocaust called: "The Courage to Care: The Holocaust 1933–1945." The online exhibition features sections on the Jews, the Nazis, history of World War II, resistance movements, rescuers, and much more. In addition, teachers can access full-length books on topics such as Kristallnacht and scholarly essays about the Holocaust and Nazi Germany from the *Simon Wiesenthal Center Annual*, Volumes 1–7. All told, these two Web sites are worth extensive examination.

Internationally, there are some museum-based Web sites worth examining. The Web site of Israel's national Holocaust museum and memorial, Yad Vashem, is located at <http://www.yad-vashem.org.il/>, and the museum itself can be visited in Jerusalem. The Web site currently offers very little in the way of resources for students and teachers outside of some educational materials in Hebrew. A notice on the Web page promises an expanded, updated version in the future. Because of Yad Vashem's stature in the field of international Holocaust studies, it would be worth revisiting this site in the future to explore what additions have been made.

For German Holocaust museums and memorials, the best resource is a site created by the Topography of Terror memorial museum in Berlin called "Memorial Museums for the Victims of National Socialism in Germany." This site, located at <http://www.dhm.de/ausstellungen/ns_gedenk/e/index.html>, provides historical details and general information concerning Holocaust memorials and museums in Germany.

A number of private entities also operate Holocaust Web pages that might be worth considering. Perhaps the largest of these is the "Cybrary of the Holocaust" located at <http://www.remember.org>. The "Cybrary of the Holocaust" is one of the largest Web sites dedicated to targeting its information directly at students and teachers. As its name suggests, it aims to be a cyberspace-based library of information concerning the Holocaust. The Cybrary site, at first glance, offers an impressive amount of information concerning the Holocaust. It provides an almost encyclopedic offering of historical information, much of which is relevant and accurate, although very confusing to navigate. It offers curriculum guidelines, provides a lesson plan for teaching about Anne Frank, and includes excerpts of testimonies from Holocaust survivors and transcripts of Nazi speeches and official documents. It also contains historical photographs and artwork created by students reflecting their feelings about the Holocaust.

Unfortunately, the Cybrary also offers a classic case study of one of the main problems of the World Wide Web. It is a site created by a company called "Inetdesign" with no apparent links to any Holocaust research centers. Its creators offer no credentials for their work in the Holocaust. This is not to suggest that the Cybrary has hired unqualified people to create this site. Nor is it being suggested that certain academic credentials are imperative for creating a factually and pedagogically sound Web site. But one would feel more comfortable knowing at the outset this organization's mission, intentions, and the background of its authors. Is the purpose of the site to document and teach the Holocaust? Or, is it rather a promotional vehicle for its umbrella company "Inetdesign" to promote its Web-based business?

Primary sources posted in the Cybrary have no context. For example, the Cybrary has an original transcript of the 1942 Wannsee Conference Protocol. At the Wannsee Conference, called by Reinhard Heydrich in January 1942, the Nazis coordinated and formalized their plans to carry out the extermination of European Jewry. Another Cybrary link below this points to a document concerning Einsatzgruppen operations in Lithuania in 1941, when mobile units of the Security Police and SS Security Service murdered Jews in the wake of Germany's invasion of the Soviet Union in June 1941. No source is provided for this document, and in both cases, there is no contextual information. An astute student might wonder why Jews were being killed in Lithuania in 1941 before the Nazis solidified their plans for the Holocaust at the Wannsee Conference in January 1942. Of course, this is part of a much broader and complicated series of historical issues. But, suffice it to say, *offering these documents entirely out of historical context makes them valuable only to someone who is already familiar with the historical issues involved and is simply seeking to locate the raw text.*

Much like the Cybrary of the Holocaust, the History Place site at <http://www.historyplace.com> is not exactly forthcoming concerning its authorship, mission, and reasons for existing. The .com designation indicates that it is likely a commercial entity. After fifteen minutes of extensive searching, this author managed to locate the following statement under the section devoted to "Awards": "The History Place is a private, independent, Internet-only publication based in the Boston area that is not affiliated with any political group or organization. We present a fact based, common sense approach in the presentation of the history of humanity, prepared by knowledgeable writers and historians. Great care is always given to accuracy in the construction and maintenance of our exhibits." That sounds good and may very well be true. But why not be more explicit and state exactly who these knowledgeable writers and historians are? Additionally, the only way to contact The History Place is via e-mail, with no names or addresses given.

But again, like the Cybrary, the amount of information presented is substantial and one would be foolish to disregard this site entirely. This Web site offers a large component called "Nazi Germany/World War II in Europe." There is information here on Adolf Hitler's rise to power, including a chapter-by-chapter biographical summary leading up to Hitler's rise to power in Germany in 1933. There are biographical sketches of other Nazi leaders including Adolf Eichmann, Rudolf Hess, and Reinhard Heydrich. There are timelines of World War II in Europe and the Holocaust, replete with hyperlinks to more detailed summaries of key events. Generally speaking, this author found little to quibble with the focus of the site, but there were enough small blunders to make him question the historical accuracy of the site.

An important German Web site worth investigating is the "Memorial Museums for the Victims of National Socialism in Germany" page located at <http://www.dhm.de/ausstellungen/ns_gedenk/e/index.html>. This page, published in both German and English by Thomas Lutz of the Topography of Terror museum in Berlin, provides historical summaries, contact information, and direct links to a large number of memorial sites throughout Germany. It is especially useful for investigating specific concentration camps in Germany and to evaluate how Germany has commemorated this history over the past fifty years. Among the many links offered here, one can navigate to the Web page for the Dachau Concentration Camp located outside of Munich. This Web page is located at <http://www.infospace. de/gedenkstaette/english/index.html> and provides a short history of the camp.

One of the best Web sites operated by a Holocaust memorial is the Austrian Mauthausen Concentration Camp Memorial Web site located at <http://www. mauthausen-memorial.gv.at/engl/index.html>. This site serves several purposes. It provides practical information for visitors to the actual memorial in Austria. It also effectively utilizes the interactive features of the World Wide Web. Once a visitor to this site accesses the main Web page and clicks on "The Mauthausen Concentration Camp 1938–1945," the visitor is directed to a historical summary of the camp replete with numerous hyperlinks to various topics concerning the history of the camp. For example, visitors to this site can learn about the various physical components of the concentration camp, the history of its construction—including its several satellite camps—and details about the type of forced labor that was performed there. Other links lead to informative paragraphs detailing such issues as what daily life in the camp would have been like for prisoners, an overview of the camp population with a detailed breakdown of the nationalities of various prisoners interned there, and even details concerning health issues such as disease and nutrition. Further links lead to information detailing the camp's administration, discussions of forced labor and medical experiments, frank explanations of how prisoners were killed, the liberation of the camp, and statistical information concerning prisoner populations and deaths. A final section offers excerpts from written testimony and reports by former prisoners offering a look into Mauthausen in the words of former prisoners. All in all, this is a well-conceived and smartly presented Web site that deserves a visit.

Ben Austin, a sociology professor at Middle Tennessee State University, designed one of the first Holocaust Web sites <http://www.mtsu.edu/~baustin/holo.html> to complement his class, "The Sociology of Genocide and the Holocaust." One of Austin's intentions in creating this Web site was to document the uniqueness of the Holocaust. He offers primary source information on a number of specific historical topics relating to the Holocaust including the Nuremberg laws, Kristallnacht, the "Euthanasia Program," children in the Holocaust, Gypsies, homosexuals, and postwar trials. Professor Austin features documents from the Yad Vashem archive that deal with Nazi death camps. Return visitors to this Web site will observe that Austin has made few improvements since his initial construction of the site several years ago.

V. Concerns for Teachers Using the Internet

As mentioned earlier in this chapter, one of the greatest dangers to students on the World Wide Web is the presence of hate groups and Holocaust denial groups. Although it is not the purpose here to mention or evaluate such Web pages, being aware of their presence and their message is essential for any teacher thinking of turning to the Web for assistance in teaching the Holocaust. There are, however, some prominent Web sites that strive to combat antisemitism, hate groups, and Holocaust deniers on the Web. Perhaps the most famous of these is Kenneth McVay's Web page, "The Nizkor Project," which can be found at <http://www. nizkor.org>.[11] This Web site is difficult to evaluate, as it is one of the most uneven Web pages encountered in research for this chapter.

To his credit, McVay clearly provides information outlining his agenda and history of publishing on the Web. McVay describes his motivations for combating falsehoods on the Internet as beginning with a 1992 episode in which he encountered antisemitic propaganda and vowed to combat it. He calls himself "a leader in developing and implementing community-based, grass roots strategies for countering the lies of those promoting hatred on the Internet." Perhaps a better way of classifying McVay is as a "lone wolf Web battler." Clearly, "The Nizkor Project" is the work of a well-intentioned individual who has invested a great deal of time and energy. But it also has some serious shortcomings that make its overall impression weak. For example, there are a series of ill-conceived hyperlinks that direct the user away from the main purpose of the site. One example is a link to an AltaVista search summary page for the Piltdown man. Although this is a Web page, it does offer a tremendous amount of material on Holocaust deniers and hate groups. McVay presents material from these groups in their own words, so that the user knows who they are and how they argue their position.

For more advanced students, the Avalon Project at the Yale Law School offers access to a substantial number of primary source documents on topics of eighteenth-, nineteenth-, and twentieth-century American history.[12] Virtually every major event in American history is covered with primary source documents. For World War II and the Holocaust, a number of documentary sources are available. A short list indicates the breadth and scope of this collection: "World War II—Documents, 1940–1945," "A Decade of American Foreign Policy—Basic Documents 1941–1949," "The Munich Pact and Associated Documents," "The Stroop Report: The Warsaw Ghetto Is No More," "International Military Tribunal and Postwar Documents," and "Nazi-Soviet Relations 1939–1941: Documents from the Archives of the German Foreign Office."

VI. Final Considerations about the Use of Technology

As we have seen, the access and breadth of sources available at students' and teachers' fingertips is staggering. Without question, Internet technology offers tremendous possibilities for education. If it sparks students' creativity and curiosity, all the better.

The incredible pace at which technology changes requires constant reconsideration of Internet sources and options. When this author was first approached to write this chapter, there seemed to be a battle emerging between the use of interactive CD-ROMs and the use of the Internet. It has become apparent that CD-ROM is losing the battle, with the Internet charging ahead full-speed.

A few Web sites devoted to the Holocaust have turned into literally hundreds. Some, as has been noted, are very good; others are constantly changing and improving; others should be avoided. Hopefully, in the future, persistent problems such as slow speeds for many users, and missing or moved Web sites will become less noticeable. It is hoped that some of the considerations and criteria herein for Web site evaluation will assist educators in locating resources that will help them in the classroom.

NOTES

1. The audience for this chapter is primarily teachers of grades seven to twelve. At this stage, it seems fairly clear that the World Wide Web has dwarfed other forms of computer technology, including CD-ROMs. As a result, this chapter will focus exclusively on Web resources, although lessons can be applied to CD-ROM resources.

2. Victoria Benning, "Internet Access Weaves a Tangled Web for Schools," *The Washington Post,* May 30, 1996:B5.

3. For a good introduction to the Web for absolute beginners, see Pasadena Public Library, "World Wide Web Tutorial for First-Time Users," July 31, 1998, <http://www.ci.pasadena.ca.us/library/tutorial.html>.

4. To learn more about the history of the World Wide Web, visit <http://www.nmsi.ac.uk/usage/histweb.html>.

5. For a good overview of Holocaust-specific CD-ROM possibilities for your classroom, this author recommends visiting the Florida Center for Instructional Technology Web site. The section, "A Teacher's Guide to the Holocaust" provides abstracts of several CD-ROM products: <http://fcit.coedu.usf.edu/Holocaust/resouRce/software.htm>.

6. To locate and subscribe to a Listserv or bulletin board of interest to you, you can try searching either Liszt Select (<http://www.liszt.com>), which currently has over ninety thousand mailing lists in a searchable directory, or TileNet (<http://www.qcfurball.com/engines/tilenet.html>).

7. For a good Web-based introduction to using the Internet in the classroom, visit: <http://web/syr.edu/~djleu/sites.html>.

8. There are several useful Web sites that offer suggestions for critically evaluating other Web pages. Two that I found very informative are: Alexander, Janet and Marsha Tate, *Checklist for an Informational Web Page,* The Wolfgram Memorial Library at Widener University, posted 1996, Rev. 1997 <http://www.science.widener.edu/~withers/inform.htm> and Kathy Schrock, *Critical Evaluation of a Web Site: Secondary School Level,* Kathy Schrock's Guide for Educators (Posted 1996). Schrock's Web site offers many resources, including bibliographies and other tools and links for critically evaluating Web pages. <http://www.capecod.net/schrockguide/evalhigh.htm>

9. See: Alex Jonas, and Darren Minarek, *Untangling the Web,* Close-Up Foundation Web Site, <http://www.closeup.org/ncss-stu.htm>.

10. David Klevan, a Holocaust education specialist responsible for high school programs at the United States Holocaust Memorial Museum, offers teachers a handout with a set of criteria for evaluating Web sites. Much of the following discussion is based on points raised in this handout and from conversations the author has had with Klevan.

11. As McVay notes on his homepage, the Hebrew word *nizkor* means, "we will remember."

12. William C. Fray and Lisa A. Spar, Codirectors, "The Avalon Project at the Yale Law School," <http://www.yale.edu/lawweb/avalon/avalon.htm>, 1998.

ANNOTATED CD-ROM BIBLIOGRAPHY

Lest We Forget: A History of the Holocaust (Endless Interactive, Logos Research Systems), <http://www.logos.com>.   A powerful testimony to the Holocaust, this CD-ROM uses rare archival film footage, historical speeches, original music, and documentary photographs to elicit powerful emotions that writing alone cannot achieve.

Historical Atlas of the Holocaust (United States Holocaust Memorial Museum), <http://www.ushmm.org>.   This interactive CD-ROM contains more than 230 full-color maps with accompanying text to chronicle the history of the Holocaust from 1933 to postwar Europe in 1949–1950.

The Complete Maus (Voyager Publishing), <http://www.learntech.com/learntech>.   The Pulitzer Prize-winning graphic memoir about the Holocaust, enriched with conversations with artist/creator Art Spiegelman, audio interviews of his father, and other original documents from which this work evolved.

The Yellow Star (Kush Multimedia) <http://www.compucity.com>.   This CD-ROM tells the story of the persecution of the Jews in Europe from 1933 to 1945. The viewer is presented with a virtual book containing a timeline of events related to the Holocaust. Each page has a photograph, text, and a movie. An index and glossary are also available from the control bar.

The Holocaust (Quanta Press CD-ROMs), Inquiries through Social Studies School Service <http://www.socialstudies.com>.   Through the use of archival newsreel footage and historical photographs, a graphic documentation of the Holocaust is made available. A text reference section contains a wealth of original documents, including interviews with liberating soldiers, correspondence from camp prisoners, and the Nuremberg Tribunal Report. Warning: This is not recommended for unprepared audiences.

11

The Inclusion of Art in a Study of the Holocaust

SHARI ROSENSTEIN WERB

A work of art can be a powerful, thought-provoking tool for educators faced with the challenge of bringing Holocaust history to the classroom. Unlike the printed text, which unfolds over time, pictorial art can speak volumes at a glance, stimulating students to explore and respond to the variety of perspectives critical to an understanding of Holocaust history. For this reason and others, teachers should seriously consider the inclusion of art in their lessons and units on the Holocaust.

For purposes of this discussion, four categories of Holocaust-period art will be examined: *Nazi Art*, as exemplified in posters and illustrated books for children, which reveals the Nazi racist ideology; *Art "From the Outside,"* which uses the political cartoon as a means of investigating world responses to events occurring within Nazi Germany and Europe; *Victim Art*, which documents the Holocaust from the viewpoint of those who suffered under Nazi persecution; and *Aftermath: Art as Memory*, which explores the legacy of the Holocaust as interpreted by artists (survivors and others) working in the postwar period.

Although this chapter will delineate the many benefits of using art in the classroom, it is imperative to note that artistic works must be placed in their historical context. A piece of Nazi propaganda art, for example, can potentially convey to one's students the same hateful message it had originally transmitted to the German citizenry. On a different note, the strong factional biases of a political cartoon published fifty-five or sixty years ago may be misunderstood without an explanation. On yet another note, victim art can sometimes be called into question by the student: How, after all, did people suffering under such terrible conditions find the materials and opportunity to create works of art? Finally, since art created in the aftermath of the Holocaust often portrays subjects and themes also found in victim art, students must be reminded of the critical distinction between the two categories. The Nazis did not approve of victims documenting their experiences during the Holocaust, so it was extremely dangerous for them to create art. After the Holocaust, when creating art could not lead to physical harm (although it could perhaps open emotional wounds), many survivors documented their experiences. Readers should keep these issues in mind while reading the rest of this chapter.

Each section is followed by a select annotated bibliography of works and images appropriate for classroom use. Those selections particularly effective with students are highlighted and accompanied by suggestions for displaying and discussing them. Most of the examples are chosen from materials held in the Collections Division of the United States Holocaust Memorial Museum because these items are readily available to educators.

Nazi Art

The fate of art and artists under the Nazi regime can serve as a metaphor for German society as a whole during the years 1933 to 1945. To Nazi authorities, a work of art fell into one of two categories: acceptable or unacceptable. An acceptable painting or sculpture was one that conformed to the tastes of the German dictator. Hitler, himself a failed artist who blamed his lack of success on what he conceived to be the "liberal" artistic establishment, strongly opposed modernist tendencies in the arts. For example, he disliked the expressionist style of artists such as Paul Klee and Max Beckmann, who were influential in Germany during the 1920s. Instead, he preferred straightforward, representational (if idealized) portraits and scenes drawn from nature.

Quite apart from any set of aesthetic criteria, however, an artist in Hitler's Germany needed first and foremost to be an ethnic German to win the Nazi government's stamp of approval.

Art unacceptable to the German authorities was deemed "degenerate," "Bolshevik," or "Jewish." Such works were exposed to ridicule on a national scale (as in the notorious "Degenerate Art" exhibit of 1938), and eliminated—often along with their creators—from public view. Artists whose works were associated with the Degenerate Art exhibit were forbidden to exhibit their artwork or to teach, and many of the artists were interned in concentration camps. This exhibit represented the end for many artists' careers at the time. Many of these works by banned artists such as Marc Chagall, Paul Klee, and Wassily Kandinsky, found their way into major museums throughout the world and, although certain artists may not have survived the Nazis, much of their artwork has outlived the Third Reich.

It is possible to teach a minilesson about Holocaust history based on the experiences of an individual artist whose works were deemed "degenerate." Students should begin with an examination of the artist's world prior to Hitler's takeover in Germany, then analyze how that world changed as the Nazi government increasingly enforced its conception of what was an "acceptable" work of art, and, not long later, who was an "acceptable" human being. Another approach is to have students examine works by various artists active during this period in order to arrive at a definition of "degenerate art." Entartete Kunst ("degenerate art"), to Germany's cultural guardians, generally referred to works of abstract and expressionist art, or art manifesting a leftist political sensibility. The concise definition offered in *The Encyclopedia of the Third Reich*, "Forms of modern art to which Hitler objected," however, is perhaps the most accurate (Synder, 1989, p. 85).

Although the work of many so-called degenerate artists may not appeal to all, this activity serves to foster student reflection on larger, perennial issues, such as censorship and freedom of expression. (These lessons can be supplemented with examples of victim art, which point out the powerful human urge for self-expression, even at the risk of one's life.)

An examination of art created and controlled by the Nazis can be both a disturbing and a rewarding exercise. Veneration of Hitler, hatred of Jews, state-sanctioned terrorism, "racial science," and the uses of propaganda are among the topics that may be effectively introduced to the classroom through a study of the art the Nazis deemed "acceptable." First, however, a caveat: Nazi-sanctioned art has in the past proved all too successful in its propagandistic intent, and it retains some of its power to this day. *It is the instructor's obligation to keep students mindful of the manipulative nature of this art, and to assure that Nazi racist stereotypes are not perpetuated, however unintentionally.*

Because of the wide availability of examples in the form of photo reproductions or slides, propaganda art and Nazi architecture are, perhaps, the two categories of "acceptable art" best suited for use in the classroom. While other styles of art can also serve effectively (these are described in the bibliography), the present discussion will be limited to these two categories.

Propaganda Art.   The Nazi press, controlled by Joseph Goebbels's Ministry of Propaganda, published and distributed many books that featured ludicrously stereotyped depictions of Jews. The familiar styles of the cartoonist and caricaturist were employed in these works to incite hatred and disgust on the part of ordinary Germans toward their Jewish fellow citizens, whose presence in the Third Reich suddenly constituted an "alien menace." Caricature was used in promotional posters for the antisemitic films *The Eternal Jew* and *Jud Süss*, and in books geared toward the young, such as *The Poison Mushroom (Der Giftpilz)* (see Figure 11.1) and *The Sly Fox*. The books were used in classrooms to instruct children on how to identify and isolate their Jewish classmates. In a calculated attempt to indoctrinate the masses, caricatures of Jews were displayed throughout Nazi Germany—in public spaces, on magazine pages, in schools, and at the workplace.

Teachers can use a poster-sized reproduction of the cover to the children's book *The Poison Mushroom* to introduce students to Nazi propaganda. As most students will not likely be able to read the German cursive script on the book's cover, ask them to describe what they see in the picture. After they list the more straightforward details, such as the caricatured (hook-nosed and bearded) Jewish man positioned within a mushroom, ask them to discuss the relationship of the illustration's different elements. Then spend some time speculating on what the book's title may be, and to what purpose the book may have been written. Only at this point should the translated title of the book be revealed, as well as the fact that it is a work intended for children. Ultimately, these disclosures prepare the class for a full discussion of the insidious nature of Nazi propaganda. Taking part in this activity stimulates students to identify the intended audience of propaganda art and to explore the meaning behind its stereotyped imagery.

FIGURE 11.1 *Der Giftpilz* (The Poison Mushroom). Book cover. Reprinted, with permission, from the collections of the United States Holocaust Memorial Museum.

Propaganda art was pervasive in Nazi Germany. Political posters and murals served to glorify Hitler's storm troopers, portraying them not as the thugs they were but as Germany's saviors. Reproductions of political posters can be used to show students how a particular artistic style is capable of persuasively "selling" a deadly political message. Indeed, comparisons may well be made between the Nazi's use of vivid graphics and pithy slogans to promote their ideology and the techniques of modern commercial advertising. Furthermore, teachers may wish to ask students to consider the means by which the Nazis, through popular political art, were able to convince the German masses of the nobility of their cause.

Nazi Architecture.   In addition to its functional aspects, architecture has a symbolic value that the Nazis recognized and used to their advantage. Hitler's personal love of this applied art, documented by his chief architect Albert Speer (1970) in *Inside the Third Reich*, assured that architecture would play an important role in the New Germany. Reflected in its monumental government buildings, coliseums, and public spaces, the image of Germany the Nazis conveyed both to the outside world and to the German citizenry was one of power, permanence, and self-assurance. Symbolism aside, a study of Nazi architecture also offers the opportunity to investigate events pertinent to Holocaust history, such as mass party rallies, for which these structures served as the ideal backdrop. Anticipating the propaganda value of these events, Hitler's architects incorporated into their designs special set-off areas from which the state-controlled media could photograph and film the events.

Despite their monumental aspirations, many of these buildings were, in fact, constructed in haste and with inferior material. Due to lack of manpower, time, and supplies, others were never finished; still others were destroyed during the war. During a visit with a group of students to the site of the infamous Nazi Party rally in Nuremberg, this author personally encountered one of the Nazi era's most ambitious attempts at awe-inspiring architecture: an enormous stadium built beside a manmade lake. From a position on the rally grounds, the edifice appeared quite magnificent, but a short walk around the lake and closer inspection of the structure revealed something quite different. The impressive facade turned out to have been fabricated of low-grade, crumbling stone—and behind it lay nothing more than a patch of weeds. The scene reminded one of a movie set. The guide reported that the Nazis had never completed the stadium; its facade alone sufficed to satisfy the people's need to believe that they lived in a prosperous era overflowing with exciting possibilities.

Conclusion.   Before embarking on a unit about Nazi art, it is highly recommended that instructors take the time to familiarize themselves with its various genres (not all of which are discussed here), and the political purposes this art served. One can only relate the innocuous landscapes and scenes of German family life that characterize Nazi-approved art to the violence and criminality of Hitler's regime by "reading" this body of work in the light of Nazi ideology. Only then will the student reach a deeper understanding of this complex subject. The bibliography below includes a number of excellent reference books, and also a fine film, that deal specifically with art, and the fate of artists, during the Third Reich.

Teaching Resources

Adams, Peter. *Art of the Third Reich*. New York: Harry Abrams Publishers, 1992. This book was written following the acclaimed Adams's 1988 BBC film documentary entitled "Art in the Third Reich." Both the film and the book cover topics such as "The Great German Art Exhibitions," "The Exhibition of 'Degenerate Art'," "The Visualization of National Socialist Ideology," and "Hitler and the Architects." Adams succeeds in producing a valuable survey of Hitler's influence over all of the arts in Nazi Germany. The film, which is a good classroom resource, provides a visually stimulating overview of this subject supported by insightful narration.

Barron, Stephanie. *Degenerate Art: The Fate of the Avant-Garde in Nazi Germany.* Los Angeles, CA: Los Angeles County Museum of Art, 1991. This book served as an exhibition catalogue for the exhibit entitled "Degenerate Art: The Fate of the Avant-Garde in Nazi Germany," which was organized by the Los Angeles County Museum of Art. It contains a wealth of information about all forms of art the Nazis deemed degenerate, including paintings, sculpture, architecture, music, and film. The essay entitled "Entartete Kunst, Munich 1937: A Reconstruction" offers photographs that chronicle the installation and opening of the original exhibition. An insert describes in great detail the original exhibition space and a catalogue of the works displayed. This catalogue explains why these works were included as part of the exhibition.

Hinz, Berthold. *Art in the Third Reich.* New York: Pantheon Books, 1979. This book is written from an art historian's point of view. It deals with genre painting, National Socialist painting, photography, mass media, and architecture from the Third Reich, and contains both color and black-and-white images. The author weaves Nazi philosophy throughout his interpretation of the artwork, thereby placing this art into its proper context. Although the language used in this book is often technical, and might be considered advanced for secondary students, there are many interesting photographs of artwork and architecture to use for classroom activities.

Art "From the Outside"

World reaction to Hitler's regime was frequently communicated through the lively medium of the political or editorial cartoon, of which thousands were printed in newspapers and journals during the years 1933 to 1945. A well-chosen selection of cartoons can offer teachers an effective means of making Holocaust history more accessible to students.

Political art from *outside* the Third Reich serves to deflate the rhetoric and stereotypes promoted by the Nazis. While some of these cartoons attack Nazi German tactics, many others, in the great tradition of political caricature, take aim at the physical appearance of major figures in the Nazi party. Artists who targeted such characteristics often stressed the discrepancy between the ideal "Aryan" type familiar from Nazi propaganda, and Hitler's actual appearance, which many outside Germany thought quite ridiculous.

The cartoon captioned ". . . the greatest educator of the German nation is the Fuehrer," originally published in the American magazine, *Labor Front,* in 1936, sav-

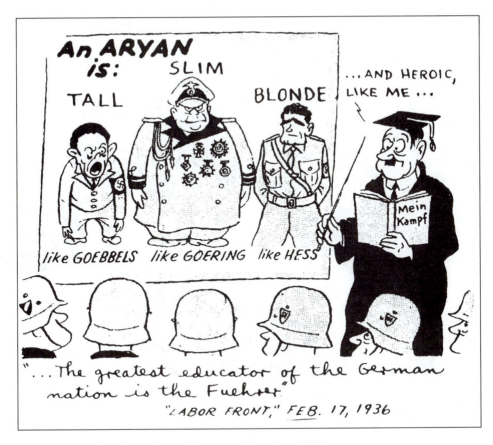

FIGURE 11.2 "An Aryan is . . ." Cartoon. *Labor Front*, 1936.

ages the whole issue of "racial science." The cartoon depicts Hitler in a cap and gown pointing out the attributes of the ideal "Aryan" type (tall, strong, and blonde) to a group of Nazi soldiers. Under a diagram chart labeled "An Aryan Is" stand his paragons: short, apish Josef Goebbels, bloated Hermann Goering, and the dark-haired Rudolf Hess. Students often inquire about the incongruity between the Nazi ideal and its party leadership. Contemporary illustrations such as this one validate this observation about the fundamental hypocrisy of Nazism.

Global politics are the concern of a second political cartoon, printed in the *New York Times* on July 3, 1938, in the "The News of the Week in Review" (p. E3). In this piece, a poor but dignified looking Jew (labeled "non-Aryan") rests wearily at a crossroads—the "cross" being the twisted Nazi emblem of the swastika. He leans against a traffic post, atop which four "Go" signs point in four directions. At each terminus, four "Stop" signs mark four dead ends. But salvation glimmers at the

THE NEW YORK TIMES, SUNDAY, JULY 3, 1938.

WILL THE EVIAN CONFERENCE GUIDE HIM TO FREEDOM?

FIGURE 11.3   "Will the Evian Conference Guide Him to Freedom?" Cartoon. *The New York Times*, 3 July 1938.

horizon, where imposed in a rising sun motif are the words "Evian Conference." The cartoon is captioned: "Will the Evian Conference Guide Him to Freedom?" The Conference, organized by the U.S. State Department to provide an international forum to discuss the fate of Jews seeking refuge outside Germany and Austria, unfortunately did not result in a coordinated program of rescue and sanctuary. As previously mentioned, students will not appreciate this or other topical cartoons without first understanding their historical context. Rather than simply filling in the missing information, however, instructors should seize the opportunity to guide student inquiry into the unfamiliar subjects and issues these drawings raise. Concerning the present example, students will wonder about the Evian Conference: What was it? When did this conference take place? They also might ask about the symbolic purport of the traffic signs, or the reason why the central figure, clearly portrayed as Jewish, is labeled "non-Aryan." (I have successfully employed the "Artifact Inquiry Activity Worksheet," prepared by the U.S. Holocaust Memorial Museum/Education Department, in my own teaching; it is offered as a supplement to this section [Appendix].)

Finally, locally published political cartoons allow students to explore Holocaust history from the "outsider" perspective of their home communities. An assignment can send students to their local library, where, browsing hometown newspapers from the period from 1933 to 1945, they will uncover a fascinating range of graphic art (as well as articles and editorials) reporting and commenting on the situation in Europe. Based on this material, teachers might assign students to create a timeline recounting this history through a series of political cartoons. Another activity could draw on the political cartoon's function as a barometer of public opinion. Undertaking a survey of cartoons created in response to Holocaust history, students can gain unique insight into the changing moods and attitudes of the people over time.

Teaching Resources

Douglas, Roy. *The World War 1939–1945: The Cartoonists' Vision.* London: Routledge, 1990. Douglas selected political cartoons from various countries and provides background and interpretive information. Although only a few cartoons deal specifically with the Holocaust, most comment on the events of the war and the many personalities involved. This book can provide students with a look at a range of viewpoints of the concerned countries.

Zeman, Zbynek. *Heckling Hitler: Caricatures of the Third Reich.* Hanover, NH: University Press of New England, 1987. This book is organized chronologically, starting with caricatures of Hitler as he was coming into power; it includes the Nazi movement, its leadership, and Germany's position in World War II. These political satirists helped shape public opinion of Nazi Germany, and a close examination of the works included in this book can illuminate how perceptions of Hitler changed over time.

Victim Art

Classroom teachers rarely have time to offer an in-depth survey of the Holocaust period. Instead, they tend to focus on a few events, such as Hitler's rise to power, the adoption of anti-Jewish legislation in Germany, and the establishment of the concentration camps or the horrors in the camps. Although this framework may provide an adequate overview of Holocaust history, students feel more "connected" to the subject when given details about the lives of individuals who were persecuted by the German State. One way of providing that connection is to introduce and discuss works of art created by these victims of Nazism. Because a work of art can address several issues simultaneously, bringing victim art to the classroom offers the instructor an efficient means of approaching the complex issues and themes of Holocaust history.

Victims were not allowed to possess cameras, paintbrushes, or sketchpads, in part because these were the tools by which the outside world might learn of Germany's crimes against humanity. Yet, many victims managed secretly to create a durable record of their experiences by painting, sketching, or, in rare instances, photographing the scenes that they witnessed. They smuggled crayons or canvases past ghetto watchmen and traded precious food rations for access to art supplies from camp storehouses. Some even fashioned their own materials: charcoal from bits of burnt wood, paintbrushes from strands of their own hair. They produced telling portraits of prisoners and persecutors, and documented the brutalization of a people through straightforward depictions of everyday life. A careful study of works by victim-artists can help teachers bridge many gaps in student awareness of Holocaust history. This author has used artistic creations such as the three examples discussed below to enable educators and students to: (1) better understand the nature of human relations within the ghettos and camps; (2) investigate the phenomenon of art created and preserved by persons under extreme duress; (3) gain insight into the life story of an individual artist; and (4) perceive the significance of seemingly minor events.

Example 1: Lodz Ghetto Policeman.   This ink drawing, by an artist known only as "Kurant," is an excellent means of introducing students to the role the Jewish Councils (*Judenrat*) and Jewish Police played in the ghettos. Students with some background knowledge of ghetto life will note that the man portrayed clearly does not look like a "typical" ghetto inhabitant. He is conspicuously well-groomed, sports a distinctive cap, is suitably dressed for the cold Polish winter, and is, to all appearances, in good health and even well-fed. Some students also may observe that the policeman's yellow Star of David is worn as an armband, whereas most Lodz ghetto dwellers were obliged to sew this demeaning badge of identification directly onto their clothing. Each of these details relates in some way to the privileged status of the ghetto elite, which included members of the Jewish police force. The portrait, at first glance, appears respectful and admiring. But is it really so? Who, anyway, were the Jewish Police? Did they work to benefit the ghetto dwellers, or were they collaborators who sold out their fellow Jews for more food and better clothes? Did the artist, in turn, exchange his services for some extra rations, or perhaps a better set of paintbrushes?

For discussion units about "ghetto life," this author makes use of a slide reproduction of the "Lodz Ghetto Policeman" from the United States Holocaust Memorial Museum's Collection to lead into such unfamiliar topic areas as the Judenrat and the Ghetto Police. My procedure is to draw attention to the portrait's date, 1941, and to the artist's signature, both on the lower right-hand corner. I explain that the portrait was sketched in the Lodz Ghetto, in German-occupied Poland, that the original artwork is quite small in size, and that we possess very little information about the artist or his creation, which was concealed in the ghetto and retrieved after the war. Students are then invited to examine the portrait for clues about its origins and to relate their findings to what they already have learned of Holocaust history.

I prompt the students analyzing the portrait by asking: "Does the subject look like a 'typical' ghetto inhabitant?" The response may include some of the details mentioned above: the man's robust appearance, neatly trimmed hair, fur-lined coat, self-possessed demeanor, and—perhaps most striking of all—his uni-

FIGURE 11.4 Kurant.
Lodz Ghetto Policeman.
Drawing, 1941. Reprinted,
with permission, from the
collections of the United
States Holocaust
Memorial Museum.

form. Once the police attire has been noted, I inquire: "Who do you think this uniformed man was?" and "What do you think he did in the ghetto?" At this point I might also ask students to think about the sociology of portrait painting, both in general terms ("Why do people have their portraits made?"), and within the special context of the ghetto ("Why might someone paint this man's portrait?"). Other prompts/questions could include: "Do you think this portrait was created on commission?" and "Does the artist reveal any feelings toward his subject?" During the course of the discussion I make it a point to introduce detailed information about the Ghetto Police (and also to provide reading materials and a list of resources for students wishing to conduct further research on their own).

At this point in the discussion, it is helpful to provide specific information regarding the role of Jewish Police in the ghettos. I do this either in the form of an inquiry, where students ask questions to find out more information, by encouraging students to do their own research on the topic, or providing materials for students to read. Armed with more information about the topic, we complete the analysis of this work by considering the purpose of creating the artwork at the time (from the perspectives of the victims, perpetrators, and bystanders) and how this work contributes to our understanding of Holocaust history today.

Finally, we also consider the purposes the portrait may have served from the triple perspective of victim, perpetrator, and bystander. I have found that a critical examination to this single work of art, beyond addressing the still-controversial role played by the Ghetto Police, often opens onto the broader subject of social hierarchy within the ghetto—an important but frequently neglected theme in discourse about the Holocaust.

Example 2: The Last March of Janusz Korczak and the Children on Their Way to Deportation.   Halina Olamucki was a young art student in Warsaw when her studies were interrupted by the German conquest of Poland. Interned in the Warsaw Ghetto and detailed to a labor brigade on the "Aryan" side, Olamucki—at great personal risk—began to smuggle art supplies into the ghetto. At the same time, she passed along her covertly created sketches and paintings of ghetto life to her confidants outside the ghetto walls.

Olamucki's pencil sketch, "The Last March of Janusz Korczak and the Children [on Their Way to Deportation]" (1943), is the only surviving contemporary graphic documentation of this dramatic, historic event. A contextual study of the sketch can reveal many layers of information and meaning; its title alone may stimulate student curiosity about the situation of children in the ghetto, the significance of the term "deportation," or the fascinating figure of the orphanage director and educator Korczak, who chose to go to his death with his children. Students investigating the story behind the picture soon piece its various elements into a compelling and poignant narrative. They may learn, for example, the reason why Korczak holds two of the youngest children in his arms, and discover the source of the green banners borne by the children at the rear of the procession. (These were the emblems of the child-ruler King Matt, the hero of Korczak's popular novel of the same name.)

A more general but equally worthwhile response to Olamucki's artwork would be to encourage students to speculate on the artist's rationale. Why, for example, did Olamucki persist in creating her graphic chronicles of life within the Warsaw Ghetto, considering the torture and death she faced were she caught? And what motives might Olamucki have had for dating and signing her initials to her work? This drawing works best in "ghetto life" units when used in conjunction

FIGURE 11.5 Halina Olamuscki. *Le dernier chemin Korczak et les enfants* (The Last March of Janusz Korczak and the Children [on Their Way to Deportation]). Drawing, 1943. Reprinted, with permission, from the collections of the United States Holocaust Memorial Museum.

with a brief narrative by Hanna Mortkowicz-Olczakowa, a colleague and acquaintance of Korczak's, entitled "Yanosz Korczak's Last Walk." (The latter is included in Glatstein, Knox, and Margoshes [Eds.], *Anthology of Holocaust Literature*. New York: Atheneum, 1982, pp. 134–137.) I first have students read this account, asking them to underscore any passages that help them visualize the "last march." I then introduce Olamucki's artwork, noting that it was sketched the same year (1943) that Korczak and the children were deported from the ghetto, and request them to look for details that parallel what they have just read. I have found that using the written account in this fashion has the advantage of clarifying in advance some of the drawing's potentially obscure points of reference.

Example 3: Uniform Tailor Shop.   Theresienstadt (Terezín) is the site educators most often associate with the theme "Art in the Holocaust." Although it is true that, for a time, the arts flourished in the Theresienstadt Ghetto in occupied Czechoslovakia, it is important that students understand why this state of affairs was tolerated—even authorized—by the Nazis. The reason, succinctly, was that Theresienstadt, which its cynical rulers dubbed the "paradise ghetto," functioned as a propaganda tool, whereby Germany would prove to the outside world its supposed superior treatment of political detainees. Although it is true that Theresienstadt's prisoners, the inhabitants of this lie, were permitted a variety of cultural and recreational activities, these could scarcely mask the malnutrition,

FIGURE 11.6   Petr Kien. *Uniformschneiderei* (Uniform Tailor Shop). Print. Reprinted, with permission, from the collections of the United States Holocaust Memorial Museum.

disease, and deportations to death camps that marked the reality of their lives in the ghetto. (This subject is covered in greater detail in several of the bibliographic references.)

When working with students, this author makes a point of distinguishing between three categories of victim art: "Assigned Art" (artwork ordered by the

Nazis as part of an official job or task, such as counterfeiting documents or creating maps); "Acceptable Art" (artwork permitted by the Nazis, for example, landscapes, still-lifes or portraits); and "Clandestine Art" (artwork created in defiance of the Nazis—secret documentation of scenes from daily life). Familiarity with these categories can help students contextualize a particular work of art and identify the restrictions and risks involved in its creation. Because artists in Theresienstadt moved frequently between these three categories, their work provides a model opportunity to define and discuss the character of victim art.

The portfolio of Petr Kien, who was an author as well as an artist, includes drawings and sketches from each of the three categories of victim art. As deputy director of the Theresienstadt Drawing Office, Kien was obliged to produce technical drawings (such as charts, blueprints, and posters) and other official work on order of the Nazi command. But Kien's high-ranking position also gave him the means and opportunity to express himself in more personal terms. Whether Uniform Tailor Shop falls into the category of Assigned, Acceptable, or Clandestine art is a matter for debate. In the classroom, however, it is instructive to capitalize on such uncertainty.

A cursory look at this ink drawing is enough to suggest that Kien had access to conventional art supplies, and sufficient time to complete his work with a fair degree of professional polish. The drawing's apparent subject matter (as well as its title) tells us that uniforms were manufactured and repaired in Terezín. From the composition it becomes evident that the individuals toiling away are not Kien's primary interest but, rather, the work process itself. Scanning the image, one's eyes are drawn first to the black sewing machine in the foreground, its brand name, "Singer," then down toward a garment being gathered and stitched, and, finally, toward the background, where two workers lean against a far wall.

Kien's emphasis on work rather than character might suggest that he had created the sketch on assignment from his office. But other interpretations are also possible. For example, Kien may have created this "motion study" for his own amusement, or, possibly, to test his technical skills. Or, perhaps, in calling attention to the sewing machine, Kien had a more subversive point in mind. After all, the Jewish slaves depicted in the ghetto shop are mending uniforms for soldiers of the Third Reich with a machine manufactured in an enemy nation, the United States, by a company founded and owned by Jews. Might this not be construed as an ironic comment on self-styled "Aryan" superiority? At any event, the objective here is not to find the "correct answer," for there is none. Rather, the point is to inspire students to think about the categories of victim art, and the particular circumstances of its creation.

Before leaving the subject of Theresienstadt, a word should be offered about the well-known children's art that originated there. These drawings and paintings may be used to advantage in the classroom, as most young students find their imagery both familiar and appealing. But, although they contain some fascinating impressions of ghetto life, these artworks should not be mistaken for factual documents about Theresienstadt or the Holocaust. Indeed, Terezín's art instructors counseled their students not to make their ghetto experience a theme for their art but rather to portray scenes of normal domestic life from before the war, or to imagine and depict their lives after liberation. The surviving artwork, however, offers a rare glimpse into the emotional world of their young creators. This author uses the following examples because they are on display in the United States Holocaust Memorial Museum's Permanent Exhibition: One drawing, for example, depicts a house floating through the sky on a colossal leaf; another portrays a group of girls at a prewar (or postliberation) social gathering, the yellow Star of David emblazoned on each glamorous party dress. The fact that imprisoned teachers in Theresienstadt encouraged children to indulge in escapist fantasies can itself form the basis of a provocative classroom discussion about the purpose and meaning of art during the Holocaust. It also might be noted that the artistic medium itself can offer clues about the inner emotional state of these children and insight into their tragically constricted existence: witness the preponderance of muted tones in the color sketches, or the collage-piece featuring "snowy mountains" fashioned from papers discarded by the Ghetto Administrative Office.

Teaching Resources

Amishai-Maisels, Ziva. *Depiction and Interpretation: The Influence of the Holocaust on the Visual Arts.* Oxford and New York: Pergamon Press, 1993. The primary aim of this ambitious study is to detail the impact Nazism and the Holocaust made on Western art. Seeking to answer the question "How does one deal with the Holocaust in art?" the author discusses and analyzes works by major artists such as Chagall, Rothko, Picasso, Shahn, Grosz, and Beckmann. The book also includes sections on imprisoned artists, exiled artists, and the creative output of Holocaust survivors.

Blatter, Janet & Sybil Milton. *Art of the Holocaust.* New York: Routledge Press, 1981. This authoritative book on the subject includes over 350 works of art created by victims of the Nazis in ghettos, concentration camps, and in hiding. The two introductions give detailed answers to questions about Holocaust art—who the "artists" were, why they created artwork, what is meant by Holocaust art, and where this art may be found. Because it contains so many illustrations, this book, currently out of print, is worth obtaining through an interlibrary loan before starting a section on Holocaust art.

Costanza, Mary. *The Living Witness: Art in the Concentration Camps and Ghettos.* New York: Free Press, 1982. This book is organized in such a way as to provide the reader with detailed information about the different types of artists ("assigned" and "secret"), the places where art was made, the materials artists used, and how the artwork was recovered. It includes many examples of art ideal for use in the classroom to help students learn about the Holocaust through the eyes of the victims.

Czarnecki, Joseph P. *Last Traces: The Lost Art of Auschwitz.* New York: Atheneum, 1989. This book provides insight into the resourcefulness of people imprisoned in Auschwitz and the importance of self-expression for those forced to live in a concentration camp. Czarnecki takes the reader on a tour of the barracks, offices, and gas chambers to provide examples of artwork created within these conditions.

Green, Gerald. *The Artists of Terezin: Illustrations by the Inmates of Terezin.* New York: Hawthorn Books, 1969. The author describes the Terezin Ghetto, the experiences of the artists imprisoned in Terezin, and includes over one hundred black and white reproductions of their artwork. It also includes reproductions from a book entitled *Tommy,* created by Bedrich Fritta, an inmate in Terezin, for his son Tommy on his third birthday.

Salomon, Charlotte [introduced by Judith Herzberg], *Charlotte, Life or Theater?* New York: Viking Press, 1981. Charlotte Salomon painted more than seven hundred watercolors during the years 1939 to 1941 as an autobiographical account of her life. The graphic portrayal of her life before and during the Holocaust, overlaid by text and musical selections, enables the viewer to witness Charlotte's interpretation of her personal development, her artistic maturity, and her experiences during the Holocaust. Although aspects of this enormous collection of artwork provide insights into Charlotte's experiences during the Holocaust, it is (equally) filled with memories unrelated to the Holocaust. If one chooses to use this book in the classroom, it is important to identify this as a unique example of art created during the Holocaust, in that Charlotte had access to art supplies, time, and a reasonably safe place to paint. Her series of paintings can be best used as part of a more in-depth study of the Holocaust rather than an introduction.

Volavkova, Hana, & the United States Holocaust Memorial Museum. "*. . . I Never Saw Another Butterfly": Children's Drawings and Poems from Terezin Concentration Camp 1942–1944.* Expanded Edition. New York: Schocken Books, 1993. This compilation of childrens' poetry and artwork from Terezin is only a small part of the complete collection in Prague. Friedl Dicker-Brandeis, a Bauhaus-trained artist, was one of the many teachers who provided art education for the children forced to live in Terezin. While the art is relatively unsophisticated, it is possible, through the variety of images, to learn about the world—imaginary and real—in which these children lived. The poetry, although written by children under thirteen, is quite profound and explores the issues these children were confronting daily.

Kantor, Alfred. *The Book of Alfred Kantor: An Artist's Journal of the Holocaust.* New York: Schocken Books, 1987. Alfred Kantor sketched scenes during his internment in Terezin (which were saved) and other concentration camps (which were lost). While he was living in a displaced persons camp after the war, Kantor recreated hundreds of these drawings from memory. The illustrations and handwritten commentary give the reader an "insider's" account of life in the camps. In one scene, in which two prisoners are outside the barracks fishing through an overturned barrel, the caption reads: "Women carrying 'dinner' were allowed to scrape out barrels after food-distribution. Cold soup and full of splinters but it's food."

Krizkova, Marie Rut, Kurt Jiri Kotouc, & Zdenek Ornest. *We Are Children Just the Same: Vedem, the Secret Magazine by the Boys of Terezin.* Philadelphia, PA: Jewish Publication Society, 1995. This book is a compilation of stories, essays, poems, letters, and drawings by a group of thirteen- to fifteen-year-old boys, imprisoned in Terezin, who managed to produce a weekly underground magazine called *Vedem* ("In the

Lead"). Many young people contributed material to *Vedem,* but only fifteen of them survived Terezin. This book, read in its entirety, takes the reader through a range of experiences and provides depth to one's understanding of Terezin. Because the entries have separate authors and artists, each one offers a glimpse into the minds of individual teenage boys. Various editions of the magazine included such topics as "Rambles through Terezin," "The Hearse," and "Preparing for the High Holiday."

Massachusetts College of Art. *Seeing through "Paradise": Artists and the Terezin Concentration Camp. Exhibition Catalogue.* Boston: Massachusetts College of Art, 1991. This exhibition catalogue contains six essays and over forty illustrations describing different aspects of life in Terezin, including biographies and portraits of artists imprisoned there. The purpose of the exhibit, "Seeing through Paradise," was to contrast the propaganda art of Terezin that imprisoned artists were forced to depict for the outside world with the secret work of the artists showing the reality of life in Terezin. The artwork included in this catalogue provides only a glimpse into the world in which these artists were forced to live and how determined they were, at the risk of their own life, to record the truth. Although many people are familiar with the children's artwork from Terezin, the story of Friedl Dicker Brandeis, the Bauhaus-trained art educator who served as drawing instructor and mentor for these children, and hundreds of adults, is not well known. The book contains an essay by Al Hurwitz describing Brandeis's life, art, and philosophy for teaching young people.

Spiritual Resistance: Art from Concentration Camps 1940–1945: A Selection of Drawings and Paintings from the Collection of Kibbutz Lohamei Haghetaot, Israel. New York: The Union of American Hebrew Congregations, 1981. This catalogue reflects a small percentage of the three thousand works of art housed in this museum's collection. It contains large reproductions of the artwork with accompanying biographies of the artists, most of whom perished during the Holocaust. There are some extremely interesting works that can be used in a classroom to show specific details from life in the ghettos and concentration camps in color and in black and white. An essay by Miriam Novitch, the museum's curator and coiner of the term "spiritual resistance," provides insight into how many of the works were acquired.

Toll, Nelly S. *Behind the Secret Window: A Memoir of a Hidden Childhood during World War II.* New York: Dial Books, 1993. While *The Diary of Anne Frank* is the most widely used text that depicts a teenager coming of age while in hiding from the Nazis, *Behind the Secret Window* is another noted work created in hiding. Nelly Toll kept two journals during her thirteen months hiding in a small bedroom in Lwow, Poland: a written one kept track of her impressions of daily events and feelings about her life in hiding, and an illustrated journal documented the dream world into which she was able to escape for brief periods of time. The drawings reflect scenes from her happy life before she went into hiding and also include scenes from her imagination showing her desire to play outside with children her own age. A few drawings actually express her innermost fears such as the one called "Master Beating Alicia the Slave Girl." Toll writes, "I painted a series of pictures about the slave

Alicia's experiences after reading *Uncle Tom's Cabin*. Although at that time in Poland I had never seen black people, I identified with their suffering."

Toll, Nelly. *Without Surrender: Art of the Holocaust*. Philadelphia, PA: Running Press, 1978. Art supplies in ghettos and concentration camps were so scarce that the artists had to use and reuse inferior quality materials. Many of the works of art in this book have dual purposes, such as musical scores combined with illustrations, cartoons decorating outgoing letters, an illustrated diary in addition to charcoal, pencil, and watercolor works. The book concludes with an essay and black-and-white versions of Nelly's childhood drawings crafted in hiding.

The Aftermath: Art as Memory

As noted in the section on "Victim Art," many persons risked their lives to create works of art, which, they hoped, would inform the world about the horrors of the Nazi ghettos and camps. Among victim artists who survived, several continued through the postwar years to bear witness by means of their creative endeavors. Such works fall into our final category, "Aftermath Art," which also includes art by victims whose first surviving artistic efforts date from after liberation, as well as the creations by artists with no direct experience of the Holocaust.

One effective way to acquaint students with Aftermath Art is to survey a group of works by a single artist. Although this activity is best accomplished in a gallery setting, the opportunity to visit an appropriate exhibition rarely presents itself. A number of quite suitable examples, however, may be found within the monographs and anthologies noted in the bibliography. This author often uses artwork by the Hungarian artist Gyorgy Kadar in her own lecture-demonstrations, as this material is both persuasive and available in the form of slide transparencies. (For additional information about the slide transparencies, contact The Holocaust Lecture Series, Vanderbilt University, Nashville, Tennessee.) Kadar, a survivor of Auschwitz, began recreating scenes of his wartime ordeals immediately after liberation, and by 1946 had completed a cycle of fifty-seven autobiographical drawings. During the next forty-two years, while his reputation rose in the international art world, he remained silent on the subject of the Holocaust. In 1988, however, Kadar began work on a second cycle, which he completed two years later and includes sixteen drawings.

Surveying Kadar's output, from his earliest postwar creations to the retrospective works of his late maturity, students can judge how the artist's approach to his subject matter altered over time. Sybil Milton's (1990) essay, "The Obligation of Memory: Gyorgy Kadar's Second Holocaust Suite" (in the exhibition catalogue entitled *Kadar: The Haunted Imagination*), is a valuable guide to the artist's evolving methods and objectives. As Milton (1990) explains, the young Kadar was motivated to bear witness for, and memorialize, the victims, whereas the mature artist's concerns were "indicting the Nazi system, linking the perpetrators directly to their crimes" (p. 14), and making certain that the public would understand his message. Thus, the abstract style of the early works yielded to the blunt, unambiguous realism of the second set. (Both cycles are linked by Kadar's decision to work almost exclusively in black and white.) Instructors may point to style, theme, and medium as areas for discussion. They also may remark on survivor psychology as an aspect of Aftermath Art. Feelings of guilt at having survived when friends and family did not, and the need to purge nightmarish images from the conscious mind, are important factors in the creative lives of many survivors.

The work of Karl Stojka also may be effectively used in a classroom setting. An Austrian Roma (Gypsy) who had been deported to Auschwitz-Birkenau while still a child, Stojka's autobiographical art both complements and contrasts with Kadar's. Stojka began painting in 1970 and has since produced over one hundred canvasses documenting his and his family's persecution in Nazified Vienna and subsequent experiences during the war. This artwork, in contrast to the pencil-and-charcoal sketches created by Kadar, is filled with rich colors that reflect Stojka's vocation as a dealer in Oriental carpets. He makes particularly compelling use of the red, green, purple, pink, and yellow tints that mark the identity patches worn by the prisoners in the camps.

Because Stojka's art chronicles the Roma experience of the Holocaust, it can serve to introduce or illustrate the important topic of Nazi Germany's non-Jewish victims. A major retrospective of his paintings was mounted in Vienna in 1990, from which an exhibition catalogue, *The Story of Karl Stojka: A Childhood in Birkenau*, was later issued. This catalogue, published by the U.S. Holocaust Memorial Museum in 1992, includes a section with suggestions for teachers wishing to use Stojka's works as a classroom resource.

Aftermath Art by "second-hand witnesses," such as the children of survivors, or by other individuals who feel emotionally drawn to the subject of the Holocaust, offers a different perspective—one most closely resembling that of the majority of students and educators. The creators of these works often make use of symbolic devices to express their response to Holocaust history and their compassion for the victims of Nazism. Among the more frequently encountered images are barbed wire, crematoria smokestacks, the Nazi swastika, and the Jewish Star of David. Recurrent too, are allusions to biblical events and religious themes: the Hebrews enslaved by Pharaoh; the opening of the Heavens on Judgment Day; and the crucifixion of Jesus Christ.

In his comic book epic, *Maus*, Art Spiegelman (1986 and 1991), a child of survivors, weds such imagery to a narrative that is both a chronicle of his father's life and his own tale of growing up in a traumatized household. Historically accurate and compellingly readable, Maus is rightly considered by students familiar with the comic book form to be an "easy introduction" to the subject of the Holocaust. But the work itself, in concept and design, is far from simple, and the instructor using art as a teaching tool might ask the class to consider how Spiegelman has organized Maus. Analyzing its structure, students will note contrasting themes (the father's story; the son's story) and timeframes (past and present). In terms of Aftermath Art, however, the lesson Maus most impressively conveys concerns the emotional legacy of the Holocaust, underscored by the uneasy relationship of father and son. Using comic book imagery (panel drawings, captions, dialogue balloons) and characters (anthropomorphized animals, notably cat and mouse stand-ins for Germans and Jews), Spiegelman makes a major statement about survivor trauma and its mechanism of transmission from one generation to the next.

Finally, many educators encourage students to respond to their study of the Holocaust by creating their own works of Aftermath Art. This exercise, which should be assigned only after the instructor is certain that students are strongly grounded in the subject, can be an illuminating activity. For students, fashioning a meaningful work of art means confronting and synthesizing all the information—and all the emotions—they have accumulated during their course of study.

As founding coordinator of the National Art Contest at the United States Holocaust Memorial Museum, this author has had the opportunity to examine thousands of pieces of student art, ranging from pencil sketches on loose-leaf notebook paper, to massive framed canvasses, to graphics generated entirely by computer. Since instructors tend to uncritically submit artworks from every student participant, we look to these entries for clues about the general quality of Holocaust education in the American classroom. Although the Art Contest entries have not yet received a systematic study, follow-up conversations with teachers have proved enlightening. For example, when the subject turns out to have been taught in a superficial manner—perhaps with a brief unit dealing with Hitler, the death camps, and liberation—student art tends to be violent, gruesome, and quite impersonal. By contrast, when an instructor fostered student identification with the German's victims (perhaps by assigning class members to imagine the experiences of Jews or Gypsies caught up in the Holocaust), the entries tend to aim for emotional effect, with little or no regard for historical accuracy. It is almost superfluous to note that each year's outstanding entries were created by students who had learned from a variety of media (including artifacts, films, photography, music, works of art), and who had benefited from critical analysis of the history with an informed and involved instructor.

Teaching Resources

Bohm-Duchen, Monica. *After Auschwitz: Responses to the Holocaust in Contemporary Art.* Exhibition Catalog. London: Northern Centre for Contemporary Art, 1995. This catalog contains excellent essays and examples of artwork on the subjects of Holocaust art, Holocaust Memorials, and the fifty years that followed the Holocaust. The exhibition of the same name traveled throughout England during 1995.

Furth, Valerie Jakober. *Cabbages and Geraniums: Memories of the Holocaust.* Boulder, CO: Social Science Monographs, 1989. This autobiographical anthology consists of works by Valerie Furth created thirty-six years after being liberated from Auschwitz.

Milton, Sybil. *The Story of Karl Stojka: A Childhood in Birkenau.* Exhibition Catalog from the Austrian Embassy. Washington, DC: United States Holocaust Memorial Museum, 1992. This catalogue provides biographical information about the Roma

(Gypsy) survivor, Karl Stojka, who, along with his immediate family, was perse-cuted during the Holocaust. Stojka's artwork is autobiographical, recounting episodes from his experiences in concentration camps from 1943 to 1945. The art-work from this catalogue introduces the experiences of Gypsies being persecuted because they were viewed as "non-Aryans" by the Nazis.

Kadar, Gyorgy. *Gyorgy Kadar Survivor of Death, Witness to Life.* Exhibition Catalog of the Vanderbilt University Collection of Holocaust Art. Nashville, TN: Vanderbilt University Press, 1988.

Kadar, Gyorgy. *The Haunted Imagination, New Holocaust Images by Gyorgy Kadar.* Exhibition Catalog of the Vanderbilt University Collection of Art. Nashville, TN: Vanderbilt University Press, 1990. These catalogs and slide versions of the artwork are available through Vanderbilt University. The first cycle represents the work of Gyorgy Kadar immediately following his liberation from Buchenwald and the sec-ond is reflective of his work over forty years later. Each provides excellent intro-ductory essays.

Spiegelman, Art. *Maus: A Survivor's Tale* and *Maus II: A Survivor's Tale: And Here My Troubles Began.* New York, Pantheon, 1986 and 1991. Spiegelman, whose parents survived the Holocaust, chronicles his parents' experiences and the effect of these experiences on his own life through a series of comic strips. This format presents a unique and accessible way for students to learn about how the Holocaust affected Spiegelman's family. The two volumes are also available on CD-ROM, which con-tain oral interviews with Spiegelman's father and original sketches from which the comic strips were later drawn.

Conclusion

Exposure to artworks such as those identified in this chapter can help students "view" Holocaust history from a different perspective than those offered by narra-tive or photographic documentation. Capable of weaving complex, disparate themes into an integrated whole, a work of testimonial art encompasses the artist's external reality and subconscious world, plus the interplay of these two. Such cre-ations simultaneously encapsulate and expand on aspects of Holocaust history, providing instructors with an effective means for addressing this multifaceted subject. Holocaust art mediates history, foremost by its appeal to the emotions. Ideally, instructors should take this initial, emotional response as a cue to begin guiding students in their search for meaning in an artist's work. For some stu-dents, this quest will involve exploring the story behind a commissioned ghetto portrait. For others, it might entail contemplating the obstacles prisoners had to surmount to obtain art supplies and to assure that their works might survive. For yet others, this search might lead to an examination of propaganda art, or to the creation of an original work "from the aftermath." But whatever the nature of their response, it is almost certain that a close investigation of Holocaust-related art will enhance student understanding of this difficult and forbidding subject.

REFERENCES

Glatstein, Jacob, Israel Knox, & Samuel Margoshes (Eds.). (1982). *Anthology of Holocaust Literature.* New York: Atheneum.

Milton, Sybil. (1990). "The Obligation of Memory: Gyorgy Kadar's Second Holocaust Suite." In *Kadar: The Haunted Imagination* (pp. 11–18). Nashville, TN: Vanderbilt University Press.

Milton, Sybil. (1992). *The Story of Karl Stojka: A Childhood in Birkenau.* Washington, DC: United States Holocaust Memorial Museum.

Synder, Louis. (1989). *The Encyclopedia of the Third Reich.* New York: Paragon House.

Speer, Albert. (1970). *Inside the Third Reich.* New York: Macmillan.

Spiegelman, Art. (1986 & 1991). *Maus: A Survivor's Tale* and *Maus II: A Survivor's Tale: And Here My Troubles Began.* New York: Pantheon.

APPENDIX

United States Holocaust Memorial Museum
Critical Thinking: Inquiry Activity

The Permanent Exhibition at the United States Holocaust Memorial Museum displays hundreds of artifacts and photographs from the Holocaust that, when taken out of context, may appear to be very familiar, or have several explanations. When these artifacts and photographs are put into the context in which they were used or in which the event happened, however, interpretations are completely altered. The activity below helps viewers begin to understand how historical events changed the function of everyday objects and the nature of seemingly ordinary events in photographs. Viewers first use past experience to make associations, then look closer at physical details; continue by putting the object into the historical context of the Holocaust; and finally make connections between the actual object or photograph and the history. We hope that this exercise encourages viewers to examine other objects and photographs in the exhibition more critically in order to gain a deeper understanding of the Holocaust.

Using What We Already Know: Making Associations

Have students look at a reproduction of an object or photograph from the Museum's Permanent Exhibition.

For an object: state the nature of the object (i.e., this is a milk can); ask students to discuss the familiar uses for this type of object and what kind of people might use such an object.

For a photograph: state the nature of the scene portrayed in the photograph (i.e., two uniformed men walking with a dog); ask students to discuss possible explanations for what might be happening and what kind of people might be involved in a scene such as this one.

Looking Closer

Invite students to look closer at the reproduction of the object or photograph.

For objects: a close examination enables students to identify details that may indicate why the object was chosen to be used or provide evidence that it was used during the Holocaust. Encourage students to use the physical details of the object to determine what materials were used to make it; the level of quality involved in its construction; whether there are specific identifying marks; its current condition; and the difference between this particular object and similar objects.

For photographs: a close examination enables students to identify details that may indicate how specific scenes reflect individual or group activities that contributed to or characterized aspects of the Holocaust. Encourage students to use physical details within the photograph to determine who is in the photograph (look at foreground, background, edges); who may have taken the photograph; style and quality of clothing; the difference between this scene and similar scenes; and evidence of staged versus informal photographs.

Putting It into Context

Encourage students to ask questions that will produce historical information about the object or photograph. Provide facts that help students place the object or photograph into its historical context. Students may be able to answer each other's questions using evidence from their observations and examinations of the object or photograph.

For the object include: who used the object; the purpose of the object; and where, when and why this particular object was used.

For the photograph include: who is in the scene; what the scene shows; and where, when, and why this scene was photographed.

Making Connections

Have students make connections between the object or scene and its historical relevance. Students may provide additional examples of objects or scenes and their historical relevance.

Once the students have the factual information related to the object or scene portrayed in the photograph, it is essential for them to consider the implications of the object or scene during the Holocaust from various viewpoints such as the "perpetrator," "victim," or "bystander." It is also important for students to make a connection between the object or scene and its relevance to our understanding of the Holocaust today. Students also may construct a title for an exhibit that contains either the object or the photograph as a way of reinforcing an important theme or concept.

For example: Does this scene reveal anything about the "perpetrators," "victims," or "bystanders"?

12 Drama Activities and the Study of the Holocaust

BELARIE ZATZMAN

Drama activities offer educators a language for remembering, for negotiating meaning with their students in the midst of anguish and suffering. The arts offer a form for shaping memory and memorial, by placing us in someone else's shoes and, in so doing, creating a landscape of knowledge and empathy. Drama provides a critical opportunity to reflect on the relationship between ourselves and others by providing a means for students to express a personal connection to the material.

According to Robert Skloot (1982), a professor at the University of Wisconsin at Madison who specializes in Holocaust drama, plays about the Holocaust struggle

> to educate us to the history of that time, to move us with the stories of the perished millions, to raise crucial moral questions for us to ponder, to demonstrate the human action that can be taken in times of extreme stress and how it can be evaluated, and to suggest ways in which the darkest hours of our night-filled century can be kept from descending again. (p. 35)

In drama and theater, issues of representation are often explored by a juxtaposition of the real and the fictional; a tenuous but significant balance which can provide students and teachers access to the Holocaust. Indeed, drama allows for a multiplicity of structures and opportunities for reflection, in which fact and fiction stand as different forms of revealing difficult truths. Again, Skloot (1982) asserts that theater of the Holocaust scripts, for example,

> . . . express their understanding of the historical facts and individual interpretations of those facts; by their nature, the plays are not history, but they would not stand apart from history. Although we can learn about history from them, their significance is that they search for meaning, or at least intelligibility, in an event which, from nearly every angle, shelters some kind of profound truth about us all. (p. 21)

Teaching concepts and facts about the Holocaust serves as the foundation for the drama work presented here. *Indeed, it is essential that historical context support thoughtful and critical improvisation.* In the activities detailed in this chapter, students can make symbolic links between historical events and dramatic contexts as a way of creating significant personal meaning. My experience in using drama to teach the Holocaust is that Holocaust plays and drama activities can raise crucial historical and moral questions and make them more immediate. Traces of lives, real or imagined, help us become intimately involved in characters' actions, choices, bravery, and suffering; in so doing, drama links us to our own histories and provides a means for understanding ourselves.

As Bjorn Krondorfer (1988) of the Jewish German Dance Theatre notes, *it is critical not to marginalize the history:*

> We hoped to find common ground without minimizing history. We then formed and analyzed concepts; we would avoid staging a naturalistic play, and instead interweave biographical stories, historical reenactments, and our own relationships. We felt that a straight docudrama about the Holocaust would not reflect our contemporary struggle with the past. Ultimately, we would not comprehend the Shoah. Our coming to terms with the Holocaust had to take place via our relationships, and both past and present ought to be part of the final performance. (p. 239)

Historical knowing is a way of understanding ourselves. How does one begin to interact with the materials of the past? How can we use these fragments, traces of the past, to construct ideas about who we are in the present? Drama has the power to help us negotiate issues of past and present, by providing opportunities for meaning-making, for finding forms that can hold the needs of bearing witness, of honoring the unspeakable while facing the limits of representation.

Whether working with plays from the theater of the Holocaust or designing activities for the classroom, students' work in this area can assume many forms "because from the raw material can be drawn differing interpretations of the same historical event, and because no single form can accurately portray that event" (Skloot, 1982, p. 21). Not only do I expose students to a range of primary sources (e.g., diary, autobiography, memoir, interviews, survivor video testimony), examine the relationship between source materials and the students' artistic reflections about them (e.g., through writing, improvisation, or visual art activities), but, most important, I use these artistic responses to help them find a language to articulate a personal connection to the Holocaust.

The development of the drama work described here has been interdisciplinary and community-based. To facilitate this connection, teachers should maintain regular contact with a Holocaust museum and/or resource centers, for the survivors associated with them are always a welcome addition to the class. If teachers do not have access to a Holocaust survivor, there are several archives of survivor testimony, including the Fortunoff Video Archive for Holocaust Testimonies, Yale University and the United States Holocaust Memorial Museum (USHMM) repository. Local Jewish federations and community centers also can offer video testimonies of individuals who live in the local community, a project often conducted by volunteers. Such programs have collected an enormous and moving record of individual survivors' stories that can serve as an important resource for classrooms. When working with senior students, I also invite in artists—either survivors or children of survivors—so that students may see how others have found a way to speak through their art.

When developing theatrical structures, I am always aware of the need to tread carefully; weighing every artistic decision, neither wishing to trivialize nor offend. With caution and hesitancy, I also move forward with the knowledge that creating these kinds of drama moments is "not to diminish its importance but rather to alter the route by which we approach" the Shoah (Langer, 1995, p. 3). Teachers combining dramatic technique with Holocaust-related subjects should also take great care that their drama activities are explored with the requisite seriousness that the subject of the Holocaust demands. The key to avoiding trivilization is to ensure that the drama work does not degenerate into games and giggling. Only with a mature and deeply focused approach can teachers create dramatic events that stand as strong pedagogical tools.

Using drama to teach about the Holocaust provides our children with an opportunity to take ownership of the knowledge they construct, to question, and to deepen their engagement. What follows is an invitation to participate in memory and history. These drama events, all of which have been used in middle school, secondary, and university classrooms, are ways to integrate drama into the curriculum. All of the drama activities include a reflective component, so that student journals become a requirement for recording the process of learning and creating.

1. Survivor Testimony

Regardless of whether I am working with Jewish or non-Jewish students, I always bring survivors to talk with my class, and these meetings become central to the students' experience of understanding and remembering. I have discovered that the students' response to the survivors is so powerful that it helped all of us face the resistance to working with this difficult subject. In the act of retelling through the recollections of survivors, and in imaginatively entering the world of "what if," we create a bridge between public memory and private memory.

Clearly, given that the generation of witnesses is passing, there is an increasing urgency to tell their story. Once heard, their story of the Holocaust becomes part of one's legacy; one shares in the responsibility to remember and retell. One becomes a "witness." Retelling through the arts is a potent form of maintaining our legacy since "throughout history, art has been a means of such telling" (Feinstein, 1994, p. 10).

The students should be asked to develop their experience of "witnessing" the survivors testimony in two steps:

A. Reflection Students should create journal entries based on their personal response to the survivors recollections. These should be recorded in the journals both during and after the session with the survivor. Each journal should document particular events, emotions, moments of decision, and strong images that are important to the student in response to "witnessing" the survivor's story. In this

FIGURE 12.1   Arnold Kramer. "Railway Car." Photograph of authentic freight car used to deport Jews. Reprinted, with permission, from the collections of the United States Holocaust Memorial Museum.

way, the students directly select that which connects their life to the survivor, and in turn, the Holocaust. This is particularly significant, as the present is the site of all representation, not the past.

Maintaining a reflective journal when working with the Holocaust not only serves to chart the development of artistic ideas or historical source material for role play or improvisation, for example, but the reflective writing also functions to give voice to students' reaction to difficult material. For example, Jordana wrote:

Today was a very emotional day for me. Though we have been doing alot [*sic*] of reading, to actually see survivors makes it all the more real. I can't get their life stories out of my mind. I want to cry but force myself not to. I came home and told everyone some of the stories I heard today. They were so honest and I felt their determination and their suffering. I wonder how I would cope if I was given their circumstances.

B. Characters   Using the survivor testimony as a base, the students should develop "in-role writing" for a fictional character they create. Writing-in-role is a powerful tool, in which the student takes on the role of a character to write "in-role," using the first-person voice to describe circumstances or feelings from that character's point of view. "Writing-in-role" provides another perspective through which students can express their personal connection to the Holocaust.

"In-role writing" can be extended by creating an improvisational scene for the character. Improvisation can allow students to examine the life of a character by creating a spontaneous response to a dramatic situation, or, too, by carefully planning particular key moments to explore so that their improvisations allow for deeper insight and discovery. The improvised scenes might involve one or more characters, verbal and nonverbal activity, movement and role playing, in order to help build meaning.

Layering writing and drama activities—allowing one experience to build on reflections of the other—deepens the richness of the students' work and prepares them to experience multiple perspectives, by taking on a range of different roles, relationships, or situations from a variety of points of view, as do the drama activities throughout this chapter. Clearly, the opportunity to develop writing through drama is yet another significant goal in using drama to teach about the Holocaust.

The influence of shared memory and reflective writing is profound, as evidenced by journal entries that document students' strong feelings about meeting with survivors. Indeed, the act of remembering is tangible throughout the journals. For example, William wrote: "I met four Holocaust survivors and I felt amazed and ashamed for having not cared enough. History is about people, not places and dates."

The parallels between in-role and out-of-role writing are also important to examine. In her reflective journal, Arielle focused on her right to freedom and grappled with an ambivalence about her Jewish identity. She wondered how it was possible to be judged by something she, herself, was not even certain about. Writing about her own experience, Arielle stated:

> I'm really affected by the material we've gone over. I've gone to sleep with dreams of people taking away my freedom. About what life is about, what should I be concerned about. Mostly I think about that if I were there in Europe in the 40s—I would be persecuted, even though I don't feel a strong link with my religion.
>
> It wouldn't matter—nothing would matter. The unfairness strikes me. I feel like I would want to scream for the people's lives who were lost. It isn't fair. It isn't fair.

Drama becomes the means of retelling, placing the student in the role of interpreter rather than simply, as one teacher commented, "regurgitating information"; they "learn the craft of history and to personalize the facts." The students' entries record their in-depth and perceptive efforts to understand the experience

FIGURE 12.2 Arnold Kramer. "Shoes." Photograph of shoes confiscated from prisoners in Majdanek. Reprinted, with permission, from the collections of the United States Holocaust Memorial Museum.

of the survivors (see Zatzman, 1998). In response, they shape their own narratives, questioning that which is inherently a part of their own identities.

2. Sign Language

This drama exercise, based upon a site specific memorial to the now-absent Jewish population in the Berlin neighborhood of Schoneberg, may prove to be quite powerful. The first version (1991) of this memorial began as cardboard signs, which were hung on buildings of that neighborhood. The signs recorded facts: names, dates, ages, deportation dates of the Jewish residents who had once inhabited those dwellings. A subsequent 1993 permanent installation, by artists Stih and Schnock, extended this idea by creating a set of eighty signs that documented the insidious loss of rights between 1933 and 1945. These signs are found mounted, almost inconspicuously, on lampposts throughout the town (Wiedmer, 1995). It is a palpable way not only of remembering, but of recording the "day-to-day events of a neighbourhood from which 6,000 people vanished virtually without a trace." These signs or "markers" were designed as "stumbling blocks" to the community's consciousness of such a time (Wiedmer, 1995, p. 10).

To prepare themselves for this activity, students should study all source material from which they can draw in order to select information they wish to record on each sign. For example, they might conduct research into the Nuremberg Laws (1935) or the 1941 Yellow Star of David decree.

The markers should be designed to show text on one side, image on the other. The students may paint, draw, or use collage. The minimal text is intentionally juxtaposed against the advertising-like and contemporary presentation of the signs.

Some examples for creating these powerful markers might include posting a sign in the classroom which reads:

- "Aryan and non-Aryan children are forbidden to play together. 1938," or
- a marker that is paired with a picture of a kitten, and a text that reads "Jews may no longer keep pets," or
- an image of a bench that reads: "Jews may only use those benches at the Bayerischer Platz which are marked in yellow" (from an eyewitness report, 1939), or
- a pair of swimming trunks partnered by a sign proclaiming: "Berlin public pools may no longer be entered by Jews, 3.12.1938," or
- "Jews not wanted here 29.1.1936," or
- "Give immediate leave to the Jewish teaching staff at all city schools 1.4.1933" (Wiedmer, 1995, pp. 10–11).

For the drama work of Sign Language, the specific site of the school is used in order to prepare a memorial based on these Berlin projects. Clearly, the texture of any North American memorial is sharply different; our memorials are not built on actual ground associated with the Holocaust. Nevertheless, we can develop performances that should not only provoke powerful discourse, but journey, by asking participants to move throughout the school community, using its lampposts, halls, library, office, playground, cafeteria, track, and gym to create public spaces of memory.

Students should observe the traffic patterns of the school and select where they wish to mount their markers to create these sites of memorial. The signs should be left up for the whole course of study, so that they are at once familiar and foreign. The markers shift us between time present and time past, if we notice them. They are reminders, are conscience, are warnings as students and staff move through the space. Because we walk past the markers as a part of our regular school routine, it is almost shocking to recognize that we stand as both witness and participant, as kind of unwilling collaborators. The simplicity of the project seems to belie its antisemitic content and the signs' apparently neutral images can easily blend into our public consciousness (Wiedmer, 1995, pp. 8–9). Reflection time should acknowledge that we participate in the memorial from the safety and security of our normal lives; and the ease with which we might come to walk down the halls should remind us that we might be at risk even today.

At lunchtime, recess, or at the end of the day, the students should animate the different spaces, so that the signs become the site for improvisation, short scenes, or the public presentation of some drama explored within the classroom. Short monologue improvs between characters from a novel study the class is working on could be presented to the audience with monologues based on characters built from survivor testimony.

Sign Language also provides an opportunity to present scenes from the repertoire of Holocaust plays developmentally appropriate for students (Stevens, Brown, and Rubin, 1995). These might include: Atlan's (1987) *Mister Fugue or Earth Sick;* Goodrich and Hackett's (1956) *The Diary of Anne Frank;* Lebow's (1988) *A Shayna Maidel;* and Raspanti's (1971) *". . . I Never Saw Another Butterfly".* A different scene might be performed each day, at different and unexpected locations in the school.

The teacher should conduct a discussion about how this memorial makes visible, in its scenes, text, and images, the level of political violence that had gone on in everyday life. The whole school community, as a part of their everyday life during this event, is therefore engaged in understanding that the destruction of the European Jewish population was not a sudden, irreversible occurrence, but rather a slow process consisting of hundreds of rules and laws. Members of the local community could be invited to journey through the performance spaces of the Sign Language memorial. Ultimately, the point is to recognize the impact of how all those rules slowly culminated in the deportation and murder of millions of people.

One is pulled into a "temporal shift," from present time to moments staged in memory and back again. When signs and scenes intersect, one is suddenly in an active memorial space in which she/he is dramatically drawn into questioning how one might have reacted had they lived in Germany at that time. Ultimately, one learns more about the historical period, and possibly how to begin to address the complex issue of neo-Nazi movements and racism today.

3. Diary

Anne Frank's famous diary is only one of many available, excellent primary sources from which to develop drama work. From Adelson (Ed.) *The Diary of Dawid Sierakowiak* (1996) to Boas's *We Are Witnesses: Five Diaries of Teenagers Who Died in the Holocaust* (1995) or Holliday's *Children in the Holocaust and World War II* (1995), each diary presents different experiences and contexts from which to examine the Holocaust. Teachers and students can create improvisations that explore a single diary or juxtapose different narratives by moving from one diary to another, as part of a dramatic structure.

Four or five different diaries should be selected as the foundation for examining the students' artistic responses to a diary. After reading the diary or diary excerpt, a decision should be made about which member of the family is to be role played. Each student should research their family and the individual they will be role playing. In each group, the family's "given circumstances," that is the factual information "given" in the original diary, should be discussed.

Research is an important component of building the diary dramas. By using photographs as well as finding "their" town or city on a map, students can locate "where they live." They should learn about the history of the country and what was happening historically and economically prior to 1939. It is up to each family to know everything about who they are by the time the war breaks out. Some simple questions to ask might include: Where do we live? What is the weather like? What kind of work do we do? How many Jews live in the same city or town? *They should find out as much background information as possible, so that when the drama work begins there will be a solid base from which to role play.*

A. Yellow Star (Anne Frank's *Diary*)

PETER: *Starts to rip off his Star of David.*

ANNE: What are you doing?

PETER: Taking it off.

ANNE: But you can't do that. They'll arrest you if you go out without your star.

PETER: Who's going out?

ANNE: Why, of course! You're right! Of course we don't need them any more. *She picks up his knife and starts to take her star off. As she pulls off her star the cloth underneath shows clearly the color and form of the star.* Look! It's still

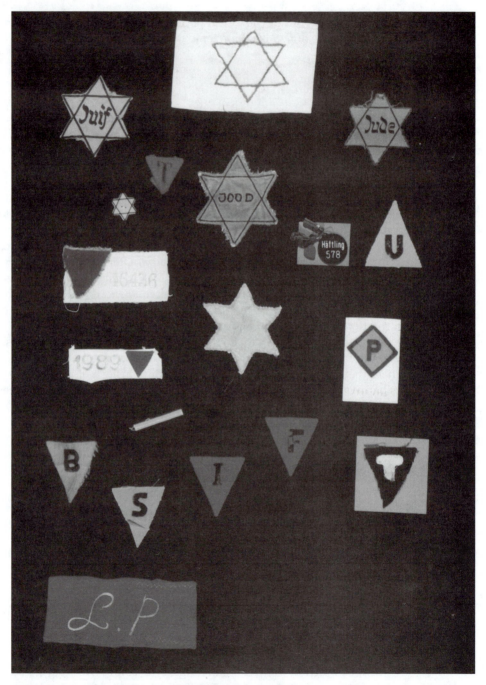

FIGURE 12.3   Arnold Kramer. "Stars, Triangles and Markings." Photograph of badges used by Nazis to identify victims. Reprinted, with permission, from the collections of the United States Holocaust Memorial Museum.

there! *Peter goes over to the stove with his star.* What are you going to do with yours?

PETER: Burn it.

ANNE: *Starts to throw hers in, and cannot.* It's funny, I can't throw mine away. I don't know why.

PETER: You can't throw . . . ? Something they branded you with . . . ? That they made you wear so they could spit on you?

ANNE: I know. I know. But after all, it is the Star of David, isn't it?

(Goodrich & Hackett, 1956, I.ii.p. 10)

A decree of September 1, 1941 required Jewish people throughout the Reich to wear the yellow Star of David badge whenever they went out in public. Children under the age of six were exempted (Berenbaum, 1993, p. 69). Students should be asked: How were the stars different in different countries? What other kinds of markings do you know about (e.g., different shapes and colors in different countries, pink triangle, tattooing)?

Next, they should be given the following directions: In role, be aware that your country has been invaded by the Nazis and each one of you must now wear a star on your clothes. Discuss how the wearing of the star was part of a systemic anti-Jewish policy, which varied from country to country across Western Europe. Then the teacher should divide the students into family groups to review the pattern in each of France, Belgium, Norway, Luxembourg, and the Netherlands. They should make and sew one star for each member of the family, taking into account the variations in color and shape. The inscription should reflect your country of origin (e.g., Jude/Juif). The teacher should have all the materials ready for this exercise to take place (e.g., felt and markers). (For information on the different wording, shapes, and colors of the markings, see the United States Holocaust Memorial Museum's *Artifact Poster Set.* Available from the USHMM Bookstore, P.O. Box 92420, Washington, DC, 20090-2420.)

Finally, a reflection-in-action discussion bridging past and present might include such questions as: Have you ever been treated differently because of your ethnicity, language, clothing, or age? How did that make you feel? Did it affect the way you acted in other situations? Where were you? In a shopping mall, or at school, or somewhere else? In small groups, the students should discuss their experiences.

4. Letters

The teacher should select a survivor, author of a diary, participant in an historical event, artist, or character from a novel or play in their Holocaust study who has greatly influenced the students. That person should be used as an inspiration for creating the following in-role improvisation ideas.

A. A Collection of Voices

The class should be gathered into a confined space in one part of the classroom. In-role, the students should be asked to write a letter to someone whom they may never see again. When everyone has finished writing, the teacher should signal each student with a tap on the shoulder, asking him or her to read his or her letter aloud. Each voice is brought in one at a time, until everyone has joined the circle of letters, and all the voices are heard at once. (In addition to being a powerful frame for giving voice to the voiceless, this is also a helpful activity for students who may have difficulty reading publicly.)

B. Suitcase Activity #1

All the letters should be used to completely cover a suitcase. These private corre-spondences should be pasted into place. The different kinds of paper, text, ink, and dates should all be visible. The "Letter Suitcase" becomes a moving memorial about displacement, memory, and relationships.

In addition, this exercise is modeled on a piece by Toronto artist Francesca Vivenza, who first created a work in which she used her personal letters from different people, at different times in her life, in this way. This exercise can be extended by making an audiotape that can be hidden inside the suitcase, which can be played while the letters on its exterior—based on accurate historical content—are being read. Ques-tions to be considered for this activity are: What might the soundscape include? Are there sounds of a public space? What modes of travel are suggested by the sounds in the environment? Are there any private conversations? Whose voices are heard? Another drama approach to working with the idea of the suitcase as a potent symbol of culture and identity, helping students to draw connections between the study of the Holocaust and their own lives, follows.

5A. The Suitcase Project

This project was originally created with students between the ages of twelve and fifteen as part of an annual Holocaust Remembrance Day. "... I Never Saw Another Butterfly," an extraordinary collection of children's drawings and poems written between 1942 and 1944, served as a primary source for this project (Volavkova, 1993). The Suitcase Project takes place in two parts; the first stage begins as each par-ticipant is given the name of an actual child who had been at Terezin Concentration Camp, and whose brief life is documented in "... I Never Saw Another Butterfly." Of the fifteen thousand children deported to Terezin, only one hundred survived.

Our students were paired with a Holocaust child who was born in the same month as their own birthdates. In a few cases, we've had exact matches, a parallel that seemed to mark this active memorial in a way that made its significance all the more poignant for the entire class. We also used the bibliographic information in "Butterfly" to provide the students with the dates of their counterpart's arrival, the length of their stay in Terezin and, finally, the date and their age at the time of their death, mostly in Auschwitz, to where they were subsequently deported.

The deliberate matching of the Terezin children with our students was a drama structure conceptualized in order to help them identify with a particular face and story. Each student was also given a poem and an accompanying drawing or painting, written by their Terezin child. Used as readers theater, the children presented the poems and artwork to the rest of the class.

Fabio Mauri's Western or Wailing Wall sculpture served as an inspiration for the next stage of the project, in which the students explore the theme of identity (and, in some cases, contemporary Jewish identity) in response to the Holocaust, and to discover ways of representing themselves and who they are. After their work with the poetry, the students' task is to construct a suitcase that might have belonged specifically to the Terezin child with whom they have been matched. The suitcases are built out of Styrofoam, then covered with paper mache, and finally, painted. Each piece of Styrofoam can be cut to approximately one foot square—with some larger and smaller pieces for visual interest. Each completed suitcase should have a tag identifying its owner by name, and any other bibliographic information they wish to include. To support this work, the students should be shown and guided in a discussion of the United States Holocaust Memorial Museum's (USHMM) poster of the suitcases. The USHMM also produces a teachers guide that accompanies the posters. The lessons in the guide could help create an anticipatory set for this suitcase activity.

Metaphorically, the luggage creates a text—images that suggest a multiplicity of possible narratives—about people forced into exile, forced to search for identity; luggage carrying uprooted and imprisoned identities, a testament to human life and complexity. The collection of baggage will also evoke Auschwitz and the heap of suitcases that was human life. Therefore, as fragments of our past, these suitcases immediately become suggestive of displacement, dislocation, and annihilation. Ultimately, the suitcases can be installed all together in a single large-scale piece, mounted on a large sheet of particleboard. It stands as a moving memorial—one that I've seen remain hanging all year, well beyond the memorial occasion it was designed to mark.

B. Packing

This drama exercise directly extends the interdisciplinary work of The Suitcase Project, by asking the students to actively engage in the action of packing itself. It asks the students to consider how they set priorities and what they value and to consider issues that individuals might have faced as they prepared to leave their homes. Directions to be given to the students for this activity are:

1. You must pack your suitcase within a limit of fifteen minutes. You do not know where you are going.
2. You MUST be able to carry your suitcase for at least ten miles.
3. List on a piece of paper every item you will pack.

4. Next to the items that you pack, write why you have packed that item.
5. Name the items you decided to pack, but either changed your mind or had to leave behind because there wasn't enough room for them or your suitcase would have been too heavy to carry. Please list and state the reason(s) why you did not take them.
6. If you have a scale at home, please weigh your suitcase and record its weight.

Next, the students should research the actual suitcases. They should be asked what people were forced to write on suitcases. How much weight were they allowed? What were they allowed to pack and not pack, and why?

Following that, this entry from Anne's diary should be read aloud:

Wednesday July 8, 1942
Hiding . . . where would we hide? In the city? In the country? In a house? In a shack? When, where, how . . . ? These were questions I wasn't allowed to ask, but they still kept running through my mind. Margot and I started packing our most important belongings into a schoolbag. The first thing I stuck in was this diary, and then curlers, handkerchiefs, schoolbooks, a comb and some old letters. Preoccupied by the thought of going into hiding, I stuck the craziest things in the bag, but I'm not sorry. Memories mean more to me than dresses. (Frank, 1991, p. 20)

6. Photographs

Photographs, too, are an excellent source for drama. As the specific intention of using drama to teach the Holocaust is to deepen the students' connection to the voices of children and adults lost, one caution would be to avoid photos that are horrific, which may alienate or desensitize students.

Instead, a teacher should opt to use pictures that seem to hold a narrative, or that suggest interesting relationships between people, events, or environment. For drama, one can make use of photographs that range from prewar images of Jewish cultural life to photos from the Warsaw Ghetto to images of partisans.

A famous photograph of Hans and Sophie Scholl and Christoph Probst, leaders of the "White Rose" resistance group inside Germany, provides a good example of photography as a source for drama. These three young people founded the White Rose movement in June 1942. The were outraged that educated Germans did nothing to protest Nazi anti-Jewish policies. Because they distributed anti-Nazi flyers and painted "Freedom!" slogans throughout the University of Munich, they were arrested in February 1943 and executed four days later. The photograph was taken in the summer of 1942, when they were twenty-four, twenty-two, and twenty-four, respectively (Bachrach, 1994, p. 69).

To help students learn to interpret and construct meaning, they should be shown this White Rose photograph and asked to pull as many clues from the photograph as possible, questioning everything they see. In the image of Sophie, Hans, and Christoph talking together, for example, they might consider: Who is the girl? How old do you think she is? Who is she talking to? What is her relationship to them? What do you think they are discussing? What might be at stake? Who else is in the photo? Where are they? Where might she be going after the discussion is finished? One variation of this exercise is to wait to tell the students its historical background only after they have analyzed the photo.

The instruction to vary the point of entry when using photographs is an important drama strategy. Drama can be introduced at different points in a photograph's timeline, in order to deepen the students' understanding of the events. An improvisation could be created that begins a few minutes or even days, *before* the photo was taken; or the point of view could be varied by developing an improv that begins after the photograph has been shot, in order to explore what might happen next, for example. Next, the students could compare their analysis of the situation with the real events or relationships depicted.

It is important to note that not all improvisations need to be shared with the whole class, and so these exercises can be developed simultaneously by all the groups. When the improvs are complete, however, the students can reflect on their experience and share their discoveries with the larger group. Each individual group can be encouraged to talk about their work. The teacher can also address questions, in-role, specifically to all the Sophies, to all the Hans, to all the Christophs. All the Sophies, for example, can step into an inner circle, so that they have a special way to reflect on their role and to talk to the rest of the group. In this way, the students build a collective representation as well as a personal interpretation of these historical figures.

James Young (1993) explains that memorials depend on their capacity to adapt to new times (p. 281). If we hope for the life of the memory to be enduring, then drama can help us encompass multiple memories, renew meanings, and create community. Each time I work with a group of students I am reminded again: the power of using drama in the classroom is that it can cast new—and sometimes unexpected—light on the Holocaust. This power can move both students and teachers emotionally, spiritually, and intellectually; through art-making it can promote discussion and debate; and it can help our children to produce their own culture of reflection and action (Booth, 1994).

Using drama to teach the Holocaust means than we have the possibility of meeting Augusto Boal's (1992) challenge to recognize theater as a form of knowledge that can transform society. Drama can help us to examine memory and history, allowing us to discover those moments where public and private experiences intersect. In the drama events presented here, those intersections become part of their lived experience, so that students using theater to study the Holocaust have the opportunity of creating meaning by "doing" (which is defined as the deeper "knowledge in") rather than simply by "talking" (which is defined as "knowledge about") (Courtney, 1989, p. 188). Finally, through drama we invite the students' participation in remembering as an active and collective force:

> The theatre above all other forms of artistic practice insists on the life of the community; it cannot be made without it. Each play presented here enacts a rite of mourning for the lost community of Jewry and, by extension, for the threatened

human community whose doom the Holocaust may foreshadow. That rite cannot take place without the participation of the community of spectators as living witness. In the very act of representing the annihilation of the human community, then, the theatre itself offers a certain fragile potentiality for re-creation. (Fuchs, 1987, p. xxii)

REFERENCES

Adelson, Alan. (Ed.). (1996). *The Diary of Dawid Sierakowiak: Five Notebooks From the Lodz Ghetto.* Trans. Kamil Turowski. New York: Oxford University Press.

Atlan, Liliane (Ed.). (1987). "Mister Fugue or Earth Sick." In Elinor Fuchs (Ed.), *Plays of the Holocaust: An International Anthology.* New York: Theatre Communications Group.

Bachrach, Susan. (1994). *Tell Them We Remember: The Story of the Holocaust.* Boston, MA: Little, Brown.

Berenbaum, Michael. (1993). *The World Must Know: The History of the Holocaust as Told in the United States Holocaust Memorial Museum.* Boston, MA: Little, Brown and Company.

Boal, Augusto. (1992). *Games for Actors and Non-Actors.* London: Routledge.

Boas, Jacob. (Ed.). (1995). *We Are Witnesses: Five Diaries of Teenagers Who Died in the Holocaust.* New York: Henry Holt.

Bohm-Duchen, Monica. (1995). *After Auschwitz: Responses to the Holocaust in Contemporary Art.* London: Northern Centre for Contemporary Art.

Booth, David. (1994). *Drama and the Making of Meanings.* Newcastle upon Tyne: National Drama Publications.

Clenman, Donia Blumenfeld. (1995, July). "Poetry Reading for Department of Fine Arts," Theatre, Atkinson College, York University.

Courtney, Richard. (1989). *Play, Drama and Thought.* Toronto: Simon & Pierre.

Edelheit, Abraham J. & Herschel Edelheit. (1994). *History of the Holocaust: A Handbook and Dictionary.* Boulder, CO: Westview Press.

Feinstein, Stephen. (1994). *Witness and Legacy: Contemporary Art About the Holocaust.* Minneapolis, MN: Lerner Publications.

Frank, Anne. (1991). *The Diary of A Young Girl: The Definitive Edition.* New York: Doubleday.

Fuchs, Elinor. (Ed.). (1987). *Plays of the Holocaust: An International Anthology.* New York: Theatre Communications Group.

Goodrich, Frances & Hackett, A. (1956). *The Diary of Anne Frank.* New York: Random House.

Holliday, Laurel. (Ed.). (1995). *Children in the Holocaust and World War ll: Their Secret Diaries.* New York: Simon & Schuster.

Kesselman, Wendy. (1988). *I Love You, I Love You Not.* New York: Samuel French.

King, Nancy. (1993). *Storymaking and Drama.* Portsmouth, NH: Heinemann.

Kraus, Joanna Halpert. (1989). *Remember My Name.* New York: Samuel French.

Krondorfer, Bjorn. (1988). "Experimental Drama and the Holocaust: The Work of the Jewish-German Dance Theatre and its Application to the Teaching of the Holocaust." In A. L. Berger & R. Libowitz (Eds.), *Methodology in the Academic Teaching of the Holocaust.* Lantham, MD: University Press of America.

Krondorfer, Bjorn. (1995). *Remembrance and Reconciliation.* New Haven, CT: Yale University Press.

Langer, Lawrence. (Ed.). (1995). *Art from the Ashes: A Holocaust Anthology.* New York: Oxford University Press.

Lebow, Barbara. (1988). *A Shayna Maidel.* New York: NAL Penguin.

Raspanti, Celeste. (Ed.). (1971). ". . . I Never Saw Another Butterfly." New York: Dramatic Publishing Company.

Stevens, E. C., Brown, J. E., & Rubin, J. E. (1995). *Learning About The Holocaust: Literature and Other Resources for Young People.* North Haven, CT: The Shoe String Press.

Skloot, Robert. (1988). *The Darkness We Carry: The Drama of the Holocaust.* Madison: University of Wisconsin Press.

Skloot, Robert. (Ed.). (1982). *The Theatre of the Holocaust.* Madison: University of Wisconsin Press.

Tandy, Miles. (1995). *Curriculum Guide: World War II.* London: EDS Publications.

Volavkova, Hana. (Ed.). (1993). *". . . I Never Saw Another Butterfly": Children's Drawings and Poems from Terezin Concentration Camp, 1942–1944.* New York: Schocken Books.

Wiedmer, Caroline. (1995, December). "Designing Memories." In Rebecca Comay (Ed.), "Fascism and its Ghosts." A special issue of *Alphabet City Magazine of Toronto.* Numbers 4 & 5, pp. 6–14.

Young, James. (1993). *The Texture of Memory: Holocaust Memorials and Meaning.* New Haven, CT: Yale University Press.

Zatzman, Belarie. (1998). "Holocaust Stories." In D. Booth & J. Neelands (Eds.), *Writing in Role* (pp. 78–86). Hamilton: Caliburn Enterprises.

Zatzman, Belarie. (Ed.). (1997). *Study Guide: The Diary of Anne Frank.* Toronto: Educational Services, Young People's Theatre.

Zatzman, Belarie & Dobson, W. (1997). "Lessons for the Living" in J. Clark, W. Dobson, T. Goode, & J. Neelands (Eds.), *Lessons for the Living: Drama and the Integrated Curriculum* (pp. 68–82). Clark, Newmarket, Ontario: Mayfair Cornerstone.

ACKNOWLEDGMENTS

I would like to thank the many fine teachers and students who contributed their ideas and experience to this work, particularly Patterson Fardell, Jack Lipinsky, Margie Marmor, Yvonne Singer, Darlene Mignacco, and Suzanne Caines.

13 Including Music in a Study of the Holocaust

ROSELLE K. CHARTOCK

The role of music and song is germane to teaching about the Holocaust, in that music and song represent significant primary sources that reflect the very souls of the people who created or performed them. Furthermore, students can learn a great deal about the victims and the perpetrators during the Holocaust by focusing on the music generated by both groups and the purposes to which they put their music. Because of their own contact with contemporary music, students are already aware of the fact that music can influence human emotion and behavior. Through the incorporation of music and song into a study of the Holocaust, students can be assisted to recognize the Holocaust victims' feelings of despair and hope for survival as well as the hate and perverse pride of the oppressors.

This chapter, accompanied by an extensive bibliography, presents background knowledge about the roles played by music during the Holocaust, and a rationale for utilizing such materials in a study of the Holocaust. Following the rationale is a delineation of numerous instructional strategies, learning activities, and musical resources that even those teachers who are least comfortable and knowledgeable about music can use to enrich their lessons and units on the Holocaust.

Background: The Role of Music during the Holocaust

Joseph Goebbels, Hitler's propaganda minister, considered music to be the "most German of arts" (Goebbels at the Reich Music Festival, 1938, quoted in Rabbiner, 1993, p. 13). Germans basked in the glory of such historic figures as Bach, Beethoven, Brahms, Wagner, and Bruckner. With this heritage in mind, the Nazis recognized the utility of music as a propaganda tool for arousing a nationalistic revival and for controlling and manipulating human behavior. Music, like all of the fine arts, was to be one of the mediums for demonstrating Germany's "moral and cultural superiority," which the Nazis perceived as threatened by an international modernism associated with world Jewry (Rabbiner, 1993, p. 11). In effect, the

Nazis led an assault on the arts from 1933 to 1945, censoring certain works and glorifying others in order to assert political power.

As part of their assault on the arts, the Nazis staged a "Degenerate Music" exhibition in 1938, in Dusseldorf, in conjunction with the national music festival, the Reichsmusiktage, a "musical olympics" that featured Richard Wagner, Hitler's favorite composer, as well as contemporary composers such as Werner Egk. "Entartete Musik" (Degenerate Music), organized by Nazi arts administrator Hans Severus Ziegler, presented antimodernist attacks on jazz, the "musical-Bolshevist" *Threepenny Opera* of Kurt Weill, and the experimental, atonal music of Arnold Schonberg, all of which were labeled as alien, racially degenerate elements to be purged from German music (Rabbiner, 1993, p. 11). Many composers were attacked by the Nazis, including Paul Hindemith—a non-Jew opposed to Nazi ideology—and sought refuge in other countries, particularly the United States (Rabbiner, 1993, p. 11). At the Reichsmusiktage, Goebbels declared that "German musical life has now been purged of the last traces of Jewish domination . . ." (Rabbiner, 1993, p. 13). By 1936, Jewish composers who had remained in Germany had been removed from their positions, as well as from the Reich Music Chamber, in which membership was required in order for a person to work in the field of music.

There is little doubt about the fact that Hitler had found in composer Richard Wagner's (1813–1883) music and words a prototype of his antisemitic sentiments (Katz, 1986, p. 2). Many of Wagner's operatic works contained underlying antisemitic symbols, such as the Jew as hoarding capitalist and the cause of all evil in the world. For example, the character Mime in *The Ring* is the "excessively unattractive foster father of Siegfried, the mythical German hero" (Von Oppen, 1980, p. 213). A symbol of greed, Mime is portrayed through language and music as the operatic equivalent of "the Jew," who, in Wagner's essay on "The Jew in Music," is said to be "incapable of human speech and therefore of music" (Von Oppen, 1980, pp. 213–214).

A number of songs were chosen by the Nazis to arouse people's passions and generate an unhealthy patriotism and racism. These songs placed blame for Germany's problems on the Jews and other minorities (von Hugli & Ischi, 1975, pp. 14, 20; Feig, 1979, p. 96). Many of these songs were intended to influence young Germans recruited for Hitler Youth groups, and teenagers sang marching songs composed especially for them. One such song was "Deutschland erwache" or "Awaken, Germany," which contained strong antisemitic, nationalistic sentiments:

> Awaken, Germany from your bad dream
> Don't give the foreign Jews any room in your empire.
> We want to fight for your resurrection
> Aryan blood should not be wasted
>   (von Hugli & Ischi, 1975, p. 14).[1]

Apart from the propagandistic purposes to which the Nazis put music, there was the diabolical role music played in deceiving the victims as they arrived at the death camps. For example, the new arrivals at Auschwitz-Birkenau were told to disrobe in order to take showers but were, in fact, often marched into gas chambers to the sounds of Beethoven played by the camp orchestra composed of other inmates (Gilbert, 1985, p. 686; Miller, 1981). The beauty of the music established an illusion of well-being and camouflaged the real intentions of the Nazis. Also in the camps, Nazi doctors, like the notorious Dr. Mengele, sadistically used music as they conducted experiments to determine the nature of the responses of the insane to musical stimuli. After the observation sessions, these unsuspecting people were gassed and replaced by other victims (Miller, 1981). At the end of a day's work, SS officers were entertained by music provided by prisoners like violinists Lepold and Henry Rosner. In such ways, music, the product of human creativity, became a beastly and deadly instrument of the Nazis.

By contrast, music played a benevolent and nurturing role among the victims. Music was central to Jewish life in the ghetto and camps just as it had been in Jewish cultural life before the Holocaust.

Playing music had been a part of both the secular and religious life of Jews before they were forced into the ghettos. They brought their music into ghettos and this music helped to bring some normality to their new, and disorienting environment. More specifically, for Jews in the ghetto, music served as an expression of hope, passive protest, and spiritual resistance. Songs accompanied the activities of adults at work in the ghetto and youth organizations at play (Flam, 1992). There were songs expressing hatred, desire for revenge, hope for victory, and determination to fight to the death for it (Belsky, 1979, p. 91). Music was also a major source of strength and a means of attempting to overcome the dehumanizing conditions of the ghettos and camps. Singing traditional songs, organizing lessons and secretly playing in ensembles enabled many Jews to maintain their dignity.

In ghetto schools, children learned to play, sing, dance, and act. "The schools themselves became bracing cultural centers for the whole [Warsaw] ghetto. Dramatic, choral, and musical performances by schoolchildren, which proved particularly popular, were produced to raise funds for social welfare programs [established in the ghetto]" (Dawidowicz, 1975, p. 255). The sights and sounds of these children engendered high morale and a hope that these children would survive.

The Lodz Ghetto had an underground symphony orchestra, the Kovno Ghetto a mandolin orchestra, the Warsaw Ghetto several string quartets, and most ghettos had adult and children's choruses (Dawidowicz, 1975, p. 257; Flam, 1992, pp. 18–23). Flam (1992) notes that the survivors she interviewed recalled street singers who offered "social and political satire, humor and parodies of popular songs" (p. 25) that reflected daily life in the ghetto.

Lullabies were one of the most popular song genres. Not only were traditional lullabies sung but many were written in the ghetto and performed in ghetto theaters (Flam, 1992, p. 148). "Clearly the central value of music in the ghetto [was] its vital human expression. Within an inhuman environment, the voice that continued to sing . . . became the cry of the inmates for recognition as human beings. . . . The act of singing, which is fundamentally an act of creation . . . was an assertion of freedom as well as of life and of community" (Flam, 1992, p. 185).

This assertion for freedom was reflected in songs that "inspire[d] purposeful defiance of the Nazi war machine with words such as

And those who were hidden
In fear only yesterday,
Now march right long with us, not alone.
   (Meltzer, 1976, p. 173)

In the concentration camps, songs were composed and sung that enabled the prisoners to attempt to cope with the pain they endured. Songs gave many people strength. Often the words contained hidden messages of hope that helped the victims fight to retain their humanity in spite of the desolation around them. One such song was "Peat Bog Soldiers," which was sung by political prisoners as they marched to and from work in the peat bog where they were used to dry out peat bog swamps.[2] "Peat Bog Soldiers" was written by political prisoners in the Borgermoor Camp, near Hanover, Germany, in 1933, and was the first known song ever written in a Nazi concentration camp (Kalisch & Meister, 1985, p. 92). "In keeping with an old German military tradition, prisoners were forced to sing while marching to and from work. In the concentration camps, however, only Nazi soldier songs were allowed, but prisoners began to write their own marching songs" (Kalisch and Meister, 1985, p. 92) like this one, which German political prisoners sang with such enthusiasm that this last verse was finally forbidden:

But for us there is no complaining,
Winter will in time be past;
One day we shall cry rejoicing,
Homeland dear, you're mine at last.
   (Hill, 1965, p. 24)

Prisoners sang as they worked in freezing temperatures without overcoats, and their songs conveyed the nature of their suffering: ". . . we lie in the ditches . . . we have the fever . . " (Meltzer, 1976, pp. 93–94).

There were also a number of songs created by partisans while they were living in the forests of Eastern Europe and carrying on guerilla warfare in an effort to undermine the Nazis. Their music also stirred passions for survival and hope for a future where little evidence existed that such a future was possible (Meltzer, 1976, pp. 158–160).

Music was, however, only a temporary respite from the suffering. The story of the camp at Terezin is perhaps the most tragic example of this fact. "The most agonizing of music's helplessness was the fate of the artistic community in Theresienstadt" in Czechoslovakia, (Dawidowicz, 1975, p. 137) which was "formed into a Jewish ghetto in 1941 as a propaganda tool to convince foreign observers that Jews were being treated well" (Dawidowicz, 1975, p. 137). There, children engaged in musical and artistic activities, and composers continued to create symphonies.

Few of them, however, escaped being transported to death camps. Of the fifteen thousand children who passed through Terezin, only one hundred survived. What did survive were some of the children's poems and drawings and some of the classical works that these composers recorded on scraps of paper. The string quartets, for example, of Pavel Haas (1894–1944) and Hans Krasa (1899–1944) have been played in concerts during the last few years (Ross, 1995, pp. 25, 31).

Interestingly, concentration camp orchestras were a haven for keeping some of these composers and musicians alive during their entire internment (Miller, 1981). One of these was Fania Fenelon, who, as a member of the Women's Orchestra in the Auschwitz-Birkenau (Poland) concentration camp, was thus spared the gas chambers. In *Playing for Time*, the screenplay by Arthur Miller (1981), which was based on Fenelon's book (1979), it becomes clear that music was a means of "buying" survival time for orchestra members who played for Nazi officers. Whereas music meant survival for many of these musicians, ironically, it also signaled death for those who marched to the "showers" accompanied by their music (Gilbert, 1985, pp. 500–501).

Overall, however, for the victim, music and song symbolized survival—life over death. The songs, and their singing, tell us the story of their bravery and their spiritual resistance, their will to live and to prevail (Flam, 1992, p. 185).

Rationale for Integrating Music into a Study of the Holocaust

There are several key reasons for integrating music/songs into the teaching of any historical subject. First, songs composed during a historical period by the participants constitute important historical documents. They are primary sources in the truest sense, because they come from the lips of the people whose experiences and feelings gave rise to their expression. Such was the case of the song, "Peat Bog Soldiers" (referred to earlier), which was created from a poem written by one of the prisoners in the Borgermoor camp by the name of Esser, a miner who wrote it in response to a particularly vicious assault on the inmates by drunken SS men (Kalisch & Meister, 1985, p. 93). Among the many songs about Jews by Jews during this period—all of which can be accessed via the United States Holocaust Memorial Museum's Learning Center (USHMM, Learning Center, 100 Raoul Wallenberg Place SW, Washington, DC 20024-2140)—are the following: *Undzer shtetl brent* (Our Town is Burning), *Ikh benk ahem* (I Long for Home), *Friling* (Springtime), *Shtiler, shtiler* (Quiet, Quiet), *Dos elnte kind* (The Lonely Child), *S'iz gut* (It's Good), *A yidish kind* (A Jewish Child), *Nit keyn rozhinkes, nit keyn mandlen* (No More Raisins, No More Almonds), *Minutn fun bitokhn* (Moments of Hope), and *Yugnt-himen* (Hymn of Youth).

Second, B. Lee Cooper (1981), a social studies educator who has extensively written about the utility of integrating songs into the teaching of social studies, notes that "If [the study of history] is to become a forum for the reflective examination of the [causes and effects] of social change, [then musical] presentations [can] provide relevant personal and historical illustrations for students" (p. 2). Continuing, he asserts that the challenge for teachers who plan to employ songs in their lessons and units is "to convince their students of the academic legitimacy of the investigation of songs and lyrics" (p. 2). The best argument that can be made is that a student of history cannot afford to overlook the role of songs as primary sources that can convey the ideas, values, and emotions of people during a particular period of history.

Third, as Bates, Sanabria, Watrous, and Ulin (1986), who were involved in developing an integrated arts curriculum, have pointed out, ". . . songs are another way of describing events. . . . Many songs tell stories, and have chronicled a people's history and heritage . . ." (pp. 10–11).

Fourth, music has the power to convey the emotions behind the words created by those who experienced certain events. As Belsky (1979) has noted, Yiddish songs coming out of the Holocaust "are part of a vast body of music created by persecuted and oppressed people throughout history [and more] than any other means of expression the song can convey to us the suffering of the men, women and children . . " (p. 89).

Often the melody, rhythm, and form are as significant as the lyrics. For example, the melody of the Yiddish lullaby, "Oyfn Pripetshok," which mothers sang to their babies in the ghettos and camps, contains both an upbeat, affirmative sound and a sadder, more morose one, and this combination reflects the mix of emotions inherent in the messages contained in the song. Reflected in the melody is the sadness that comes with the possibility of future persecution: "When you children will be exiled/and be tortured, may you gain strength from these letters/Study, look into them now" (Warshawsky in Silber, 1963, pp. 134–135). But there is also the message that with the study of the Torah (Jewish law), they will be happy and will be rewarded.

Referring to the use of folk songs, Laurence Seidman (1985) noted that "When [students] sing these songs, they step into the shoes of people they sing about. They feel their pains and joys; they live their hopes and despairs" (Seidman, 1985, p. 580). In the case of the Holocaust, they can empathize with the child in the ghetto and gain a sense of what aroused the members of the Hitler Youth.

Songs convey not only the emotions of those who sang them but often arouse the emotions of the students, thus reaching them on the affective level. Words convey to students historical information, but the music can stir their emotions, which brings us to the fifth reason why teachers can effectively use music in the teaching of history. *If presented with historical information in the form of a song, students who may have resisted more traditional means may be motivated to find out more about the topic by consulting more academic texts.* By impacting their emotions, the students are sparked intellectually. "They [will then] want to know more about the times and incidents in the songs" (Seidman, 1985, p. 580).

A sixth reason for integrating songs/music is that they have the power to help students remember what they are learning. Hitler knew well the propagandistic power of music and employed the music of Haydn with a powerful nationalistic message by Hoffmann von Fallersleben, in the anthem, "Deutschland Über

Alles" ("Germany Over All"), the anthem of the Third Reich, and perhaps the most successful piece of music for unifying Germans under Hitler (von Hugli & Ischi, 1975, p. 20). So powerful was the effect of this song that the version sung by Germans during the Third Reich is outlawed in Germany today. As a tool for keeping Nazi goals ever-present in the minds of Germans, this anthem proved most effective.

It is, of course, the pedagogical—as opposed to the propagandistic—advantages of music that teachers should consider when incorporating music into the teaching of the Holocaust. If students are able to listen to the songs of both the victims and the perpetrators—or even memorize a stanza or two—this material will likely remain with them long after their formal study of the Holocaust has ended. One song or even one line of one song is easily retained and can facilitate their recall of the larger issues.

Finally, songs can be utilized in a language arts context, social studies context, or in art and photography classes. They can be used on all secondary grade levels and are effective as "a universal teaching tool with all types of students . . " (Seidman, 1985, p. 581).

Overall, music/songs of the Holocaust period can address and complement the issues contained in the larger study and can offer teachers a springboard for exploring those issues.

Instructional Activities for Incorporating Music into the Study of the Holocaust

The following teaching and learning activities involving musical resources can assist students in analyzing and comprehending the complexities of the Holocaust. There are many ways in which teachers can integrate music into Holocaust curricula. Teachers may opt to use one or more of these ideas, depending on the amount of time available for teaching about the subject.

If teachers are able to sing these songs, if they choose to play tapes, or if they locate a music teacher who can sing the songs with the students, that is all well and good, but, first and foremost, the songs should be thought of as works that can be read, discussed, and evaluated. As previously mentioned, it is significant that even without the melodies, the songs are primary sources that convey the powerful emotions of the victims, the perpetrators, and the commemorators of the Holocaust.

Among the suggested instructional activities that follow are those that involve discussion, small group work, research, debates, creative writing, and artistic exploration. The focus of the activities is organized chronologically: (1) Music of the Perpetrators (1933–1945); (2) Music of the Victims during the Holocaust (1935–1945); and (3) Post-Holocaust Music of Remembrance and Renewal (1945–present). The majority of these methods have been successfully implemented by the author and other educators at the middle and secondary levels.

1. *Assessing the role of a national anthem*   "Deutschland Über Alles" ("Germany Over All") was perhaps the most powerful and pervasive piece of music sung before and during the time of the Holocaust. It was the national anthem of the Third Reich, which Germans sang with patriotic fervor.

The tune to "Deutschland Über Alles" was originally written by noted composer Joseph Haydn (1732–1809) as a hymn; and this song, with its original words, can still be found in hymnals today. From its role as a hymn, the song went on to become the Austrian national anthem. Then new words were composed by August Heinrich Hoffmann von Fallersleben (1798–1874), a poet of children's verse. His message, written before the separate German city-states unified in 1871, implies the fierce nationalistic belief that Germany must unify and spread its power beyond its borders. The song became the German anthem after unification under Otto von Bismarck, and the song continued to convey the poet's message. Hitler knew that the words and music could arouse his people into pushing for the expansion of its borders.

> Germany, Germany over all
> Above everything (else) in the world
> If it holds (stays) together fraternally
> For protection and (comfort?)
> From the Maas to the Memel
> From the Etsch to the Belt[3]
> Germany, Germany above everything (else)
> Everything (else) in the world.
> German women, German loyalty
> German wine and German song
> Shall retain their beautiful old sound
> (and) Shall inspire us to noble deed
Our whole lives
German women, German loyalty
German wine and German song.
Unity, Justice and Freedom
For the German fatherland
Toward this let us strive together.
Fraternally with heart and hand
Unity, Justice and Freedom
Are the foundation of happiness
Prosper in the splendor (glow) of happiness
Prosper (flourish) German Fatherland.
> Text: Hoffmann von Fallersleben
> Music: Joseph Haydn
> Translation: Charles L. Hamilton
> (Original German version: Von Hugli & Ischi, 1975, p. 20)

Today still another version of this anthem exists. In 1950 the Federal Republic adopted the following verses as the official words and, with the unification of East and West Germany in 1990, this version continues to be in effect:

Unity and right and freedom
For the German fatherland;
Let us all pursue the purpose
Brotherly, with heart and hands.
Unity and right and freedom
Are the pawns of happiness.
Flourish in this blessing's glory
Flourish, German fatherland!
 (Shaw & Coleman, 1960, p. 186)

There are many activities that might evolve from the use of this anthem. First, students could read the words aloud in unison. Second, they should be asked: "What are the implications of this title for both Germans *and* non-Germans?" and then required to respond in writing. Both small group and large group discussions could follow. Third, they could develop an artistic response to the title, words, and sentiments in the first song.

2. *Richard Wagner and the Nazis*   Not only did Richard Wagner—and Hitler— blame the Jews for all that was bad in society, but both believed during their respective life times that one of the purposes of his music should be to further German nationalism. Wagner's music was played at Nazi Party rallies, and it is not surprising that "the Berlin opera celebrated Hitler's arrival in power with a Wagner opera" (Von Oppen, 1980, p. 214).

Students should listen to part of Wagner's *The Ring*. Even though most will not understand the German lyrics, they will sense the power of the music. Students can be asked to describe Wagner's music in terms of its possible emotional appeal for people, and its ability to arouse patriotic feelings. They could analyze why Hitler may have found Wagner's music both useful and beautiful. Particularly controversial is the question of whether or not a work of music can be judged apart from its composer. That is, should people shun Wagner's work due to the fact that his operatic symbolism was antisemitic? A good source that examines the connection between Wagner and Hitler is the essay by Von Oppen (1980) referred to here, and the biography of Wagner by Derek Watson (1979). A short article about the Wagner-Hitler connection, "Politics and Music: Wagnerian Music and Thought in the Third Reich" (included in Chartock and Spencer (Eds.), 1995, pp. 176–183) is also capable of generating a lively discussion among the students.

3. *Assessing the Role of Patriotic Songs in Children's Lives*   Hitler knew that music was a powerful means to get his message across to young people. In fact, school textbooks, some of which included music, were rewritten to further the goals of the Nazis and to arouse in young people fervent loyalty to Hitler and his mission. To produce a generation of dedicated Nazis, the "reeducation" began in elementary schools.

The following song, "You (Our) Dear Fuhrer," was contained in a songbook for children published in Germany in 1940 (Rabbiner, 1933, p. 44).

(The song was written—with different words—in 1884. New words were created during the Nazi period. The words below constitute the Nazi version.)

"You (our) dear Fuhrer"
("Du Lieber Führer du")

You dear Fuhrer
We the young boys or girls
of all towns and cities
We celebrate you.
You dear Fuhrer
You are so good to
us, your little ones
That we will always be yours and
will remain so forever.
    (Translation by Charles Hamilton)

Elsewhere in this book, Samuel Totten has pointed out the critical need to provide a historical context for reading Holocaust literature, and this is just as true regarding songs about the Holocaust. More specifically, and ideally, students should be well informed of the rise of the Nazis, the Nazi dictatorship, the propaganda campaign undertaken by the Nazis, and the adulation that the Nazis tried to instill in the general populace for Hitler. It also would be valuable for the students to know of Hitler's bellicosity and disdain for those deemed "Other," and what resulted from this: waging war and depriving people of their basic civil and human rights, including their freedom and lives. Then and only then will students be able to appreciate the significance of such a song.

Once the above is assured, students should read the translation of the song. Then, they might be required to do any of the following and/or additional activities: They could be asked to write a response to the question How would you feel about singing such a song? Explain your answer in a good amount of detail. Next, they could discuss—first in small groups and then in a whole class discussion—their responses. A follow-up discussion could focus on how such a song could be used to instill loyalty to Hitler and/or patriotism.

On a different note, they could create an artistic response in regard to how they would feel being required to sing such a song. The response could take virtually any form from a song, a drawing, a pantomime, a short story, a playlet, and so on.

This song also could be used as a springboard for reading about Hitler Youth as portrayed in Hans Peter Richter's (1972) book, *I Was There*. Used together, this book and the songs can help students address the issue as to why many young people eagerly joined organizations like the Hitler Youth.

4. *Making Connections to the Victims*   "The song was the only truth. The Nazis could take everything away from us, but they could not take singing from us. This remained our only human expression" (Miriam Harel, survivor of the Lodz Ghetto in Poland, in Flam, 1992, p. 1).

Samuel Totten has noted that this is an excellent quote to have students respond to after they have studied life and death in the Nazi-organized ghettos and/or the concentration and death camps. Once the students have completed such key preparatory work, they could respond in writing by noting specific examples of the ghetto dwellers' and concentration and death camp prisoners' lives that provide evidence as to why Harel might make such an assertion as the above. What the students should be asked to note in particular are any and all aspects of the prisoners' lives which were denied or stripped from them by the Nazis.

5. *Interpreting Cultural Beliefs through Song*   The music of a culture is often the link to its past, its beliefs, values, and aspirations. The lullaby "Ofyn Pripet-shok" ("On the Hearth") is an example of such a song. Written by Russian-born Mark Warshawsky, it was sung by mothers to their babies from the time of its creation in the late nineteenth century. Warshawsky was one of the most popular Yiddish folk bards of that time, and this lullaby "so effectively captured the Yiddish mood and idiom, that the folk adopted [it] . . . within the composer's lifetime" (Silber, 1963, p. 134).

Have the students read the words to the song and help them to interpret what these words can tell them about Jewish culture. (The song conveys the importance of education and the Torah, the basis of Jewish laws and doctrine. It also identifies the three functions of the Torah and of education, which are to provide (1) a source of happiness; (2) a source of strength in the face of oppression; and (3) a link to the Jewish past and tradition.)

> *Chorus*
> On the hearth a little fire burns
> And it is hot in the house,
> And the "rebe" is teaching the little children,
> The a-b-c.
> *Ofyn pripetshok brent a fayerld un in shtub is heys*
> *Under rebe le rent kleyne kinderlech*
> *dem a-lef-beys;*
> *under rebe lerent kleyne kinderlech*
> *dem a-lef-beys.*
>
> See now little children, remember dear ones,
> What you are learning here;
> Say it over and over again:
> "A" with a "kometz" spells "O!"
> Study children, with great interest,
> That is what I tell you;
> The one who will know his "Ivre" first
> Will get a banner (for a prize).
>
> *Chorus*
>
> Study children, do not fear,
> Every beginning is difficult;
> Happy is the one who studies Torah,
> Need a man more?
>
> *Chorus*

When you children will be exiled,
And be tortured,
May you gain strength from these letters,
Study, look into them now.

Chorus

When you will grow older, children,
You will understand,
How many tears lie in these letters
And how much weeping.

Chorus

(Silber, 1968, pp. 134–135)

Useful references that address Jewish culture are: Lucy S. Dawidowicz, *The Golden Tradition: Jewish Life and Thought in Eastern Europe* (Syracuse, NY: Syracuse University Press, 1996); Michael Katz and Gershon Schwartz, *Swimming in the Sea of Talmud: Lessons for Everyday Life* (Philadelphia, PA: Jewish Publication Society, 1998); and Mark Zborowski and Elizabeth Herzog, *Life Is With People: The Culture of the Shtetl* (New York: Schocken Books, 1995).

6. *Parallels to Other Times and Places*   After reading and singing the song "Peat Bog Soldiers," part of which appears below, discuss with students other examples in history when there were crises such as war or persecution when the victims created "music out of pain." For example, every war, including the American Revolution, the Civil War, World War I, and Vietnam, resulted in songs. Slavery in the United States also resulted in the development of songs. Slaves, for example, sang underground railroad songs in much the same way as prisoners of the Nazis sang this song, with an eye toward freedom and a belief that their liberation would someday be realized. Escaping slaves sang "Follow the Drinking Gourd," the drinking gourd referring to the "Big Dipper in the night sky, always pointing to the North Star and to freedom" (Seeger and Reiser, 1985, p. 39). An example of a Revolutionary lament is "Johnny Has Come for a Soldier," which expresses the hardships of the women left behind by the soldiers (Scott, 1994/1995, p. 46). Students should locate some of these songs and compare and contrast their messages with the one below.

First verse
Far and wide as the eye can wander
Heath and bog are every where
Not a bird sings out to cheer us
Oaks are standing gaunt and bare.

Chorus
We are the peat bog soldiers;
We're marching with our spades to the bog.

Third Verse
But for us there is no complaining,
Winter will in time be past;

One day we shall cry rejoicing,
Homeland dear, you're mine at last.

Chorus
Then will the peat bog soldiers
March no more with our spades to the bog.
(Hill, 1965, p. 24; Kalisch & Meister, 1985, pp. 94–96)

7. *Illustrating Songs*   Students could respond to one of the following "political songs," such as "Mein Vater Wird Gesucht" (My Father Was Sought Out) or "Peat Bog Soldiers," in artistic form such as a drawing, collage, mobile, or sculpture. They also could illustrate one of the songs, thereby bringing into view some of the images contained in the songs. For some of the students, the songs may remain an abstraction until they can interpret the words in a more concrete format. Once they create a piece of art, they could write a short piece about the connection between their artwork and the song. Students could also construct a bulletin board using the words of the songs as the center and surround it with the images they have drawn.

The words for "Mein Vater Wird Gesucht" (My Father Was Sought Out), which was composed by two German émigrés named Hans Drach (the text) and Gerda Kohlmey (the melody) in 1936, are as follows:

My father is sought out,
He can't come to our home;
They hunt for him with hounds,
Perhaps he has been found—
And never will come home.

The SA often comes
To ask us where he is;
This we cannot tell them,
So they take us and they beat us—
But we'll never talk.

Still, Mother does break down
When we read a report
That says Father had been captured,
and hung himself soon after;
But I don't believe that.

He'd sworn to all of us
That this he'd never do.
Party members say that
The SA simply shot him—
Without a trial, too.

Today I know just why
They did that thing to him;
We'll strive and we'll accomplish
The work he couldn't finish—
And father's goals live on.

This song was printed in a Prague German-language newspaper published for Communist refugees from Germany. It was one of the best-known songs among German exiles between 1936 and 1945.

8. *Creating Their Own Songs*   Students may be able to express their understanding of written materials on the Holocaust through the vehicle of original musical expression. Have them write a song reflecting their response to a film, a work of literature or other resource they may have used during their study of the Holocaust. Some students who find writing papers difficult may be able to succinctly and personally express what they learned in the simple form of a song. For example, if the students have read certain first-person accounts, a poem, a piece of fiction, or a memoir—such as Elie Wiesel's *Night*—they could create a song that that tells one of their respective stories.

9. *Sing the Songs*   After distributing the words of a song, in this case, "Yugnt-himen" (Hymn of Youth), which was composed by Shmerke Kaczerginski (text) and Basye Ruin (music) in the Vilna Ghetto in 1942, read them aloud with the students and define key terms, answer questions, and explain the origins. After the content of the song is grasped by students, play the song on the guitar and sing it, or play a tape of the song. Then repeat the song and have the students sing only the chorus/refrain until they are comfortable with the part that is repeated. Nod when they are to join in. During the many times this author has led this song, students have always participated. If anyone absolutely refuses to sing, encourage him/her to tap his/her foot or finger to the beat of the song, or hum it. Then have him/her join in on the whole song. Most will join. Compliment them. This generally leads to more participation and singing with more feeling.

The words of the English version of "Yugnt-himen" (Hymn of Youth) are:

> Our song is filled with grieving,
> Bold our step, we march along.
> Though the foe the gateway's watching,
> Youth comes storming with their song.
>
> *Refrain*
> Young are they, are they, are they
> whose age won't bind them.
> Years don't really mean a thing,
> Elders also, also, also, can be children
> In a newer, freer, spring.
>
> Those who roam upon the highways,
> Those whose step with hope is strong,
> From the ghetto youth salutes them,
> And their greetings send along
>
> *Refrain*
>
> We remember all our tyrants,
> We remember all our friends,

And we pledge that in the future,
Our past and present blend.

Refrain

So we're girding our muscles,
In our ranks we're planting steel,
Where a blacksmith, builder marches
We will join them with our zeal!

Refrain

The above English version is from Mlotek and Gottlieb, *We Are Here* (New York: Workmen's Circle, 1983).

For other songs, such as "Ofyn Pripetshok," which is in Yiddish, again have students read the words aloud; then play the tape several times and have students follow along with the songsheets that have been distributed. Next, lower the music and have the students sing along with the tape. After a few times, students will able to sing the song without any accompaniment.

Teachers could ask the students what people hearing the warning that is implied in the song could have done, if anything, to prevent further disaster. *Again, it is imperative that such a task be provided in a historical context (that is, the students need to know exactly what the Jews faced in the regard to the Nazi juggernaut). Without such information this activity become nothing more than a guessing game, which is unconscionable during a study of the Holocaust.*

10. *Interpreting Symbols and Metaphors* A Jewish partisan song by Hirsch Glik, "Zog Nit Keinmol" ("Never Say That You Are Treading the Final Path"), provides a unique view into the history of the Holocaust, and offers students an opportunity to learn how symbolism and metaphor were used by the partisans. As noted earlier, the partisans were resistance fighters, Jews and non-Jews, in different countries who fought the Nazis in the forests and lived by their wits. (Some of the Jewish partisans had to endure periodically the antisemitism of peasants and other partisans on whom they depended for - support.) "Songs were one of their weapons . . ." (Belsky, 1979, p. 92), and Glik's song became their official hymn. ". . . [with] almost magical speed it was caught up by all the concentration camps . . . and by a score of other peoples as well" (Belsky, 1979, p. 92). Glik's song reflected his own experience as a partisan in the Vilna Ghetto where he was killed during an encounter with Nazi troops in 1944.

In an excerpt from "Zog Nit Keinmol" (a song associated with the Youth Club in the Vilna Ghetto), students can be helped to interpret what the "sun" stands for (victory), "leaden skies" (despair), "days of blue" (a better future, freedom), as well as other terms and lyrics. Before providing students with the answers, the students should be asked to respond to the song in terms of what they see, hear, and feel. They could also be asked to "rewrite" the song by replacing certain words (e.g., sun, leaden skies, days of blue, etc.) with what they symbolize or stand for. A discussion could ensue to ascertain the different students' interpretations, and then the latter could be compared and contrasted with the above meanings.

Using this song as a springboard, students could also do research on the resistance movements of the partisans. They could be required to discuss the roles played by young people in these movements.

"Zog Nit Keinmol"
("Never Say")

Never say that there is only death for you
Though leaden skies may be concealing days of blue—
Because the hour we have hungered for is near;
Beneath our tread the earth shall tremble: We are here!

We'll have the morning sun to set our day aglow,
And all our yesterdays shall vanish with the foe,
And if the time is long before the sun appears,
Then let this song go like a signal through the years.

So never say that there is only death for you.
Leaden skies may be concealing days of blue—
Yet the hour we have hungered for is near;
Beneath our tread the earth shall tremble: We are here!

(Friedlander, 1968, pp. 280–281; Meltzer, 1976, p. 159;
Silverman, 1983, p. 203. Translated from the Yiddish by Aaron Kramer.)

11. *"Choral" Reading*   Students can also read one or more of the songs in unison, as opposed to singing them together. For example, a choral reading of "Ofyn Pripetshok" (On the Hearth") or "Zog Nit Keinmol" ("Never Say") can often help students experience the emotions in the songs and share in common the hopes and the determination expressed in the songs, which, in many cases, is what Jews and others did when they sang together.

12. *Listening to Post-Holocaust Music of Remembrance.*   In 1951, a song, "Babi Yar," was written by the Russian Jewish poet Shike Driz and the musician Rivka Boyarska to commemorate the massacres of 33,771 Jews that took place in the area on the outskirts of Kiev in Russia in September 1941, by Germans under the supervision of SS officers (Kalisch & Meister, 1985, p. 23). "No official recognition of the mass murders of Babi Yar had been given by the Russians until Yevgeny Yevtushenko gained worldwide attention with his poem 'Babi Yar'" (Kalisch & Meister, 1985, p. 24).

In 1962, Dmitri Shostakovich integrated this poem into his Thirteenth Symphony, which is a powerful expression of sorrow, protest, and spiritual resistance to oppression that he, too, experienced under a totalitarian communist regime. For him, as for the Jews during the Holocaust, music was an important outlet for emotions.

Samuel Totten has noted that there are various ways to approach this symphony in the classroom. First, he suggests that *students should become conversant with the actual incident at Babi Yar. That is, there is a need to contextualize both the poem and the music about this tragedy. In order to do so, students could read a historical account of the massacre at Babi Yar.* Several good sources for such information are the following works: Michael Berenbaum's *The World Must Know: The Holocaust as Told in the United States Holocaust Memorial Museum* (Boston, MA: Little, Brown, 1993, pp. 99–101; *Tell Them We Remember: The Story of the Holocaust* by Susan D. Bachrach (Boston, MA: Little, Brown, 1994, pp. 42–43); or *The Black Book of Soviet Jewry,* by Ilya Ehrenburg and Vasily Grossman (Eds.) (New York: Holocaust Library, 1981).

Next, students could read the poem and respond to it by writing down notes about their initial *and* personal reaction to the poem. That could be followed by both small group and whole class discussion of such ideas.

Conversely, and this more approximates a reader response type activity, the students could initially respond to the poem by writing a personal reaction to it in which they write a letter to the poet regarding any aspect of the poem they want and/or their reaction to it. (For a detailed discussion of a reader response activity around a poem, see Samuel Totten's [2000], " 'Written in Pencil in the Sealed Railway-Car': Incorporating Poetry into a Study of the Holocaust via Reader Response Theory," in *Teaching Holocaust Literature* [Boston, MA: Allyn and Bacon]).

After the students have discussed their personal, written reactions in both small group and large group discussions, they could read a historical account of the tragedy at Babi Yar and then compare their personal response with the facts that influenced the writing of the poem.

Finally, the students could listen to the first movement of the Symphony. After doing so, they could either draw or write about what they "see" as they listen to the music. The poem (1961) can be found in a collection of Yevtushenko's poetry (1964).

13. *Learning about Holocaust Music from Survivors*   Invite a survivor of the Holocaust to class to speak about music in the camps and/or music's role in their lives.

14. *Comparing the Songs to the Readings*   Students can develop a list of the basic facts, themes and/or concepts they learned from the songs and then compare/contrast them with the ideas contained in the readings, photographs and other resources they may be using. This activity will help to reinforce the learning that students experience as a result of using diverse sources of information.

15. *Concluding Activities*   A unit on the Holocaust could be concluded by having students write an original song synthesizing the many concepts and events they studied through their historical texts and/or literature. Divide students into groups, assigning each one to write a stanza about a particular aspect of the Holocaust (the tune chosen could be one familiar to most students; however, it should not be a tune that is "cute," "flip," or one likely to degenerate into disrespect for the history). If possible, the students should perform their musical composition for other classes.

Conclusion

Integrating music into a study of the Holocaust enables teachers to address the topic from two perspectives, that of the perpetrator and that of the victim. Hitler and the German Nazis used music to further their goals of racial and political dominance. They turned music, one of the most moving expressions of human creativity, into a weapon to further oppress innocent people.

By contrast, music played a more nurturing role in the fragile lives of the victims who sought refuge, sustenance, and comfort in their songs and, in so doing, exemplified how music can serve as a powerful form of spiritual resistance. The victims sang songs that had been a part of their heritage and then contributed their own songs to that heritage. They left behind a musical legacy that both informs and inspires.

As a result of this exploration, students will likely begin to recognize music's connections to the past and the present. They may begin to listen to songs with a keener ear for the meaning of lyrics, both hidden and explicit. Undoubtedly, they will have gained insight into the motivations of those who use music to arouse attitudes and emotions for good or evil.

NOTES

1. Jews had, in fact, been living in Germany for over six centuries at that time.
2. Although the Jews of Europe were the primary and major target of the Nazis' "Final Solution," other groups were also interned and brutalized, if not killed, in camps, including Gypsies, Poles and other Slavs, Soviet prisoners of war, homosexuals, Jehovah's Witnesses, and political prisoners who had resisted Hitler and his regime.
3. The references to the Maas River in France, Belgium, and the Netherlands, the Mermel River in Eastern Europe, the Etsch River in upper Italy, and the Belt, which refers to two channels in the Baltic, imply that as far back as the mid-nineteenth century, Germans like Fallerslebenn were thinking in terms of German expansion throughout Europe.

REFERENCES

Allport, Gordon W. (1958). *The Nature of Prejudice*. New York: Anchor.

Bates, Davis, Diane Sanabria; Beth Gilden Watrous, & Donald Ulin. (1986). *"Sing Me a Story of History": An Integrated Arts Curriculum*. Northampton, MA: Pioneer Valley Folklore Society and Massachusetts School Union 18.

Belsky, Gilbert. (1979). *The Holocaust: A Teacher Resource*. Philadelphia, PA: Philadelphia School District. (Unit 5 of 6, pp. 71–94, "Jewish Resistance to the Holocaust.") [Available on ERIC microfiche, #ED 224733]

Blood, Peter & Annie Patterson. (Eds.). (1992). *Rise Up Singing*. Bethlehem, PA: Sing Out Corp.

Bor, Joseph. (1978). *The Terezin Requiem*. New York: Avon Bard.

Botstein, Leon. (1995, December). "The Involuntary Ghetto: Jewish Musical Life Under the Third Reich. Remembering the Jewish Cultural Alliance (1933–41)." *Program Notes*. New York: Albany Symphony Chamber Players.

Chartock, Roselle K. & Jack Spencer. (Eds.). (1995). *Can It Happen Again? Chronicles of the Holocaust*. New York: Black Dog and Leventhal.

Cooper, B. Lee. (1981). *Popular Music in the Social Studies Classroom: Audio Resources for Teachers.* How to Do It Series, #2, No. 13. Washington, DC: National Council for the Social Studies.

Dawidowicz, Lucy S. (1975). *The War Against the Jews 1933–1945.* New York: Holt, Rinehart and Winston.

Di Meglio, John E. (1971, January). "Music in World History Classes." *The History Teacher* 4(5):4–56.

Feig, Konnilyn G. (1979). *Hitler's Death Camps: The Sanity of Madness.* New York: Holmes and Meier.

Fenelon, Fania. (1979). *Playing for Time.* New York: Berkeley Books.

Flam, Gila. (1992). *Singing for Survival: Songs of the Lodz Ghetto, 1940–45.* Chicago: University of Illinois Press.

Friedlander, Albert H. (1968). *Out of the Whirlwind: A Reader of Holocaust Literature.* New York: Doubleday.

Gilbert, Martin. (1985). *The Holocaust.* New York: Holt, Rinehart and Winston.

Hill, Waldemar. (1965). *The People's Songbook.* New York: Oak Publications, 1965.

Kalisch, Shoshana with Meister, Barbara. (Eds.). (1985). *Yes, We Sang! Songs of the Ghettos and Concentration Camps.* New York: Harper and Row.

Karas, Joza. (1985). *Music in Terezin, 1941–1945.* New York: Beaufort Books.

Katz, Jacob. (1986). *Darker Side of Genius: Richard Wagner's Anti-Semitism.* Hanover, NH: University Press of New England for Brandeis University Press.

Kenneally, Thomas. (1983). *Schindler's List.* New York: Penguin.

Kren, George N. & Rappaport, Leon. (1980). *The Holocaust and the Crisis of Human Behavior.* New York: Holmes and Meier.

MacKenzie, Jo-Anne. (1996, April 11). "Confronting Guilt: A Child of the Third Reich Comes to Terms with Her Past." *Rutland Daily Herald,* p. 19.

Mayer, Michael. (1975). "The Nazi Musicologist as Myth Maker in the Third Reich." *Journal of Contemporary History* 10(4):649–665.

Meltzer, Milton. (1976). *Never to Forget: The Jews of the Holocaust.* New York: Harper Collins.

Miller, Arthur. (1981). *Playing for Time.* New York: Bantam.

Mlotek, Eleanor & Gottlieb, Malke. (Eds.). (1983). *We Are Here: Songs of the Holocaust.* New York: Hippocrene Books and Workmen's Circle Education Department.

Rabbiner, Susan. (Ed.). (1993). *Assault on the Arts: Culture and Politics in Nazi Germany, Educator's Guide.* New York: New York Public Library.

Ramati, Alexander. (1986). *And the Violins Stopped Playing: A Story of the Gypsy Holocaust.* New York: Franklin Watts.

Richter, Hans Peter. (1972). *I Was There.* New York: Holt.

Ross, Alex. (1995, August 20). "In Music, Though, There Were No Victories," *New York Times,* Arts and Leisure Section, pp. 25, 31.

Rubin, Ruth. (1973). *Voices of a People.* New York: McGraw-Hill.

Rubin, Ruth. (1965). *Jewish Folksongs in Yiddish and English.* New York: Oak Publications.

Scott, John Anthony. (1994/1995). "The American Revolution Through Its Songs and Ballads." In John Anthony Scott's *Folksong in the Classroom.* Sturbridge, MA: Folksong in the Classroom. (P.O. Box 925, Sturbridge, MA 01566.)

Seeger, Pete, & Reiser, Bob. (1985). *Carry It On! A History in Song and Picture of the Working Men and Women of America.* New York: Simon and Schuster.

Seidman, Laurence I. (1985, October). "Folksongs: Magic in Your Classroom," *Social Education,* 49(7):580–587.

Shaw, Martin & Henry Coleman. (1960). *National Anthems of the World.* New York: Pitman Publishing.

Shirer, William. (1985). *The Nightmare Years, 1930–1940: 20th Century Journey.* New York, Bantam.

Shirer, Willliam. (1960). *The Rise and Fall of the Third Reich.* New York: Simon and Schuster.

Silber, Irwin (Ed.). (1963). *Hootenanny Song Book.* Reprints from *Sing Out! The Folk Magazine.* New York: Consolidated Music Publishers, Inc.

Silverman, Jerry. (1983). *The Yiddish Songbook.* New York: Stein and Day.

Stein, R. Conrad. (1985). *Warsaw Ghetto.* New York: Children's Press.

Steiner, Eric. (1950). *Hebrew Songs.* New York: Mills Music.

Steinhorn, Harriet. (1983). *Shadows of the Holocaust: Plays, Readings, and Program Resources.* New York: Kar-Ben Copies.

Stephens, Elaine C., Brown, Jean E. & Rubin, Janet E. (1995). *Learning About . . . the Holocaust: Literature and Other Resources for Young People.* North Haven, CT: Library Professional Publications.

Szonyi, David M. (1985). *The Holocaust: An Annotated Bibliography and Resource Guide.* New York: KTAV Publishing House.

Talty, Stephan. (1996, February 25). "The Method of a Neo-Nazi Mogul," *New York Times Magazine*, pp. 40, 42–43.

Totten, Samuel. (2000). "'Written in Pencil in the Sealed Railway-Car': Incorporating Poetry into a Study of the Holocaust via Reader Response Theory." In Samuel Totten (Ed.), *Teaching Holocaust Literature.* Boston, MA: Allyn and Bacon.

Volavkova, Hana (Ed.). (1962). ". . . I Never Saw Another Butterfly": Children's Drawings and Poems (Terezin, 1942–44).* New York: McGraw Hill.

Von Hugli, S. & Ischi, B. (Eds.). (1975). *Der Nationalsozialosmus.* Bad Godesberg, Germany: Kultureller Tonbanddienst.

Von Oppen, Beate Ruhm. (1980). "The Intellectual Resistance." In Henry Friedlander and Sybil Milton (Eds.), *The Holocaust: Ideology, Bureaucracy and Genocide* (pp. 207–218). Millwood, NY: Kraus.

Watson, Derek. (1979). *Richard Wagner: A Biography.* New York: Schirmer.

Wiesel, Elie. (1970). *Night.* New York: Bantam Books.

Wolff, Virginia Euwer. (1993). *The Mozart Season.* New York: Scholastic.

Wulffson, Don L. (1970). "Music to Teach Reading," *Journal of Reading,* December. 14(3):179–182.

Yevtushenko, Yevgeny. (1964). *Yevtushenko, Selected Poems.* New York: Penguin Books.

ANNOTATED BIBLIOGRAPHY

Compact Disks:

"Chants. Mystiques." (1995). Available: Poly Gram Group Distribution, 825 Eighth Avenue, New York, NY 10019. Contains pieces representative of three thousand years of traditional Hebrew chants, hidden treasures of a continuing tradition. Includes "Ani Ma'Amin," ["I Believe in the Coming of the Messiah]," which was a chant sung by thousands of Jews as they walked into the gas chambers.

"Entartete Musik" (Degenerate Music). (1994). Available: The Decca Record Co. Ltd., c/o Bayside Distribution, 885 Riverside Parkway, West Sacramento, CA 95605. This combination booklet and CD consists of music by composers suppressed or displaced by the Third Reich 1933–1945. Composers and musicians, Pavel Haas (1899–1944) and Hans Krasa (1899–1944), were brought together by tragic fate in the Terezin Ghetto and both died on October 16, 1944. They played music while in Terezin and also composed new pieces. The Terezin Chamber Music Foundation, founded and directed by Mark Ludwig, has brought their music and the history surrounding it to schools and concert halls. Ludwig is a member of the Boston Symphony Orchestra and the Hawthorne Quartet.

"Is Gewein a Folk, Songs and Dances of the Jews," Vol. 1. (1995). Available: ARC Music US, P.O. Box 11288, Oakland, CA 94611. Includes the instrumental version for one of the most popular Jewish folk dances, the Hora, which traditionally is danced at Jewish weddings and celebrations.

"In the Fiddler's House." (1995). Available: Angel Records, 810 Seventh Avenue, New York, NY 10019. Features Yiddish/Klezmer music played by Brave Old World, Andy Statman Klezmer Orchestra, The Klezmatics and The Klezmer Conservatory Band with violinist Itzhak Perlman. Klezmer is music with an old-world sound. With origins in Eastern Europe, Klezmer music flourished in America among Jewish immigrants early in the twentieth century and also was played by musical groups that were formed in the ghettos.

"Jewish Lullabies." (1992). Available: Brentwood Music, 316 Southgate Court, Inc., Brentwood, TN 37027. Sung in English and interwoven with Yiddish, the German-Hebrew language spoken by Eastern European Jews, many of whom continued to sing these lullabies in the ghettos and concentration camps. English lyrics with transliteration of Yiddish are enclosed. Contains the instrumental version of "Ahf'n Pripitchik" ("On the Hearth") and "Tum-Balalayka" ("Play, Balalaika").

"A Lid for Every Pot." (1995). Available: Tzimmes: 12-719 East 31st Avenue, Vancouver, British Columbia, Canada. Contains "Ofyn Pripetshok" ("On the Hearth"), a lullaby sung in the camps and ghettos.

"Maramaos—The Lost Jewish Music of Transylvania." (1994). Available: United States Holocaust Memorial Museum Shop, P.O. Box 92420, Washington, DC 20090-2420; 1-800-259-9998. The Music of Jewish Klezmers from the Hungarian province of Transylvania thought to have been obliterated along with its performers during the Holocaust. Performed by Hungarian folk ensemble Muzsikas.

"Mordecai Gebirtig—Krakow Ghetto Notebook." (1995). Available: United States Holocaust Memorial Museum Shop, P.O. Box 92420, Washington, DC 20090-2420; 1-800-259-9998. Gebirtig was a Yiddish songwriter murdered in the Krakow Ghetto in 1942. Singer/guitarist Daniel Kempin presents Gebirtig's songs of spiritual resistance discovered in his notebook that survived the war. Includes annotation and translation. (Also available from: The Jewish Book Center of the Workmen's Circle, 45 East 33rd Street, New York, NY 10016; 1-800-922-2558, ext. 285.)

"Old World Beat." (1991). Available: Rounder Records Corp, One Camp Street, Cambridge, MA 02140. The Klezmer Conservatory Band plays the Klezmer music that originated in Eastern Europe and remained alive throughout the Holocaust, in spite of the attempts to eradicate Jewish culture.

"Our Town Is Burning: Cries from the Holocaust" edited by Leon Lishner (1995). Available: The Jewish Book Center of the Workmen's Circle, 45 East 33rd Street, New York, NY 10016; 1-800-922-2558, ext. 285. Contains several songs from the camps and ghettos, including the song in the title "Es Brent" (literally "It Burns") by Mordecai Gebirtig. The song is more commonly referred to as "Our Town (or Shetel) Is Burning."

"Raisins and Almonds." (1995). Available: Omega Record Group, 27 West 72nd Street, New York, NY 10023. New York. Martha Schlamme sings Yiddish and Jewish folksongs, many of which came from Eastern Europe and were sung by Jews in the ghettos.

" 'Remember the Children' ": Songs for and by Children of the Holocaust." (1996). Available: United States Holocaust Memorial Museum Shop, P.O. Box 92420, Washington, DC 20090-2420; 1-800-259-9998. These songs were created and sung by Jews in the ghettos of Eastern Europe during the Holocaust period. They were either dedicated to or written by children who had seen parents suffer. The songs depict the tragic events of the Holocaust and reflect the children's search for comfort in the Yiddish tradition. Includes booklet with words in Yiddish and English.

"Rise Up and Fight." (1997). Available: United States Holocaust Memorial Museum Shop, P.O. Box 92420, Washington, DC 20090-2420; 1-800-259-9998. Theodore Bikel and other folk singers present the spiritual songs of the Eastern European resistance fighters. Comes with an illustrated booklet with words of the songs in Yiddish and English. Includes "Zog Nit Keinmol," ("Never Say You Are Treading the Final Path").

Sidor Belarsky Sings Songs of the Holocaust. (1995). Available: United States Holocaust Memorial Museum Shop, P.O. Box 92420, Washington, DC 20090-2420; 1-800-259-9998.) The late Sidor Belarsky performs songs inspired by the Holocaust. Includes "Zog Nit Keinmol," "The Partisans' Song," and several works by the poet Mordecai Gebirtig. Also available from: The Jewish Book Center of the Workmen's Circle, 45 East 33rd Street, New York, NY 10016; (1-800-922-2558, ext. 285).

"Songs of Our Fathers." (1995). Available: Acoustic Disc, Box 4143, San Rafael, CA 94913. Collection of Yiddish and Hebrew Songs with a thirty-six-page illustrated booklet.

"Symphony No. 13. (Babi Yar)." (1995). Elektra Enterainment, 75 Rockefeller Plaza, New York, NY: This is the symphony by Dmitri Shostakovich that was inspired by Russian poet Yevgeny Yevtushenko's protest poem, "Babi Yar," the name of a ravine near Kiev, in Ukraine, where tens of thousands of Jews were massacred by the German army during World War II.

"Terezin: The Music 1941–1944." (1995). Available: United States Holocaust Memorial Museum Shop, P.O. Box 92420, Washington, DC 20090-2420; 1-800-259-9998. A collection of music from the Terezin Concentration Camp, near Prague, now in the Czech Republic. The recordings include chamber music created at Terezin by Viktor Ullmann, Pavel Haas, and Gideon Klein as well as Hans Krasa's children's opera "Brundibar."

"The Thirteenth Anniversary Album." (1993). Available: Rounder Records Corp, One Camp Street, Cambridge, MA 02140. The Klezmer Conservatory Band "live" playing traditional Klezmer music including the lullaby "Tum Balalayka." Includes a twenty-nine-page booklet of complete texts and transliterations of many of the songs that were sung in the ghettos and survived the Holocaust.

"We Shall Live! Yiddish Songs of the Holocaust." (1995). Available: The Jewish Book Center of the Workmen's Circle, 45 East 33rd Street, New York, NY 10016, 1-800-922-2558, ext. 285. As indicated by the title, this is a collection of songs that came out of the Holocaust. Includes words in Yiddish and English.

Cassette Tapes:

"Der Nationalsozialismus." (National Socialism or Nazism) (1975). Available: Inter Nationes, Audiotape Service, 5300 Bonn-Bad Godesberg, Kennedyallee 91–103, Germany. A series of cassette tapes and booklets. Number two contains Band #3, "Hitler in the Political Arena," in which S. von Hugli, and B. Ischi, present the actual songs and music played and sung during the Third Reich, songs that were intended to inspire nationalistic and antisemitic attitudes.

Williams on Williams. (1995). Available: SONY Music Entertainment, Inc., 550 Madison Avenue, New York, NY 10022. John Williams and the Boston Pops Orchestra play "The Classic Spielberg Scores." It includes the film score for *Schindler's List*, the film based on the Thomas Kenneally book about Oskar Schindler, the German industrialist who helped over a thousand Jews survive the Holocaust.

Films/Videos:

Playing for Time. (148 minutes, color. The film is available in most video stores.) Produced in 1980, this is the true story of Fania Fenelon and a group of women prisoners in Auschwitz who survived by forming a small orchestra and performing for Nazi officers. Vanessa Redgrave plays the role of Fenelon.

Music of Auschwitz. (Sixteen minutes; available for purchase or rental from The Anti-Defamation League, 823 United Nations Plaza, New York, NY 10017.) In this "60 Minutes" segment originally televised over CBS-TV, newsman Morley Safer accompanies Auschwitz survivor Fania Fenelon on her return to the Auschwitz concentration camp.

Drama/Plays

Miller, Arthur. (1981). *Playing for Time.* New York: Bantam. This play, by the noted American playwright Arthur Miller, is based on the book and life of Fania Fenelon, who survived the death camp because of her role as a musician in the Women's Orchestra at Auschwitz-Birkenau in Poland. The book delineates characters and their speaking parts and thus can be used in class readings or role playing.

Song Books That Contain Holocaust-Related Songs

Hill, Waldemar. (1965). *The People's Songbook.* New York: Oak Publications. Contains "Peat Bog Soldiers," words and music, which has been mentioned frequently in this chapter as an example of a song created by inmates of a concentration camp.

Shaw, Martin and Henry Coleman. (1960). *National Anthems of the World.* New York: Pitman Publishing. Contains the modern version of the German national anthem, "Deutschland Über Alles," as well as national anthems from many other countries. It includes the music as well as the words in English.

Silber, Irwin (Ed.). (1963). *Hootenanny Song Book.* Reprints from *Sing Out: The Folk Magazine.* New York: Consolidated Music Publishers. Contains "Ofyn Pripetshok" (pp. 134–135), which is included in this chapter. It contains the music as well as words.

Silverman, Jerry. (1983). *The Yiddish Songbook.* New York: Stein and Day. Contains Yiddish songs that span two centuries, including twelve songs from the Holocaust period.

Books:

Flam, Gila. (1992). *Singing for Survival. Songs of the Lodz Ghetto, 1940–45.* Chicago: University of Illinois Press. This is a collection of the songs created and performed in the Lodz Ghetto of Poland during the Holocaust. Flam draws on interviews with survivors.

Kalisch, Shoshana with Barbara Meister (Eds.). (1985). *Yes, We Sang! Songs of the Ghettos and Concentration Camps.* New York: Harper and Row. Includes nearly all of the Holocaust-related songs referred to in this essay along with the background of each one.

Rubin, Ruth. (1973). *Voices of a People: The Story of Yiddish Folksong*. New York: McGraw-Hill. Includes songs and commentary about the origin, meaning, and background of over five hundred Yiddish folk songs—all are translated into English. Among them are songs sung during the Holocaust. The latter include a history of the pogroms and concentration camps. Also available from the Jewish Book Center of the Workmen's Circle, 45 East 33rd Street, New York, NY 10016; 1-800-422-2558, ext. 285.

Units/Teacher Resource Guides

Belsky, Gilbert. (1979). *The Holocaust: A Teacher Resource*. Philadelphia, PA: Philadelphia School District. Unit 5 of this secondary curriculum is entitled "Jewish Resistance to the Holocaust," (pp. 71–94) and includes "The Strength to Survive Is Expressed in Yiddish Music" (pp. 89–93). Several of the songs mentioned in this essay, including "Zog Nit Keinmol" ("Never Say You are Treading the Final Path"), a partisan song, are contained in this unit. [Available on ERIC microfiche, #ED224733.]

Rabbiner, Susan (Ed.). (1993). *Assault on the Arts: Culture and Politics in Nazi Germany*. New York: New York Public Library. This is an Educator's Guide and includes the German version of the song, "You (Our) Dear Führer" ("Du Lieber Führer du").

Seidman, Laurence I. (1985, October). "Folksongs: Magic in Your Classroom," *Social Education 49*(7):580–587. Although the focus of this article is not on Holocaust music, it includes a strong rationale for including music into the extant curriculum, as well as a solid discussion of several instructional strategies for incorporating songs in the teaching of different subject matter.

Annotated Bibliography

Szonyi, David M. (1985). *The Holocaust: An Annotated Bibliography and Resource Guide*. New York: KTAV Publishing House, Inc. for the National Jewish Resource Center. Section III, pp. 223–251, "Jewish Music Resources for Holocaust Programming," contains an extensive guide to a wide variety of music suitable for performances in commemoration of the Holocaust, including materials by the victims and survivors themselves.

Adjunct Material

Steinhorn, Harriet. (1983). *Shadows of the Holocaust: Plays, Readings and Program Resources*. New York: Kar-Ben Copies. A wide selection of short pieces that could be utilized by teachers/students interested in preparing dramatic and musical presentations about the Holocaust or in commemoration of its victims.

Holocaust Chronology

From Acquisition of Power to Nuremberg Trials 1933–1946

COMPILED BY STEPHEN FEINBERG

1933

January 30	Hitler appointed Chancellor of Germany by President Paul von Hindenburg
February 3	Hitler secretly addresses leaders of the German armed forces, outlining the aims of the new Germany
February 27	*Reichstag* fire
February 28	Civil and basic constitutional rights in Germany suspended by the Reichstag
March 5	*Reichstag* elections; Nazis win 44 percent of the vote
March 6	Emergency degree, "For The Protection of the German People," restricts opposition press and information services
March 13	Josef Goebbels becomes Reich Minister of Public Enlightment and Propaganda
March 22	First concentration camp opens at Dachau
March 24	"Enabling Law" passed by Reichstag; used to establish dictatorship. Henceforth, Hitler ruler by decree
April 1	Nationwide boycott of Jewish-owned businesses
April 7	Jews excluded from government employment; includes teachers and university professors
April 26	Gestapo (Geheime Staatspolizei) begins functioning as a state-sanctioned terror organization
May 2	Dissolution of free trade unions
May 10	Public burning of books written by Jews and opponents of Nazis
July 14	Nazi party (NSDAP) declared the only political party in Germany
July 14	"Law for the Prevention of Progency with Hereditary Diseases" (sterilization law) enacted
July 20	Concordat signed in Rome between the Vatican and the Third Reich

September 17	*"Reichsvertretung der Deutschen Juden"* (Reich Representation of German Jewry) established
October 14	German withdrawal from the League of Nations
December 1	Legal unity of German state and Nazi Party declared

1934

January 26	Ten-year nonaggression pact signed with Poland
January 30	"Law for the Reorganization of the Reich" strips German states of their sovereignty
March 21	Hitler initiates the *"Arbeitsschlacht"* (Battle for Work), emphasizing the necessity of employing jobless citizens
April 20	Himmler appointed head of the Gestapo
April 22	Reinhard Heydrich becomes head of the Gestapo central office
June 30	"Night of the Long Knives"; SA is purged
July 1	Ernst Röhm, head of the SA, is murdered
July 20	SS established as an organization independent from the SA
August 2	Death of President von Hindenburg; Hitler declares himself Führer of the German state; armed forces are required to take a personal oath of loyalty to Hitler
September 3–10	Nuremberg Party Day; filming of Leni Riefenstahl's *Triumph of the Will*

1935

March 16	In violation of Treaty of Versailles, military conscription introduced; no response from other powers
April 1	Jehovah's Witnesses banned from civil service jobs; many arrested throughout Germany
April 30	Nazi decree forbids Jews from exhibiting the German flag
July 16	Reich Interior Minister Frick instructs registrars not to solemnize any more "mixed marriages"
September 15	Swastika becomes part of official flag of the Third Reich
September 15	Nuremberg Laws announced at Nuremberg Party Days; Jews deprived of citizenship and racial laws promulgated
October 1	German Propaganda Ministry, to avoid offending Arabs, explains that Nazism is anti-Jewish rather than antisemitic
November 26	Prohibition of racially mixed marriages ("Law for the Protection of German Blood and Honor") applied to "Gypsies" and persons of African heritage
December 13	*Lebensborn* ("Spring of Life") organization founded by the SS

1936

| March 3 | Jewish doctors no longer permitted to practice in government institutions in Germany |
| March 7 | Nazi army enters Rhineland in violation of Treaty of Versailles; no response from other powers |

March 26	Jews no longer permitted to run or lease a pharmacy
June 17	Himmler appointed head of German police *(Reichsfuhrer-SS und Chef der Deutschen Polizei)*
June 26	Himmler merges the Gestapo and the Criminal Police into the Security Police under Heydrich
July 12	First arrest of German Gypsies; sent to Dachau
August 1	In anticipation of 1936 Olympic Games in Berlin, antisemitic signs removed from most public places
August 28	Mass arrest of Jehovah's Witnesses
October 25	Rome-Berlin Axis agreement signed

1937

March 14	Publication of the Papal Encyclical *Mit brennender Sorge (With Burning Sorrow)* denouncing Nazi persecution of the church and clergymen
July 19	Establishment of Buchenwald concentration camp (originally called Ettersberg); most early inmates are political prisoners
August 19	Jews in Germany may only patronize Jewish-owned bookstores, while owners are forbidden to sell works by Aryan authors
September 7	Hitler declares end of Treaty of Versailles
November 25	Political and military pact signed by Germany and Japan

1938

March 13	Austria is annexed by Germany; "Anschluss"
July 6–15	Thirty-two countries at Evian Conference discuss refugee policies; most countries refuse to let in more Jewish refugees
August 17	All Jewish men in Germany required to add "Israel" to their names; all Jewish women required to add "Sarah"
Sept. 26– Oct. 8	Seventeen thousand Jews with Polish citizenship are expelled from the German Reich, and transported to the Polish border
September 29	Munich Agreement is signed
November 7	Shooting of Ernst vom Rath in Paris by Herschel Grynszpan, a Polish Jew, whose family was forcibly deported from Germany
November 9–10	"Kristallnacht," a nationwide pogrom; thirty thousand Jews sent to concentration camps (ten thousand to Buchenwald)
November 12	Fine of one billion reichsmarks levied on Jews of Germany
November 15	All Jewish children expelled from public schools
December 2–3	Gypsies in Germany required to register with police

1939

January 24	Goring instructs Frick to establish a Reich Central Office for Jewish Emigration; Heydrich appointed Director
January 30	In a speech to the Reichstag, Hitler threatens that another war will mean the "extermination of the Jewish race in Europe"

March 15	Germans invade Czechoslovakia; no immediate response from other powers
May 15	Ravensbruck concentration camp for women established
June	Jewish refugees aboard the S.S. St. Louis denied entry to the United States and Cuba; forced to return to Europe
August 23	Hitler-Stalin Pact signed
August 25	Polish-British treaty
September 1	Germany invades Poland; World War II begins
September 2	Stutthof concentration camp established in Poland
September 3	Britain and France declare war on Germany
September 21	Reinhard Heydrich (SS) orders establishment of Judenräte and concentration of Polish Jews
September 28	Partition of Poland between Germany and USSR
October	Hitler authorizes "euthanasia program" (T-4) in Germany; doctors to kill institutionalized mentally and physically handicapped
October 8	First Polish ghetto established in Piotrkow Trybunalski
November 8	Failure of the attempt of Johann Georg Elser to assassinate Hitler in Munich

1940

January	First gassing of mentally handicapped
February 8	Establishment of Lodz Ghetto ordered
April 9	Germans invade Denmark; Danes continue to govern
April 27	Himmler (SS) orders establishment of Auschwitz concentration camp (Auschwitz I); first prisoners, mostly Poles, arrive in early June; Rudolf Höss appointed commandant
April 30	Lodz Ghetto, first enclosed ghetto, is sealed
April–May	Twenty-five hundred Sinti and Roma deported from Reich to Poland
Spring	Germans conquer Denmark, Norway, Belgium, Luxembourg, Holland, and France
September 27	Berlin-Rome-Tokyo Axis is established
October 3	Anti-Jewish laws passed by Vichy government in France
November 15	Warsaw Ghetto is sealed

1941

January 10	Dutch Jews required to register with police
March	Himmler orders construction of camp at Birkenau (Auschwitz II); construction begins in October 1941 and continues until March 1942
March 3	Krakow Ghetto established
March 24	Germans invade North Africa
April 6	Germans invade Yugoslavia and Greece
April 24	Lublin Ghetto is sealed
June 22	Operation "Barbarossa"; Germans invade the USSR

June 23	Einstazgruppen begin their mass murder of Jews, Gypsies, and communist leaders in the USSR
July 20	Minsk Ghetto established
July 24	Kishinev Ghetto established
July 31	Hermann Göring gives Reinhard Heydrich the authority to prepare a "final solution" to the "Jewish question" in Europe
August 1	Bialystok Ghetto established
August 24	"Euthanasia program" (T-4) in Germany officially halted, but unofficially continued; between seventy thousand and ninety-three thousand people had been murdered during the course of this program
September 3	The first experimental gassing of Soviet prisoners of war at Auschwitz
September 3–6	Two ghettos established at Vilna
September 19	German Jews required to war yellow badge in public
September 29–30	At Babi Yar, 33,771 Kiev Jews murdered
Oct–Nov	First deportation of German and Austrian Jews to ghettos in Eastern Europe
October	Construction of Majdanek-Lublin extermination camp
October 15	Start of the mass deportation of Jews from the Reich to ghettos in Kovno, Lodz, Minsk, and Riga
November 1	Construction of Belzec extermination camp begins
November 24	Theresienstadt (Terezin) concentration camp established
Nov–Dec	Medical experiments begin at Buchenwald
December 7	Japan attacks Pearl Harbor
December 8	Gassing operations begin at Chelmo extermination camp; vans are used
December 11	Germany and Italy declare war on the United States

1942

January	Deportations from Theresienstadt to ghettos (Riga, Warsaw, Lodz, Minsk, and Bialystok) in the East begin
January 20	Wannsee Conference; coordination of the "Final Solution" planned
February 8	First Jews from Salonika, Greece sent to Auschwitz
March 1	Construction of Sobibor extermination camp begins; Jews first killed there in May 1942
March 17	Killings begin at Belzec extermination camp
March 27	First Jews from France sent to Auschwitz
April 29	Dutch Jews ordered to wear yellow badge
April 30	Pinsk Ghetto established
June 7	Jews in occupied France ordered to wear yellow badge
July	Removal of non-Jewish population from Theresienstadt (Terezin) completed

July 15–16   First transports of Dutch Jews to Auschwitz

July 22   Treblinka extermination camp completed; by August 1943, 870,000 Jews murdered at Treblinka

July 22–   Mass deportations from Warsaw Ghetto to Treblinka
Sept. 12

July 28   Jewish fighting organization set up in Warsaw Ghetto

September   Completion of Monowitz (Auschwitz III), the I.G. Farben "Buna" synthetic oil and rubber factory

October   Deportations of Jews from Theresienstadt to Auschwitz and Treblinka begin

October 16   Over one thousand Roman Jews are deported to Auschwitz

November 24   Knowledge of the extermination of the Jews of Europe publicly announced by Rabbi Stephen S. Wise

1943

January 18–22 Jewish Fighting Organization offers armed resistance to deportation of five thousand Jews from Warsaw to Treblinka

February 2   Germans defeated at Battle of Stalingrad

February 26   First transport of Gypsies arrive at Auschwitz; Gypsy Camp established

March   Gustloff armaments works, a large factory producing aircraft parts, constructed at Buchenwald

April 19–   Warsaw Ghetto uprising; Jews resist Germans' effort to deport
May 16   them to death camps

June 21   Himmler orders the complete and final liquidation of all ghettos in the Ostland

August 2   Inmate uprising at Treblinka extermination camp

August 16   Revolt in Bialystok Ghetto

October 2   Germans attempt round-up of Danish Jews; Danish people use boats to smuggle most Danish Jews (seventy-two hundred) to neutral Sweden

October 14   Inmate revolt at Sobibor extermination camp

October 20   United Nations War Crimes Commission established

1944

March 19   Germans occupy Hungary

April 7   Alfred Wetzler and Rudolf Vrba escape from Auschwitz with detailed information about the extermination of the Jews; their report, from Slovakia, reaches the free world in June

May 2   First transport of Hungarian Jews reach Auschwitz; by July 9, over 437,000 Hungarian Jews are sent to Auschwitz; most of them are gassed upon arrival

June 6   Allied invasion of Normandy

July 20   Unsuccessful attempt made to assassinate Hitler

July 23   International Red Cross visit to Theresienstadt (Terezin)

July 24	Soviet army liberates Majdanek extermination camp
August 2	Gypsy camp at Auschwitz destroyed by Nazis; three thousand Gypsies gassed
October 6	Prisoners blow up one of the gas chambers at Auschwitz-Birkenau extermination camp

1945

January 17	Germans forcibly evacuate prisoners of Auschwitz on "death marches"
January 27	Soviet army liberates Auschwitz
April 11	Buchenwald "self-liberated" and liberated by the American army
April 15	British army liberates Bergen-Belsen concentration camp
April 28	Mussolini executed by Italian partisans
April 29	American army liberates Dachau concentration camp
April 30	Ravensbruck concentration camp liberated
April 30	Hitler commits suicide in Berlin
May 2	Soviet troops capture Berlin
May 3	Germans hand over Theresienstadt (Terezin) to the International Red Cross
May 5	American army liberates Mauthausen concentration camp
May 7	Nazi Germany surrenders; end of World War II in Europe
May 8	Theresienstadt (Terezin) liberated by Soviet troops
August 14	Japan surrenders; end of World War II
November 20	First major Nuremberg War Crimes Trials begin

1946

October 1	Conclusion of first major Nuremberg Trials; twelve Nazis to be executed, three sentenced to life imprisonment, four receive various prison terms, and three are acquitted
October 16	Execution of Nazi war criminals

SOURCES

Edelheit, Hershel & Abraham J. Edelheit. (1991). *A World in Turmoil: An Integrated Chronology of the Holocaust and World War II*. Westport, CT: Greenwood Press.

Gutman, Israel (Ed.). (1995). *Encyclopedia of the Holocaust*. New York: Macmillan.

Hilberg, Raul. (1985). *The Destruction of the European Jews*. New York: Holmes and Meier.

Kirk, Tim. (1995). *The Longman Companion to Nazi Germany*. London: Longman Group Limited.

Reitlinger, Gerald. (1953). *The Final Solution: The Attempts to Exterminate the Jews of Europe 1939–1945*. New York: Beechhurst Press.

APPENDIX B

Holocaust History, Film, Education, and Other Resources

A Select Annotated Bibliography

COMPILED BY SAMUEL TOTTEN AND STEPHEN FEINBERG

Note: In light of the fact that select annotated bibliographies accompany the chapters on art, first-person accounts, and music of the Holocaust (as well as one of the chapters on literature of the Holocaust), most publications germane to those subjects are not included in this select bibliography.

JOURNALS

Dimensions: A Journal of Holocaust Studies (published by the Anti-Defamation League's Braun Center for Holocaust Studies, New York City). An outstanding journal that regularly includes historical and, less often, pedagogical essays on various aspects of the Holocaust. The historical essays are often relatively short, highly readable, and ideal for use in the classroom.

Holocaust and Genocide Studies (published three times a year by Oxford University Press in association with the United States Holocaust Memorial Museum). An outstanding scholarly journal that regularly includes essays and book reviews on a wide variety of issues related to the Holocaust and other genocidal issues/events.

Journal of Holocaust Education (formerly the *British Journal of Holocaust Education*, this journal is published Frank Cass and Co., Limited, Ilford, Essex, England). This journal generally includes a mix of both historical and pedagogical pieces on various aspects of the Holocaust.

NEWSLETTERS

Martyrdom and Resistance (published by the International Society for Yad Vashem, 500 Fifth Avenue, Suite 1600, New York, NY 10110-1699). This newsletter (which is printed in a newspaper format) generally includes news about the work of the International Society for Yad Vashem, book reviews on various aspects of the Holocaust, information about survivor groups, general pieces on diverse aspects of the history and related issues, and an overview of campus and classroom activities vis-à-vis Holocaust education.

BIBLIOGRAPHIES

Cargas, Harry James. (Ed.). (1985). *The Holocaust: An Annotated Bibliography.* Chicago, IL: American Library Association. 196 pp. This bibliography addresses a wide array of topics/issues germane to the Holocaust. Although it is now dated, it is still a useful resource.

Darsa, Jan. (1991). "Educating about the Holocaust." In Israel Charny (Ed.), *Genocide: A Critical Bibliographic Review, Vol. 2* (pp. 175–193). London and New York: Mansell Publishers and Facts on File. Includes a thought-provoking essay and an annotated bibliography of key works on the subject of teaching about the Holocaust.

Drew, Margaret. (1988). *Facing History and Ourselves: Holocaust and Human Behavior: Annotated Bibliography.* New York: Walker and Company, 1988. 124 pp. Although dated, this bibliography, designed specifically for use by educators, is still a useful reference. The bibliography includes and "describes those books, from the profusion of Holocaust materials, that best explore the wide range of human responses to the Holocaust, on the part of victims, victimizers, and rescuers." It is divided into five key parts, including "Children's Books" and "Adult Books." It also includes useful appendices, including A. Basic Readings Lists; B. Literature as History; C. Legacy of the Holocaust: A Supplementary Reading List; and D. Human Behavior: A Supplementary Reading List.

Edelheit, Abraham, and Hershel Edelheit. (1986). *Bibliography on Holocaust Literature.* Boulder, CO: Westview Press. 842 pp. A massive bibliography that includes sections on life in prewar Europe, antisemitism, fascism, Nazism, the extermination of the Jews, and the aftermath of the Holocaust.

Edelheit, Abraham, and Hershel Edelheit (Eds.). (1990). *Bibliography on Holocaust Literature: Supplement.* Boulder, CO: Westview Press. 684 pp. A valuable and updated addition to the original bibliography.

Roskies, Diane K. (1975). *Teaching the Holocaust to Children: A Review and Bibliography.* New York: KTAV Publishing House Inc. 65 pp. An early and interesting bibliography that includes information on the following: Methodology, Pedagogical Issues, School Curricula, and Children's Literature. In her conclusion, Roskies addresses issues that she thinks curriculum developers and teachers need to consider when developing units of study on the Holocaust: antisemitism, life and death in the ghettos, East European Jewry, death and historical time, and physical resistance. The booklet concludes with a lengthy bibliography of pedagogical articles, curricula for children at the elementary and secondary levels, children's literature, and analytical pieces about various Holocaust curricula. Although dated, this short bibliography still includes much that is useful.

Shulman, William L. (Ed.). (1998). "Holocaust: Resource Guide—A Comprehensive Listing of Media for Further Study." Volume 8 in *Holocaust.* Woodbridge, CT: Blackbirch Press, Inc. 80 pp. This annotated bibliography is divided into four main parts: (1) Bibliography (General Reference Works; European Jewry Before the Holocaust;

The Holocaust: A General Overview; Country/Cultural Studies; Germany, Hitler, and the Rise of Nazism; Ghettos; Concentration and Extermination Camps; Resistance; Rescue; Perpetrators, Bystanders, and Collaborators; Other Victims of Nazi Persecution; Liberation and Judgment; Memoirs and Diaries; Survivors and the Generation After; Antisemitism; Specialized Studies); (2) Illustrated Books (which includes books on art about the Holocaust); Videos; (3) Web Sites and CD-ROMs; and (4) Museums and Resource Centers.

Szonyi, David M. (1985). *The Holocaust: An Annotated Bibliography and Resource Guide.* New York: KTAV Publishing House. 396 pp. Although dated, teachers are likely to find this bibliography to be of some use. Among the sections in the book are: Scholarship, Memoirs, and Other Nonfiction of the Holocaust; Literature of the Holocaust; Bibliographies on the Holocaust for Young People; Audio-Visual Materials on the Holocaust; An Introduction to High School Holocaust Curricula; Teacher Development; and Oral History with Holocaust Survivors.

Totten, Samuel. (1991). "First-Person Accounts of the Holocaust." In Samuel Totten (Ed.), *First-Person Accounts of Genocidal Acts Committed in the Twentieth Century: An Annotated Bibliography* (pp. 91–273). Westport, CT: Greenwood Press. Contains hundreds of annotations of diaries, letters, memoirs, autobiographies, oral histories, and video accounts.

Trynauer, Gabrielle. (Ed.). (1989). *Gypsies and the Holocaust: A Bibliography and Introductory Essay.* Montreal: Interuniversity Centre for European Studies & Montreal Institute for Genocide Studies. 51 pp. This landmark bibliography includes a wide range of works on the genocide of the Gypsies by the Nazis.

United States Holocaust Memorial Museum. (1993a). *Annotated* [Holocaust] *Bibliography.* Washington, DC: Author. 31 pp. Contains three distinct sections (middle level, high school, and adult) on general history, specialized history, biographies, fiction, memoirs, art, and general history.

United States Holocaust Memorial Museum. (1993b). *Annotated* [Holocaust] *Videography.* Washington, DC: Author. 13 pp. Includes annotations on films that address overviews of the Holocaust, life before the Holocaust, propaganda, racism and antisemitism, "enemies of the state," ghettos, camps, genocide, rescue, resistance, responses, perpetrators, liberation, post-Holocaust, Anne Frank, Janusz Korczak, and related films.

GENERAL REFERENCE TOOLS: ATLASES, DICTIONARIES, ENCYCLOPEDIAS, AND HANDBOOKS

Edelheit, Abraham J., and Hershel Edelheit (Eds.). (1994). *History of the Holocaust: A Handbook and Dictionary.* Boulder, CO: Westview Press. 524 pp. An extremely useful tool for educators and researchers, this volume is comprised of the following: Part I. History of the Holocaust (1. Antecedents; 2. World War I and Its Aftermath; 3. The Nazi Totalitarian State; 4. The Shoa; 5. The Geography of the Holocaust; 6. Jewish Responses to Persecution; 7. Jewish-Gentile Relations in Extremis; 8. International Responses; 9. Aftermath and Recovery); and Part II. Dictionary of Holocaust Terms.

Both the history (pp. 3–157) and the definitions of the terms (pp. 161–460) are highly informative.

Edelheit, Hershel and Abraham Edelheit. (1991). *World in Turmoil: An Integrated Chronology of the Holocaust and World War II.* Westport, CT: Greenwood Press. 450 pp. Spanning sixteen years, this extensive chronology includes events related to the Third Reich, the Holocaust, and World War II.

Epstein, Eric Joseph, and Philip Rosen. (1997). *Dictionary of the Holocaust: Biography, Geography, and Terminology.* Westport, CT: Greenwood Press. 416 pp. This volume is comprised of two thousand entries on major personalities, concentration and death camps, cities and countries, and significant events. It includes important terms translated from German, French, Polish, Yiddish, and twelve other languages. Biographical entries provide a brief overview of the individual and their place and/or significance vis-à-vis the period.

Friedman, Saul S. (Ed.). (1993). *Holocaust Literature: A Handbook of Critical, Historical, and Literary Writings.* Westport, CT: Greenwood Press. 677 pp. This text is divided into three sections: "Conceptual Approaches to the Holocaust," "Holocaust Area Studies," and "The Holocaust in Education and the Arts." The collection includes reflective essays by such individuals as Nora Levin ("The Relationship of Genocide to Holocaust Studies"), Shmuel Krakowski ("Relations Between Jews and Poles during the Holocaust"), and Henry James Cargas ("The Holocaust in Fiction").

Gilbert, Martin. (1991). *Atlas of the Holocaust.* New York: Pergamon Press. 256 pp. Included in this volume are 316 maps drawn by the noted historian Martin Gilbert. The atlas traces each phase of the Holocaust, starting with the antisemitic violence of prewar Germany, the ever-increasing discrimination against the Jews, and, finally, the genocide carried out in the death camps and elsewhere. More specifically, "set out herein is the spread of the early random killings, the systematic mass expulsion from thousands of towns and villages, the establishment of ghettos, the deliberate starvation of Jews trapped in these ghettos, the setting up of the death camps, the distant deportation to those camps, the slave-labour camp system, the death marches and the executions from the time of Germany's military domination to the very last days of the Allied liberation." Each map is fully annotated and based on documentary evidence from a wide range of sources. An excellent resource for use in the classroom.

Gutman, Israel (Ed.). (1995). *Encyclopedia of the Holocaust.* New York: Macmillan. Four volumes. 1,905 pp. A massive and major work, this four-part set (which is divided into two large volumes) contains entries on a wide array of critical issues by some of the most noted scholars of the Holocaust. Highly recommended for the serious student of Holocaust history.

Overy, Richard. (1996). *The Penguin Atlas of the Third Reich.* New York: Penguin. 143 pp. Making use of both maps and charts, this atlas delineates the rise and fall of Nazi Germany. It addresses a remarkably wide range of issues germane to the political, cultural, and social history of the Third Reich.

United States Holocaust Memorial Museum. (1996). *Historical Atlas of the Holocaust.* Washington, DC. 252 pp. An essential tools for teachers, the atlas presents the story of the Holocaust in more than 230 full color maps in all its specific geographical details. Maps and text explain the physical facts of the deportations, concentration camps, and the extermination of the victims of the Nazi state.

Wistrich, Robert. (1995). *Who's Who in Nazi Germany.* New York: Routledge. 312 pp. A readable and useful compilation of brief biographies of individuals who influenced wide-ranging aspects of life in Nazi Germany.

Wyman, David S. (1996). *The World Reacts to the Holocaust.* Baltimore, MD: Johns Hopkins University Press. 981 pp. A major work that chronicles the impact of the Holocaust in the post-World War II world. It includes information on twenty-two countries and explores the difficulties and controversies involved in the efforts of various nations to come to terms with the Holocaust.

REFERENCE AND HISTORICAL WORKS SPECIFICALLY FOR SECONDARY LEVEL STUDENTS

Altshuler, David. (1978). *Hitler's War against the Jews—The Holocaust: A Young Reader's Version of the War against the Jews 1933–1945 by Lucy Dawidowicz.* West Orange, NJ: Behrman House. 190 pp. Although this is a truncated and simplified version of Dawidowicz' text, it remains true to the original work. For young people, it provides a good overview of the history of the Holocaust.

Bachrach, Susan D. (1994). *Tell Them We Remember: The Story of the Holocaust.* Boston, MA: Little, Brown and Company. 109 pp. A well-written and accurate history of the Holocaust appropriate for a younger audience (upper elementary, middle level, and junior high school students). It is highly readable and packed with photos that complement the text.

Bauer, Yehuda with Nili Keren. (1982). *A History of the Holocaust.* Danbury, CT: Franklin Watts. 398 pp. Coauthored by a highly respected Israeli historian and an Israeli teacher educator, this volume presents a solid examination of the history of the Holocaust. It is comprised of fourteen chapters: 1. Who Are the Jews; 2. Liberalism, Emancipation and Antisemitism; 3. World War I and Its Aftermath; 4. The Weimar Republic; 5. The Evolution of Nazi Jewish Policy, 1933–1938; 6. German Jewry in the Prewar Era, 1933–1938; 7. Poland—The Siege Begins; 8. Life in the Ghettos; 9. The "Final Solution"; 10. West European Jewry, 1940–1944; 11. Resistance; 12. Rescue; 13. The Last Years of the Holocaust, 1943–1945; and 14. Aftermath and Revival.

Berenbaum, Michael. (1993). *The World Must Know: The History of the Holocaust as Told in the United States Holocaust Memorial Museum.* Boston, MA: Little, Brown and Company. 240 pp. Written by the former Director of Research at the United States Holocaust Memorial Museum, this is an engaging and highly readable historical work that is thoroughly accessible to secondary-level students. Color and black-and-white photographs complement the text. *Highly recommended as a class text for a high school course on the Holocaust.*

Friedman, Ina R. (1990). *The Other Victims: First-Person Stories of Non-Jews Persecuted by the Nazis.* Boston, MA: Houghton Mifflin Company. 214 pp. Specifically written for students in grades five through nine, this volume includes first-person accounts about individuals such as a Gypsy, a Jehovah's Witness, a deaf person, a Czech schoolboy, a Christian and Jewish couple, a dissenter, and a young boy who was forced into slave labor.

Gilbert, Martin. (1987). *The Holocaust: A History of the Jews of Europe during the Second World War.* New York: Henry Holt and Company. 959 pp. A powerful book in which Gilbert interweaves first-person testimony throughout the text in order to illustrate the impact that the Nazis' policy had on individuals and communities.

Hilberg, Raul. (1985). *The Destruction of the European Jews.* Student Edition. New York: Holmes & Meier. 360 pp. This is the student edition of Hilberg's highly acclaimed three-volume set, *The Destruction of the European Jews.* Commenting on the three-volume set, Holocaust scholar David Wyman asserted that it constitutes "the standard text in the field."

Kirk, Tim. (1994). *The Longman Companion to Nazi Germany.* Reading, MA: Addison-Wesley. 277 pp. A compilation of facts and commentary about German society, culture, and economy during the Nazi period. It includes a useful glossary, concise biographies, and an annotated bibliography.

KEY HISTORICAL WORKS

Books

Bartov, Omer. (1992). *Hitler's Army: Soldiers, Nazis, and War in the Third Reich.* New York: Oxford University Press. 238 pp. A provocative book that challenges the view that the Wehrmacht was an apolitical professional fighting force, having little to do with the Nazi party and the fulfillment of Nazi racial policy.

Berenbaum, Michael, & Peck, Abraham J. (Eds.). (1998). *The Holocaust and History: The Known, The Unknown, The Disputed, and The Reexamined.* Bloomington and Indianapolis: Indiana University Press. 836 pp. This is an outstanding collection of fifty-four essays by noted scholars such as Raul Hilberg, Yehuda Bauer, Michael R. Marrus, Hans Mommsen, Christopher R. Browning, Henry Friedlander, Sybil Milton, Randolph L. Brahm, Susan S. Zuccotti, and Nechama Tec. The book is comprised of eleven parts, each of which includes a series of essays: Probing the Holocaust: Where We Are, Where We Need to Go; Antisemitism and Racism in Nazi Ideology; The Politics of Racial Health and Science; The Nazi State: Leadership and Bureaucracy; "Ordinary Men": The Sociopolitical Background; Multiple Voices: Ideology, Exclusion and Coercion; Concentration Camps: Their Task and Environment; The Axis, the Allies, and the Neutrals; Jewish Leadership, Jewish Resistance; The Rescuers; and The Survivor Experience.

Berenbaum, Michael. (Ed.). (1990). *A Mosaic of Victims: Non-Jews Persecuted and Murdered by the Nazis.* New York: New York University Press. 244 pp. This book includes a series of highly readable and informative essays on non-Jewish victims of the Nazis, including Gypsies, Poles, other Slavs, Soviet prisoners of war, non-Jewish children, Jehovah's Witnesses, pacifists, and homosexuals. A particularly outstanding essay for use in a high school classroom is Konnilyn Feig's "Non-Jewish Victims in the Concentration Camps."

Bratton, Fred Gladstone. (1994). *The Crime of Christendom: The Theological Sources of Christian Anti-Semitism.* Santa Barbara, CA: Fithian Press. 241 pp. A very accessible and easy to read account of the theological foundations and the growth of Christian antisemitism.

Breitman, Richard. (1991). *The Architect of Genocide: Himmler and the Final Solution.* Hanover, NH: Brandeis University Press and the University Press of New England. 335 pp. Based on a wide array of sources—many of them used in a historical study for the first time—Breitman "conclusively counters efforts to portray the Holocaust as unpremeditated, the result of bureaucratic improvisations under wartime constraints. . . . He finds Himmler and Hitler to be complementary figures: Hitler envisioned the Nazi policy toward the Jews, and Himmler, the master organizer who controlled the SS and security forces, turned it into horrific reality." Noted Holocaust scholar Yehuda Bauer asserts that it is "a truly path-breaking book, one of the few that will have a lasting impact on historical research of the period. It shows both the primacy of Hitler as the motivating force in the mass murder, and the way in which his initiatives were accepted and internalized by the SS, on the basis of ideology."

Breitman, Richard. (1998). *Official Secrets: What the Nazis Planned, What the British and Americans Knew.* New York: Hill and Wang. 325 pp. Integrating new evidence with known sources, Breitman examines how Germany's leaders initiated and implemented the Holocaust and when they did so. At the same time, he assesses the British and American suppression of information about Nazi killings and the tensions between the two powers over how to respond. Much of the information used in this study was culled from previously marked "top secret" files in British archives.

Browning, Christopher R. (1992). *Ordinary Men: Reserve Police Battalion 101 and the Final Solution in Poland.* New York: HarperCollins. 231 pp. Deemed "a truly pioneering study" by Holocaust scholar George Mosse, this book examines in minute and graphic detail the sequence of events and individual actions and reactions that made it possible for ordinary men to become mass murderers—men who, in cold blood and up close, shot and killed thousands of men, women, and children.

Browning, Christopher R. (1995). *The Path to Genocide: Essays on Launching the Final Solution.* New York: Cambridge University Press. 191 pp. In this book, Holocaust scholar Christopher Browning provides "an authoritative account of the evolution of Nazi Jewish policy; and in doing so, he seeks to answer some of the fundamental questions about what actually happened and why, between the outbreak of war and the emergence of the Final Solution. Browning assesses [various] historians' interpretations and offers his own insights, based on detailed case studies."

Burleigh, Michael. (1997). *Ethics and Extermination: Reflections on Nazi Genocide.* New York: Cambridge University Press. 261 pp. A series of essays concerned with three central subjects: German relations with the "East," "euthanasia," and extermination.

Burleigh, Michael & Wipperman, Wolfgang. (1991). *The Racial State: Germany 1933–1945.* New York: Cambridge University Press. 386 pp. This book deals with the ideas and institutions that underpinned the Nazis' attempt to restructure a "class" society along racial lines.

Dawidowicz, Lucy S. (1975). *The War Against the Jews, 1933–1945.* New York: Bantam Books. 466 pp. This book presents a systematic account as to why and how the Nazis carried out its genocide of the Jews, *and* how the Jews responded to the assault—first against their rights, next their livelihood, and then their lives.

Feig, Konnilyn. (1981). *Hitler's Death Camps: The Sanity of Madness.* New York: Holmes and Meier. 547 pp. Partially based on Feig's visit to nineteen camps, this historical study of the world of Nazi concentration and extermination camps focuses on the major camps, including Auschwitz, Dachau, Buchenwald, and Majdanek.

Feingold, Henry L. (1995). *Bearing Witness: How America and Its Jews Responded to the Holocaust*. Syracuse, NY: Syracuse University Press. 322 pp. In this major study, Feingold examines why the efforts of the U.S. government and Jewish leaders were ineffective in halting or mitigating Germany's genocidal policy during the Holocaust years.

Friedlander, Henry. (1995). *The Origins of Nazi Genocide: From Euthanasia to the Final Solution*. Chapel Hill: The University of North Carolina Press. 421 pp. In this book, Holocaust scholar and survivor Henry Friedlander explores how the Nazi program of secretly exterminating the handicapped evolved into the systematic destruction of Jews and Gypsies. "Tracing the rise of racist and eugenic ideologies in Germany, he describes how the so-called euthanasia of the handicapped proved a practical model for mass murder thereby initiating the Holocaust."

Friedländer, Saul. (1997). *Nazi Germany and the Jews: The Years of Persecution, 1933–1939. Volume I.* New York: HarperCollins. 436 pp. Examining both the latest published material and a wealth of new archival findings, Friedländer describes and interprets the steadily increasing anti-Jewish persecution in Germany following the Nazis ascent to power in 1933. "[H]e demonstrates the interaction between intentions and contingencies, between discernible causes and changing circumstances. He also shows how Nazi ideological objectives and tactical policy decisions enhanced one another and always left an opening for ever more radical moves." Volume II will be entitled *The Years of Extermination*.

Glass, James M. (1997). *"Life Unworthy of Life": Racial Phobia and Mass Murder in Hitler's Germany*. New York: Basic Books. 252 pp. Glass argues that a key reason why so many "ordinary Germans" came to regard Jews as less than human and ended up taking part in the Final Solution "lies in the rise of a particular ethos of public health and sanitation that emerged from the German medical establishment and filtered down to the common people, e.g., 'racial hygiene' singled out the Jews as an infectious disease that had to be eradicated if the Aryan race were to survive."

Hayes, Peter. (Ed.). (1996). *Lessons and Legacies: The Meaning of the Holocaust in a Changing World*. Evanston, IL: Northwestern University Press. 373 pp. Among the essays in this book that may be of particular interest to educators are Saul Friedlander's "The 'Final Solution': On the Unease in Historical Interpretation"; Michael R. Marrus's "The Use and Misuse of the Holocaust"; Christopher R. Browning's "One Day in Jozefow: Initiation to Mass Murder"; Lawrence Langer's "Redefining Heroic Behavior: The Impromptu Self and the Holocaust Experience"; and Alvin H. Rosenfeld's "Popularization and Memory: The Case of Anne Frank."

Hilburg, Raul. (1985). *The Destruction of the European Jews*. New York: Holmes & Meier. Three Volumes. 1,274 pp. A major and landmark history of the Holocaust, this three-volume set provides a detailed description of the bureaucratic machinery of destruction. Extremely well organized and documented, this is an essential work for those involved in Holocaust studies. Commenting on this work, Holocaust scholar Michael R. Marrus stated: "The lasting achievement of Hilberg's volumes is his portrayal of the perpetrators, acting both individually and as part of a horrifyingly effective destructive apparatus. No other work gives such a complete and awesome sense of the Nazis' Final Solution, linking the most banal administrative tasks to mass murder. . . . In its originality, scope and seriousness of theme, this is one of the great historical works of our time."

Hilberg, Raul. (1992). *Perpetrators, Victims, Bystanders: The Jewish Catastrophe 1933–1945.* New York: HarperCollins Publishers. 340 pp. As the title suggests, this fascinating, highly informative, and important study focuses on the lives and actions (and inaction) of the perpetrators, victims, and bystanders during the Holocaust period.

Kaplan, Marion A. (1998). *Between Dignity and Despair: Jewish Life in Nazi Germany.* New York: Oxford University Press. 290 pp. A remarkable book that vividly details the ever-increasing tension and constricted lives faced by German Jews as the Nazis implemented—from 1933 onward—policy after policy aimed at isolating, disenfranchising, and, ultimately, exterminating the Jewish populace. Based on memoirs, diaries, interviews, and letters of Jewish women and men, this book provides a highly readable and intimate portrait of Jewish life in Nazi Germany. It is a must-read for anyone wishing to begin to understand the early years of Nazi rule and how the Nazi regime slowly strangled the life out of German Jewry.

Laqueur, Walter. (1983). *The Terrible Secret: Suppression of the Truth about Hitler's "Final Solution."* New York: Penguin Books. 262 pp. Laqueur examines when and how information about the genocide of the Jews became known to millions of Germans, international Jewish organizations, leaders of Jewish communities throughout Europe, and top government officials in neutral and Allied countries.

Lipstadt, Deborah E. (1986) *Beyond Belief: The American Press & the Coming of the Holocaust, 1933–1945.* New York: Free Press. 370 pp. This acclaimed work presents an examination of the American press and how it covered (and "covered up") the ever-increasing discrimination and annihilation of the Jews in Nazi-dominated Europe.

Marrus, Michael R. (1987). *The Holocaust in History.* New York: Meridian. 267 pp. This volume constitutes the first comprehensive assessment of the vast literature on the Holocaust. Drawing on the entire range of historical literature on the Holocaust and applying the tools of historical, sociological, and political analysis, Marrus examines thorny questions that have concerned scholars over the years.

Michalczyk, John (Ed.). (1994). *Medicine, Ethics, and the Third Reich: Historical and Contemporary Issues.* Kansas City, MO: Sheed and Ward. 258 pp. Prominent voices in the field of bioethics reflect on the medical experiments on human subjects during the Third Reich.

Ofer, Dalia, and Lenore J. Weitzman. (1998). *Women in the Holocaust.* New Haven, CT: Yale University Press. 402 pp. Chapters by eminent historians, sociologists, and literary experts examine Jewish women's lives in the ghettos, the Jewish resistance movement, and the concentration and death camps. The volume also includes valuable testimonies of Holocaust survivors. "By examining women's unique responses, their incredible resourcefulness, their courage, and their suffering, the book enhances our understanding of the experiences of all Jews during the Nazi era."

Ritter, Carol, & Roth, John. (Eds.). (1993). *Different Voices: Women and the Holocaust.* New York: Paragon House. 435 pp. This major anthology includes the powerful testimony of women survivors ("Voices of Experience"), insights of key scholars ("Voices of Interpretation"), and reflections of theologians, philosophers, and others ("Voices of Reflection") regarding women's experiences of the during the Holocaust. Among the contributors to this pioneering volume are Ida Fink, Etty

Hillesum, Charlotte Delbo, Olga Lengyel, Sybil Milton, Vera Laska, Gitta Sereny, Magda Trocmé, and Deborah Lipstadt.

Sofsky, Wolfang. (1997). *The Order of Terror: The Concentration Camp*. Princeton, NJ: Princeton University Press. 356 pp. In this book, a renowned German sociologist examines the Nazi concentration camp system from the "inside"—"as a laboratory of cruelty and a system of absolute power built on extreme violence, starvation, 'terror labor,' and the businesslike extermination of human beings." Using historical documents and the reports of survivors, he delineates in great detail how "arbitrary terror and routine violence destroyed personal identity and social solidarity, disrupted the very ideas of time and space, perverted human work into torture, and unleashed innumerable atrocities."

Trunk, Isaiah. (1972). *Judenrat: The Jewish Councils in Eastern Europe under Nazi Occupation*. Lincoln: University of Nebraska. 663 pp. This is the first-full length account of the *Judenrat* (the Nazi-assigned Jewish leadership councils of the ghettos). Exhaustive in its examination, Trunk describes the establishment of the ghettos, life and death in the ghettos, the role of the *Judenrat* in carrying out Nazi directives, and the many and often deadly ramifications of the latter.

Weiss, John. (1996). *Ideology of Death: Why the Holocaust Happened in Germany*. Chicago, IL: Ivan R. Dee. 427 pp. Weiss examines why the destruction of the Jews was conceived and implemented by the Germans. "Exploring the unique nature of the German experience as well as the annals of anti-Semitism, Mr. Weiss rejects the notion that the Holocaust was a product of Nazi fanaticism. He shows instead how racist ideas ingrained in German culture led to the unthinkable." Of this book, noted Holocaust scholar Raul Hilberg states, "For many readers, this book can safely take the place of an entire library."

Wyman, David S. (1984). *The Abandonment of the Jews: American and the Holocaust, 1941–1945*. New York: Pantheon Book. 444 pp. This is a major and disturbing study of the United States government's totally inadequate response to the Nazi assault on the European Jews. Thoroughly documented, this book provides answers as to why the United States miserably failed to carry out the kind of rescue effort it could have. In essence, it constitutes an indictment as to why and how the United States basically became what Wyman calls a "passive accomplice" to the annihilation of the Jews.

Yahil, Leni. (1990). *The Holocaust: The Fate of European Jewry, 1932–1945*. New York: Oxford University Press. 808 pp. This prizewinning history provides a "sweeping look at the Final Solution, covering not only Nazi policies, but also how Jews and foreign governments perceived and responded to the unfolding nightmare." Yahil presents a systematic examination of the evolution of the Holocaust in Europe, probing its politics, planning, goals, and key figures.

Books Containing Primary Documents

Aly, Gotz. (1999). *Final Solution: Nazi Population Policy and the Murder of the European Jews*. New York: Arnold Publishers and Oxford University Press. 301 pp. Using extensive primary source documents, many recently released, Aly shows the close connection between the Nazis' view of the "new Order" in Europe and the extermination of the Jews.

Arad, Yitzhak, Gutman, Yisrael, & Margaliot, Abraham. (Eds.). (1981). *Documents on the Holocaust.* Jerusalem: Yad Vashem. 504 pp. An impressive and extensive collection of primary source documents on the destruction of the Jews of Germany, Austria, Poland, and the Soviet Union. It includes documents issued by both the perpetrators and the victims (e.g., resistance organizations, leaders of the Judenräte, excerpts from diaries). This book is a must for those educators who wish to include primary documents into their curriculum on the Holocaust.

Berenbaum, Michael. (Ed.). (1997). *Witness to the Holocaust: An Illustrated Documentary History of the Holocaust in the Words of Its Victims, Perpetrators and Bystanders.* New York: HarperCollins. 364 pp. Highly useful for the classroom, this volume includes documents related to the topics listed in the chapter titles: (1) The Boycott; (2) The First Regulatory Assault against the Jews; (3) Early Efforts at Spiritual Resistance; (4) The Nuremberg Laws; (5) The Conference at Evian; (6) The November Pogroms—Kristallnacht and Its Aftermath; (7) The Beginning of Ghettoization; (8) The Judenrat; (9) A Mosaic of Victims: Non-Jewish Victims of Nazism; (10) The Einsatzgruppen; (11) Babi Yar; (12) The Call to Arms; (13) Hitler's Plan to Exterminate the Jews; (14) The Killers: A Speech, A Memoir, and an Interview; (15) Choiceless Choices; (16) The End of a Ghetto: Deportation from Warsaw; (17) The Warsaw Ghetto Uprising; (18) What Was Known in the West; (19) Why Auschwitz Was Not Bombed; (20) Liberation and Its Aftermath; and (21) The Nuremberg Trials.

Dawidowicz, Lucy. (Ed.). (1976). *A Holocaust Reader.* West Orange, NJ: Behrman House. 397 pp. A collection of documents about various facets of the Holocaust, this book is comprised of the following parts and chapters: Part I. The Final Solution (1. Preconditions: Conventional Anti-Semitism and Adolf Hitler; 2. The First Stage: Anti-Jewish Legislation; 3. The Interim Stage: "All Necessary Preparations"; 4. The Final Stage: Mass Killings, "Resettlement," Death Camps); Part II. The Holocaust (5. The First Ordeal: The Jews in Germany 1933–1938; 6. The Ordeals of the Ghettos in Eastern Europe; 7. The Ordeals of the Judenräte; 8. Confronting Death: The Ordeals of Deportation; 9. Resistance: The Ordeal of Desperation).

Housden, Martyn. (1997). *Resistance & Conformity in the Third Reich.* London and New York: Routledge. 199 pp. This book, which was designed for use with students, examines the complex relationship between ordinary Germans and the Nazi government. It includes key primary sources, including but not limited to first-person accounts by survivors, former kapos, former Hitler Youth members, a member of the Luftwaffe, and a Nazi bureaucrat; leaflets by resistance members; statements and speeches by various Nazis; sections of a report by Reinhard Heydrich; police reports and summaries of interrogation sessions; declarations by opponents of the Nazis; and copies of school curricula designed and implemented by the Nazis. In the preface, it is stated that "A distinctive feature of [this series] is the manner in which the content, style and significance of documents is analyzed. The commentary and the source are not discrete, but rather merge to become part of a continuous and integrated narrative."

Marrus, Michael R. (1997). *The Nuremberg War Crimes Trial 1945–46: A Documentary History.* Boston, MA: Bedford Books. 276 pp. A superb collection of over seventy primary documents about various facets of the Nuremberg Trials. The book is divided into nine chapters and a set of appendices: (1) Historical Precedents; (2) Background; (3) Preparations; (4) The Court; (5) Crimes against Peace; (6) War Crimes;

(7) Crimes against Humanity; (8) Last Words; and (9) Assessment. The appendices include: Chronology of Events Related to the Nuremberg Trial (1919–1946), The Defendants and Their Fate; Charges, Verdicts, and Sentences; and Selected Bibliography. Among the documents are such pieces as "Winston S. Churchill, Franklin D. Roosevelt, and Joseph Stalin, Moscow Declaration, November 1, 1943"; "Robert H. Jackson, Opening Address for the United States, November 21, 1945"; "Robert Jackson, Cross-Examination of Hermann Göring, March 18, 1946"; "Marie Claude Vaillant-Couturier, Testimony on the Gassing at Auschwitz, January 28, 1946"; "Robert H. Jackson, Cross-Examination of Albert Speer, June 21, 1946"; and "Rudolf Höss, Testimony on Auschwitz, April 15, 1946."

Milton, Sybil. (Trans. and Ann.). (1979). *The Stroop Report*. New York: Pantheon Books. *The Stroop Report* is SS leader Juergen Stroop's actual record of the battle against the Jews during the Warsaw Ghetto Uprising. It includes his summary record and daily reports of German actions, as well as over fifty photographs taken by the Germans forces at the time.

Mosse, George. (1981). *Nazi Culture: A Documentary History*. New York: Schocken Books. 386 pp. This anthology of original source material includes pieces taken from contemporary literature, diaries, newspapers, and speeches. Mosse, a noted scholar of the Holocaust, provides useful introductions to each section and selection.

Noakes, J., & Pridham, G. (1984). *Nazism 1919–1945: A Documentary Reader*. Three Volumes. Exeter, England: University of Exeter. The three volumes of this set (Volume 1. "The Rise to Power, 1919–1934"; Volume 2. "State, Economy and Society, 1933–1939," and Volume 3. "Foreign Policy, War and Racial Extermination") are comprised of a collection of documents on Nazism. All of the volumes "contain material from a wide range of sources both published and unpublished: State and Party Documents, newspapers, speeches, memoirs, letters, and diaries."

Remak, Joachim. (Ed.). (1990). *The Nazi Years: A Documentary History*. Prospect Heights, IL: Waveland Press. 178 pp. The editor reports that the ideology of and practices of National Socialism "are described by way of documents nearly all of which were written by the actors, victims, or simple witnesses of the time and at the time." Continuing, Remak asserts that the point of the book is "to tell, the whole essential story of National Socialism, from its obscure ideological beginnings to its seizure of power; to show the uses to which the power was put, at home and abroad, until the bitter end of the Third Reich" (p. vii). The eleven chapters in the book are: The Roots, The Soil, The Program, Power, The Attractions, Propaganda, The Churches, War, Eugenics, The Jews, and Resistance.

Wolfe, Robert. (1993). *Holocaust: The Documentary Evidence*. Washington, DC: National Archives and Records Administration. 37 pp. This pamphlet includes an introduction that highlights key aspects of the Nazis' ideology and exterminatory policies, as well as a set of "facsimiles" of key Nazi documents dealing with various aspects of the Holocaust years, including: a report by Reinhard Heydrich, Chief of Security Police, to Hermann Göring about the destruction that took place during Kristallnacht; a telegram from Reinhard Heydrich to chiefs of all operation commands of the Security Police regarding the "concentration of Jews from the countryside into the larger cites"; an invoice regarding the shipment of 390 canisters of Zyklon B cyanide gas to be used for "disinfection and extermination" at Auschwitz; a "Statistical Report Regarding the Final Solution of the Jewish Question in Europe"; and a speech by Heinrich Himmler on October 4, 1943. In the latter, Himmler asserted that: "The questions arose for us: what about women and children?—I decided here, too, to find a clear-cut solution. I did not believe myself justified to root out the men—say also, to kill them, or to have them killed—and to allow avengers in the form of their children to grow up for our sons and grandsons [to confront]. The hard decision had to be made for this people to disappear from the earth." Unfortunately, none of the documents are translated in their entirety. Furthermore, most of the documents are poor copies and difficult to read. Still, this is a highly valuable booklet for teachers and students for it includes key documents that illuminate key aspects of the history.

PAMPHLETS ON HISTORICAL ISSUES FOR USE IN THE CLASSROOM

United States Holocaust Memorial Museum. (n.d.-a). *Handicapped.* Washington, DC: Author. 20 pp. This pamphlet provides a highly readable and informative overview of the plight of the mentally and physically handicapped at the hands of the Nazis. It focuses on both the forced sterilizations and "euthanasia" killings suffered by the victims. It also includes primary documents and photographs.

United States Holocaust Memorial Museum. (n.d.-b). *Homosexuals.* Washington, DC: Author. 16 pp. This pamphlet provides an overview of the treatment of homosexuals by the Nazis from 1933 through 1945. It includes an excerpt from a first-person account and numerous photographs.

United States Holocaust Memorial Museum. (n.d.-c). *Jehovah's Witnesses.* Washington, DC: Author. 15 pp. An informative piece on the beliefs of the Jehovah's Witnesses, why the Nazis persecuted Jehovah's Witnesses, and the treatment the Witnesses faced at the hands of the Nazis. It includes a facsimile of a Nazi-issued document, primary documents, and photographs.

United States Holocaust Memorial Museum. (n.d.-e). *Poles.* Washington, DC: Author. 27 pp. This pamphlet provides an overview of the plight of the Polish people at the hands of the Germans. Among the many topics addressed are: The invasion and occupation of Poland, Nazi terror against the intelligentsia and clergy, expulsions and the kidnapping of children, forced labor and the terror of the camps, and Polish resistance. It includes a facsimile of a Nazi-issued document, two first-person accounts, a map, and photographs.

United States Holocaust Memorial Museum. (n.d.-f). *Sinti and Roma.* Washington, DC: Author. 21 pp. A highly informative piece about the plight of the Gypsies at the hands of the Nazis. Viewed as "asocials" (that is, as being outside "normal" society and racial "inferiors") by the Nazis and their collaborators, the Sinti and Roma were targeted for extermination. Between 220,000 to 500,000 Sinti and Roma were killed during the Holocaust period. It includes primary documents and photographs.

United States Holocaust Memorial Museum. (1999). *Voyage of the St. Louis: Refuge Denied.* Washington, DC: Author. 26 pp. A magnificent booklet for use in the classroom, it thoroughly and cogently addresses the fate of the nine hundred Jewish passengers on the *St. Louis,* a transatlantic ocean liner, who were fleeing Nazi persecution and were turned away by both Cuba and the United States. Particularly powerful is the inclusion of the personal stories of individual families.

BOOKS ON FILMS

Avisar, Ilan. (1988). *Screening the Holocaust: Cinema's Images of the Unimaginable*. Bloomington: Indiana University Press. 212 pp. Disagreeing with those theorists who believe that art cannot deal with the Holocaust in a meaningful way, Avisar examines how filmmakers have struggled with the task of depicting the atrocities of the Holocaust on film.

Doneson, Judith. (1987). *The Holocaust in American Film*. Philadelphia, PA: Jewish Publication Society. 262 pp. An investigation into the ways in which specific films influenced and reflected the Americanization of the Holocaust and how film has helped to disseminate the event in the popular culture.

Grobman, Alex, Daniel Landes, & Sybil Milton. (Eds.). (1983). *Genocide: Critical Issues of the Holocaust: A Companion to the Film* Genocide. Los Angeles, CA: The Simon Wiesenthal Center, and Chappaqua, NY: Rossel Books. 501 pp. In addition to serving as a companion volume to the film *Genocide* (which is ideal for use in the classroom as it provides a succinct but powerful overview of the Germans' polices and actions), this text also includes a discussion of how the Holocaust is portrayed through film, an examination of aspects of modern antisemitism, and implications of the Holocaust for today's world.

Insdorf, Annette. (1990). *Indelible Shadows: Film and the Holocaust*. New York: Cambridge University Press. 293 pp. Richly illustrated, this book is a valuable introduction to the ways in which filmmakers have dealt with the subject of the Holocaust. It critically examines seventy-five fictional and documentary films, and includes a list of over one hundred films and their distributors.

Lanzman, Claude. (1985). *Shoah: An Oral History of the Holocaust, The Text of the Film*. New York: Pantheon. 200 pp. This is the complete text of Lanzmann's nine and a half-hour documentary in which witnesses, survivors, former SS officers, and Polish villagers speak about their experiences vis-à-vis the Holocaust.

Leiser, Erwin. (1974). *Nazi Cinema*. New York: Macmillan. 179 pp. Through his analysis of films created by the Nazis, Leiser reveals how the use of film served as a medium for indoctrination.

Loshitzky, Yosefa. (1997). *Spielberg's Holocaust: Critical Perspectives on* Schindler's List. Bloomington and Indianapolis: Indiana University Press. 250 pp. This volume is comprised of a compilation of essays that assess the strengths and limitations of *Schindler's List*. The various authors examine the film from different perspectives and contexts, including aesthetic, religious, historical, and social.

PEDAGOGICAL RESOURCES

Books

Facing History and Ourselves. (1994). *Facing History and Ourselves: Elements of Time*. Brookline, MA: Author. 402 pp. An outstanding volume and major resource that provides a detailed and intelligent discussion as to why and how video testimony by Holocaust survivors should and can be incorporated into the classroom.

Schilling, David (Ed.). (1998). *Lessons and Legacies: Teaching The Holocaust in a Changing World*. Evanston, IL: Northwestern University Press. 233 pp. Conveniently divided into three sections ("Issues," "Resources," and "Applications"), this collection includes essay by Michael Marrus ("Good History and Teaching the Holocaust"), Gerhard Weinberg ("The Holocaust and World War II: A Dilemma in Teaching"), Christopher Browning ("Ordinary Germans or Ordinary Men? Another Look at the Perpetrators"), and Judith Doneson ("Why Film?").

Totten, Samuel (Ed.). (2001). *Teaching Holocaust Literature*. Boston, MA: Allyn and Bacon. This volume is comprised of rich narratives by secondary-level teachers (grades seven to twelve) on the process they used to teach a piece of Holocaust literature to their students. Among the contributors are noted Holocaust educators such as Rebecca Aupperle, Elaine Culbertson, Carol Danks, Peggy Drew, William Fernekes, and Karen Shawn.

Totten, Samuel. (Forthcoming). *Holocaust Education: Issues and Approaches*. Boston, MA: Allyn and Bacon. In this book, Totten addresses a host of key issues germane to teaching the Holocaust at the secondary level. Among the various chapters are: "Teaching the Holocaust: The Imperative to Move Beyond Clichés," "The Start Is as Important as the Finish: Assessing Students' Schema," "Essential Topics/Issues to Consider When Teaching the Holocaust," "'Complicating' Students' Thinking about Aspects, Facts, Concepts, Conditions, Situations, Motivations Vis-à-Vis the Holocaust," and "Minimizing, Simplifying and 'Denying' the Complexity and Horror of the Holocaust: The Questionable and Problematic Use of Simulations in an Attempt to Convey Historical Experiences."

United States Holocaust Memorial Museum. (1994). *Teaching about the Holocaust: A Resource Book for Educators*. Washington, DC: Author. 115 pp. This volume includes a host of valuable resources, including the museum's *Guidelines for Teaching about the Holocaust,* an "Annotated Bibliography," an "Annotated Videography," a set of "Frequently Asked Questions," a piece entitled "Children and the Holocaust," a historical summary of the Holocaust, and a detailed chronology.

Teaching Guidelines

Parsons, William S., & Totten, Samuel. (1994). *Guidelines for Teaching about the Holocaust.* Washington, DC: United States Holocaust Memorial Museum. 16 pp. Addresses key issues that educators ought to consider when preparing to teach about the Holocaust. Noted Holocaust educators Stephen Feinberg, William Fernekes, and Grace Caporino were major contributors to the development of this publication as well as Holocaust historian Sybil Milton.

Essays/Articles about Pedagogical Strategies, Lessons, Units, Resources

Danks, Carol. (1995, October). "Using Holocaust Stories and Poetry in the Social Studies Classroom." *Social Education* 59(6):358–361. In this article, Danks succinctly discusses certain caveats and guidelines to be taken into consideration when using short stories and poetry in a study of the Holocaust. She also explores ways to teach Ozick's "The Shawl," the short stories in Borowski's *This Way for the Gas, Ladies and Gentlemen,* and various pieces of poetry.

Darsa, Jan. (1991). "Educating about the Holocaust: A Case Study in the Teaching of Genocide." In Israel W. Charny (Ed.), *Genocide: A Critical Bibliographic Review,* Volume 2 (pp. 175–193). New York: Facts on File. While not actually a case study, this is a thought-provoking essay that raises and examines numerous key issues vis-à-vis Holocaust education. It includes an extensive and useful annotated bibliography that highlights key Holocaust curricula, adjunct resources, and essays on Holocaust pedagogy.

Drew, Margaret A. (1995, October). "Incorporating Literature into a Study of the Holocaust." *Social Education* 59(6):354–356. Among the issues Drew discusses in this piece are criteria teachers ought to use in selecting literature for use in the upper elementary and secondary classrooms, key issues that should be addressed in the study of the Holocaust, and various first-person accounts and novels that can be incorporated into such a study.

Drew, Peg. (Fall 1989). "Holocaust Literature and Young People: Another Look." *Facing History and Ourselves News,* pp. 20–21. Drew argues that in addition to reading literature students need a solid grounding vis-à-vis the history of the Holocaust. Only in that way, she argues, will they be able to make sense of the events that led up to and resulted in the Holocaust.

Farnham, James. (1983, April). "Ethical Ambiguity and the Teaching of the Holocaust." *English Journal* 72(4):63–68. A thought-provoking piece that discusses the clash between the value systems of students and actions of victims in the camps, the complexities of ethical behavior, and "ethical problems from the [Holocaust] literature."

Greeley, Kathy. (1997). "Making Plays, Making Meaning, Making Change." In Samuel Totten & Jon E. Pedersen (Eds.), *Social Issues and Service at the Middle Level* (pp. 80–103). Boston, MA: Allyn and Bacon. In this fascinating essay, Greeley discusses and explains how she involved her students in the writing and production of a play that dealt, in part, with key issues germane to the Holocaust.

Kalfus, Richard. (1990, February). "Euphemisms of Death: Interpreting a Primary Source Document on the Holocaust." *The History Teacher* 23(2):87–93. Kalfus describes a powerful learning activity in which he uses a primary document that he asserts "illustrates the all-pervasive, destructive force that was National Socialism" (p. 87). He states, "the insidious, administrative language used here is a concrete, dramatic example of how an entire caste of civil servants could become active participants in the extermination process" (p. 87). Part of the activity includes having the students replace the euphemisms with their intended meaning, for example, "*merchandise, pieces,* and *load* become Jews; *operating time* becomes annihilation; *operation* becomes gassing," and so on (p. 88).

Kettel, Raymond P. (Fall 1996). "Reflections on *The Devil's Arithmetic* by a Holocaust Survivor: An Interview with Jack Wayne—B8568." *The New Advocate* 9(4):287–295. This is a fascinating article/interview in which a survivor comments on how moved he was by Jane Yolen's novel, *The Devil's Arithmetic.* He notes that he especially appreciates the work because the protagonist's experiences are so much like his own. Information in the interview can be used by teachers to highlight and illuminate, for their students, various aspects of *The Devil's Arithmetic.*

Kimmel, E. A. (1977, February). "Confronting the Ovens: The Holocaust and Juvenile Fiction." *The Horn Book Magazine,* pp. 84–91. In his examination of juvenile fiction about the Holocaust, Kimmel notes, that as of the late 1970s, no Holocaust fiction written for children had been written about the death camps. After predicting that a novel about the death camps would eventually be written, he raises the issue as to "whether or not that novel [would] come any closer to the question at the core of all this blood and pain" (p. 91).

Meisel, Esther. (1982, September). "I Don't Want to Be a Bystander": Literature and the Holocaust." *English Journal 71*(5):40–44. Succinctly discusses the use of two poems: Nelly Sach's "The Chorus of the Rescued" and Ka-Tzetnik's "Wiedergutmahung."

National Council for the Social Studies. (1995, October). Special Issue, "Teaching about the Holocaust." *Social Education, 59*(6). Samuel Totten & Stephen Feinberg. Recipient of the EdPress Award for special topics, this issue includes "Teaching about the Holocaust: Issues of Rationale, Content, Methodology, and Resources," "Anti-Semitism: Antecedents of the Holocaust," "The Other Victims of the Nazis," "Altruism and the Holocaust," "Incorporating Literature into a Study of the Holocaust: Some Advice, Some Cautions," "Using Holocaust Short Stories and Poetry in the Social Studies Classroom," "The American Press and the Holocaust—A Unit of Study," "Anti-Semitism: A Warrant for Genocide—A Unit of Study," and "Hitler's Death Camps—A Unit of Study."

Rudman, Masha Kabakow, and Rosenberg, Susan P. (Summer 1991). "Confronting History: Holocaust Books for Children." *The New Advocate 4*(3):163–176. This article presents and discusses numerous rationales for including literature in a study of the Holocaust, issues several caveats in regard to selecting and using Holocaust literature in the classroom, and then provides a critique of various types of Holocaust literature on various subject matter.

Rushforth, Peter. (1994). "'I Even Did a Theme Once on That Anne Frank Who Kept The Diary, and Got an A Plus on It': Reflections on Some Holocaust Books for Young People." *Dimensions: A Journal of Holocaust Studies 8*(2):23–35. In this bibliographical essay, Rushforth, author of the novel *Kindergarten,* provides a thorough and intelligent critique of ten popular books used by many teachers at the upper elementary, middle, and junior high levels of schooling to teach about various facets of the Holocaust. The books he critiques are *Anton the Dove Fancier, and Other Tales of the Holocaust, Gentlehands, Journey to America, Alan and Naomi, Number the Stars, Daniel's Story, The Island on Bird Street, Friedrich, A Pocket Full of Seeds,* and *The Devil's Arithmetic. This is a valuable article that should be consulted by any teacher who is considering the use of Holocaust fiction in his/her classroom.*

Schwartz, Donald. (1993, February). "'Who Will Tell Them after We're Gone?' Reflections on Teaching the Holocaust." *The History Teacher 23*(2):95–110. A thought-provoking and well-written essay that addresses, among other issues, the place of the Holocaust in school curricula, textbook coverage of the Holocaust, and various rationales for teaching the Holocaust to school-age students.

Shawn, Karen. (1995). "Liberation: A Documentary Guide to the Liberation of Europe and the Concentration and Death Camps." *Dimensions 9*(1):G1–G23. This excellent study guide is packed with key information about the liberation of the concentration and death camps. In addition to both "questions for discussion" and "questions for further research," it includes a solid historical overview of liberation, photographs from the period, excerpts from eyewitness testimony, and a short bibliography and videography on liberation.

Shawn, Karen. (1993). "The Warsaw Ghetto: A Documentary Discussion Guide to Jewish Resistance in Occupied Warsaw 1939–1943." *Dimensions: A Journal of Holocaust Studies* 7(2): G1–G15. This discussion guide, which includes a succinct historical overview of Jewish resistance in occupied Warsaw, is packed with fascinating primary documents and photographs from the period.

Totten, Samuel. (2000). "The Critical Need to Establish an Accurate and Thorough Historical Foundation When Teaching the Holocaust." In Ted DeCoste and Bernard Schwartz (Eds.), *The Holocaust: Art, Politics, Law, Education.* Alberta, Edmonton: University of Alberta Press. The author discusses the dangers in not providing students with a historically accurate foundation of the Holocaust. He concludes with a discussion of effective ways to establish such a historical foundation when teaching the Holocaust.

Totten, Samuel. (1998a). "Examining the Holocaust through the Lives and Literary Works of Victims and Survivors: An Ideal Unit of Study for the English Classroom." In Robert Hauptman and Susan Hubbs Motin (Eds.), *The Holocaust: Memories, Research, Reference* (pp. 165–188). New York: The Haworth Press. (This article was copublished simultaneously in *The Reference Librarian,* Numbers 61/62, 1988.) This essay includes a detailed discussion as to how Totten assisted his students to begin to understand how a writer's life experiences frequently influence the stories he/she tells as well as the allusions, symbols, and motifs he/she uses in his/her works.

Totten, Samuel. (in press-a). "How They Taught the Holocaust to High School Students: A Semester-Long Course Co-Taught by a University Professor and a High School English Teacher." *Journal of Holocaust Education.* A discussion of the trials, tribulations, frustrations, compromises, methods, limitations, and successes of a team-taught course on the Holocaust.

Totten, Samuel. (1998b). "Incorporating Contemporaneous Newspaper Articles about the Holocaust into a Study of the Holocaust." In Robert Hauptman and Susan Hubbs Motin (Eds.), *The Holocaust: Memories, Research, Reference* (pp. 59–81). New York: The Haworth Press. (This article was copublished simultaneously in *The Reference Librarian,* Numbers 61/62, 1988.) The author suggests ways in which teachers can use newspaper articles from 1933 to 1945 to assist students in grappling with key aspects of Holocaust history.

Totten, Samuel. (2001). "Incorporating Poetry into a Study of the Holocaust at the High School Level Via Reader Response Theory." In Samuel Totten (Ed.), *Teaching Holocaust Literature.* Boston, MA: Allyn & Bacon. This piece highlights the way the author conducted a reader response activity around Dan Pagis's poem "Written in Pencil in the Sealed Railway-Car." Student responses are included and succinctly commented upon.

Totten, Samuel (2000). "Diminishing the Complexity and Horror of the Holocaust: Using Simulations in an Attempt to Convey Historical Experience." April *Social Education* 4(3):165–171. This article examines and decries the use of simulations by teachers to instruct their students about various facets of the Holocaust as experienced by the victims.

Totten, Samuel (in press). "Nothing About a Study of the Holocaust Should Be Perfunctory, Including Its Close: Suggestions for Closing a Lesson, Unit or Study of the Holocaust." *Social Education*. This article highlights useful and powerful strategies, other than final exams, for bringing a study of the Holocaust to a close. An emphasis is placed on authentic assessment and tasks that encourage students to reflect on the new knowledge and insights gleaned from their study.

Totten, Samuel (1998c, February). "The Start Is as Important as the Finish: Establishing a Foundation for a Study of the Holocaust." *Social Education* 62(2):70–76. In this article, Totten describes and discusses various types of opening activities that can be used to (1) assess students' current knowledge base about the Holocaust, (2) students' depth of knowledge about the history of the Holocaust, and (3) any questions and concerns about the Holocaust that they particularly wish to learn about during their course of study.

Wieser, Paul. (1995a, October). "The American Press and the Holocaust." *Social Education* 59(6):C1–C2. The purpose of this lesson by a high school social studies teacher is to engage students in a study about the fact that while news of mass killings of millions of Jews reached the United States in the early 1940s, the press gave the subject little prominence.

Wieser, Paul. (1995b, October). "Anti-Semitism: A Warrant for Genocide." *Social Education* 59(6):C4–C6. The purpose of this lesson is to engage students in an examination of the impact of the relentless buildup of Hitler's antisemitic policies and anti-Jewish legislation.

Wieser, Paul. (1995c, October). "Hitler's Death Camps." *Social Education* 59(6):374–376. The purpose of this lesson, which features a top-secret Nazi document on the shipment of used clothing and possessions taken from Jewish deportees to the Majdanek and Auschwitz camps, is to engage students in a study of the existence and function of the Nazi extermination camp system.

Yolen, Jane. (1989, March). "An Experiential Act." *Language Arts* 66(3):246–251. Discusses the value of the literary device of "time travel," especially as it relates to her Holocaust novel, *The Devil's Arithmetic*.

Zack, Vicki. (1991, January). "'It Was the Worst of Times': Learning about the Holocaust through Literature." *Language Arts* 68:42–48. Zack, a fifth-grade teacher in Canada, discusses a study of the Holocaust that she and several of her students conducted using Jane Yolen's *The Devil's Arithmetic*.

Educational Research, Criticism, and Philosophical/Pedagogical Essays

Braham, Randolph L. (Ed.). (1987). *The Treatment of the Holocaust in Textbooks: The Federal Republic of Germany, Israel, and the United States.* Boulder, CO and New York City: Social Science Monographs and the Institute for Holocaust Studies of the City University of New York. 332 pp. Although dated, this detailed study is still valuable.

Carrington, Bruce, & and Geoffrey Short. (1997). "Holocaust Education, Anti-Racism, and Citizenship. *Educational Review* 49(3):271–282. In this paper, the authors report the findings of a case study whose purpose was to "assess the potential of Holocaust education as a medium for developing; 'maximalist' notions of citizenship among students of secondary school age. . . . The sample, comprising both males and females from a variety of ethnic backgrounds, was drawn from six secondary schools in south East England. The discussion focuses on (1) the impact of Holocaust education in the students' understanding of racism (and, in particular, their ability to recognize and deconstruct stereotypes); and (2) the students' opinions on the value of Holocaust; education in preparing young people for active citizenship in a participatory pluralist democracy" (p. 271). The paper concludes with a discussion of the pedagogical implications of the study.

Dawidowicz, Lucy. (1992). "How They Teach the Holocaust." In Lucy Dawidowicz (Ed.) *What Is the Use of Jewish History?* (pp. 65–83). New York: Schocken Books. A highly critical essay on the inaccuracies, gaps, and general inadequacy of much Holocaust curricula. *This is a key essay that every educator should read and ponder prior to developing and/or teaching a curriculum, unit, or even a single lesson on the Holocaust.*

Friedlander, Henry. (1979). "Toward a Methodology of Teaching about the Holocaust." *Teacher's College Record 81*(3):519–542. An early and outstanding essay on teaching about the Holocaust. Friedlander, a noted scholar and Holocaust survivor, discusses difficulties in studying and teaching about the Holocaust, issues key caveats to educators, and suggests and discusses major issues that should be considered when teaching this history. *This is a key essay that every educator should read and ponder prior to developing and/or teaching a curriculum, unit, or even a single lesson on the Holocaust.*

Lipstadt, Deborah E. (1995, March 6). "Not Facing History." *The New Republic*, pp. 26–27, 29. Although basically a critique of the Facing History and Ourselves program, the focus of this article is germane to all educational programs whose focus is Holocaust history. Lipstadt argues that teachers and curriculum developers must avoid eliding "the differences between the Holocaust and all manner of inhumanities and injustices" (p. 27); for if they don't, instead of "making history relevant, [they] will distort [its meaning]" (p. 27).

Shawn, Karen. (1995). "Current Issues in Holocaust Education." *Dimensions: A Journal of Holocaust Studies 9*(2):15–18. Shawn cogently argues that the negative side of the proliferation of educational activity and development of resources to teach about the Holocaust is that "such rapid, broad-based popularization could conceivably dilute and diminish the impact of the Holocaust" (p. 16). In her discussion, Shawn examines the problematic nature of statewide directives for Holocaust education, current staff development programs in place purportedly for the purpose of preparing teachers to teach this history, and "the recent alarming proliferation of poorly conceived and executed textbooks, teaching aids, and lesson plans flooding our schools" (p. 18). Shawn also offers suggestions for ameliorating many of these problems.

Shawn, Karen. (Spring 1991). "Goals for Helping Young Adolescents Learn about the Shoah." *Ten Da'at 5*(2):7–11. [To obtain a copy of this article, contact the Ten Da'at office at 1-212-960-5261.] In this well-thought-out and thought-provoking article, Shawn discusses the importance of using solid rationales when teaching the Holocaust. She also addresses such issues as affective and cognitive goals, and the selection of controlling ideas or themes.

Shawn, Karen. (1994). " 'What Should They Read and When Should They Read It?': A Selective Review of Holocaust Literature for Students in Grades Two through

Twelve." *Dimensions: A Journal of Holocaust Studies 8*(2):G1–G16. Shawn provides an excellent critique of forty-seven works. The article also includes a short but thought-provoking introduction that suggests possible criteria to use when selecting Holocaust literature for classroom study. The article concludes with a section entitled "Second Thoughts, " at the outset of which Shawn notes: "The following books, while frequently recommended by critics, teachers, publications, and so on, raise, for me, anyway, troubling questions. These might involve historical content or 'message,' or tone." *This is a must-read for educators.*

Short, Geoffrey. (Winter 1995). "The Holocaust in the National Curriculum: A Survey of Teachers' Attitudes and Practices." *The Journal of Holocaust Education 4*(2):167–188. In this study, Short, a senior lecturer in education at the University of Hertfordshire, Great Britain, interviewed thirty-four secondary-level history teachers in order to ascertain their attitudes and practices in regard to teaching about the Holocaust. Among the questions Short asked his respondents were: What do you see as the main advantage and disadvantages of teaching the subject? Do you relate the Holocaust to contemporary developments—that is, the resurgence of nationalism and racism across much of Europe? Do you, and should you, draw parallels between the Holocaust and other atrocities committed against ethnic groups in the past? How do you contextualise the teaching of the Holocaust? Do you do anything to explore and undermine students' misconceptions and stereotypes about Jews and Judaism prior to teaching about the Holocaust? A key finding of the study is that "The vast majority of teacher are committed to Holocaust education, but see its value in terms of combating racism rather than anti-Semitism. In fact, the nature and history of anti-Semitism was the area most often omitted as a result of the shortage of time" (p. 186).

Short, Geoffrey. (1997). "Learning through Literature: Historical Fiction, Autobiography, and the Holocaust. *Children's Literature in Education 28*(4):179–190. In this piece, Short argues "against the common-sense view that children's literature dealing with the Jews in Nazi Germany is necessarily useful as an aid to studying the Holocaust" (p. 180). Concerned about how the history of the Holocaust is taught in British schools, Short asserts that "Ostensibly relevant literature cannot be relied upon to remedy these defects. . . . [S]ome of the literature may not, in fact, be at all informative about the attempted annihilation of European Jewry" (p. 180). Following a discussion of his research findings, Short discusses the shortcomings of two popular books—*Friedrich* and *Mischling Second Degree*—for use in teaching students about this history.

Short, Geoffrey. (1994). "Teaching the Holocaust: The Relevance of Children's Perceptions of Jewish Culture and Identity." *British Educational Research Journal 20*(4):393–405. In this study, seventy-two children between the ages of twelve and fourteen "were interviewed in order to explore their knowledge of Judaism, the nature of any misconceptions they have about the faith, the extent to which they appreciate the commonalties between Judaism and Christianity, and their awareness of anti-Semitism." Ultimately, Short argues that "for the Holocaust to be taught effectively, teachers will need some idea of how children . . . perceive Jewish culture and identity" (p. 393).

Totten, Samuel. (Winter 1998). "A Holocaust Curriculum Evaluation Instrument: Admirable Aim, Poor Result." *Journal of Curriculum and Supervision 13*(2):148–166.

This essay constitutes a critical analysis of the Association of Holocaust Organization's (AHO) *Evaluating Holocaust Curricula: Guidelines and Suggestions.*

Totten, Samuel. (1999). "Holocaust Education for K–4 Students? The Answer is No!" September/October *Social Studies and the Young Learner* 12(1):36–39. In this article, Totten argues that Holocaust education for K–4 students is untenable, due to its complexity and horrific nature. He supports those teachers who wish to teach their young charges about prejudice, discrimination, stereotyping, and focus on prejudice reduction and conflict resolution, but he suggests that they should not refer to it as Holocaust education and that such efforts should not introduce the students to the world of the Holocaust.

Totten, Samuel, and Riley, Karen. (under review). "State Department of Education Sponsored Holocaust and/or Genocide Curricula and Teaching Guides: A Critique." In this essay, Totten and Riley critique the historical accuracy of eleven state-department-sponsored and/or -developed curricula for use in secondary-level schools. The key findings are that many of the curricula are rife with errors and/or address key concepts in a sorely inadequate manner.

Wegner, Gregory. (Winter 1998). " 'What Lessons Are There from the Holocaust for My Generation Today?' Perspectives on Civic Virtue from Middle School Youth." *Journal of Curriculum and Supervision* 13(2):167–183. An interesting study that examined two hundred essays by eighth graders, which addressed the question: "What lessons from the Holocaust are there for my generation today?"

Adjunct Resources

Littell, Franklin H. (Ed.). (1997). *Hyping the Holocaust: Scholars Answer Goldhagen.* Merion Station, PA: Merion Westfield Press International. 177 pp. This volume includes a collection of often scathing critiques of Daniel Goldhagen's *Hitler's Willing Executioners.* Among the contributing essayists are Franklin H. Littell, Hubert G. Locke, Hans Mommsen, Jacob Neusner, Didier Pollefeyt, and Roger W. Smith.

Totten, Samuel (Ed.). (forthcoming). *Examining the Past to Protect the Future: The Personal Stories of Holocaust Educators on the Genesis and Evolution of Their Pedagogical Endeavors* (working title). Westport, CT: Bergin & Garvey. This book is comprised of the personal stories of noted Holocaust educators across the globe in which they discuss their pedagogical efforts vis-à-vis the Holocaust. Among those included in the volume are Sid Bolkosky, Steve Cohen, Ephraim Kaye, Nili Keren, Marcia Littell, Leatrice Rabinsky, Stephen Smith, Karen Shawn, Margo Stern-Strom, Samuel Totten, and Paul Wieser.

INDEX